E.J. PRATT: COMPLETE POEMS

PART 2

THE COLLECTED WORKS OF E.J. PRATT
GENERAL EDITORS: SANDRA DJWA and R.G. MOYLES

The aim of this edition is to present a critical annotated text of
the collected works of E.J. Pratt – complete poetry; selected prose
and correspondence – fully collated and with a textual apparatus
that traces the transmission of the text and lists variant readings.

E.J. PRATT

Complete Poems
Part 2

Edited by Sandra Djwa and R.G. Moyles

UNIVERSITY OF TORONTO PRESS
Toronto Buffalo London

© University of Toronto Press 1989
Toronto Buffalo London
Printed in Canada

ISBN 0-8020-5775-6

Printed on acid-free paper

Canadian Cataloguing in Publication Data

Pratt, E.J. (Edwin John), 1882–1964
Complete poems

(The Collected works of E.J. Pratt)
Includes bibliographical references and index.
ISBN 0-8020-5775-6 (SET)

I. Djwa, Sandra, 1939–   . II. Moyles, R.G.
(Robert Gordon), 1939–   . III. Title. IV. Series:
Pratt, E.J. (Edwin John), 1882–1964. The collected
works of E.J. Pratt.

PS8531.R3A17 1989   c811'.52   c88-093068-3
PR9199.2.P73A17 1989

This book has been published with the help of a grant from the Canadian
Federation for the Humanities, using funds provided by the Social
Sciences and Humanities Research Council of Canada. Publication has
also been assisted by the Canada Council and the Ontario Arts Council
under their block grant programs.

Contents

vi Contents

Preface

This is Part 2 of an edition of *E.J. Pratt: Complete Poems*. Part 1 contains the 'Introduction,' poems arranged chronologically up to *The Titanic* (1935), a list of variants and emendations and a set of annotations for those poems. Part 2 contains the remainder of Pratt's poetry – from 'Silences' (1936) to 'The Unromantic Moon' (1953) – a list of variants and emendations, a set of annotations for those poems, three appendices containing unpublished poetry and drama, and a descriptive bibliography that provides a textual history of every Pratt poem.

E.J. PRATT: COMPLETE POEMS

PART 2

Silences

There is no silence upon the earth or under the earth like the silence
    under the sea;
No cries announcing birth,
No sounds declaring death.
There is silence when the milt is laid on the spawn in the weeds and
    fungus of the rock-clefts;
And silence in the growth and struggle for life.
The bonitoes pounce upon the mackerel,
And are themselves caught by the barracudas,
The sharks kill the barracudas
And the great molluscs rend the sharks,
And all noiselessly –   10
Though swift be the action and final the conflict,
The drama is silent. .

There is no fury upon the earth like the fury under the sea.
For growl and cough and snarl are the tokens of spendthrifts who
    know not the ultimate economy of rage.
Moreover, the pace of the blood is too fast.
But under the waves the blood is sluggard and has the same
    temperature as that of the sea.

There is something pre-reptilian about a silent kill.

Two men may end their hostilities just with their battle-cries,
'The devil take you,' says one.
'I'll see you in hell first,' says the other.   20
And these introductory salutes followed by a hail of gutturals
    and sibilants are often the beginning of friendship, for who would
    not prefer to be lustily damned than to be half-heartedly blessed?
No one need fear oaths that are properly enunciated, for they
    belong to the inheritance of just men made perfect, and, for all we
    know, of such may be the Kingdom of Heaven.
But let silent hate be put away for it feeds upon the heart of the hater.

4

Today I watched two pairs of eyes. One pair was black and the
    other grey. And while the owners thereof, for the space of five
    seconds, walked past each other, the grey snapped at the black and
    the black riddled the grey.
One looked to say – 'The cat,'
And the other– 'The cur.'
But no words were spoken;
Not so much as a hiss or a murmur came through the perfect enamel
    of the teeth; not so much as a gesture of enmity.
If the right upper lip curled over the canine, it went unnoticed.
The lashes veiled the eyes not for an instant in the passing.   30
And as between the two in respect to candour of intention or
    eternity of wish, there was no choice, for the stare was mutual and
    absolute.
A word would have dulled the exquisite edge of the feeling.
An oath would have flawed the crystallization of the hate.
For only such culture could grow in a climate of silence –
Away back before emergence of fur or feather, back to the unvocal
    sea and down deep where the darkness spills its wash on the
    threshold of light, where the lids never close upon the eyes, where
    the inhabitants slay in silence and are as silently slain.

March 1936

Seen on the Road

The pundit lectured that the world was young
As ever, frisking like a spring-time colt
Around the sun, his mother. The class hung
Upon his words. I listened like a dolt,

And muttered that I saw the wastrel drawn
Along the road with many a pitch and bump
By spavined mules – this very day at dawn!
And heading for an ammunition dump.

5

The savant claimed I heckled him, but – Hell!
I saw the fellow in a tumbril there,
Tattered and planet-eyed and far from well,
With winter roosting in his Alpine hair.   May 1936

The Baritone

He ascended the rostrum after the fashion of the Caesars:
His arm, a baton raised oblique,
Answering the salute of the thunder,
Imposed a silence on the Square.
For three hours
A wind-theme swept his laryngeal reeds,
Pounded on the diaphragm of a microphone,
Entered, veered, ran round a coil,
Emerged, to storm the passes of the ether,
Until, impinging on a hundred million ear-drums,   10
It grew into the fugue of Europe.

Nickel, copper and steel rang their quotations to the skies,
And down through the diatonic scale
The mark hallooed the franc,
The franc bayed the lira,
With the three in full flight from the pound.
And while the diapasons were pulled
On the *Marseillaise*,
The *Giovanezza*,
And the *Deutschlandlied*,   20
A perfect stretto was performed
As the *Dead March* boomed its way
Through *God Save the King*
And the *Star Spangled Banner*.

Then the codetta of the clerics
(Chanting a ritual over the crosses of gold tossed into the crucibles
   to back the billion credit)
Was answered by
The clang of the North Sea against the bows of the destroyers,
The ripple of surf on the periscopes,
The grunt of the Mediterranean shouldering Gibraltar,   30
And the hum of the bombing squadrons in formation under Orion.

And the final section issued from the dials,
WHEN –
Opposed by contrapuntal blasts
From the Federated Polyphonic Leagues
Of Gynecologists,
Morticians,
And the Linen Manufacturers –
The great Baritone,
Soaring through the notes of the hymeneal register,   40
Called the brides and the grooms to the altar,
To be sent forth by the Recessional Bells
To replenish the earth,
And in due season to produce
Magnificent crops of grass on the battlefields.   December 1936

Puck Reports Back

OBERON
Much have I longed for thy return, my sprite:
This greenwood, once the stage of elfin pranks
And welkin-splitting laughter, has become
A desert in thy absence. Now these stories
Burrow beneath my ribs and chase away
The bile, for they reveal a madder world
Than what Lysander knew and Hermia.
Poor Bottom in his downiest moments saw

No visions such as these that thou relatest –
That fire should burn in water; mortals fly   10
Throughout the empyrean on the backs
Of birds; and whales with whirling fins should leave
Their native element and take the air
Across the land and sea with greater speed
Than falcons; and that lovers could exchange
Their vows in whispers at the self-same instant,
Though separate a thousand ocean leagues –
These tales would tax my own too credulous ears,
As though I heard accounts of wrathful capons
Tracking Hyrcanian tigers to their lairs.   20
Hast thou another fable in thy scrip?

PUCK
My Prince of Shadows, these reports I've brought
Are more than fantasies that might disturb
The reason through the love-juice of a herb.
I saw the strangest duel ever fought –
Sir Guy, Knight of the Garter, famous knight,
Has challenged valiant Boris, famous count,
To settle a reckoning in single fight.
Boris not only questioned the amount,
The nature and occasion of the debt,   30
But forwarded a diplomatic note
To the knightly challenger that, when they met,
He would be pleased to take him by the throat,
With many a courtly phrase which might imply
His general opinion of Sir Guy.
So, to collect, a journey was begun,
Which, for the distance under broiling sun
And pelting rain, had the same pith of sense
As if a man might barter pounds for pence.
At last when they appeared in mutual sight   40
Upon two neighbouring hills where a ravine
That ended in a quagmire lay between,

The count began to bellow at the knight
With fearful imprecations while Sir Guy
Called Boris a bat, a polecat and a kite,
A worm, an adder and a wart-hog – Why
They should attack each other with such words
I know not, but when finished with the birds
And all the noxious animals, they hurled
The missiles of the vegetable world.   50
And while they cursed they put more armour on
Their steeds, beyond all war caparison,
And on themselves already over-weight:
For every oath they added some new plate
To some new part of their anatomy,
And when they had their beavers down, no hint
Of mortal man escaped captivity
Save through the eye-slits where the sovereign glint
Of reason peered blasted with ecstasy.

OBERON
This is the visitation of the moon!   60
But, prithee, how with such accoutrement
Climbed they up to the saddles of their coursers?

PUCK
A dozen robust yeomen by main force
Managed to get Sir Guy upon his horse.
As many knights accomplished the same feat –
Placing against the withers of the mount
A ladder, they pushed up the angry count
And got him fastened well astride his seat.
Nor was this all: To see through their disguise
And find the men, I had to rub my eyes.   70
As though the armour were not yet complete,
The henchmen brought another piece of mail
Shaped like a conduit or a metal hose
And screwed it to each gladiator's nose.

Far-off it might have been a dragon's tail,
But on a closer view it had the look
Of an elephant's trunk, when it recurved
On the cuirass – What was the purpose served?
The devil knows; so crazed it was I shook
With laughing paroxysms, then with fright,   80
For suddenly the day became as night,
The curses took on corporal form – so rank
The poisonous emanations were, they swept
Across the gap and up the hills and stank
Like an Irish fen. The squires, they broke and wept;
The knights, they choked; while I ran off for cover
To an acorn cup and drew a rose-leaf over.

OBERON
Whither did all this lead, my gentle Puck?
Did they sit howling on those hills forever?

PUCK
I went to sleep within my nest of oak   90
To rinse the portent through a dream, then woke,
Uncuddled, and stole forth to banks I knew,
Where violets, musk-rose and wild thyme grew:
I filched them from their beds and sent them out
(With a million glow-worms lighting up the air)
To pour their distillation through the rout
Of wind and stench. Anon, I looked and there
Unmoved, the same infuriated pair –
Sir Guy, rigid, barking his challenge still,
And Boris booming, bellowing from the hill.   100

OBERON
This story would outwit all tricks of mirth
Known to the gullible within my realm.
Such folly falling on a broken mirror
Could scarce distort its own insane grimaces.
How were they loosened from their pedestals?

PUCK

My lord! I scouted round the clover fields
And drove out from their lazy honey yields
A furious colony of humble-bees.
I fanned them up both hills and bade them squeeze
Through rivet cracks and joints, and stick like leeches   110
To the bare lard within the warriors' breeches.
I then fled to a pine tree top and heard
A pandemonium of oaths and screeches,
And by the buckle creakings and the gird
Of the loin plates upon their rusty hinges,
I knew how well my squads clapped on the twinges.
But this, my master, could not get them parted
From their incorporate posts, and so I tried
A prank that I devised one Hallowtide
Which never failed to get two fighters started.   120
Changing myself into a gamecock, I
With bristling hackles, and my comb blood-red,
Settled upon the helmet of Sir Guy,
Until the proud arch of my neck and head
Assumed the tautness of a Parthian bow.
With such inflammatory mien, I crew
Six notes contemptuous at Boris who
Stiffened and took the insult like a blow.
In half a second, like a meteorite,
I landed on the county's helm and shrilled   130
The fiery syllables back at the knight.
Thou shouldst have heard my clarion as I drilled
Helmet and skull to pierce the globèd brain.
Each lusty crow held triumph and disdain:
I nearly tore my wattles when I blew it,
For my restored ears still feel the pain.
Zounds, sir, the way the count and knight went to it!

OBERON

The impact of those mighty opposites,
Spurred to their wrath by such a vent of scorn,
Must have, like an Olympian avalanche,   140
Brought terror to the battlements of Jove.

PUCK

Nay, nay, your Majesty – 'twas no such fun.
Never indeed was there a tilt begun
With heraldry like this, that ended so.
The rivals did not strike a single blow.
When once they started off, they could not stop.
They did not seem to ride so much as drop
To the solid earth, then rise, bound through the air,
Which angry at their overweening pride
Bounced them from knoll to knoll, made them collide   150
With their own saddles, till the exhausted pair –
Pitched from their stallions which, poor jades, were wrecked
By the very iron bands meant to protect
The fetlocks – took one final somersault
Into the miry bottom of the vault.
I watched them wallowing like drunken grooms,
Pursuing a blind orbit in the mud,
Only the gesture of their fighting blood
Waving defiance from the bankrupt plumes.
Count Boris' nozzle sent a farewell blast,   160
Claiming a fatuous triumph, while a high
Blue feather from the proud knob of Sir Guy,
Striving to keep erect, gave up the last
Frail effort of heroic pantomime,
To fall like a snapped water-flag and lie
Prone in the sea-green bubbles on the slime.

OBERON

Enough, my romping elf! I pray, enough!
In these reports there's matter to regale
Titania through many a sulky moon.
Had Nestor heard them, he'd have cracked his sides.   170
The sport that night in the Athenian grove,
Compared with this, was but episcopal.
There's not a planet left that keeps its course;
The distaff cracks; the dizzy earth is run
By three inebriated witches – Stay!

PUCK

Another tale of men I could recite –
Of winged-clipped human eagles living in holes
Under the ground in envy of the moles...
But I shall leave that for a winter night.

OBERON

I know not what thou hast in mind to say,   180
But hold! It is not well those jests should come
In troops – They have a boding sentry face
And smell too strongly of mortality.   October 1937

The Fable of the Goats

One half a continental span,
The Aralasian mountains lay
Like a Valkyrian caravan
At rest along the Aryan Way.
And central to the barrier,
Rising in mottled columns, were
The limestone ramparts of the heights –
The Carolonian Dolomites.
Over those scaffolds nothing passed
But navigators of the sky: 10
Those crags were taken only by

The sun and moon and the wind's blast,
By clouds and by the eagles' wings
Out on their furthest venturings.
So rooted in geography
The natural frontier, it could be
A theme for neither god nor beast
To argue that one side was east
And that the other side was west.
Yet with this knowledge manifest,   20
We must record a truth as strange
As any fact or myth that can
Inflict mortality on man.

The middle section of this range
For endless centuries had been
Earth's most dramatic *mise en scène*
For lawless indeterminate fights.
Both avalanche and cataract
With Time compounding had attacked
The lowest of the Dolomites   30
With spring's recurrent cannonade;
Had deepened crater and crevasse,
Torn down the gorges and had laid
The canyon of St Barnabas.
Along this canyon's northern edge,
One hundred feet in length, a ledge
Of schist, known as the Capra Pass,
Projected from the mountain wall.
This slippery stretch might well appall
The tread of cloven-footed things   40
In their most cautious pedallings,
But as a ground on which to stage
The fortunes of a battle rage,
That ledge of Capra might reveal
A tale which, for perversity,
Could tame the Kyber Route or steal

The title from Thermopylae.
The country which those peaks divide
Was noted for its rich terrains,
Its sweeping uplands and its wide 50
Deltas and undulating plains.
Millions of hornèd ruminants
Roebucks and elks and argalis
Upon this vast inheritance
Had founded aristocracies,
Which ruled the commons till, between
Their slaughterous feuds internecine
And foreign raids, they lost their lead
To a lusty more endurant breed –
A new totalitarian horn 60
Known as the genus capricorn.

The Aralasian country west,
Described as Carob, was possessed
By a remarkable race of goats
With lyrate horns and shaggy coats.
Unyielding individualists
At first by nature they had learned
The folly of obstructionists
Within their tribal ranks and turned
To federal virtues for the wise 70
Conduct of corporate enterprise.
And of this wide domain the head
Was Cyrus. It was he who led
The bucks against the bulls in that
Perfidious effort to profane
The purity of the racial strain:
'Twas he, the high-born aristocrat,
Who rounded up intransigents,
Drove out all civil disputants,
And bent the proletariat 80
Under a regimen of drill
To his authoritarian will.

And on the east there was a spot
As fertile as the Carob land,
Where goats likewise had won command –
The ancient dynasty of Gott.
Straight-horned those tribes, of wiry coat,
They had outmatched their canine foes,
Then turned upon the yaks and smote
The harts and put to shame the does.   90
Inebriated by success,
With numbers vastly multiplied,
They built a citadel of pride
About a national consciousness,
Outran their borders to possess
The lush exotic harvest yields
Of hitherto unvanquished fields,
Until they had from that wild shore
Of the Fallopian corridor
Down to the grey Ovidian Sea   100
Established their hegemony.

Now when the veterans returned
Flushed with their foreign victories,
The hearts of all the generals burned
With personal antipathies.
All scrambled for the seats of power,
Some wanted this, some wanted that,
And some they knew not what – whereat
Uprose the leader of the hour,
A buck who by right of descent,   110
As by his natural temperament,
Had never recognized retreat.
A scion of a Caliphate,
He knew the strategy to beat
The factions by a stroke of state
And quell diversity of bleat,
For of all lands, the realm of Gott
Indubitably was polyglot.

His stroke of state, his *coup d'état*
Was nature's oldest formula.   120
It was the leader's bright idea
To send them forth to find their grub
On fetid moors and desert scrub
Where tuber roots of Ipomoea
Purga – the standard panacea
For disaffections of the mind –
Became their diet, which, combined
With seeds of Croton Tiglium,
Restored their equilibrium.
The mightiest hybrid of his race   130
Was this ballista of the herd;
The orient framework of his face
Had been through generations blurred
By a gigantic Ural trek –
For unlike Cyrus, Prince of Carob,
The Gottite leader's stream was stirred
By elements from Turk and Arab:
Tincture of Tartar, touch of Czech
Lay in the great Abimelech.

So with the martial banners furled   140
At all the frontiers in debate,
It seemed as if the caprine world
Might manage to domesticate
The gains imperial and release
Their bucking energies for peace
Under a wise duumvirate –
Two cousins far removed but loined
From the same root, the god-like Pan,
Abimelech and Cyrus joined
In a world reconstruction plan!   150
But goats like men have never found
Much standing room on neutral ground,

Once let a point of honour rise
And death stalks in on compromise.
Those Gottites and the Carobites
Stood pat upon their natural rights,
And here we must at once admit
Three rocks on which a League might split.

It seemed that Nature had designed,
When first she fixed a Gottite mind,   160
Or pitched the Carob brain, and bent
The bony bulwarks round about,
Into a three-inch armament,
That compromise should never find
An alley either in or out.
For when in any age was born
A freak without a cloven hoof,
Or with palmated frontal roof
That blossomed points along the horn –
Some civilized concessive goat   170
Who carried democratic stripes
Upon his softly textured coat –
The uniformitarian types,
Who strove to dominate the breed,
Exiled him from the herds. Indeed,
One had appeared like this to show
Progressive softening of the brain
By urging tolerance towards the foe
At the finish of a great campaign.
Now, inasmuch as he was not   180
Pure Carob or acknowledged Gott,
By some form of a large jerboa
Derived from stray spermatozoa,
They tore his carcass joint from joint
And sheared him to the fourteenth point.
That goats were laid down for dissent
Was clearly, whether right or wrong,

An architectural intent.
Those picket horns were three feet long –
What was their purpose but reproof?   190
And what the skull's, if not for shock?
As axiomatic as the hoof
For stance upon the mountain rock!

Moreover, Nature – quirky dame –
Had planted in their disposition
A sacred but a smoky flame
Of uncontrollable ambition.
Nomads from zoologic time,
The race grew conscious that they must
Give to an aimless wanderlust   200
The sublimation of a climb.
Valleys and plains were nurseries
Which full-grown goats might leave behind
For the wild gully routes that wind
Up to the mountain crags and screes –
Places of habitation where
Ancestral bands of satyrs shook
Lascivious lightnings from their hair.
They marvelled with exalted look
At things that voyaged through the air;   210
They worshipped clouds and glorified
The golden eagles as they took
The solar orbit in their stride.

Joined with this instinct of ambition
There was a problem called nutrition,
A knotty, vexed consideration
Not yet resolved by sublimation.
Of all the animals that faced
The question of a food supply,
The goat had the most catholic taste   220
That crops could ever satisfy.

It could be proved by any test
He had no rival at a feast;
He craved the foliage of the west
To vary pastures of the east,
New barks and fresher rinds: the sight
Of grasses inaccessible
Was whetstone to the appetite.
The more he had, the more he wanted;
A taste unrecognized, a smell   230
Still unappropriated, haunted
The rumen like a ghostly spell.
The eastern tribes had often stared
Up at the peaks and wondered what
Those vapours were their nostrils flared,
What herbs and blossoms there might be –
Was it goatleaf or bergamot,
Red clover or sweet cicely?
And likewise when the east wind blew
Over the Carolonian summit,   240
The herds from western uplands drew
Intoxicating essence from it.
Was that bay laurel, was it thyme
That floated from the mountain span?
Their eyes were fastened on the climb,
Their noses quivered with the sniff,
Yes, by the beard of the first Khan,
There was no error in that whiff,
They knew it, every buck and dam,
'Twas lavender and marjoram.   250

On one crisp morning when the heights
Were diamond brilliant with their snows,
When dawn had flushed with a deep rose
The panels of the Dolomites,
And atmospheric odours tart
Made tonic impact on the heart,

A common inspiration struck
Concurrently each monarch buck:
It was the Ledge, the unconquered Ledge,
The sanguinary Capra Pass,   260
That sent its challenge from the edge
Of the canyon of Saint Barnabas.

Abimelech and Cyrus led
Their troops up the opposing sides,
Past fell and scaur and watershed,
Over the small and great Divides.
The marching bleat from every corps
Combined into their battle roar,
Excelsior! Excelsior!
Such stout morale, such fine *élan*   270
Was never seen since time began.
By noon both tribes became aware
Through subtle changes in the air
Caused by the sharp reverberant sound
Of hoofs upon untimbered ground,
And by the Carob-Gottite smell,
A mixture indescribable,
That they might any moment close
With their hereditary foes.
They reached the hollow where the green   280
Ledge like a boa lay between
The twin peaks of the Dolomites.
Massed by prophetic signals, kites
And buzzards in a storm of wings
Swept up and down the great ravine,
Impatient for their scavengings.
Upon that very ledge were fought
Thousands of battles that had wrought
The drama of a racial glory,
With nothing in the strife more certain   290
Than that each act of the long story

Should close upon a carrion curtain.
And yet – was there a goat dismayed
In all that spiral cavalcade?
No – not a buck, nor could there be
From stock designed for battery
And built like Carthaginian rams,
Although that thousand feet of drop
Sheer from the Carolonian top
Put curds within the milcher dams.   300
With pawing hoofs and sweating flanks,
Each chieftain as the duellist
Of his own herd stepped from the ranks
To try the quarrel on the schist.
Abimelech himself had seen
His sires – grands and great-grands – fall,
Locked with the lyrates, down the wall,
Plumb to the crypts in the ravine,
Dropping like frenzied bacchanals,
Hitting their corrugated globes   310
So bloodily, the frontal lobes
Came out through their occipitals.
But so intense the patriot fire,
And so magnificent the roll,
The youth had felt the same desire
Kindle the torches of his soul.
And had not Cyrus felt as well
The potent ritual of the spell,
The phobias of his spirit burn
In the white heat of discipline,   320
As he had watched his kith and kin
In their inexorable turn
Perish? How splendidly they fell!
And how the witenagemot
Would hallow this immortal spot!
And had he not gone back to tell
The nursing dams who would convey

To generations then unborn
The story? How they would portray
That plunge! And had not Cyrus sworn 330
Upon the blood script of the laws,
That on some sacrificial day
He would go forth his father's way,
Crusading downward to be torn
By canyon jags and vulture claws,
Maintaining to the end The Cause,
The exaltation of The Horn?
And now the fatal hour had struck.
Abimelech, that eastern buck
With all the pride of a Mogul, 340
His anger rising in a storm
Of snorts, superbly true to form,
Moved to the centre, lowered his skull –
The famous Gottite cranium –
To meet the Carobite Defender,
The noble Cyrus who had come
To die but never to surrender.

Come all ye hair-dividers, wise
To ways of nature and of art,
Who know how to anatomize 350
The fine vagaries of the heart,
Come bring your lore and make it plain –
This riddle in the Carob brain.
In that weird passage from the dark
Matrix that shaped the Carobite
And stratified his skull for fight,
Up to this present hour, the spark
Had never failed the dynamite.
Ye cannot say that Cyrus knew
Just what he was about to do. 360
For nowhere in his long descent
Was there a trace of one rehearsal
Which might account for this reversal

Of military precedent.
Folly it is to speculate
Upon the food that Cyrus ate,
That inland buds of evergreen
With valley shoots could mitigate
A million years of feudal hate
From Irish Moss and carrageen;   370
Or that the Adriatic weed
By working on the thyroid freed
The activators in his blood;
That something in the morning cud
Gentled his lymph towards his foes –
A steadying digitalis flip
To the heart when he paused to nip
The foxglove. Tell us he that knows.
Or failing every shibboleth
Of blood or ductless glands or such,   380
Did reason enter in to touch
The senses with the thought of death,
And flash across goat-leaden eyes
Glimpse of futilitarian skies?
The vultures with their ten-foot spread,
Their hairless necks and crimson lids,
Were at their business half-a-mile
Below among the ancient dead
Or roosting on the pyramids.
And some were mounting the defile   390
To flank the Pass of Capra where
They lounged like lizards on the air;
And one black wing had come so near
The Rock, its tip had brushed the coat
Of the Carob leader as it passed:
And had that brush, so leisured, cast
The only one acknowledged fear
Within the history of the goat?
Or was it fear? Did Cyrus know

That neither courage, strength nor will 400
Behind the battle urge to kill
Was proof against a flying foe?
That every time when honour wronged
Secured revenge upon the peaks,
Inevitably the spoils belonged
To the swiftest wings and sharpest beaks—
The harpies and the cormorants
Who, compensating for their theft
Of blood and flesh and fat, had left
The glory to the ruminants? 410
But do not reason why the mind
Should save the soul or seek to find
Within the evolutionary dream
An optimistic phagocyte,
That cleaning up the corporate stream,
Had scrubbed a conscience into light,
The conscience of a Carobite –
An Aryan working overtime
Beating the Tartar to the climb!
Ye cannot know what Cyrus felt; 420
Ye only know that Cyrus knelt.
Knelt! Hocks and knees! The body lay
Prone – lengthwise – on the Capra Pass,
As if beside his dam – the way
He went to sleep in summer grass.

Now let pathologists explain
What happened to the other brain.
After a close look at the head,
A momentary sniff at hoof
And beard which gave Abimelech proof 430
That Cyrus was by no means dead,
A flash of understanding thrown
Like a dagger of apocalypse,
Had pierced the Gottite cranial bone

And crashed his spiritual eclipse.
Was it a glint of chivalry
Nurtured under the eastern climes,
A throw-back to the Gobi times,
When someone in his ancestry
Had set a fashion for the race,   440
Made it a stigma of disgrace
To foul a fallen enemy?
Let him declare it who can tell
Whether in Palestinian lands
Some new conciliatory cell
Had been evolved while roving bands
Converged upon the desert sands
To share the water from a well.

The chieftain saw the road was thrown
Wide open: it was his alone   450
To take possession in his stride –
'Twas his alone, this flush of pride
In a great conquest which would place
Him as the hero of his race.
But all the arrogance and scorn
On which his tribal soul was bred,
Spurn of the hoof, flaunt of the horn
That was Abimelech's, had fled,
And in its place a strangely warm
Infusion – a considerate care   460
That would not harm a single hair.
He sniffed once more the prostrate form
Of Cyrus. Then as if he feared
He might do violence to the head
Or bring pollution to the beard,
He stepped so lightly over, cleared
Knees, hoofs and rump with that sure tread
Which never yet had made him miss
His foothold on a precipice.

Clean over? Yes, beyond his foe! 470
None could deny the deed was done,
The Carolonian summit won,
The Capra Pass without a blow!

Cyrus looked up and in his eyes
Was an incredulous surprise.
He could not find his enemy.
He shook himself and blinked awhile,
Then straightened up and gingerly
He made the perilous defile.
Reaching the safety of the bend, 480
He stopped and, curious, craned his neck,
Only to see Abimelech
Watching him at the other end.
The eyes of those two hierarchs
Were four interrogation marks.
No record in the family tree
Illumined this epiphany.
Five minutes motionless and mute
They stood with that hypnotic stare
That only puzzled goats could wear; 490
And then in reverent salute
As though their eyes had shed their scales,
And each had recognized a brother
Bidding Good Morning to the other,
They waved their beards and stubby tails,
And turning took their downward trails,
Accompanied by their retinue,
Alive to the redemptive clue –
Cyrus to where the wild thyme grew,
And where he could at his sweet beck 500
Tread acres of the cistus-tree
And lavender; Abimelech
To bergamot and barberry,
And where he could, up to his neck,
Crop billowing leagues of cicely. 1937

Under the Lens

Along the arterial highways,
Through the cross-roads and trails of the veins
They are ever on the move –
Incarnate strife,
Reflecting in victory, deadlock and defeat,
The outer campaigns of the world,
But without tactics, without strategy.

Creatures of primal force,
With saurian impact
And virus of the hamadryads,   10
The microbes war with the leucocytes.

Physicians watch the conflict –
Advance, respite, recession and advance –
They shake their heads and murmur,
'Body versus organism,'
'A question of endurance,'
'Try out transfusion,'
'Pour in fresh troops.'

With flush and pallor alternating,
Pulses racing, slowing, flickering,   20
The body sinks,
Like a derelict with a mutinous crew,
Steamless and rudderless,
Taking its final drubbing from the sea.

Once it was flood and drought, lightning and storm and earthquake,
Those hoary executors of the will of God,
That planned the monuments for human faith.
Now, rather, it is these silent and invisible ministers,
Teasing the ear of Providence
And levelling out the hollows of His hands,
That pose the queries for His moral government.   1937

The Old Organon (1225 A.D.)

When Genghis and his captains
Built their pyramids of skulls
Outside Bokhara and Herat,
And sacked Otrar and Samarcand,
There was no sophistry between the subject and the verb;
For what the Khan said, he meant.
Behind the dust were the hoofs of his cavalry,
Behind the smoke was his fire.
And when Mohammed and Jehal-ud-Din,
In their flight from the Indus to the Caspian,   10
Appealed to Allah for protection,
Even the Great God of Islam
Could find no escape for the faithful,
When he knew the flight was regimented
To the paces of a Mongol syllogism.   1937

The New (1937 A.D.)

Now when the delegates met around the tables
And lifted up their voices,
The subjects were the civilizing tasks,
The fulfilment of historic missions,
The redemption of the national honour,
And the emancipation of the slaves.
But flaws were hidden in the predicates,
And in the pips of the adverbials,
And the rhetorical adjectives
Assumed the protective colouring   10
Of the great cats against the jungle grass –
THEREFORE,
In all the wealth of their possessive pronouns,
Not a syllable was spared
For the oil reported in the foreign shales.   1937

The Illusion

All patterns of the day were merged in one –
Clouds, wings and faces, dunes and harbour bars –
In a swift blur of vision as the sun
Went down at noon upon a drift of spars.

In such a lightless hour the sea had cleft
A heart, fumbling its way as through a strait,
Then passed, bequeathing to the common weft
No record but its arid distillate.

Though when night comes with sleep there still remains
Enough of daylight and of surf to trace   10
The artisan outside the storm-swept panes,
Refashioning the pallor of his face
To softer lines which thread my nescient mood
With the illusion of beatitude.   1937

The Impatient Earth

Back to the earth would we come
In the fullness of years,
As we return home at dusk
When our eyes are dim with day
And our feet tired with stubble.
We would come with slow step
Along the cool loam of lanes,
Home to your heart
With the mellow toll of bells in the west.

But not as today would we come   10
To the trumpet's unnatural summons,
With our loins girt for a longer race
And our faces set for a different goal,
With our feet strung to the measures of life,
To a riot of bells in the east.

This is the season for blood-root and bud-break,
For freshets and resinous airs,
For the mating migrations
Of swallows and whitethroats,
For the scaling of crags,   20
For the plangent call of the surf
Where ospreys are building their nests.

Then why should we come out of season
To take the long lease of your heart,
When the swift irresponsible trespass
Of our feet above ground
Is cut short by the halt of the sentry?
There are months still to go for the autumn,
And months for the poppies to bloom,
Though hate and greed have grown to their harvest,   30
Though tolerance, forgiveness and love are forgotten
Like scars on the body of Christ –
Too soon in the morning for youth
To take the deep draught of your opiate!   November 1938

The Submarine

The young lieutenant in command
Of the famous submarine, the K–
148, had scanned
The sea circumference all day:
A thousand times or so his hand
Revolved the prism in the hope
That the image of the ship expected,
But overdue, might be reflected
Through the lenses of his periscope.
'Twas getting late, and not a mark   10
Had troubled the monotony
Of every slow expanding arc

Of the horizon. Suddenly
His grip froze to the handle! What
Was that amorphous yellow spot
To the north-east? Was it the lift
Of a wave, a curl of foam, a drift
Of cloud? Too slow for foam, too fast
For cloud. A minute more. At last
The drift was taking shape; his stroke   20
Of luck had fallen – it was SMOKE!

An hour of light in the western sky,
And thirty seconds for descent;
The quarry ten miles off. Stand by!
The valves were opened – flood and vent –
And the water like a rumble of thunder
Entered the tanks. Two generators
Sparked her fins and drove her under
Down the ocean escalators.

No forebear of the whale or shark,   30
No saurian of the Pleiocene,
Piercing the sub-aquatic dark
Could rival this new submarine.
The evolution of the sea
Had brought forth many specimens
Conceived in horror – denizens
Whose vast inside economy
Not only reproduced their broods,
But having shot them from their wombs,
Devoured them in their family feuds   40
And passed them through their catacombs.
But was there one in all their race
Combined such terror with such grace,
As this disturber of the glooms,
This rapid sinuous oval form
Which knew unerringly the way

To sound and circumvent a storm
Or steal a march upon her prey?
No product she of Nature's dower,
No casual selection wrought her   50
Or gave her such mechanic power
To breathe above or under water.

In her thoracic cavities
One hundred tons of batteries
Were ready, on the dive, to start
The musculation of the heart.
And where outside a Ming museum
Could any antiquarian find
An assemblage such as here was shrined
Within the vault of her peritoneum?   60
Electric switches, indicators,
Diving alarm-horns, oscillators,
Rudder controls, and tubes and dials,
Yellow, white, magenta vials,
Pipes to force out battery gases,
Pressure gauges, polished brasses,
Surrounded human figures caught
At their positions, silent, taut,
Like statues in the tungsten light,
While just outside the cell was night   70
And a distant engine's monotone
Tapping at a telephone.
And now two hundred feet below
She held her bearings towards her foe,
While silence and the darkness flowed
Along an unnavigated road.

In half an hour she stopped and blew
The water ballast with her air,
Rose stealthily to surface where
Upon the mirror in full view,   80
Cutting an Atlantic swarth

The trail of smoke turned out to be
A fat mammalian of the sea,
Set on a course north-east by north,
And heavy with maternity.
Within her framework iron-walled
A thousand bodies were installed,
A snug and pre-lacteal brood
Drawing from her warmth and food,
Awaiting in two days or three   90
A European delivery.
Blood of tiger, blood of shark,
What a prey to stalk and strike
From an ambush in the dark
Thicket of the sea!

       Now like
The tiger-shark viviparous
Who with her young grown mutinous
Before the birth-hour with the smell
Of blood inside the mother, will expel
Them from her body to begin   100
At once the steerage of the fin,
The seizure of the jaw, the click
Of serried teeth fashioned so well
Pre-natally to turn the trick
Upon a shoal of mackerel –
So like the shark, the submarine
Ejected from her magazine
The first one of her foetal young.
It ran along the trolley, swung
Into a flooded tube and there   110
Under a jet of compressed air
It found the sea. A trip-latch in
The tube a second later sprung
A trigger, and the turbine power
Acting on the driving fin
Paced it at fifty miles per hour.

So huge and luscious was this feast,
The 148 released
Three others to offset the chance
Of some erratic circumstance   120
Of aim or speed or tide or weather.
And during this time nothing was seen
Except to an eye in the submarine
Of that bevy of sharks on the sea together,
So accurately spaced one after the other,
And driven by thirst derived from the mother.
Each seemed on the glass a tenuous feather
Of gold such as a curlew in flight
Would make with its nether wing skimming the swell;
Not a hint of a swerve to the left or right,   130
The gyros were holding the balance so well.

The rich-ripe mammal was swimming straight
On the course of her chart with unconcerned leisure,
Her steady keel and uniform rate
Combining so perfectly with the deep black
Of the hull – silhouette against the back–
Drop of the sunset to etch and measure
The target – when three of those shafts of foam
At the end of their amber stretch struck home.
The first one barely missed – to plough   140
A harmless path across her bow:
The next tore like a scimitar
Through flesh to rip the jugular;
Boilers and bulkheads broke apart
When the third torpedo struck the heart;
And with what logic did the fourth
Cancel the course north-east by north,
Hitting abaft the beam to rut
The exploding nitrates through her gut.

The young commander's time was short   150
To log the items for report.
Upon the mirror he descried
Three cavernous wounds in the mammal's side –
Three crumbled dykes through which the tide
Of a gluttonous Atlantic poured;
A heavy starboard list with banks
Of smoke fluted with steam which soared
From a scramble of pipes within her flanks;
Twin funnel-nostrils belching red,
A tilting stern, a plunging head,   160
The foundering angle in position,
And the sea's reach for a thousand souls
In the last throe of the parturition.

Now with her hyper-sensitive feel
Of her master's hands on the controls –
A pull of a switch, a turn of a wheel,
The submarine, like the deep-sea shark,
Went under cover, away from the light
And limn of the sunset, from the sight
Of the stars, to a native lair as dark   170
As a kraken's grave. She took her course
South-west by south – for what was the source
Of that hum to the port picked up by the oscillator?
A rhythm too rapid, too hectic for freighter
Or liner! This was her foe, not her prey:
Faster and louder, and heading her way!
Beyond the depth where the tanks could flood'er,
She drove her nose down with the diving rudder,
Far from the storm of shells or thrust
Of the ram, away from the gear-wrenching zone   180
Of the depth-bomb, away from the scent and lust
Of a killer whose might was as great as her own.   December 1938

The Anomaly

The plan on which this life is built
Is somewhat like a patchwork quilt,
As crazy as may be –
Two colours stand out in the scheme:
To one we give the name of dream,
To one reality.

For when in sleep man leaves behind
His polished economic mind,
A pauper though he be,
He turns a Sultan overnight,   10
Takes all the wealth of life at sight,
And holds a realm in fee.

But when within his waking state,
As one of the electorate,
Though hungry as can be,
He gathers in his harvest store,
Fills up the pantry, locks the door,
Then throws away the key.   1938

The Stag

Branched head lifted and poised,
Ears cupped, vibrating,
Nostrils flaring,
Body shafted to the muscle-strings –
He leaped to the bay of hounds
And took the runway to the lake.
Trailing a drift of vapour,
From flanks and lungs
In the crisp November morning,
He measured up his stamina   10

Against those footling mongrels,
And tossed them off his easy margins
Of speed and wind.

Water – through the birches!
And the challenge of the swim!

Both barrels – at thirty yards!
Through eyes, sockets, and skull to the brains,
Crash of knees,
Spate of nostrils,
Antlers ploughing through underbrush.   20
'Dead as a stump!'

'What a spread!'
'Thirty-five points. No, thirty-six, thirty-seven;
For the oak panels
Over the west door of the Imperial';
'Ought to fetch fifty dollars,
God – what sport!'   1938

Old Harry

Along the coast the sailors tell
The superstition of its fame –
Of how the sea had faceted
The Rock into a human head
And given it the devil's name.

And much there was that would compel
A wife or mother of a seaman
To find a root in the belief
The rock that jutted from the reef
Was built to incarnate a demon.   10

But there's a story that might well
Receive a share of crediting,
And make the title fit the look
Of vacancy the boulder took
Under the ocean's battering.

Within that perforated shell
Of basalt worn by wave and keel
The demon ruler of the foam
One night upon returning home
Was changed into an imbecile,   20

Ordered to stay within his cell,
Clutch at the spectres of the air,
Listen to shrieks of drowning men,
And stare at phantom ribs and then
Listen again and clutch and stare.

So like a sea-crazed sentinel,
Weary of sailors and their ships,
Old Harry stands with salt weed spread
In matted locks around his head,
And foam forever on his lips.   February 1939

The Dying Eagle

A light had gone out from his vanquished eyes;
His head was cupped within the hunch of his shoulders;
His feathers were dull and bedraggled; the tips
Of his wings sprawled down to the edge of his tail.
He was old, yet it was not his age
Which made him roost on the crags
Like a rain-drenched raven
On the branch of an oak in November.

Nor was it the night, for there was an hour
To go before sunset. An iron had entered   10
His soul which bereft him of pride and of realm,
Had struck him today; for up to noon
That crag had been his throne.
Space was his empire, bounded only
By forest and sky and the flowing horizons.
He had outfought, outlived all his rivals,
And the eagles that now were poised over glaciers
Or charting the coastal outlines of clouds
Were his by descent: they had been tumbled
Out of their rocky nests by his mate,   20
In the first trial of their fledgling spins.

Only this morning the eyes of the monarch
Were held in arrest by a silver flash
Shining between two peaks of the ranges –
A sight which galvanized his back,
Bristled the feathers on his neck,
And shot little runnels of dust where his talons
Dug recesses in the granite.
Partridge? Heron? Falcon? Eagle?
Game or foe? He would reconnoitre.   30

Catapulting from the ledge,
He flew at first with rapid beat,
Level, direct; then with his grasp
Of spiral strategy in fight,
He climbed the orbit
With swift and easy undulations,
And reached position where he might
Survey the bird – for bird it was;
But such a bird as never flew
Between the heavens and the earth   40
Since pterodactyls, long before
The birth of condors, learned to kill
And drag their carrion up the Andes.

The eagle stared at the invader,
Marked the strange bat-like shadow moving
In leagues over the roofs of the world,
Across the passes and moraines,
Darkening the vitriol blue of the mountain lakes.
Was it a flying dragon? Head,
Body and wings, a tail fan-spread   50
And taut like his own before the strike;
And there in front two whirling eyes
That took unshuttered
The full blaze of the meridian.
The eagle never yet had known
A rival that he would not grapple,
But something in this fellow's length
Of back, his plated glistening shoulders,
Had given him pause. And did that thunder
Somewhere in his throat not argue   60
Lightning in his claws? And then
The speed – was it not double his own?
But what disturbed him most, angered
And disgraced him was the unconcern
With which this supercilious bird
Cut through the aquiline dominion,
Snubbing the ancient suzerain
With extra-territorial insolence,
And disappeared.

So evening found him on the crags again,   70
This time with sloven shoulders
And nerveless claws.
Dusk had outridden the sunset by an hour
To haunt his unhorizoned eyes.
And soon his flock flushed with the chase
Would be returning, threading their glorious curves
Up through the crimson archipelagoes
Only to find him there –

Deaf to the mighty symphony of wings,
And brooding
Over the lost empire of the peaks.   Winter 1939

The Radio in the Ivory Tower
(1937–Sept. 1939)

This is the castle of peace,
And this its quietest hour;
There isn't a cry from the gathering dusk,
There isn't a stir in the mist;
The fog has scarfed the moon and stars,
The curtains are drawn on the tides;
There isn't a wave at the curve of the shore;
A granite-grey silence covers the land,
And the gulls are asleep on a soundless swell.

Nor is there a sign that under this Rock,   10
At the heart of the earth, the volcanoes
Await the word of the Lord of Misrule
To renew their ancient carnival;
Nor is there a sign above the Rock
That the earth responds to the whip of the sun,
Directing its pace and its orbit.
This is the cloister of the world,
Reduced to a cell in the fortress of peace
In the midst of anonymous, infinite darkness.

A slight turn of a dial,   20
And night and space and the silence
Thronged and tongued with life –
As the hosts might swarm through a lens
From a blood drop
Or a spot of dust in the heavens.
Out of the void they came

To storm the base of the tower,
To hammer the walls of the cell
And tap at the mullioned panes.

Polaris, the scout of Orion,   30
Was frigidly, jealously
Watching a speck on the frontier.
Adjusting a monocle,
He focused a stare which had often congealed
The blood of explorers,
And frozen their hands to the sextants
Till their bodies starched on the parallels.
He flashed to his chief
That a pair of Muscovite eagles
Had taken his stare without blinking,   40
Had rifled the pole right under his nose,
And, southward advancing, had brushed with their wings
One-half the floor of the world.
Nor would it be long, he predicted,
Before complaints would come from the stars,
All the way from zenith to nadir,
That their eyes had been blinded by grit,
The moment those birds had swept
All the dust from the planet Tellurian
With one whiff of their insolent tails.   50

A civilized group from the west,
Lithe, sleek and genteel
And ambassadorial,
Silked from their speech to the rim of their cuffs,
Were joined by a rout from the east:
Battered, uncouth and down at the heel,
Reeking with smoke from Nanking,
Weathering typhoons off Shanghai and Burma,
They filled the night with their clamour,
And spattered the shirts of the Cabinet Ministers   60
With sludge from the bed of the Yangtze.

From the south, south-east and south-west
Came the ghosts of the master of rapture,
Invoked by their master executants.
Through larynx and fingers and lips,
From catgut and silver and brass,
They were harassed by spirits still in the flesh
Who strove through auditions
With tap-dance and croon, with yodel and bleat,
To grind out an art cacophonic.   70
And choirs arrayed in white robes
Who had heard of blood that redeemed,
Of fires that refined
And of glory that sanctified dying,
Were massed in their anthem formation
To peal forth their late Hallelujahs
To a sovereign of love, law and order.

Tenore robusto and coloratura,
Deep-chested contralto and basso profundo
Entered to sing of their balcony lovers,   80
Of jealousies, hates and neurotic farewells,
Of picadors, passionate gypsies,
Of damsels anaemic waiting at windows
For exiles that never returned.
. . . . .
The moon waxed and waned,
And came again to the full,
Till the sea arose to the equinox.
But only ferrets of sound
Came out of the fog
To worm themselves through the cracks in the cobbles.   90
The waters leaped at the splayed bastions –
The might of the waters
Against the weight of the concrete,
Against the strength of the steel –
But only the dull reverberation of their paws
Disturbed the insulation of the tower;

Only the faintest echoes seeped through the copper roof
As the gulls screamed around the weather-vane.

(September 1939)
The dial swung to the 69,
And with the sprint of light   100
On the last lap of the kilocycles
Blew in the great syllabic storm of the age.
Slow in the deep bass started the overture,
Heavy with guttural chords
And growling consonants that raked the cuspids
With timed explosions.
A crash of the dental mutes
Was followed by the pour of the open vowels
Along a huge Teutonic corridor.
And when the serried sibilants struck High G,   110
A child ran from the room of the tower,
An Alsatian bristled his neck,
A Dachshund slunk under a chair;
And the period ended with a frenzy
Of thirty thousand voices orchestrated
To reduce the Gotterdammerung
To a trundle lullaby.
O master mason! What was wrong with the mortar
That, built to withstand the siege of the sea,
Should crumble beneath the roar from a throat?   120

Another turn, and the static combined
With the music of march and the roll of drums,
To prelude the close of a civilized aeon.
With a new salute and macabre step,
Chaos came in at the call of the horns.
No longer did news pause to rest on the journey,
Relayed through the stations in story and comment,
To be combed and groomed by the censors
In the leisured light of the studios:

But straight from the rape of the liners,   130
From the listed decks of the cruisers,
From trenches and plants and fields,
Came the grind from the lurch of the life-boats,
The sputter of salt from the throats,
The caterpillar crunch of the tanks,
The cries that out-blared the burst of the shells,
And the wheeze from the lungs that followed the sirens
In the smother of black-outs that covered the world.

Then Time shedding his mask,
His lazy hour-glass, his rusty scythe,   140
And all his tattered mortalities
Curved over bowed decrepit shoulders
Assumed the stature of a young Apollyon.
He rose to be the Paragon of Power.
A set of golden keys
Closing all doors of life,
Fitting the wards of death,
Hung from a girdle at his waist;
And as he led his mad aerial legions
Around the turret,   150
What thunders tarried in his fists!
What voltage in the dark tips of his wings!   December 1939

Fire-Worship

Many a morning had I watched this bay
Rifle the jewels which the Dawn outrolled,
And then deliver to the god of Day
The plunder for a smock of woven gold.

But never had this picture struck my eyes
At any bargain counters of the east –
Such sacrificial use of merchandise,
The vision of a bandit turning priest –

46

Until this morning when the ocean learned
To hold a Mass before the highest name   10
In pagan hierarchies, and returned
Its transubstantial gems to flame.   February 1940

Dunkirk

So long as light shall shine upon a world
Which has a human sage for the lyre,
A pennant at the masthead left unfurled,
A name, a title to be writ in fire;
So long as there is drama on the earth
And the wild pulses leap to the grand themes
That dignify our voyaging from birth
To death along the highway of our dreams;
This name shall be the symbol for the soul,
A new Promethean triumph in defeat,   10
And find its place in the historic scroll
That lists the immortal stand, the great retreat,
Attending causes ultimately won –
Thermopylae, Corunna or Verdun.   July 1940

Brébeuf and His Brethren

I

The winds of God were blowing over France,
Kindling the hearths and altars, changing vows
Of rote into an alphabet of flame.
The air was charged with song beyond the range
Of larks, with wings beyond the stretch of eagles.
Skylines unknown to maps broke from the mists
And there was laughter on the seas. With sound
Of bugles from the Roman catacombs,

The saints came back in their incarnate forms.
Across the Alps St Francis of Assisi   10
In his brown tunic girt with hempen cord,
Revisited the plague-infected towns.
The monks were summoned from their monasteries,
Nuns from their convents; apostolic hands
Had touched the priests; foundlings and galley slaves
Became the charges of Vincent de Paul;
Francis de Sales put his heroic stamp
Upon his order of the Visitation.
Out of Numidia by way of Rome,
The architect of palaces, unbuilt   20
Of hand, again was busy with his plans,
Reshaping for the world his *City of God*.
Out of the Netherlands was heard the call
Of Kempis through the *Imitatio*
To leave the dusty marts and city streets
And stray along the shores of Galilee.
The flame had spread across the Pyrenees –
The visions of Theresa burning through
The adorations of the Carmelites;
The very clouds at night to John of the Cross   30
Being cruciform – chancel, transept and aisle
Blazing with light and holy oracle.
Xavier had risen from his knees to drive
His dreams full-sail under an ocean compass.
Loyola, soldier-priest, staggering with wounds
At Pampeluna, guided by a voice,
Had travelled to the Montserrata Abbey
To leave his sword and dagger on an altar
That he might lead the *Company of Jesus*.

The story of the frontier like a saga   40
Sang through the cells and cloisters of the nation,
Made silver flutes out of the parish spires,
Troubled the ashes of the canonized

In the cathedral crypts, soared through the nave
To stir the foliations on the columns,
Roll through the belfries, and give deeper tongue
To the *Magnificat* in Notre Dame.
It brought to earth the prophets and apostles
Out of their static shrines in the stained glass.
It caught the ear of Christ, reveined his hands   50
And feet, bidding his marble saints to leave
Their pedestals for chartless seas and coasts
And the vast blunders of the forest glooms.
So, in the footsteps of their patrons came
A group of men asking the hardest tasks
At the new outposts of the Huron bounds
Held in the stern hand of the Jesuit Order.

And in Bayeux a neophyte while rapt
In contemplation saw a bleeding form
Falling beneath the instrument of death,   60
Rising under the quickening of the thongs,
Stumbling along the Via Dolorosa.
No play upon the fancy was this scene,
But the Real Presence to the naked sense.
The fingers of Brébeuf were at his breast,
Closing and tightening on a crucifix,
While voices spoke aloud unto his ear
And to his heart – *per ignem et per aquam.*
Forests and streams and trails thronged through his mind,
The painted faces of the Iroquois,   70
Nomadic bands and smoking bivouacs
Along the shores of western inland seas,
With forts and palisades and fiery stakes.
The stories of Champlain, Brulé, Viel,
Sagard and Le Caron had reached his town –
The stories of those northern boundaries
Where in the winter the white pines could brush
The Pleiades, and at the equinoxes

Under the gold and green of the auroras
Wild geese drove wedges through the zodiac. 80
The vows were deep he laid upon his soul.
'I shall be broken first before I break them.'
He knew by heart the manual that had stirred
The world – the clarion calling through the notes
Of the Ignatian preludes. On the prayers,
The meditations, points and colloquies,
Was built the soldier and the martyr programme.
This is the end of man – *Deum laudet*,
To seek and find the will of God, to act
Upon it for the ordering of life, 90
And for the soul's beatitude. This is
To do, this not to do. To weigh the sin;
The interior understanding to be followed
By the amendment of the deed through grace;
The abnegation of the evil thought
And act; the trampling of the body under;
The daily practice of the *counter virtues*.
'In time of desolation to be firm
And constant in the soul's determination,
Desire and sense obedient to the reason.' 100

The oath Brébeuf was taking had its root
Firm in his generations of descent.
The family name was known to chivalry –
In the Crusades; at Hastings; through the blood
Of the English Howards; called out on the rungs
Of the siege ladders; at the castle breaches;
Proclaimed by heralds at the lists, and heard
In Council Halls: – the coat-of-arms a bull
In black with horns of gold on a silver shield.
So on that toughened pedigree of fibre 110
Were strung the pledges. From the novice stage
To the vow-day he passed on to the priesthood,
And on the anniversary of his birth
He celebrated his first mass at Rouen.

April 26, 1625

And the first clauses of the Jesuit pledge
Were honoured when, embarking at Dieppe,
Brébeuf, Massé and Charles Lalemant
Travelled three thousand miles of the Atlantic,
And reached the citadel in seven weeks.
A month in preparation at Notre Dame   120
Des Anges, Brébeuf in company with Daillon
Moved to Three Rivers to begin the journey.
Taking both warning and advice from traders,
They packed into their stores of altar-ware
And vestments, strings of colored beads with knives,
Kettles and awls, domestic gifts to win
The Hurons' favour or appease their wrath.
There was a touch of omen in the warning,
For scarcely had they started when the fate
Of the Franciscan mission was disclosed –   130
News of Viel, delivered to Brébeuf –
Drowned by the natives in the final league
Of his return at Sault-au-Recollét!

Back to Quebec by Lalemant's command;
A year's delay of which Brébeuf made use
By hardening his body and his will,
Learning the rudiments of the Huron tongue,
Mastering the wood-lore, joining in the hunt
For food, observing habits of speech, the ways
Of thought, the moods and the long silences.   140
Wintering with the Algonquins, he soon knew
The life that was before him in the cabins –
The troubled night, branches of fir covering
The floor of snow; the martyrdom of smoke
That hourly drove his nostrils to the ground
To breathe, or offered him the choice of death
Outside by frost, inside by suffocation;
The forced companionship of dogs that ate

From the same platters, slept upon his legs
Or neck; the nausea from sagamite,   150
Unsalted, gritty, and that bloated feeling,
The February stomach touch when acorns,
Turk's cap, bog-onion bulbs dug from the snow
And bulrush roots flavoured with eel skin made
The menu for his breakfast-dinner-supper.
Added to this, the instigated taunts
Common as daily salutations; threats
Of murderous intent that just escaped
The deed – the prologue to Huronia!

July 1626

Midsummer and the try again – Brébeuf,   160
Daillon, de Nouë just arrived from France;
Quebec up to Three Rivers; the routine
Repeated; bargaining with the Indians,
Axes and beads against the maize and passage;
The natives' protest when they saw Brébeuf,
High as a totem-pole. What if he placed
His foot upon the gunwale, suddenly
Shifted an ounce of those two hundred pounds
Off centre at the rapids! They had visions
Of bodies and bales gyrating round the rocks,   170
Plunging like stumps and logs over the falls.
The Hurons shook their heads: the bidding grew;
Kettles and porcelain necklaces and knives,
Till with the last awl thrown upon the heap,
The ratifying grunt came from the chief.
Two Indians holding the canoe, Brébeuf,
Barefooted, cassock pulled up to his knees,
Planted one foot dead in the middle, then
The other, then slowly and ticklishly
Adjusted to the physics of his range   180
And width, he grasped both sides of the canoe,
Lowered himself and softly murmuring
An *Ave*, sat, immobile as a statue.

So the flotilla started – the same route
Champlain and Le Caron eleven years
Before had taken to avoid the swarm
Of hostile Iroquois on the St Lawrence.
Eight hundred miles – along the Ottawa
Through the steep gorges where the river narrowed,
Through calmer waters where the river widened,   190
Skirting the island of the Allumettes,
Thence to the Mattawa through the lakes that led
To the blue waters of the Nipissing,
And then southward a hundred tortuous miles
Down the French River to the Huron shore.
The record of that trip was for Brébeuf
A memory several times to be re-lived;
Of rocks and cataracts and portages,
Of feet cut by•the river stones, of mud
And stench, of boulders, logs and tangled growths,   200
Of summer heat that made him long for night,
And when he struck his bed of rock – mosquitoes
That made him doubt if dawn would ever break.
'Twas thirty days to the Georgian Bay, then south
One hundred miles threading the labyrinth
Of islands till he reached the western shore
That flanked the Bay of Penetanguishene.
Soon joined by both his fellow priests he followed
The course of a small stream and reached Toanché,
Where for three years he was to make his home   210
And turn the first sod of the Jesuit mission.

'Twas ploughing only – for eight years would pass
Before even the blades appeared. The priests
Knew well how barren was the task should signs,
Gestures and inarticulate sounds provide
The basis of the converse. And the speech
Was hard. De Nouë set himself to school,
Unfalteringly as to his Breviary,

Through the long evenings of the fall and winter.
But as light never trickled through a sentence,   220
Either the Hurons' or his own, he left
With the spring's expedition to Quebec,
Where intermittently for twenty years
He was to labour with the colonists,
Travelling between the outposts, and to die
Snow-blind, caught in the circles of his tracks
Between Three Rivers and Fort Richelieu.

Daillon migrated to the south and west
To the country of the Neutrals. There he spent
The winter, fruitless. Jealousies of trade   230
Awoke resentment, fostered calumnies,
Until the priest under a constant threat
That often issued in assault, returned
Against his own persuasion to Quebec.

Brébeuf was now alone. He bent his mind
To the great end. The efficacious rites
Were hinged as much on mental apprehensions
As on the disposition of the heart.
For that the first equipment was the speech.
He listened to the sounds and gave them letters,   240
Arranged their sequences, caught the inflections,
Extracted nouns from objects, verbs from actions
And regimented rebel moods and tenses.
He saw the way the chiefs harangued the clans,
The torrent of compounded words, the art
Concealed within the pause, the look, the gesture.
Lacking all labials, the open mouth
Performed a double service with the vowels
Directed like a battery at the hearers.
With what forebodings did he watch the spell   250
Cast on the sick by the Arendiwans:
The sorcery of the Huron rhetoric

Extorting bribes for cures, for guarantees
Against the failure of the crop or hunt!
The time would come when steel would clash on steel,
And many a battle would be won or lost
With weapons from the armoury of words.
Three years of that apprenticeship had won
The praise of his Superior and no less
Evoked the admiration of Champlain.   260
That soldier, statesman, navigator, friend,
Who had combined the brain of Richelieu
With the red blood of Cartier and Magellan,
Was at this time reduced to his last keg
Of powder at the citadel. Blockade,
The piracy of Kirke on the Atlantic,
The English occupation of Quebec,
And famine, closed this chapter of the mission.

II

1629

Four years at home could not abate his zeal.
Brébeuf, absorbed within his meditations,   270
Made ready to complete his early vows.
Each year in France but served to clarify
His vision. At Rouen he gauged the height
Of the Cathedral's central tower in terms
Of pines and oaks around the Indian lodges.
He went to Paris. There as worshipper,
His eyes were scaling transepts, but his mind,
Straying from window patterns where the sun
Shed rose ellipses on the marble floor,
Rested on glassless walls of cedar bark.   280
To Rennes – the Jesuits' intellectual home,
Where, in the *Summa* of Aquinas, faith
Laid hold on God's existence when the last

Link of the Reason slipped, and where Loyola
Enforced the high authoritarian scheme
Of God's vicegerent on the priestly fold.
Between the two nostalgic fires Brébeuf
Was swung – between two homes; in one was peace
Within the holy court, the ecstasy
Of unmolested prayer before the Virgin,   290
The daily and vicarious offering
On which no hand might dare lay sacrilege:
But in the other would be broken altars
And broken bodies of both Host and priest.
Then of which home, the son? From which the exile?
With his own blood Brébeuf wrote his last vow –
'Lord Jesus! You redeemed me with your blood;
By your most precious death; and this is why
I make this pledge to serve you all my life
In the Society of Jesus – never   300
To serve another than Thyself. Hereby
I sign this promise in my blood, ready
To sacrifice it all as willingly
As now I give this drop.' – Jean de Brébeuf.

Nor did the clamour of the *Thirty Years*,
The battle-cries at La Rochelle and Fribourg,
Blow out the flame. Less strident than the names
Of Richelieu and Mazarin, Condé,
Turenne, but just as mighty, were the calls
Of the new apostolate. A century   310
Before had Xavier from the Indies summoned
The world to other colours. Now appeals
Were ringing through the history of New France.
Le Jeune, following the example of Biard
And Charles Lalemant, was capturing souls
By thousands with the fire of the *Relations*:
Noble and peasant, layman, priest and nun
Gave of their wealth and power and personal life.

Among his new recruits were Chastellain,
Pijart, Le Mercier, and Isaac Jogues,   320
The Lalemants – Jerome and Gabriel –
Jerome who was to supervise and write,
With Ragueneau, the drama of the Mission;
Who told of the survivors reaching France
When the great act was closed that 'all of them
Still hold their resolution to return
To the combat at the first sound of the trumpets.'
The other, Gabriel, who would share the crown
With Jean Brébeuf, pitting the frailest body
Against the hungers of the wilderness,   330
The fevers of the lodges and the fires
That slowly wreathed themselves around a stake.

Then Garnier, comrade of Jogues. The winds
Had fanned to a white heat the hearth and placed
Three brothers under vows – the Carmelite,
The Capuchin, and his, the Jesuit.
The gentlest of his stock, he had resolved
To seek and to accept a post that would
Transmit his nurture through a discipline
That multiplied the living martyrdoms   340
Before the casual incident of death.

To many a vow did Chabanel subject
His timid nature as the evidence
Of trial came through the Huronian records.
He needed every safeguard of the soul
To fortify the will, for every day
Would find him fighting, mastering his revolt
Against the native life and practices.
Of all the priests he could the least endure
The sudden transformation from the Chair   350
Of College Rhetoric to the heat and drag
Of portages, from the monastic calm

To the noise and smoke and vermin of the lodges,
And the insufferable sights and stinks
When, at the High Feast of the Dead, the bodies
Lying for months or years upon the scaffolds
Were taken down, stripped of their flesh, caressed,
Strung up along the cabin poles and then
Cast in a pit for common burial.
The day would come when in the wilderness, 360
The weary hand protesting, he would write
This final pledge – 'I, Noel Chabanel,
Do vow, in presence of the Sacrament
Of Thy most precious blood and body, here
To stay forever with the Huron Mission,
According to commands of my Superiors.
Therefore I do beseech Thee to receive me
As Thy perpetual servant and to make
Me worthy of so sublime a ministry.'

And the same spirit breathed on Chaumonot, 370
Making his restless and undisciplined soul
At first seek channels of renunciation
In abstinence, ill health and beggary.
His months of pilgrimages to the shrines
At Rome and to the Lady of Loretto,
The static hours upon his knees had sapped
His strength, turning an introspective mind
Upon the weary circuit of its thoughts,
Until one day a letter from Brébeuf
Would come to burn the torpors of his heart 380
And galvanize a raw novitiate.

III

1633

New France restored! Champlain, Massé, Brébeuf
Were in Quebec, hopes riding high as ever.

Davost and Daniel soon arrived to join
The expedition west. Midsummer trade,
The busiest the Colony had known,
Was over: forty-three canoes to meet
The hazards of return; the basic sense
Of safety, now Champlain was on the scene;
The joy of the Toanché Indians   390
As they beheld Brébeuf and heard him speak
In their own tongue, was happy augury.
But as before upon the eve of starting
The path was blocked, so now the unforeseen
Stepped in. A trade and tribal feud long-blown
Between the Hurons and the Allumettes
Came to a head when the Algonquin chief
Forbade the passage of the priests between
His island and the shore. The Hurons knew
The roughness of this channel, and complied.   400

In such delays which might have been construed
By lesser wills as exits of escape,
As providential doors on a light latch,
The Fathers entered deeper preparation.
They worked incessantly among the tribes
In the environs of Quebec, took hold
Of Huron words and beat them into order.
Davost and Daniel gathered from the store
Of speech, manners, and customs that Brébeuf
Had garnered, all the subtleties to make   410
The bargain for the journey. The next year
Seven canoes instead of forty! Fear
Of Iroquois following a recent raid
And massacre; growing distrust of priests;
The sense of risk in having men aboard
Unskilled in fire-arms, helpless at the paddles
And on the portages – all these combined
To sharpen the terms until the treasury
Was dry of presents and of promises.

1634

The ardours of his trip eight years before   420
Fresh in his mind, Brébeuf now set his face
To graver peril, for the native mood
Was hostile. On the second week the corn
Was low, a handful each a day. Sickness
Had struck the Huron, slowing down the blades,
And turning murmurs to menaces
Against the Blackrobes and their French companions.
The first blow hit Davost. Robbed of his books,
Papers and altar linens, he was left
At the Island of the Allumettes; Martin   430
Was put ashore at Nipissing; Baron
And Daniel were deserted, made to take
Their chances with canoes along the route;
Yet all in turn, tattered, wasted, with feet
Bleeding – broken though not in will – rejoined
Their great companion after he had reached
The forest shores of the Fresh Water Sea,
And guided by the sight of smoke had entered
The village of Ihonatiria.

A year's success flattered the priestly hope   440
That on this central field seed would be sown
On which the yield would be the Huron nation
Baptized and dedicated to the Faith;
And that a richer harvest would be gleaned
Of duskier grain from the same seed on more
Forbidding ground when the arch-foes themselves
Would be re-born under the sacred rites.
For there was promise in the auspices.
Ihonatiria received Brébeuf
With joy. Three years he had been there, a friend   450
Whose visit to the tribes could not have sprung
From inspiration rooted in private gain.

He had not come to stack the arquebuses
Against the mountains of the beaver pelts.
He had not come to kill. Between the two
– Barter and battle – what was left to explain
A stranger in their midst? The name *Echon*
Had solved the riddle.

                    So with native help
The Fathers built their mission house – the frame
Of young elm-poles set solidly in earth;   460
Their supple tops bent, lashed and braced to form
The arched roof overlaid with cedar-bark.
'No Louvre or palace is this cabin,' wrote
Brébeuf, 'no stories, cellar, garret, windows,
No chimney – only at the top a hole
To let the smoke escape. Inside, three rooms
With doors of wood alone set it apart
From the single long-house of the Indians.
The first is used for storage; in the second
Our kitchen, bedroom and refectory;   470
Our bedstead is the earth; rushes and boughs
For mattresses and pillows; in the third,
Which is our chapel, we have placed the altar,
The images and vessels of the Mass.'
It was the middle room that drew the natives,
Day after day, to share the sagamite
And raisins, and to see the marvels brought
From France – marvels on which the Fathers built
A basis of persuasion, recognizing
The potency of awe for natures nurtured   480
On charms and spells, invoking kindly spirits
And exorcising demons. So the natives
Beheld a mass of iron chips like bees
Swarm to a lodestone: was it gum that held
Them fast? They watched the handmill grind the corn;
Gaped at a lens eleven faceted

That multiplied a bead as many times
And at a phial where a captive flea
Looked like a beetle. But the miracle
Of all, the clock! It showed the hours; it struck   490
Or stopped upon command. *Le Capitaine*
Du Jour which moved its hands before its face,
Called up the dawn, saluted noon, rang out
The sunset, summoned with the count of twelve
The Fathers to a meal, or sent at four
The noisy pack of Indians to their cabins.
'What did it say?' 'Yo eiouahaoua –
Time to put on the cauldron.' 'And what now?'
'Time to go home at once and close the door.'
It was alive: an *oki* dwelt inside,   500
Peering out through that black hub on the dial.

As great a mystery was writing – how
A Frenchman fifteen miles away could know
The meaning of black signs the runner brought.
Sometimes the marks were made on peel of bark,
Sometimes on paper – in itself a wonder!
From what strange tree was it the inside rind?
What charm was in the ink that transferred thought
Across such space without a spoken word?

This growing confirmation of belief   510
Was speeded by events wherein good fortune
Waited upon the priestly word and act.

August 27, 1635

A moon eclipse was due – Brébeuf had known it –
Had told the Indians of the moment when
The shadow would be thrown across the face.
Nor was there wastage in the prayers as night,
Uncurtained by a single cloud, produced
An orb most perfect. No one knew the lair

Or nest from which the shadow came; no one
The home to which it travelled when it passed.   520
Only the vague uncertainties were left –
Was it the dread invasion from the south?
Such portent was the signal for the braves
To mass themselves outside the towns and shoot
Their multitudes of arrows at the sky
And fling their curses at the Iroquois.
Like a crow's wing it hovered, broodily
Brushing the face – five hours from rim to rim
While midnight darkness stood upon the land.
This was prediction baffling all their magic.   530
Again, when weeks of drought had parched the land
And burned the corn, when dancing sorcerers
Brought out their tortoise shells, climbed on the roofs,
Clanging their invocation to the Bird
Of Thunder to return, day after day,
Without avail, the priests formed their processions,
Put on their surplices above their robes,
And the Bird of Thunder came with heavy rain,
Released by the nine masses at Saint Joseph.

Nor were the village warriors slow to see   540
The value of the Frenchmen's strategy
In war. Returning from the eastern towns,
They told how soldiers had rebuilt the forts,
And strengthened them with corner bastions
Where through the embrasures enfilading fire
Might flank the Iroquois bridging the ditches,
And scaling ramparts. Here was argument
That pierced the thickest prejudice of brain
And heart, allaying panic ever present,
When with the first news of the hated foe   550
From scouts and hunters, women with their young
Fled to the dubious refuge of the forest

From terror blacker than a pestilence.
On such a soil tilled by those skilful hands
Those passion flowers and lilies of the East,
The *Aves* and the *Paternosters* bloomed.
The *Credos* and the *Thou-shalt-nots* were turned
By Daniel into simple Huron rhymes
And taught to children, and when points of faith
Were driven hard against resistant rock,   560
The Fathers found the softer crevices
Through deeds which readily the Indian mind
Could grasp – where hands were never put to blows
Nor the swift tongues used for recrimination.

Acceptance of the common lot was part
Of the original vows. But that the priests
Who were to come should not misread the text,
Brébeuf prepared a sermon on the theme
Of Patience: – 'Fathers, Brothers, under call
Of God! Take care that you foresee the perils,   570
Labours and hardships of this Holy Mission.
You must sincerely love the savages
As brothers ransomed by the blood of Christ.
All things must be endured. To win their hearts
You must perform the smallest services.
Provide a tinder-box or burning mirror
To light their fires. Fetch wood and water for them;
And when embarking never let them wait
For you; tuck up your habits, keep them dry
To avoid water and sand in their canoes. Carry   580
Your load on portages. Always appear
Cheerful – their memories are good for faults.
Constrain yourselves to eat their sagamite
The way that they prepare it, tasteless, dirty.'

And by the priests upon the ground all dots
And commas were observed. They suffered smoke
That billowed from the back-draughts at the roof,
Smothered the cabin, seared the eyes; the fire
That broiled the face, while frost congealed the spine;
The food from unwashed platters where refusal   590
Was an offence; the rasp of speech maintained
All day by men who never learned to talk
In quiet tones; the drums of the Diviners
Blasting the night – all this without complaint!
And more – whatever sleep was possible
To snatch from the occasional lull of cries
Was broken by uncovenanted fleas
That fastened on the priestly flesh like hornets.
Carving the curves of favour on the lips,
Tailoring the man into the Jesuit coat,   600
Wrapping the smiles round inward maledictions,
And sublimating hoary Gallic oaths
Into the *Benedicite* when dogs
And squaws and reeking children violated
The hours of rest, were penances unnamed
Within the iron code of good Ignatius.
Was there a limit of obedience
Outside the jurisdiction of this Saint?
How often did the hand go up to lower
The flag? How often by some ringing order   610
Was it arrested at the halliard touch?
How often did Brébeuf seal up his ears
When blows and insults woke ancestral fifes
Within his brain, blood-cells, and viscera,
Is not explicit in the written story.

But never could the Indians infer
Self-gain or anything but simple courage
Inspired by a zeal beyond reproof,
As when the smallpox spreading like a flame

Destroying hundreds, scarifying thousands,   620
The Fathers took their chances of contagion,
Their broad hats warped by rain, their moccasins
Worn to the kibes, that they might reach the huts,
Share with the sick their dwindled stock of food –
A sup of partridge broth or raisin juice,
Inscribe the sacred sign of the cross, and place
A touch of moisture from the Holy Water
Upon the forehead of a dying child.

Before the year was gone the priests were shown
The way the Hurons could prepare for death   630
A captive foe. The warriors had surprised
A band of Iroquois and had reserved
The one survivor for a fiery pageant.
No cunning of an ancient Roman triumph,
Nor torment of a Medici confession
Surpassed the subtle savagery of art
Which made the dressing for the sacrifice
A ritual of mockery for the victim.
What visions of the past came to Brébeuf,
And what forebodings of the days to come,   640
As he beheld this weird compound of life
In jest and intent taking place before
His eyes –the crude unconscious variants
Of reed and sceptre, robe and cross, brier
And crown! Might not one day baptismal drops
Be turned against him in a rain of death?
Whatever the appeals made by the priests,
They could not break the immemorial usage
Or vary one detail. The prisoner
Was made to sing his death-song, was embraced,   650
Hailed with ironic greetings, forced to state
His willingness to die.
                              'See how your hands
Are crushed. You cannot thus desire to live.

No.
     Then be of good courage – you shall die.

True! What shall be the manner of my death?

By fire.
      When shall it be?
              Tonight.
                       What hour?
At sunset.
        All is well.'
            Eleven fires
Were lit along the whole length of the cabin.
His body smeared with pitch and bound with belts
Of bark, the Iroquois was forced to run   660
The fires, stopped at each end by the young braves,
And swiftly driven back, and when he swooned,
They carried him outside to the night air,
Laid him on fresh damp moss, poured cooling water
Into his mouth, and to his burns applied
The soothing balsams. With resuscitation
They lavished on him all the courtesies
Of speech and gesture, gave him food and drink,
Compassionately spoke of his wounds and pain.
The ordeal every hour was resumed   670
And halted, but, with each recurrence, blows
Were added to the burns and gibes gave place
To yells until the sacrificial dawn,
Lighting the scaffold, dimming the red glow
Of the hatchet collar, closed the festival.

Brébeuf had seen the worst. He knew that when
A winter pack of wolves brought down a stag
There was no waste of time between the leap
And the business click upon the jugular,
Such was the forthright honesty in death   680

Among the brutes. They had not learned the sport
Of dallying around the nerves to halt
A quick despatch. A human art was torture,
Where reason crept into the veins, mixed tar
With blood and brewed its own intoxicant.
Brébeuf had pleaded for the captive's life,
But as the night wore on, would not his heart,
Colliding with his mind, have wished for death?
The plea refused, he gave the Iroquois
The only consolation in his power.   690
He went back to his cabin, heavy in heart.
To stem that viscous melanotic current
Demanded labour, time, and sacrifice.
Those passions were not altered over-night.
Two plans were in his mind – the one concerned
The seminary started in Quebec.
The children could be sent there to be trained
In Christian precepts, weaned from superstition
And from the savage spectacle of death.
He saw the way the women and their broods   700
Danced round the scaffold in their exaltation.
How much of this was habit and how much
Example? Curiously Brébeuf revolved
The facets of the Indian character.
A fighting courage equal to the French –
It could be lifted to crusading heights
By a battle speech. Endurance was a code
Among the braves, and impassivity.
Their women wailing at the Feast of Death,
The men sat silent, heads bowed to the knees.   710
'Never in nine years with but one exception,'
Wrote Ragueneau, 'did I see an Indian weep
For grief.' Only the fires evoked the cries,
And these like scalps were triumphs for the captors.
But then their charity and gentleness
To one another and to strangers gave

A balance to the picture. Fugitives
From villages destroyed found instant welcome
To the last communal share of food and land.
Brébeuf's stay at Toanché gave him proof   720
Of how the Huron nature could respond
To kindness. But last night upon that scaffold!
Could that be scoured from the heart? Why not
Try out the nurture plan upon the children
And send the boys east, shepherded by Daniel?

The other need was urgent – labourers!
The villages were numerous and were spread
Through such a vast expanse of wilderness
And shore. Only a bell with a bronze throat
Must summon missionaries to these fields.   730
With the last cry of the captive in his ears,
Brébeuf strode from his cabin to the woods
To be alone. He found his tabernacle
Within a grove, picked up a stone flat-faced,
And going to a cedar-crotch, he jammed
It in, and on this table wrote his letter.
'Herein I show you what you have to suffer.
I shall say nothing of the voyage – that
You know already. If you have the courage
To try it, that is only the beginning,   740
For when after a month of river travel
You reach our village, we can offer you
The shelter of a cabin lowlier
Than any hovel you have seen in France.
As tired as you may be, only a mat
Laid on the ground will be your bed. Your food
May be for weeks a gruel of crushed corn
That has the look and smell of mortar paste.
This country is the breeding place of vermin.
Sandflies, mosquitoes haunt the summer months.   750
In France you may have been a theologian,
A scholar, master, preacher, but out here

You must attend a savage school; for months
Will pass before you learn even to lisp
The language. Here barbarians shall be
Your Aristotle and Saint Thomas. Mute
Before those teachers you shall take your lessons.
What of the winter? Half the year is winter.
Inside your cabins will be smoke so thick
You may not read your Breviary for days.   760
Around your fireplace at mealtime arrive
The uninvited guests with whom you share
Your stint of food. And in the fall and winter,
You tramp unbeaten trails to reach the missions,
Carrying your luggage on your back. Your life
Hangs by a thread. Of all calamities
You are the cause – the scarcity of game,
A fire, famine or an epidemic.
There are no natural reasons for a drought
And for the earth's sterility. You are   770
The reasons, and at any time a savage
May burn your cabin down or split your head.
I tell you of the enemies that live
Among our Huron friends. I have not told
You of the Iroquois our constant foes.
Only a week ago in open fight
They killed twelve of our men at Contarea,
A day's march from the village where we live.
Treacherous and stealthy in their ambuscades,
They terrorize the country, for the Hurons   780
Are very slothful in defence, never
On guard and always seeking flight for safety.

'Wherein the gain, you ask, of this acceptance?
There is no gain but this – that what you suffer
Shall be of God: your loneliness in travel
Will be relieved by angels overhead;
Your silence will be sweet for you will learn
How to commune with God; rapids and rocks

Are easier than the steeps of Calvary.
There is a consolation in your hunger   790
And in abandonment upon the road,
For once there was a greater loneliness
And deeper hunger. As regards the soul
There are no dangers here, with means of grace
At every turn, for if we go outside
Our cabin, is not heaven over us?
No buildings block the clouds. We say our prayers
Freely before a noble oratory.
Here is the place to practise faith and hope
And charity where human art has brought   800
No comforts, where we strive to bring to God
A race so unlike men that we must live
Daily expecting murder at their hands,
Did we not open up the skies or close
Them at command, giving them sun or rain.
So if despite these trials you are ready
To share our labours, come; for you will find
A consolation in the cross that far outweighs
Its burdens. Though in many an hour your soul
Will echo – "Why hast Thou forsaken me,"   810
Yet evening will descend upon you when,
Your heart too full of holy exultation,
You call like Xavier – "Enough, O Lord!"'

This letter was to loom in history,
For like a bulletin it would be read
In France, and men whose bones were bound for dust
Would find that on those jagged characters
Their names would rise from their oblivion
To flame on an eternal Calendar.
Already to the field two young recruits   820
Had come – Pijart, Le Mercier; on their way
Were Chastellain with Garnier and Jogues
Followed by Ragueneau and Du Peron.

On many a night in lonely intervals,
The priest would wander to the pines and build
His oratory where celestial visions
Sustained his soul. As unto Paul and John
Of Patmos and the martyr multitude
The signs were given – voices from the clouds,
Forms that illumined darkness, stabbed despair,   830
Turned dungeons into temples and a brand
Of shame into the ultimate boast of time –
So to Brébeuf had Christ appeared and Mary.
One night at prayer he heard a voice command –
'Rise, Read!' Opening the *Imitatio Christi*,
His eyes 'without design' fell on the chapter,
Concerning the royal way of the Holy Cross,
Which placed upon his spirit 'a great peace.'
And then, day having come, he wrote his vow –
'My God, my Saviour, I take from thy hand   840
The cup of thy sufferings. I invoke thy name;
I vow never to fail thee in the grace
Of martyrdom, if by thy mercy, Thou
Dost offer it to me. I bind myself,
And when I have received the stroke of death,
I will accept it from thy gracious hand
With all pleasure and with joy in my heart;
To thee my blood, my body and my life.'

IV

The labourers were soon put to their tasks –
The speech, the founding of new posts, the sick: 850
Ihonatiria, a phantom town,
Through plague and flight abandoned as a base,
The Fathers chose the site – Teanaostayé,
To be the second mission of St Joseph.
But the prime hope was on Ossossané,
A central town of fifty cabins built

On the east shore of Nottawasaga Bay.
The native council had approved the plans.
The presence of the priests with their lay help
Would be defence against the Iroquois.   860
Under the supervision of Pijart
The place was fortified, ramparts were strengthened,
And towers of heavy posts set at the angles.
And in the following year the artisans
And labourers from Quebec with Du Peron,
Using broad-axe and whipsaw built a church,
The first one in the whole Huronian venture
To be of wood. Close to their lodge, the priests
Dug up the soil and harrowed it to plant
A mere handful of wheat from which they raised   870
A half a bushel for the altar bread.
From the wild grapes they made a cask of wine
For the Holy Sacrifice. But of all work
The hardest was instruction. It was easy
To strike the Huron sense with sound and colour –
The ringing of a bell; the litanies
And chants; the surplices worn on the cassocks;
The burnished ornaments around the altar;
The pageant of the ceremonial.
But to drive home the ethics taxed the brain   880
To the limit of its ingenuity.
Brébeuf had felt the need to vivify
His three main themes of God and Paradise
And Hell. The Indian mind had let the cold
Abstractions fall: the allegories failed
To quicken up the logic. Garnier
Proposed the colours for the homilies.
The closest student of the Huron mind,
He had observed the fears and prejudices
Haunting the shadows of their racial past;   890
Had seen the flaws in Brébeuf's *points*; had heard
The Indian comments on the moral law

And on the Christian scheme of Paradise.
Would Iroquois be there? Yes, if baptized.
Would there be hunting of the deer and beaver?
No. Then starvation. War? And feasts? Tobacco?
No. Garnier saw disgust upon their faces,
And sent appeals to France for pictures – one
Only of souls in bliss: of *âmes damnées*   900
Many and various – the horned Satan,
His mastiff jaws champing the head of Judas;
The plummet fall of the unbaptized pursued
By demons with their fiery forks; the lick
Of flames upon a naked Saracen;
Dragons with scarlet tongues and writhing serpents
In ambush by the charcoal avenues
Just ready at the Judgment word to wreak
Vengeance upon the unregenerate.
The negative unapprehended forms   910
Of Heaven lost in the dim canvas oils
Gave way to glows from brazier pitch that lit
The visual affirmatives of Hell.

Despite the sorcerers who laid the blame
Upon the French for all their ills – the plague,
The drought, the Iroquois – the Fathers counted
Baptisms by the hundreds, infants, children
And aged at the point of death. Adults
In health were more intractable, but here
The spade had entered soil in the conversion   920
Of a Huron in full bloom and high in power
And counsel, Tsiouendaentaha
Whose Christian name – to aid the tongue – was Peter.
Being the first, he was the Rock on which
The priests would build their Church. He was baptized
With all the pomp transferable from France
Across four thousand miles combined with what
A sky and lake could offer, and a forest

Strung to.the *aubade* of the orioles.
The wooden chapel was their Rheims Cathedral. 930
In stole and surplice Lalemant intoned –
'If therefore thou wilt enter into life,
Keep the commandments. Thou shalt love the Lord
Thy God with all thy heart, with all thy soul,
With all thy might, and thy neighbour as thyself.'
With salt and water and the holy chrism,
And through the signs made on his breast and forehead
The Huron was exorcised, sanctified,
And made the temple of the Living God.

The holy rite was followed by the Mass 940
Before the motliest auditory known
In the annals of worship. Oblates from Quebec,
Blackrobes, mechanics, soldiers, labourers,
With almost half the village packed inside,
Or jammed with craning necks outside the door.
The warriors lean, lithe, and elemental,
'As naked as your hand' but for a skin
Thrown loosely on their shoulders, with their hair
Erect, boar-brushed, matted, glued with the oil
Of sunflower larded thickly with bear's grease; 950
Papooses yowling on their mothers' backs,
The squatting hags, suspicion in their eyes,
Their nebulous minds relating in some way
The smoke and aromatics of the censer,
The candles, crucifix and Latin murmurs
With vapours, sounds and colours of the Judgment.

v

(*The Founding of Fort Sainte Marie*)

1639

The migrant habits of the Indians
With their desertion of the villages

Through pressure of attack or want of food
Called for a central site where undisturbed   960
The priests with their attendants might pursue
Their culture, gather strength from their devotions,
Map out the territory, plot the routes,
Collate their weekly notes and write their letters.
The roll was growing – priests and colonists,
Lay brothers offering services for life.
For on the ground or on their way to place
Themselves at the command of Lalemant,
Superior, were Claude Pijart, Poncet,
Le Moyne, Charles Raymbault, René Menard   970
And Joseph Chaumonot: as oblates came
Le Coq, Christophe Reynaut, Charles Boivin,
Couture and Jean Guérin. And so to house
Them all the Residence – Fort Sainte Marie!
Strategic as a base for trade or war
The site received the approval of Quebec,
Was ratified by Richelieu who saw
Commerce and exploration pushing west,
Fulfilling the long vision of Champlain –
'Greater New France beyond those inland seas.'   980
The fort was built, two hundred feet by ninety,
Upon the right bank of the River Wye:
Its north and eastern sides of masonry,
Its south and west of double palisades,
And skirted by a moat, ran parallel
To stream and lake. Square bastions at the corners,
Watch-towers with magazines and sleeping posts,
Commanded forest edges and canoes
That furtively came up the Matchedash,
And on each bastion was placed a cross.   990
Inside, the Fathers built their dwelling house,
No longer the bark cabin with the smoke
Ill-trained to work its exit through the roof,
But plank and timber – at each end a chimney
Of lime and granite field-stone. Rude it was

But clean, capacious, full of twilight calm.
Across the south canal fed by the river,
Ringed by another palisade were buildings
Offering retreat to Indian fugitives
Whenever war and famine scourged the land.   1000

The plans were supervised by Lalemant,
Assigning zones of work to every priest.
He made a census of the Huron nation;
Some thirty villages – twelve thousand persons.
Nor was this all: the horizon opened out
On larger fields. To south and west were spread
The unknown tribes – the Petuns and the Neutrals.

VI

(*The mission to the Petuns and Neutrals*)

1640–1641

In late November Jogues and Garnier
Set out on snow-obliterated trails
Towards the Blue Hills south of the Nottawasaga,   1010
A thirty mile journey through a forest
Without a guide. They carried on their backs
A blanket with the burden of the altar.
All day confronting swamps with fallen logs,
Tangles of tamarack and juniper,
They made detours to avoid the deep ravines
And swollen creeks. Retreating and advancing,
Ever in hope their tread was towards the south,
Until, 'surprised by night in a fir grove,'
They took an hour with flint and steel to nurse   1020
A fire from twigs, birch rind and needles of pine;
And flinging down some branches on the snow,
They offered thanks to God, lay down and slept.

Morning – the packs reshouldered and the tramp
Resumed, the stumble over mouldering trunks
Of pine and oak, the hopeless search for trails,
Till after dusk with cassocks torn and 'nothing
To eat all day save each a morsel of bread,'
They saw the smoke of the first Indian village.

And now began a labour which for faith   1030
And triumph of the spirit over failure
Was unsurpassed in records of the mission.
Famine and pest had struck the Neutral tribes,
And fleeing squaws and children had invaded
The Petun villages for bread and refuge,
Inflicting on the cabins further pest
And further famine. When the priests arrived,
They found that their black cassocks had become
The symbols of the scourge. Children exclaimed –
'Disease and famine are outside.' The women   1040
Called to their young and fled to forest shelters,
Or hid them in the shadows of the cabins.
The men broke through a never-broken custom,
Denying the strangers right to food and rest.
Observing the two priests at prayer, the chief
Called out in *council voice* – 'What are these demons
Who take such unknown postures, what are they
But spells to make us die – to finish those
Disease had failed to kill inside our cabins?'
Driven from town to town with all doors barred,   1050
Pursued by storms of threats and flying hatchets,
The priests sought refuge through the forest darkness
Back to the palisades of Sainte Marie.

As bleak an outlook faced Brébeuf when he
And Chaumonot took their November tramp –
Five forest days – to the north shores of Erie,
Where the most savage of the tribes – the Neutrals –

Packed their twelve thousand into forty towns.
Evil report had reached the settlements
By faster routes, for when upon the eve   1060
Of the new mission Chaumonot had stated
The purpose of the journey, Huron chiefs,
Convinced by their own sorcerers that Brébeuf
Had laid the epidemic on the land,
Resolved to make the Neutral leaders agents
Of their revenge: for it was on Brébeuf,
The chieftain of the robes, that hate was centred.
They had the reason why the drums had failed
The hunt, why moose and deer had left the forest,
And why the Manitou who sends the sun   1070
And rain upon the corn, lures to the trap
The beaver, trains the arrow on the goose,
Had not responded to the chants and cries.
The magic of the 'breathings' had not cured
The sick and dying. Was it not the prayers
To the new God which cast malignant spells?
The rosary against the amulet?
The Blackrobes with that water-rite performed
Upon their children – with that new sign
Of wood or iron held up before the eyes   1080
Of the stricken? Did the Indian not behold
Death following hard upon the offered Host?
Was not *Echon* Brébeuf the evil one?
Still, all attempts to kill him were forestalled,
For awe and fear had mitigated fury:
His massive stature, courage never questioned,
His steady glance, the firmness of his voice,
And that strange nimbus of authority,
In some dim way related to their gods,
Had kept the bowstrings of the Hurons taut   1090
At the arrow feathers, and the javelin poised
And hesitant. But now cunning might do
What fear forbade. A brace of Huron runners

Were sped to the Neutral country with rich bribes
To put the priests to death. And so Brébeuf
And his companion entered the first town
With famine in their cheeks only to find
Worse than the Petun greetings – corn refused,
Whispers of death and screams of panic, flight
From incarnated plague, and while the chiefs   1100
In closest council on the Huron terms
Voted for life or death, the younger men
Outside drew nearer to the priests, cursed them,
Spat at them while convulsive hands were clutching
At hatchet helves, waiting impatiently
The issue of that strident rhetoric
Shaking the cabin bark. The council ended,
The feeling strong for death but ruled by fears,
For if those foreign spirits had the power
To spread the blight upon the land, what could   1110
Their further vengeance not exact? Besides,
What lay behind those regimental colours
And those new drums reported from Quebec?
The older men had qualified the sentence –
The priests at once must leave the Neutral land,
All cabins to be barred against admission,
No food, no shelter, and return immediate.
Defying threats, the Fathers spent four months,
Four winter months, besieging half the towns
In their pursuit of souls, for days their food   1120
Boiled lichens, ground-nuts, star-grass bulbs and roots
Of the wild columbine. Met at the doors
By screams and blows, they would betake themselves
To the evergreens for shelter over-night.
And often, when the body strength was sapped
By the day's toil and there were streaks of blood
Inside the moccasins, when the last lodge
Rejected them as lepers and the welts
Hung on their shoulders, then the Fathers sought

The balm that never failed. Under the stars,   1130
Along an incandescent avenue
The visions trembled, tender, placid, pure,
More beautiful than the doorway of Rheims
And sweeter than the Galilean fields.
For what was hunger and the burn of wounds
In those assuaging healing moments when
The clearing mists revealed the face of Mary
And the lips of Jesus breathing benedictions?

At dawn they came back to the huts to get
The same rebuff of speech and club. A brave   1140
Repulsed them at the palisade with axe
Uplifted – 'I have had enough,' he said,
'Of the dark flesh of my enemies. I mean
To kill and eat the white flesh of the priests.'
So close to death starvation and assault
Had led them and so meagre of result
Were all their ministrations that they thought
This was the finish of the enterprise.
The winter ended in futility.
And on their journey home the Fathers took   1150
A final blow when March leagued with the natives
Unleashed a northern storm, piled up the snow-drifts,
Broke on the ice the shoulder of Brébeuf,
And stumbled them for weeks before she sent
Them limping through the postern of the fort.
Upon his bed that night Brébeuf related
A vision he had seen – a moving cross,
Its upright beam arising from the south –
The country of the Iroquois: the shape
Advanced along the sky until its arms   1160
Cast shadows on the Huron territory,
'And huge enough to crucify us all.'

VII

(*The Story of Jogues*)

Bad days had fallen on Huronia.
A blight of harvest, followed by a winter
In which unusual snowfall had thinned out
The hunting and reduced the settlements
To destitution, struck its hardest blow
At Sainte Marie. The last recourse in need,
The fort had been a common granary
And now the bins were empty. Altar-ware,   1170
Vessels, linens, pictures lost or damaged;
Vestments were ragged, writing paper spent.
The Eucharist requiring bread and wine,
Quebec eight hundred miles away, a war
Freshly renewed – the Iroquois (Dutch-armed
And seething with the memories of Champlain)
Arrayed against the French and Huron allies.

1642

The priests assessed the perils of the journey,
And the lot fell on Jogues to lead it. He,
Next to Brébeuf, had borne the heaviest brunt –   1180
The Petun mission, then the following year,
The Ojibway where, after a hundred leagues,
Canoe and trail, accompanied by Raymbault,
He reached the shores of Lake Superior,
'And planted a great cross, facing it west.'
The soundest of them all in legs, he gathered
A band of Huron traders and set out,
His task made double by the care of Raymbault
Whose health had broken mortally. He reached
Quebec with every day of the five weeks   1190

A miracle of escape. A few days there,
With churches, hospitals, the Indian school
At Sillery, pageant and ritual,
Making their due impression on the minds
Of the Huron guides, Jogues with his band of forty
Packed the canoes and started back. Mohawks,
Enraged that on the east-bound trip the party
Had slipped their hands, awaited them, ambushed
Within the grass and reeds along the shore.

(*The account of Jogues' capture and enslavement by the Mohawks
as taken from his letter to his Provincial, Jean Filleau, dated
August 5, 1643.*)

'Unskilled in speech, in knowledge and not knowing   1200
The precious hour of my visitation,
I beg you, if this letter chance to come
Unto your hands that in your charity
You aid me with your Holy Sacrifices
And with the earnest prayers of the whole Province,
As being among a people barbarous
In birth and manners, for I know that when
You will have heard this story you will see
The obligation under which I am
To God and my deep need of spiritual help.   1210
Our business finished at Quebec, the feast
Of St Ignatius celebrated, we
Embarked for the Hurons. On the second day
Our men discovered on the shore fresh tracks
Thought by Eustache, experienced in war,
To be the footprints of our enemies.
A mile beyond we met them, twelve canoes
And seventy men. Abandoning the boats,
Most of the Hurons fled to the thick wood,
Leaving but twelve to put up the best front   1220
We could, but seeing further Iroquois

Paddling so swiftly from the other shore,
We ceased from our defence and fled to cover
Of tree and bulrush. Watching from my shelter
The capture of Goupil and Indian converts,
I could not find it in my mind to leave them;
But as I was their comrade on the journey,
And should be made their comrade in their perils,
I gave myself as prisoner to the guard.
Likewise Eustache, always devoted, valiant,   1230
Returned, exclaiming "I praise God that He
Has granted me my prayer – that I should live
And die with you." And then Guillaume Couture
Who, young and fleet, having outstripped his foe,
But finding flight intolerable came back
Of his free will, saying "I cannot leave
My father in the hands of enemies."
On him the Iroquois let loose their first
Assault for in the skirmish he had slain
A chief. They stripped him naked; with their teeth   1240
They macerated his finger tips, tore off
The nails and pierced his right hand with a spear,
Couture taking the pain without a cry.
Then turning on Goupil and me they beat
Us to the ground under a flurry of fists
And knotted clubs, dragging us up half-dead
To agonize us with the finger torture.
And this was just the foretaste of our trials:
Dividing up as spoils of war our food,
Our clothes and books and vessels for the church,   1250
They led or drove us on our six weeks' journey,
Our wounds festering under the summer sun.
At night we were the objects of their sport –
They mocked us by the plucking of our hair
From head and beard. And on the eighth day meeting
A band of warriors from the tribe on march
To attack the Richelieu fort, they celebrated

By disembarking all the captives, making
Us run the line beneath a rain of clubs.
And following that they placed us on the scaffolds,   1260
Dancing around us hurling jests and insults.
Each one of us attempted to sustain
The other in his courage by no cry
Or sign of our infirmities. Eustache,
His thumbs wrenched off, withstood unconquerably
The probing of a stick which like a skewer
Beginning with the freshness of a wound
On the left hand was pushed up to the elbow.
And yet next day they put us on the route
Again – three days on foot and without food.   1270
Through village after village we were led
In triumph with our backs shedding the skin
Under the sun – by day upon the scaffolds,
By night brought to the cabins where, cord-bound,
We lay on the bare earth while fiery coals
Were thrown upon our bodies. A long time
Indeed and cruelly have the wicked wrought
Upon my back with sticks and iron rods.
But though at times when left alone I wept,
Yet I thanked Him who always giveth strength   1280
To the weary (I will glory in the things
Concerning my infirmity, being made
A spectacle to God and to the angels,
A sport and a contempt to the barbarians)
That I was thus permitted to console
And animate the French and Huron converts,
Placing before their minds the thought of Him
Who bore against Himself the contradiction
Of sinners. Weak through hanging by my wrists
Between two poles, my feet not touching ground,   1290
I managed through His help to reach the stage,
And with the dew from leaves of Turkish corn
Two of the prisoners I baptized. I called

To them that in their torment they should fix
Their eyes on me as I bestowed the sign
Of the last absolution. With the spirit
Of Christ, Eustache then in the fire entreated
His Huron friends to let no thought of vengeance
Arising from this anguish at the stake
Injure the French hope for an Iroquois peace.   1300
Onnonhoaraton, a youthful captive,
They killed – the one who seeing me prepared
For torture interposed, offering himself
A sacrifice for me who had in bonds
Begotten him for Christ. Couture was seized
And dragged off as a slave. René Goupil,
While placing on a child's forehead the sign
Of the Cross was murdered by a sorcerer,
And then, a rope tied to his neck, was dragged
Through the whole village and flung in the River.'   1310

(*The later account*)

A family of the Wolf Clan having lost
A son in battle, Jogues as substitute
Was taken in, half-son, half-slave, his work
The drudgery of the village, bearing water,
Lighting the fires, and clad in tatters made
To join the winter hunt, bear heavy packs
On scarred and naked shoulders in the trade
Between the villages. His readiness
To execute his tasks, unmurmuring,
His courage when he plunged into a river   1320
To save a woman and a child who stumbled
Crossing a bridge made by a fallen tree,
Had softened for a time his master's harshness.
It gained him scattered hours of leisure when
He set his mind to work upon the language
To make concrete the articles of Faith.

At intervals he stole into the woods
To pray and meditate and carve the Name
Upon the bark. Out of the Mohawk spoils
At the first battle he had found and hid   1330
Two books – *The Following of Christ* and one
Of Paul's *Epistles*, and with these when 'weary
Even of life and pressed beyond all measure
Above his strength' he followed the 'running waters'
To quench his thirst. But often would the hate
Of the Mohawk foes flame out anew when Jogues
Was on his knees muttering the magic words,
And when a hunting party empty-handed
Returned or some reverse was met in battle,
Here was the victim ready at their door.   1340
Believing that a band of warriors
Had been destroyed, they seized the priest and set
His day of death, but at the eleventh hour,
With the arrival of a group of captives,
The larger festival of torture gave
Him momentary reprieve. Yet when he saw
The holocaust and rushed into the flames
To save a child, a heavy weight laid hold
Upon his spirit lasting many days –
'My life wasted with grief, my years with sighs;   1350
Oh wherefore was I born that I should see
The ruin of my people! Woe is me!
But by His favour I shall overcome
Until my change is made and He appear.'

This story of enslavement had been brought
To Montmagny, the Governor of Quebec,
And to the outpost of the Dutch, Fort Orange.
Quebec was far away and, short of men,
Could never cope with the massed Iroquois;
Besides, Jogues' letter begged the Governor   1360
That no measures 'to save a single life'

Should hurt the cause of France. To the Provincial
He wrote – 'Who in my absence would console
The captives? Who absolve the penitent?
Encourage them in torments? Who baptize
The dying? On this cross to which our Lord
Has nailed me with Himself am I resolved
To live and die.'

          And when the commandant
Of the Dutch fort sent notice that a ship
At anchor in the Hudson would provide   1370
Asylum, Jogues delayed that he might seek
Counsel of God and satisfy his conscience,
Lest some intruding self-preserving thought
Conflict with duty. Death was certain soon.
He knew it – for that mounting tide of hate
Could not be checked: it had engulfed his friends;
'Twould take him next. How close to suicide
Would be refusal? Not as if escape
Meant dereliction: no, his early vows
Were still inviolate – he would return.   1380
He pledged himself to God there on his knees
Before two bark-strips fashioned as a cross
Under the forest trees – his oratory.
And so, one night, the Indians asleep,
Jogues left the house, fumbling his darkened way,
Half-walk, half-crawl, a lacerated leg
Making the journey of one-half a mile
The toil of half a night. By dawn he found
The shore, and, single-handed, pushed a boat,
Stranded by ebb-tide, down the slope of sand   1390
To the river's edge and rowed out to the ship,
Where he was lifted up the side by sailors
Who, fearful of the risk of harbouring
A fugitive, carried him to the hatch
And hid him with the cargo in the hold.

The outcry in the morning could be heard
Aboard the ship as Indians combed the cabins,
Threatened the guards and scoured the neighbouring woods,
And then with strong suspicion of the vessel
Demanded of the officers their captive.   1400
After two days Jogues with his own consent
Was taken to the fort and hid again
Behind the barrels of a store. For weeks
He saw and heard the Mohawks as they passed,
Examining cordage, prying into casks,
At times touching his clothes, but missing him
As he lay crouched in darkness motionless.
With evidence that he was in the fort,
The Dutch abetting the escape, the chiefs
Approached the commandant – 'The prisoner   1410
Is ours. He is not of your race or speech.
The Dutch are friends: the Frenchmen are our foes.
Deliver up this priest into our hands.'
The cries were countered by the officer –
'He is like us in blood if not in tongue.
The Frenchman here is under our protection.
He is our guest. We treat him as you treat
The strangers in your cabins, for you feed
And shelter them. That is also our law,
The custom of our nation.' Argument   1420
Of no avail, a ransom price was offered,
Refused, but running up the bargain scale,
It caught the Mohawks at three hundred livres,
And Jogues at last was safely on the Hudson.

The tale of Jogues' first mission to the Hurons
Ends on a sequel briefly sung but keyed
To the tune of the story, for the stretch
Home was across a wilderness, his bed

A coil of rope on a ship's open deck
Swept by December surge. The voyage closed   1430
At Falmouth where, robbed by a pirate gang,
He wandered destitute until picked up
By a French crew who offered him a tramp fare.
He landed on the shore of Brittany
On Christmas Eve, and by New Year he reached
The Jesuit establishment at Rennes.

The trumpets blew once more, and Jogues returned
With the spring expedition to Quebec.
Honoured by Montmagny, he took the post
Of peace ambassador to hostile tribes,   1440
And then the orders came from Lalemant
That he should open up again the cause
Among the Mohawks at Ossernenon.
Jogues knew that he was travelling to his death,
And though each hour of that former mission
Burned at his finger stumps, the wayward flesh
Obeyed the summons. Lalemant as well
Had known the peril – had he not re-named
Ossernenon, the Mission of the Martyrs?
So Jogues, accompanied by his friend Lalande   1450
Departed for the village – his last letter
To his Superior read: 'I will return
Cost it a thousand lives. I know full well
That I shall not survive, but He who helped
Me by His grace before will never fail me
Now when I go to do His holy will.'
And to the final consonant the vow
Was kept, for two days after they had struck
The town, their heads were on the palisades,
And their dragged bodies flung into the Mohawk.   1460

VIII

(Bressani)

1646

The western missions waiting Jogues' return
Were held together by a scarlet thread.
The forays of the Iroquois had sent
The fugitive survivors to the fort.
Three years had passed – and where was Jogues? The scant
Supplies of sagamite could never feed
The inflow from the stricken villages.
The sparse reports had filtered to Quebec,
And the command was given to Bressani
To lead the rescue band to Sainte Marie.   1470
Leaving Three Rivers in the spring when ice
Was on the current, he was caught like Jogues,
With his six Hurons and a French oblate,
A boy of twelve; transferred to Iroquois'
Canoes and carried up the Richelieu;
Disbarked and driven through the forest trails
To Lake Champlain; across it; and from there
Around the rocks and marshes to the Hudson.
And every time a camp was built and fires
Were laid the torment was renewed; in all   1480
The towns the squaws and children were regaled
With evening festivals upon the scaffolds.
Bressani wrote one day when vigilance
Relaxed and his split hand was partly healed –
'I do not know if your Paternity
Will recognize this writing for the letter
Is soiled. Only one finger of the hand
Is left unburned. The blood has stained the paper.
My writing table is the earth; the ink
Gunpowder mixed with water.' And again –   1490

This time to his Superior – 'I could
Not have believed it to be possible
That a man's body was so hard to kill.'
The earlier fate of Jogues was his – enslaved,
But ransomed at Fort Orange by the Dutch;
Restored to partial health; sent to Rochelle
In the Autumn, but in April back again
And under orders for the Huron mission,
Where he arrived this time unscathed to take
A loyal welcome from his priestly comrades.   1500

Bressani's presence stimulated faith
Within the souls of priests and neophytes.
The stories burned like fuel of the faggots –
Jogues' capture and his rock stability,
And the no less triumphant stand Eustache
Had made showing the world that native metal
Could take the test as nobly as the French.
And Ragueneau's letter to his General stated –
'Bressani ill-equipped to speak the Huron
Has speech more eloquent to capture souls: 1510
It is his scars, his mutilated hands.
"Only show us," the neophytes exclaim,
"The wounds, for they teach better than our tongues
Your faith, for you have come again to face
The dangers. Only thus we know that you
Believe the truth and would have us believe it".'

IX

In those three years since Jogues' departure doubts
Though unexpressed had visited the mission.
For death had come to several in the fold –
Raymbault, Goupil, Eustache, and worse than death   1520
To Jogues, and winter nights were bleaker, darker
Without the company of Brébeuf. Lion

Of limb and heart, he had entrenched the faith,
Was like a triple palisade himself.
But as his broken shoulder had not healed,
And ordered to Quebec by Lalemant,
He took the leave that seven years of work
Deserved. The city hailed him with delight.
For more than any other did he seem
The very incarnation of the age –   1530
Champlain the symbol of exploring France,
Tracking the rivers to their lairs, Brébeuf
The token of a nobler chivalry.
He went the rounds of the stations, saw the gains
The East had made in converts – Sillery
For Indians and Notre Dame des Anges
For the French colonists; convents and schools
Flourished. Why should the West not have the same
Yield for the sowing? It was labourers
They needed with supplies and adequate   1540
Defence. St Lawrence and the Ottawa
Infested by the Iroquois were traps
Of death. Three bands of Hurons had been caught
That summer. Montmagny had warned the priest
Against the risk of unprotected journeys.
So when the reinforcements came from France,
Brébeuf set out under a guard of soldiers
Taking with him two young recruits – Garreau
And Chabanel – arriving at the fort
In the late fall. The soldiers wintered there   1550
And supervised defensive strategy.
Replaced the forlorn feelings with fresh hopes,
And for two years the mission enterprise
Renewed its lease of life. Rumours of treaties
Between the French and Mohawks stirred belief
That peace was in the air, that other tribes
Inside the Iroquois Confederacy
Might enter – with the Hurons sharing terms.

This was the pipe-dream – was it credible?
The ranks of missionaries were filling up: 1560
At Sainte Marie, Brébeuf and Ragueneau,
Le Mercier, Chastellain and Chabanel;
St Joseph – Garnier and René Menard;
St Michel – Chaumonot and Du Peron;
The others – Claude Pijart, Le Moyne, Garreau
And Daniel.
          What validity the dream
Possessed was given by the seasonal
Uninterrupted visits of the priests
To their loved home, both fort and residence.
Here they discussed their plans, and added up   1570
In smiling rivalry their tolls of converts:
They loitered at the shelves, fondled the books,
Running their fingers down the mellowed pages
As if they were the faces of their friends.
They stood for hours before the saints or knelt
Before the Virgin and the crucifix
In mute transfiguration. These were hours
That put the bandages upon their hurts,
Making their spirits proof against all ills
That had assailed or could assail the flesh,   1580
Turned winter into spring and made return
To their far mission posts an exaltation.
The bell each morning called the neophytes
To Mass, again at evening, and the tones
Lured back the memories across the seas.
And often in the summer hours of twilight
When Norman chimes were ringing, would the priests
Forsake the fort and wander to the shore
To sing the *Gloria* while hermit thrushes
Rivalled the rapture of the nightingales.   1590

The native register was rich in name
And number. Earlier years had shown results
Mainly among the young and sick and aged,
Where little proof was given of the root
Of faith, but now the Fathers told of deeds
That flowered from the stems. Had not Eustache
Bequeathed his record like a Testament?
The sturdiest warriors and chiefs had vied
Among themselves within the martyr ranks: –
Stories of captives led to sacrifice,   1600
Accepting scaffold fires under the rites,
Enduring to the end, had taken grip
Of towns and clans. St Joseph had its record
For Garnier reported that Totiri,
A native of high rank, while visiting
St Ignace when a torture was in progress,
Had emulated Jogues by plunging through
The flaming torches that he might apply
The Holy Water to an Iroquois.
Garreau and Pijart added lists of names   1610
From the Algonquins and the Nipissings,
And others told of Pentecostal meetings
In cabins by the Manitoulin shores.

Not only was the faith sustained by hopes
Nourished within the bosom of their home
And by the wish-engendered talk of peace,
But there outside the fort was evidence
Of tenure for the future. Acres rich
In soil extended to the forest fringe.
Each year they felled the trees and burned the stumps,   1620
Pushing the frontier back, clearing the land,
Spading, hoeing. The stomach's noisy protest
At sagamite and wild rice found a rest
With bread from wheat, fresh cabbages and pease,
And squashes which when roasted had the taste

Of Norman apples. Strawberries in July,
October beechnuts, pepper roots for spice,
And at the bottom of a spring that flowed
Into a pond shaded by silver birches
And ringed by marigolds was water-cress   1630
In chilled abundance. So, was this the West?
The Wilderness? That flight of tanagers;
Those linguals from the bobolinks; those beeches,
Roses and water-lilies; at the pools
Those bottle-gentians! For a time the fields
Could hypnotize the mind to scenes of France.
Within five years the change was wrought. The cocks
Were crowing in the yards, and in the pasture
Were sheep and cows and pigs that had been brought
As sucklings that immense eight hundred miles 1640
In sacks – canoed, and portaged on the shoulders.
The traders, like the soldiers, too, had heard
Of a great ocean larger than the Huron.
Was it the western gateway to Cathay?
The Passage? Master-theme of song and ballad;
The *myth* at last resolved into the *fact*!
Along that route, it was believed, French craft
Freighted with jewels, spices, tapestries,
Would sail to swell the coffers of the Bourbons.
Such was the dream though only buffalo roamed 1650
The West and autumn slept upon the prairies.

This dream was at its brightest now, Quebec
Was building up a western citadel
In Sainte Marie. With sixty Frenchmen there,
The eastern capital itself had known
Years less auspicious. Might the fort not be
The bastion to one-half the continent,
New France expanding till the longitudes
Staggered the daring of the navigators?
The priests were breathless with another space 1660

Beyond the measure of the astrolabe –
A different empire built upon the pulses,
Where even the sun and moon and stars revolved
Around a Life and a redemptive Death.
They pushed their missions to the north and west
Further into Algonquin territories,
Among the Ottawas at Manitoulin,
And towards the Ojibways at Sault Sainte Marie.
New village groups were organized in stations –
St Magdalen, St Jean, and St Matthias.   1670
Had Chabanel, ecstatic with success,
Not named one fort the Village of Believers?
Brébeuf was writing to his General –
'Peace, union and tranquility are here
Between the members of our Order. We need
More workers for the apostolic field,
Which more than ever whitens for the harvest.'
And to this call came Gabriel Lalemant,
Bonin, Daran, Greslon, besides a score
Of labourers and soldiers. In one year   1680
Twelve hundred converts, churches over-crowded,
With Mass conducted in the open-air!

And so the seasons passed. When the wild ducks
Forsook the Huron marshes for the south,
It was the signal for the priests to pack
Their blankets. Not until the juncos came,
And flickers tapped the crevices of bark,
And the blood-root was pushing through the leaf-mould,
Would they reset their faces towards their home.

x

While Ragueneau's *Relations* were being sent   1690
Homeward, picturing the promise of the west,
The thunder clouds were massing in the east

Under the pounding drums. The treaty signed
Between the Iroquois and Montmagny
Was broken by the murder of Lalande
And Jogues. The news had drifted to the fort –
The prelude only to the heavier blows
And deeper treachery. The Iroquois,
Infesting lake and stream, forest and shore,
Were trapping soldiers, traders, Huron guides: 1700
The whole confederacy was on the march.
Both waterways were blocked, the quicker route –
St Lawrence, and the arduous Ottawa.
They caught the Hurons at their camps, surprised
Canoe-fleets from the reeds and river bends
And robbed them, killed them on the portages.
So widespread were their forays, they encountered
Bands of Algonquins on the hunt, slew them,
Dispersed them from their villages and sent
Survivors to the northern wilderness.   1710
So keen their lust for slaughter, they enticed
The Huron chieftains under pledge of truce
And closed negotiations with their scalps.

As the months passed the pressure of attack
Moved grimly towards the west, making complete
The isolation of Huronia.
No commerce with Quebec – no traveller
For a whole year came to the Residence.
But constant was the stream of fugitives
From smaller undefended villages,   1720
Fleeing west and ever west. The larger towns,
The deluge breaking down their walls, drove on
The surplus to their neighbours which, in turn,
Urged on the panic herd to Sainte Marie.
This mother of the missions felt the strain
As one by one the buffers were destroyed,
And the flocks came nearer for their pasturage.

There could be only one conclusion when
The priests saw the migration of the missions –
That of St Jean four times abandoning   1730
Its stations and four times establishing
New centres with a more improved defence;
That of St Ignace where a double raid
That slaughtered hundreds, lifted bodily
Both town and mission, driving to their last
Refuge the ragged remnants. Yet Ragueneau
Was writing – 'We are here as yet intact
But all determined to shed blood and life
If need be. In this Residence still reigns
The peace and love of Heaven. Here the sick   1740
Will find a hospital, the travellers
A place of rest, the fugitives, asylum.
During the year more than three thousand persons
Have sought and found shelter under our roof.
We have dispensed the Bread of Life to all
And we have fed their bodies, though our fare
Is down to one food only, crushed corn boiled
And seasoned with the powder of smoked fish.'

Despite the perils, Sainte Marie was sending
Her missionaries afield, revisiting   1750
The older sites, establishing the new,
With that same measure of success and failure
Which tested courage or confirmed a faith.
Garreau, sick and expecting death, was brought
By Pijart and a French assistant back
From the Algonquin wastes, for thirteen days
Borne by a canoe and by his comrades' shoulders.
Recovering even after the last rites
Had been administered, he faced the task
Again. Fresh visits to the Petun tribes   1760
Had little yield but cold and starving days,
Unsheltered nights, the same fare at the doors,
Savoured by Jogues and Garnier seven years

Before. And everywhere the labourers worked
Under a double threat – the Iroquois,
And the Huron curse inspired by sorcerers
Who saw black magic in the Jesuit robes
And linked disaster with their ritual.
Between the hammer and the anvil now
Huronia was laid and the first priest   1770
To take the blow was Daniel.
                            Fourteen years
This priest had laboured at the Huron mission.
Following a week of rest at Sainte Marie
He had returned to his last post, St Joseph,
Where he had built his church and for the year
Just gone had added to his charge the hundreds
Swarming from villages stormed by the foe.
And now in that inexorable order,
Station by station, town by town, it was
St Joseph's turn. Aware that the main force   1780
Of Huron warriors had left the town,
The Iroquois had breached the palisade
And, overwhelming the defenders, sacked
And burned the cabins. Mass had just been offered,
When the war yells were heard and Daniel came
Outside. Seeing the panic, fully knowing
Extinction faced the town with this invasion,
And that ten precious minutes of delay
Might give his flock the refuge of the woods,
He faced the vanguard of the Iroquois,   1790
And walked with firm selective dignity
As in the manner of a parley. Fear
And wonder checked the Indians at the sight
Of a single dark-robed, unarmed challenger
Against arrows, muskets, spears and tomahawks.
That momentary pause had saved the lives
Of hundreds as they fled into the forest,
But not the life of Daniel. Though afraid
At first to cross a charmed circumference

To take a struggle hand-to-hand, they drove   1800
Their arrows through him, then in frenzied rush
Mastering their awe, they hurled themselves upon
The body, stripped it of its clothes and flung it
Into the burning church. By noon nothing
Remained but ashes of the town, the fort,
The cabins and their seven hundred dead.

XI

July 1648

Ragueneau was distraught. He was shepherd-priest.
Daniel was first to die under his care,
And nigh a score of missionaries were lost
In unprotected towns. Besides, he knew   1810
He could not, if he would, resist that mob
That clamoured at the stockades, day by day.
His moral supervision was bound up
With charity that fed and warmed and healed.
And through the winter following Daniel's death
Six thousand Indians sought shelter there.
The season's crops to the last grain were garnered
And shared. 'Through the kind Providence of God,
We managed, as it were, to draw both oil
And honey from the very stones around us.   1820
The obedience, patience of our missionaries
Excel reward – all with one heart and soul
Infused with the high spirit of our Order;
The servants, boys, and soldiers day and night
Working beyond their strength! Here is the service
Of joy, that we will take whatever God
Ordains for us whether it be life or death.'
The challenge was accepted, for the spring
Opened upon the hardest tragic blows
The iron in the human soul could stand.   1830

St Louis and St Ignace still remained
The flying buttresses of Sainte Marie.
From them the Residence received reports
Daily of movements of the Iroquois.
Much labour had been spent on their defence.
Ramparts of pine fifteen feet high enclosed
St Louis. On three sides a steep ravine
Topped by the stakes made nigh impregnable
St Ignace; then the palisaded fourth,
Subject alone to a surprise assault,   1840
Could rally the main body of defenders.
The Iroquois, alert as eagles, knew
The weakness of the Hurons, the effect
On the morale of unexpected raids
Committing towns to fire and pushing back
The eastern ramparts. Piece by piece, the rim
Was being cracked and fissures driven down
The bowl: and stroke by stroke the strategy
Pointed to Sainte Marie. Were once the fort
Now garrisoned by forty Frenchmen taken,   1850
No power predicted from Quebec could save
The Huron nation from its doom. St Ignace
Lay in the path but during the eight months
After St Joseph's fall the enemy
Had leisurely prepared their plans. Their scouts
Reported that one-half of the town's strength
Was lost by flight and that an apathy,
In spite of all the priests could do to stem it,
Had seized the invaded tribes. They knew that when
The warriors were hunting in the forest   1860
This weaker palisade was scalable.
And the day came in March when the whole fate
That overtook St Joseph in July
Swept on St Ignace – sudden and complete.
The Mohawks and the Senecas uniting,
A thousand strong, the town bereft of fighters,

Four hundred old and young inside the stakes,
The assault was made two hours before the dawn.
But half-aroused from sleep, many were killed
Within their cabins. Of the four hundred three
Alone managed to reach the woods to scream
The alarm to the drowsed village of St Louis.

At nine o'clock that morning – such the speed
Of the pursuit – a guard upon the hill
Behind the Residence was watching whiffs
Of smoke to the south, but a league away.
Bush fires? Not with this season's depth of snow.
The Huron bivouacs? The settlements
Too close for that. Camps of the Iroquois?
Not while cunning and stealth controlled their tactics.
The smoke was in the town. The morning air,
Clearing, could leave no doubt of that, and just
As little that the darkening pall could spring
Out of the vent-holes from the cabin roofs.
Ragueneau rushed to the hill at the guard's call;
Summoned Bressani; sheets and tongues of flame
Leaping some fifty feet above the smoke
Meant to their eyes the capture and the torch –
St Louis with Brébeuf and Lalemant!

Less than two hours it took the Iroquois
To capture, sack and garrison St Ignace,
And start then for St Louis. The alarm
Sounded, five hundred of the natives fled
To the mother fort only to be pursued
And massacred in the snow. The eighty braves
That manned the stockades perished at the breaches;
And what was seen by Ragueneau and the guard
Was smoke from the massed fire of cabin bark.

Brébeuf and Lalemant were not numbered
In the five hundred of the fugitives.

1870

1880

1890

1900

They had remained, infusing nerve and will
In the defenders, rushing through the cabins
Baptizing and absolving those who were
Too old, too young, too sick to join the flight.
And when, resistance crushed, the Iroquois
Took all they had not slain back to St Ignace,
The vanguard of the prisoners were the priests.

March 16, 1649

Three miles from town to town over the snow,
Naked, laden with pillage from the lodges,
The captives filed like wounded beasts of burden,   1910
Three hours on the march, and those that fell
Or slowed their steps were killed.
                                                     Three days before
Brébeuf had celebrated his last mass.
And he had known it was to be the last.
There was prophetic meaning as he took
The cord and tied the alb around his waist,
Attached the maniple to his left arm
And drew the seamless purple chasuble
With the large cross over his head and shoulders,
Draping his body: every vestment held   1920
An immediate holy symbol as he whispered –
'Upon my head the helmet of Salvation.
So purify my heart and make me white;
With this cincture of purity gird me,
O Lord.
            May I deserve this maniple
Of sorrow and of penance.
                                  Unto me
Restore the stole of immortality.
My yoke is sweet, my burden light.
                                        Grant that
I may so bear it as to merit Thy grace.'

Entering, he knelt before as rude an altar   1930
As ever was reared within a sanctuary,
But hallowed as that chancel where the notes
Of Palestrina's score had often pealed
The *Assumpta est Maria* through St Peter's.
For, covered in the centre of the table,
Recessed and sealed, a hollowed stone contained
A relic of a charred or broken body
Which perhaps a thousand years ago or more
Was offered as a sacrifice to Him
Whose crucifix stood there between the candles.   1940
And on the morrow would this prayer be answered: –
'Eternal Father, I unite myself
With the affections and the purposes
Of Our Lady of Sorrows on Calvary.
And now I offer Thee the sacrifice
Which Thy Beloved Son made of Himself
Upon the Cross and now renews on this,
His holy altar...
                    Graciously receive
My life for His life as he gave His life
For mine...
              This is my body.
                        In like manner...   1950
Take ye and drink – the chalice of my blood.'

XII

No doubt in the mind of Brébeuf that this was the last
Journey – three miles over the snow. He knew
That the margins as thin as they were by which he escaped
From death through the eighteen years of his mission toil
Did not belong to this chapter: not by his pen
Would this be told. He knew his place in the line,
For the blaze of the trail that was cut on the bark by Jogues
Shone still. He had heard the story as told by writ

And word of survivors – of how a captive slave   1960
Of the hunters, the skin of his thighs cracked with the frost,
He would steal from the tents to the birches, make a rough cross
From two branches, set it in snow and on the peel
Inscribe his vows and dedicate to the Name
In 'litanies of love' what fragments were left
From the wrack of his flesh; of his escape from the tribes;
Of his journey to France where he knocked at the door of the
     College
Of Rennes, was gathered in as a mendicant friar,
Nameless, unknown, till he gave for proof to the priest
His scarred credentials of faith, the nail-less hands   1970
And withered arms – the signs of the Mohawk fury.
Nor yet was the story finished – he had come again
Back to his mission to get the second death.
And the comrades of Jogues – Goupil, Eustache and Couture,
Had been stripped and made to run the double files
And take the blows – one hundred clubs to each line –
And this as the prelude to torture, leisured, minute,
Where thorns on the quick, scallop shells to the joints of
     the thumbs,
Provided the sport for children and squaws till the end.
And adding salt to the blood of Brébeuf was the thought   1980
Of Daniel – was it months or a week ago?
So far, so near, it seemed in time, so close
In leagues – just over there to the south it was
He faced the arrows and died in front of his church.

But winding into the greater artery
Of thought that bore upon the coming passion
Were little tributaries of wayward wish
And reminiscence. Paris with its vespers
Was folded in the mind of Lalemant,
And the soft Gothic lights and traceries   1990
Were shading down the ridges of his vows.
But two years past at Bourges he had walked the cloisters,

Companioned by St Augustine and Francis,
And wrapped in quiet holy mists. Brébeuf,
His mind a moment throwing back the curtain
Of eighteen years, could see the orchard lands,
The *cidreries*, the peasants at the Fairs,
The undulating miles of wheat and barley,
Gardens and pastures rolling like a sea
From Lisieux to Le Havre. Just now the surf   2000
Was pounding on the limestone Norman beaches
And on the reefs of Calvados. Had dawn
This very day not flung her surplices
Around the headlands and with golden fire
Consumed the silken argosies that made
For Rouen from the estuary of the Seine?
A moment only for that veil to lift –
A moment only for those bells to die
That rang their matins at Condé-sur-Vire.

By noon St Ignace! The arrival there   2010
The signal for the battle-cries of triumph,
The gauntlet of the clubs. The stakes were set
And the ordeal of Jogues was re-enacted
Upon the priests – even with wilder fury,
For here at last was trapped their greatest victim,
Echon. The Iroquois had waited long
For this event. Their hatred for the Hurons
Fused with their hatred for the French and priests
Was to be vented on this sacrifice,
And to that camp had come apostate Hurons,   2020
United with their foes in common hate
To settle up their reckoning with *Echon*.
. . . . .
Now three o'clock, and capping the height of the passion,
Confusing the sacraments under the pines of the forest,
Under the incense of balsam, under the smoke
Of the pitch, was offered the rite of the font. On the head,

The breast, the loins and the legs, the boiling water!
While the mocking paraphrase of the symbols was hurled
At their faces like shards of flint from the arrow heads –
'We baptize thee with water...
                        That thou mayest be led   2030
To Heaven...
            To that end we do annoint thee.
We treat thee as a friend: we are the cause
Of thy happiness; we are thy priests; the more
Thou sufferest, the more thy God will reward thee,
So give us thanks for our kind offices.'

The fury of taunt was followed by fury of blow.
Why did not the flesh of Brébeuf cringe to the scourge,
Respond to the heat, for rarely the Iroquois found
A victim that would not cry out in such pain – yet here
The fire was on the wrong fuel. Whenever he spoke,   2040
It was to rally the soul of his friend whose turn
Was to come through the night while the eyes were uplifted
   in prayer,
Imploring the Lady of Sorrows, the mother of Christ,
As pain brimmed over the cup and the will was called
To stand the test of the coals. And sometimes the speech
Of Brébeuf struck out, thundering reproof to his foes,
Half-rebuke, half-defiance, giving them roar for roar.
Was it because the chancel became the arena,
Brébeuf a lion at bay, not a lamb on the altar,
As if the might of a Roman were joined to the cause   2050
Of Judaea? Speech they could stop for they girdled his lips,
But never a moan could they get. Where was the source
Of his strength, the home of his courage that topped the best
Of their braves and even out-fabled the lore of their legends?
In the bunch of his shoulders which often had carried a load
Extorting the envy of guides at an Ottawa portage?
The heat of the hatchets was finding a path to that source.

In the thews of his thighs which had mastered the trails of
  the Neutrals?
They would gash and beribbon those muscles. Was it the blood?
They would draw it fresh from its fountain. Was it the heart?   2060
They dug for it, fought for the scraps in the way of the wolves.
But not in these was the valour or stamina lodged;
Nor in the symbol of Richelieu's robes or the seals
Of Mazarin's charters, nor in the stir of the *lilies*
Upon the Imperial folds; nor yet in the words
Loyola wrote on a table of lava-stone
In the cave of Manresa – not in these the source –
But in the sound of invisible trumpets blowing
Around two slabs of board, right-angled, hammered
By Roman nails and hung on a Jewish hill.   2070

The wheel had come full circle with the visions
In France of Brébeuf poured through the mould of St Ignace.
Lalemant died in the morning at nine, in the flame
Of the pitch belts. Flushed with the sight of the bodies, the foes
Gathered their clans and moved back to the north and west
To join in the fight against the tribes of the Petuns.
There was nothing now that could stem the Iroquois blast.
However undaunted the souls of the priests who were left,
However fierce the sporadic counter attacks
Of the Hurons striking in roving bands from the ambush,   2080
Or smashing out at their foes in garrison raids,
The villages fell before a blizzard of axes
And arrows and spears, and then were put to the torch.

The days were dark at the fort and heavier grew
The burdens on Ragueneau's shoulders. Decision was his.
No word from the east could arrive in time to shape
The step he must take. To and fro – from altar to hill,
From hill to altar, he walked and prayed and watched.
As governing priest of the Mission he felt the pride
Of his Order whipping his pulse, for was not St Ignace   2090

The highest test of the Faith? And all that torture
And death could do to the body was done. The Will
And the Cause in their triumph survived. Loyola's mountains,
Sublime at their summits, were scaled to the uttermost peak.
Ragueneau, the Shepherd, now looked on a battered fold.
In a whirlwind of fire St Jean, like St Joseph, crashed
Under the Iroquois impact. Firm at his post,
Garnier suffered the fate of Daniel. And now
Chabanel, last in the roll of the martyrs, entrapped
On his knees in the woods met death at apostate hands.   2100

The drama was drawing close to its end. It fell
To Ragueneau's lot to perform a final rite –
To offer the fort in sacrificial fire!
He applied the torch himself. 'Inside an hour,'
He wrote, 'we saw the fruit of ten years' labour
Ascend in smoke – then looked our last at the fields,
Put altar-vessels and food on a raft of logs,
And made our way to the island of St Joseph.'
But even from there was the old tale retold –
Of hunger and the search for roots and acorns;   2110
Of cold and persecution unto death
By the Iroquois; of Jesuit will and courage
As the shepherd-priest with Chaumonot led back
The remnant of a nation to Quebec.

THE MARTYRS' SHRINE

Three hundred years have passed, and the winds of God
Which blew over France are blowing once more through the pines
That bulwark the shores of the great Fresh Water Sea.
Over the wastes abandoned by human tread,
Where only the bittern's cry was heard at dusk;
Over the lakes where the wild ducks built their nests,   2120
The skies that had banked their fires are shining again
With the stars that guided the feet of Jogues and Brébeuf.

The years as they turned have ripened the martyrs' seed,
And the ashes of St Ignace are glowing afresh.
The trails, having frayed the threads of the cassocks, sank
Under the mould of the centuries, under fern
And brier and fungus – there in due time to blossom
Into the highways that lead to the crest of the hill
Which havened both shepherd and flock in the days of their trial.
For out of the torch of Ragueneau's ruins the candles   213(
Are burning today in the chancel of Sainte Marie.
The Mission sites have returned to the fold of the Order.
Near to the ground where the cross broke under the hatchet,
And went with it into the soil to come back at the turn
Of the spade with the carbon and calcium char of the bodies,
The shrines and altars are built anew; the *Aves*
And prayers ascend, and the Holy Bread is broken.   194(

The Invaded Field

They brought their youth up on the lore
Of the Phoenix and the pyre,
Of birth from death and gold from fire
And the myth of the Aryan spore.

They measured life in metric tons,
Assessed both man and beast,
And with their patriot sweat they greased
The breechblocks of their guns.

They took their parables from mud –
How pure the crocus grows!   1C
See how the fragrance of a rose
May spring from buried blood!

So, on the promise of this yield
The youth swung down the road,
Goose-stepping to their songs, and sowed
Their bodies on the field.
. . . . .
Now if a brier should here be born
In some ironic hour,
Let life infect both leaf and flower
But death preserve the thorn.

April 1941

Come Away, Death

Willy-nilly, he comes or goes, with the clown's logic,
Comic in epitaph, tragic in epithalamium,
And unseduced by any mused rhyme.
However blow the winds over the pollen,
Whatever the course of the garden variables,
He remains the constant,
Ever flowering from the poppy seeds.

There was a time he came in formal dress,
Announced by Silence tapping at the panels
In deep apology.   10
A touch of chivalry in his approach,
He offered sacramental wine,
And with acanthus leaf
And petals of the hyacinth
He took the fever from the temples
And closed the eyelids,
Then led the way to his cool longitudes
In the dignity of the candles.

His mediaeval grace is gone –
Gone with the flame of the capitals   20
And the leisured turn of the thumb
Leafing the manuscripts,
Gone with the marbles
And the Venetian mosaics,
With the bend of the knee
Before the rose-strewn feet of the Virgin.
The *paternosters* of his priests,
Committing clay to clay,
Have rattled in their throats
Under the gride of his traction tread.   30

One night we heard his footfall – one September night –
In the outskirts of a village near the sea.
There was a moment when the storm
Delayed its fist, when the surf fell
Like velvet on the rocks – a moment only;
The strangest lull we ever knew!
A sudden truce among the oaks
Released their fratricidal arms;
The poplars straightened to attention
As the winds stopped to listen   40
To the sound of the motor drone –
And then the drone was still.
We heard the tick-tock on the shelf,
And the leak of valves in our hearts.
A calm condensed and lidded
As at the core of a cyclone ended breathing.
This was the monologue of Silence
Grave and unequivocal.

What followed was a bolt
Outside the range and target of the thunder,   50
And human speech curved back upon itself
Through Druid runways and the Piltdown scarps,

Beyond the stammers of the Java caves,
To find its origins in hieroglyphs
On mouths and eyes and cheeks
Etched by a foreign stylus never used
On the outmoded page of the Apocalypse.   April 1941

Dunkirk

The English May was slipping into June
With heralds that the spring had never known.
Black cavalry were astride the air;
The Downs awoke to find their faces slashed;
There was blood on the hawthorn,
And song had died in the nightingales' throats.

Appeasement is in its grave: it sleeps well.
The mace had spiked the parchment seals
And pulverized the hedging *ifs* and *wherefores*,
The wheezy adverbs, the gutted modifiers.   10
Churchill and Bevin have the floor,
Whipping snarling nouns and action-verbs
Out of their lairs in the lexicon,
Bull-necked *adversatives* that bit and clawed,
An age before gentility was cubbed.

A call came in from the Channel
Like the wash of surf on sand,
Borne in by the winds against the chalk escarpments,
Into the harbours, up the rivers, along the estuaries,
And but one word in the call.   20

Three hundred thousand on the beaches,
Their spirit-level vision training West!
A vast patience in their eyes,
They had fought pig-iron, manganese, tungsten, cobalt;

And their struggle with hunger, thirst,
And the drug of sleep,
Had multiplied the famine in their cheeks
For England,
By forty miles divided from her brood.

Seven millions on the roads in France,   30
Set to a pattern of chaos
Fashioned through years for this hour.
Inside the brain of the planner
No tolerance befogged the reason –
The *reason* with its clear-swept halls,
Its brilliant corridors,
Where no recesses with their healing dusk
Offered asylum for a fugitive.
The straightedge ruled out errors,
The tremors in the sensory nerves,   40
Pity and the wayward impulses,
The liberal imbecilities.
The reason reckoned that the allied guns
Would not be turned upon the roads
To clear the path for the retreat.
It reasoned well.

REGATTA AND CREW

Millenniums it had taken to make their stock.
Piltdown hung on the frontals of their fathers.
They had lain as sacrifices
Upon the mortuary slabs of Stonehenge.   50
Their souls had come to birth out of their racial myths.
The sea was their school; the storm, their friend.
Foot by foot and hand to hand
They had met the legions
On the beaches and in the surf.
Great names had been delivered unto them;

Caractacus,
Taking his toll of the invaders
In his retreat to the fens and hills;
Boadicea,   60
The storming of Londinium and Verulamium,
And the annihilation of the Roman *ninth*;
Alban, Alfred, Athelney, Edington!
And in the march of their survival
They had fought the poll-tax and burned
The manor rolls under Ball and Tyler.
They had led the riots against the Enclosures.
They had sung ballads to the rhythms of the gibbets.
The welts had been around their necks and ankles.
They had swept the Main with Hawkins and Drake.   70
Morgan-mouthed vocabularians,
Lovers of the beef of language,
They had carved with curse and cutlass
Castilian grandees in the Caribbean.
They had signed up with Frobisher,
Had stifled cries in the cockpits of Trafalgar.
They had emptied their veins into the Marne.
Freedom to them was like the diver's lust for air.
Children of oaths and madrigals,
They had shambled out of caves   80
To write the clauses of the Charters,
To paint the Channel mists,
To stand hushed before the Canterbury tapers.

THE RACE ON THE CHANNEL

The Royal Yacht squadrons of the Thames and Cowes,
Those slim and rakish models of the *wave-line theory*,
Flying the ensign with their Club devices –
Grand-daughters of *Genesta* and the *Galatea*
Whose racing spinnakers
Outsilvered and outflew the sea-gulls off the Isle of Wight.
Cutters, the pride of Folkestone and Sheerness   90

With their press balloon-jibs,
Their billows of flax and hemp
Smothering their single masts
And straight-running bowsprits.

Excursion paddlers –
Last of the family known as the *fleet of the butterflies*,
Purveyors of moonlight sonatas and Sunday siestas.

The fireboats from the London Fire Brigade.
Luggers with four-sided sails bent to the yards
And slung obliquely to the masts,   100
Smelling of the wharves of Deal.
Smacks that built the Grimsby name.
Yawls with their handy mizzen-sails –
The Jacks-of-all-trades on the English coast.
Barges spritsail-rigged with jigger booms.
Bluff-bowed billyboys and Norfolk wherries,
Skiffs that stank of herring roes and Yarmouth.
Dutch scoots and square-stemmed bawleys rank
With kelp, fish-scales and the slime of eels.
And with them all, the merchantmen,   110
Three-funnel liners turbine-driven,
Cabin cruisers, with whaleboats, rafts and dories
Tied to the grimy tails of barges drawn by tugs.

A Collingwood came from Newcastle-on-Tyne,
Trelawney and Grenville of the Cornish Line,
And Raleigh and Gilbert from the Devon Seas
With a Somerset Blake. They met at the quays –
McCluskey, Gallagher, Joe Millard,
Three riveters red from Dumbarton Yard,
And Peebles of Paisley, a notary clerk,   120
Two joiners from Belfast, Mahaffy and Burke,
Blackstone and Coke of Lincoln's Inn,
A butcher from Smithfield, Toby Quinn,

Jonathan Wells, a Sheffield bricklayer,
Tim Thomas of Swansea, a borough surveyor,
Jack Wesley, a stoker, by way of South Shields,
And Snodgrass and Tuttle from Giles-in-the-Fields,
Young Bill of Old Bill with Hancock and Reid,
Two sons of a bishop from Berwick-on-Tweed,
A landscape gardener of Tunbridge, Kent,   130
Povey, a draper from Stoke-on-Trent,
Arthur Cholmondeley Bennington-Grubbe
With Benbow of the Boodles Club,
A Ralph Abercrombie, a Fetherstonehaugh
With Smith, and Ibbs, and Jones, and Buggs –
They met on the liners, yachts and tugs:
The *Princess Maud*, the *Massy Shaw*,
The *Crested Eagle*, the *Nicholas Drew*,
The *Gurgling Jean* and the *Saucy Sue*.

Two prefects from Harrow – Dudley and Fraser   140
Fresh in their grey flannel trousers and blazer,
Helping two tanners, Muggins and Day,
To rig up a sail at a mizzen stay,
Were hailed by a Cambridge stroke – 'Ahoy!
Will you let me go on your billyboy?'

A curate from Cardiff, the Reverend Evans,
Inspired with zeal by a speech of Bevin's,
Called on a Rochester verger named Burchall,
Likewise inflamed by a speech from Churchill –
Together they went to a Greenwich jetty   150
And boarded a lighter – the *Bouncing Betty*.

Meadows, the valet, tapped at the door
Of Colonel Ramsbottom, late of Lahore:
'Twas dawn, and the Colonel was sick with a head;
'The Dean and his lordship, the Bishop, are here,
And your sloop, sir, is ready down at the pier,

And may I go with you?' Meadows said –
'No,' roared the Colonel, as he creaked out of bed,
Blasting out damns with a spot of saliva,
Yet the four of them boarded the *Lady Godiva*.   160

A captain with a Cape Horn face,
Being down on his luck without a ship,
Had spent ten years in his own disgrace
As skipper of a river ferry –
Tonight he was taking his finest trip
As master of a Norfolk wherry.

The Junior partner, Davie Scott,
Of MacTavish, MacEachren, MacGregor, and Scott,
Conspired with Murdoch, MacNutt and MacPhail
To go to Gravesend that evening and sail   170
For the Beach in Mr MacTavish's yacht.

HEARD ON THE COLLIERS

'I've been in a bit of a muss, mesen,
With my game left leg,' said Eddie Glen,
'And every night my faintin' spells,
Contracted in the Dardanelles.'

'My floatin' kidney keeps me 'ome,
My shoulder too 'as never 'ealed.'
Quoth Rufus Stirk of 'Uddersfield,
Cracked with shrapnel at Bapaume.

'Ow, wot's a kidney, look at me,   180
A bleedin' boulder in my lung,'
Said 'Umphrey 'Iggins of Bermondsey;
'A 'Igh Explosive 'ad me strung
On the top of a ruddy poplar tree
For thirty hours at Armenteers,
'Aven't spit straight nigh twenty years.'

'Now, my old woman,' said Solomon Pike,
'Says 'Itler's such a fidget like;
'E steals the cows and 'ens from the Danes,
'E rummages France, 'e chases the Poles,   190
And comes over 'ere with 'is blinkin' planes
To drive us to the 'Yde Park 'oles
Where there's nary a roof that isn't leakin',
Swipin' the pillows right under our 'eads,
Shooin' us out from our 'umble beds.'
''E's a mug, I says, in a manner o' speakin'.'

'How lang d'ye ken it'll take to get through it?'
Said a cautious drover, Angus Bain.
'It'll take a bit o' doin' to do it,
The blighters are dropping bombs like rain,'   200
Said the costermonger from Petticoat Lane.
· · · · ·
Out on the Channel –laughter died.
Casual understatement
Was driven back from its London haunts
To its clinical nakedness
Along the banks of the Ilissus.
In front of the crew were rolling mountains of smoke
Spilling fire from their Vesuvian rims;
The swaying fringes of Borealis blue;
The crimson stabs through the curtains;   210
The tracers' fiery parabolas,
The falling pendants of green from the Very lights;
The mad colours of the murals of Dunkirk.

Space, time, water, bread, sleep,
Above all – sleep;
Commodities beyond the purchase of the Rand.
Space – a thousand pounds per foot! Not up for sale

In the cabin suites or on the floors of the lighters.
The single Mole was crammed with human termites,
Stumbling, falling on the decks of the destroyers,   220
Sleeping, dying on the decks of the transports
Strung along the seaward end.
The solid black queues on the sand waited their turn
To file along the bridgehead jetties
Improvised from the army lorries,
Or waded out to swim
Or clutch at drifting gangplanks, rafts and life-belts.
Time – days, weeks of the balance of life
Offered in exchange for minutes now.

Stuff of the world's sagas in the heavens!   230
Spitfires were chasing Heinkels, one to twenty.
The nation's debt unpaid, unpayable,
Was climbing up its pyramid,
As the Hurricanes took on the Messerschmitts.

THE MULTIPEDES ON THE ROADS

Born on the blueprints,
They are fed by fire.
They grow their skin from carburized steel.
They are put together by cranes.
Their hearts are engines that do not know fatigue
In the perfection of their valves,   240
In the might of their systolic thrusts.
Their blood is petrol: oil bathes their joints.
Their nerves are wire.
From the assembly lines they are put on inspection.
They pass tests,
Are pronounced fit by the drill-sergeants.
They go on parade and are the pride of the High Command.
They take, understand and obey orders.
The climb hills, straddle craters and the barbed barricades.
They defy bullets and shells.   250

Faster than Genghis' cavalry they speed,
Crueller than the hordes of Tamburlaine,
Yet unknowing and uncaring.
It is these that the rearguards are facing –
Creatures of conveyor belts,
Of precision tools and schedules.
They breathe through carburetted lungs;
If pierced, they do not feel the cut,
And if they die, they do not suffer death.
And Dunkirk stands between the rearguards and the sea.   260
· · · · ·

Motor launches from the Port of London,
Life-boats from the liners,
Whale-boats, bottoms of shallow draught,
Rammed their noses into the silt,
Packed their loads and ferried them to scoots and drifters.
Blood and oil smut on their faces,
The wounded, dying and dead were hauled up
Over the rails of the hospital carriers
In the nets and cargo slings.

IN THE SKIES

The world believed the trap was sprung,   270
And no Geneva words or signatures of mercy
Availed the quarry on the sands.
The bird's right to dodge the barrels on the wing,
The start for the hare,
The chance for the fox to cross his scent,
For the teeth to snap at the end of the chase,
Did not belong to this tally-ho.

The proffered sword disclaimed by the victor,
The high salute at the burial of a foe
Wrapped in the folds of his flag,   280

The wreath from the skies,
Were far romantic memories.
As little chivalry here
As in the peregrines chasing the carriers,
As in the sniff of the jackals about a carcass!
Here over the dunes
The last civil rag was torn from the body of war –
The decencies had perished with the Stukas.
. . . . .
From Dover to Dunkirk,
From Dunkirk to Ramsgate,   290
And back to the dunes.
Power boats of the enemy
Were driving torpedoes into transports and colliers,
Lifting the engines clear from their beds,
Blowing the boilers, sheering the sterns,
And the jettisoned loads gathered up from the sea
Were transferred to other decks
And piled in steep confusion
On the twisted steel of the listed destroyers,
On the rough planks of the barges,   300
Into the hatches of the freighters,
Jammed against the bulkheads and riddled ventilators,
On the coils of the cables,
On quarterdecks and in the fo'c'sles,
On the mess-tables and under them.
'Was that roar in the North from the *Rodney*?
We hope to God it was.'
Drip of the leadlines on the bows –
'Two fathoms, sir, four feet, three and a half.'
'Wake up, you dead end. You're not on the feathers now.   310
Make room for this 'ere bloke.'
'Stiff as cement 'e is.' 'Git a gait on,
Or the Stukas'll be raisin' boils on your necks.'

'Ahoy, skipper, a can of petrol.'
'Compass out of gear – give us the line to Ramsgate.'
'Follow the scoots.'

The great birds, carrying under their wings
The black distorted crosses,
Plunged, straightened out.
Laid their eggs in air,   320
Hatched them in fountains of water,
In craters of sand,
To the leap of flame,
To the roar of avalanche.

And in those hours,
When Death was sweating at his lathe,
When heads and legs and arms were blown from their trunks,
When the seventh day on the dunes became the eighth,
And the eighth slumped into the dawn of the ninth,
When the sand's crunch and suck under the feet   330
Were sounds less to be endured than the crash of bombs
In that coma and apathy of horror –
It was then that the feel of a deck,   .
The touch of a spar or a halyard,
Was like a hold on the latch of the heart of God.
It's the Navy's job!
It's their turn now,
From the Beach to the ports.
Let the Stukas break their bloody necks on the Mole;
Let the fires scorch the stars –   340
For now, whether on the burnished oak of the cabins,
Or on the floor-boards of the punts,
Or in the cuddies of the skiffs,
Sleep at last has an even game with Death.

The blessed fog –
Ever before this day the enemy,
Leagued with the quicksands and the breakers–
Now mercifully masking the periscope lenses,
Smearing the hair-lines of the bomb-sights,
Hiding the flushed coveys.   350
And with it the calm on the Channel,
The power that drew the teeth from the storm,
The peace that passed understanding,
Soothing the surf, allaying the lop on the swell.
Out of the range of the guns of Nieuport,
Away from the immolating blasts of the oil-tanks,
The flotillas of ships were met by flotillas of gulls
Whiter than the cliffs of Foreland;
Between the lines of the Medway buoys
They steamed and sailed and rowed,   360
Back to the roadsteads, back to the piers
Inside the vigilant booms,
Back to the harbours,
Back to the River of London, to England,
Saved once again by the tread of her keels.   1941

Heydrich

With rolling drum and funeral flag
Befitting his Teutonic station,
They laid his body out at Prague
With full official confirmation.

Deliverer of the Panegyric,
Attended by a storm-troop staff,
The gentle Himmler wove a lyric
Into the Hangman's epitaph.

'So pure of soul, so free of hate,
His heart bled every time he slew
A man in his Protectorate,
Whether a Gentile or a Jew.

10

'To equal him in Nordic strain
The Reich has never had another;
He always wept at other's pain,
And Adolf loved him as a brother ...'

What tides of grief in Heydrich's heart,
What blood-banks in his sympathy,
Could wrench those arteries apart
And compensate for Lidice?

June 1942

The Truant

'What have you there?' the great Panjandrum said
To the Master of the Revels who had led
A bucking truant with a stiff backbone
Close to the foot of the Almighty's throne.

'Right Reverend, most adored,
And forcibly acknowledged Lord
By the keen logic of your two-edged sword!
This creature has presumed to classify
Himself – a biped, rational, six feet high
And two feet wide; weighs fourteen stone;
Is guilty of a multitude of sins.
He has abjured his choric origins,
And like an undomesticated slattern,
Walks with tangential step unknown
Within the weave of the atomic pattern.
He has developed concepts, grins
Obscenely at your Royal bulletins,
Possesses what he calls a will
Which challenges your power to kill.'

10

'What is his pedigree?'   20

'The base is guaranteed, your Majesty –
Calcium, carbon, phosphorus, vapour
And other fundamentals spun
From the umbilicus of the sun,
And yet he says he will not caper
Around your throne, nor toe the rules
For the ballet of the fiery molecules.'

'His concepts and denials – scrap them, burn them –
To the chemists with them promptly.'

                                        'Sire,
The stuff is not amenable to fire.   30
Nothing but their own kind can overturn them.
The chemists have sent back the same old story –
"With our extreme gelatinous apology,
We beg to inform your Imperial Majesty,
Unto whom be dominion and power and glory,
There still remains that strange precipitate
Which has the quality to resist
Our oldest and most trusted catalyst.
It is a substance we cannot cremate
By temperatures known to our Laboratory".'   40

And the great Panjandrum's face grew dark –
'I'll put those chemists to their annual purge,
And I myself shall be the thaumaturge
To find the nature of this fellow's spark.
Come, bring him nearer by yon halter rope:
I'll analyse him with the cosmoscope.'

Pulled forward with his neck awry,
The little fellow six feet short,
Aware he was about to die,
Committed grave contempt of court   50
By answering with a flinchless stare
The Awful Presence seated there.

The ALL HIGH swore until his face was black.
He called him a coprophagite,
A genus *homo*, egomaniac,
Third cousin to the family of worms,
A sporozoan from the ooze of night,
Spawn of a spavined troglodyte:
He swore by all the catalogue of terms
Known since the slang of carboniferous Time.   60
He said that he could trace him back
To pollywogs and earwigs in the slime.
And in his shrillest tenor he began
Reciting his indictment of the man,
Until he closed upon this capital crime –
'You are accused of singing out of key,
(A foul unmitigated dissonance)
Of shuffling in the measures of the dance,
Then walking out with that defiant, free
Toss of your head, banging the doors,   70
Leaving a stench upon the jacinth floors.
You have fallen like a curse
On the mechanics of my Universe.

'Herewith I measure out your penalty –
Hearken while you hear, look while you see:
I send you now upon your homeward route
Where you shall find
Humiliation for your pride of mind.
I shall make deaf the ear, and dim the eye,
Put palsy in your touch, make mute   80

Your speech, intoxicate your cells and dry
Your blood and marrow, shoot
Arthritic needles through your cartilage,
And having parched you with old age,
I'll pass you wormwise through the mire;
And when your rebel will
Is mouldered, all desire
Shrivelled, all your concepts broken,
Backward in dust I'll blow you till
You join my spiral festival of fire.   90
Go, Master of the Revels – I have spoken.'

And the little genus *homo*, six feet high,
Standing erect, countered with this reply –
'You dumb insouciant invertebrate,
You rule a lower than a feudal state –
A realm of flunkey decimals that run,
Return; return and run; again return,
Each group around its little sun,
And every sun a satellite.
There they go by day and night,   100
Nothing to do but run and burn,
Taking turn and turn about,
Light-year in and light-year out,
Dancing, dancing in quadrillions,
Never leaving their pavilions.

'Your astronomical conceit
Of bulk and power is anserine.
Your ignorance so thick,
You did not know your own arithmetic.
We flung the graphs about your flying feet;   110
We measured your diameter –
Merely a line
Of zeros prefaced by an integer.
Before we came

You had no name.
You did not know direction or your pace;
We taught you all you ever knew
Of motion, time and space.
We healed you of your vertigo
And put you in our kindergarten show,   120
Perambulated you through prisms, drew
Your mileage through the Milky Way,
Lassoed your comets when they ran astray,
Yoked Leo, Taurus, and your team of Bears
To pull our kiddy cars of inverse squares.

'Boast not about your harmony,
Your perfect curves, your rings
Of *pure and endless light* – 'Twas we
Who pinned upon your seraphim their wings,
And when your brassy heavens rang   130
With joy that morning while the planets sang
Their choruses of archangelic lore,
'Twas we who ordered the notes upon their score
Out of our winds and strings.
Yes! all your shapely forms .
Are ours – parabolas of silver light,
Those blueprints of your spiral stairs
From nadir depth to zenith height,
Coronas, rainbows after storms,
Auroras on your eastern tapestries   140
And constellations over western seas.

'And when, one day, grown conscious of your age,
While pondering an eolith,
We turned a human page
And blotted out a cosmic myth
With all its baby symbols to explain
The sunlight in Apollo's eyes,
Our rising pulses and the birth of pain,

Fear, and that fern-and-fungus breath
Stalking our nostrils to our caves of death –   150
That day we learned how to anatomize
Your body, calibrate your size
And set a mirror up before your face
To show you what you really were – a rain
Of dull Lucretian atoms crowding space,
A series of concentric waves which any fool
Might make by dropping stones within a pool,
Or an exploding bomb forever in flight
Bursting like hell through Chaos and Old Night.

'You oldest of the hierarchs   160
Composed of electronic sparks,
We grant you speed,
We grant you power, and fire
That ends in ash, but we concede
To you no pain nor joy nor love nor hate,
No final tableau of desire,
No causes won or lost, no free
Adventure at the outposts – only
The degradation of your energy
When at some late   170
Slow number of your dance your sergeant-major Fate
Will catch you blind and groping and will send
You reeling on that long and lonely
Lockstep of your wave-lengths towards your end.

'We who have met
With stubborn calm the dawn's hot fusillades;
Who have seen the forehead sweat
Under the tug of pulleys on the joints,
Under the liquidating tally
Of the cat-and-truncheon bastinades;   180
Who have taught our souls to rally
To mountain horns and the sea's rockets

When the needle ran demented through the points;
We who have learned to clench
Our fists and raise our lightless sockets
To morning skies after the midnight raids,
Yet cocked our ears to bugles on the barricades,
And in cathedral rubble found a way to quench
A dying thirst within a Galilean valley –
No! by the Rood, we will not join your ballet.'   December 1942

The Stoics

They were the oaks and beeches of our species.
Their roots struck down through acid loam
To weathered granite and took hold
Of flint and silica, or found their home
With red pyrites – fools' mistake for gold.
Their tunics, stoles and togas were like watersheds,
Splitting the storm, sloughing the rain.
Under such cloaks the morrow could not enter –
Their *gravitas* had seized a geologic centre
And triumphed over subcutaneous pain.   10
Aurelius! What direction did you take
To find your hermitage?
We have tried but failed to make
That cool unflawed retreat
Where the pulses slow their beat
To an aspen-yellow age.
Today we cannot discipline
The ferments ratting underneath our skin.
Where is the formula to win
Composure from defeat?   20
And what specific can unmesh
The tangle of civilian flesh
From the traction of the panzers?
And when our children cry aloud

At screaming comets in the skies, what serves
The head that's bloody but unbowed?
What are the Stoic answers
To those who flag us at the danger curves
Along the quivering labyrinth of nerves?   Winter 1942

Father Time

Worry had crept into the old man's face.
Why did he have to tilt the hour-glass
So often? Strange, he thought, this hurried pace
Of the atoms as they strove to pass
From bulb to bulb, fighting their way
From life to death in an unexplained stampede.

He had measured many tempos in his season,
But never cared for speed.
He always liked the sanitary, slow,
Grave manner of the mountains.   10
He had seen them flow
In rivulets of crystal grains
Down through this very corridor
To the deltas of the ocean shore.
He had watched the plants and trees turn into coal;
The marks of the fronds were in the veins
Resembling those of his own hands and temples.
He remembered how he used to while
Away the aeons, pondering the roll
Of the Amazon and Nile.   20
The curve of the sand dunes of Sahara,
The depositions of the layers of gneiss,
The march of the granite boulders
Under the control
Of dynasties of ice.

He thought of the prehistoric file
Of the saurians, one long and leisured day,
On the crumbling bridges from Australia to Malay.
And now this new adventurer –
Which called itself a soul,   30
With its mélange of pride,
Courage, honour, suicide,
Pursuing an eternal goal –
Had come along to wreck
His cool pre-Cambrian sense of sequence.
He shot a last glance at the trek
Of the human granules through the bottleneck,
Then rose and smashed the glass, and with the dust
Christened the knoll –
SEBASTOPOL!   March 1943

Autopsy on a Sadist
(after Lidice)

The microscope was at a loss to tell
The composition of his brain and glands –
Why blood should be like catnip to his smell,
And paws be given him instead of hands.

What toxins in a mammal's milk could serve
To manufacture luxuries out of pains,
Anesthetize the sympathetic nerve
Or turn to sleet the fluids of his veins?

Much less could it explain those pointed ears
That caught the raptures of a werewolf's howl,   10
The allegretto strains in human tears,
The hallelujahs in a tiger's growl.   Spring 1943

Niemoeller

God is my Fuehrer! What availed a phrase
In such a camp, with such an armoury?
A simple echo of Judean days
Had now become the Nordic infamy:
A look, a word, a gesture – his defence
Against the frown of Essen battlements.

No more, no less than these for allies
Had Christ before the Procurator's seat –
Only the incandescence of his eyes,
And the eternal pallor of his feet;   10
Only his side, his forehead, and his hands
To take the imprint of the Roman brands.   August 1943

Der Fuehrer's Pot-Pourri

At night infernal tunes ran through his head
With alternating sweat and shiver:
It was his meals, the doctors said,
Which lay so heavy on his liver,
And the abnormal rate
At which he drank and ate.
In lieu of prime beef of Yorkshire –
His most desired plate –
Had he not taken
That Netherlandish bacon?   10
Why did the butler serve
That Danzig flounder as *hors d'oeuvre*?
And then, *ach Gott*,
That cramping stitch
In the appendix, was it not
Those gamey pheasants which
Drug Tito or Mikhailovitch

Had sent him from the Jugo-Slavian mountains?
And had analysis not shown
Bacilli in the Vichy fountains,   20
And ptomaine in the Baltic tunny?
Besides, his *chef* had coaxed him to devour
A bannock made of raw Ukrainian flour,
Corinthian currants and Hymettus honey.

Thus with his stomach sated,
His nightmare ran to tunes he hated:
God Save the King and *Auld Lang Syne*
Played havoc with *Die Wacht am Rhein*.
'Allons enfants de la patrie'
Broke the *Horst Wessel* melody.   30
'Sprung from holy soil of Hellas,
Hail we still sweet Liberty,'
Were notes that struck like mortal pains.
He turned for solace
To *Deutschland ueber Alles*,
But heard instead the strains –
'I'm William of Nassau,
Dutch blood in my veins'... .
'King Christian stood beside the mast,
His glittering sword was swinging fast.'   40
He tried some variations all his own –
O Tannenbaum!
O Lebensraum!
But gave them up with a dismal moan.

Exiles returned, a million strong,
To sing to the Fuehrer all night long.
'The waters with a thousand homes'
Poured from a wild Norwegian throng.
Poles who with Starzynski bled,
Czechs whom Benes might have led,   50
Mustered round his gory bed,

Singing lustily –
'But we shall be free.'
That Polish *rota* drove him mad –
'We shall not leave our native land,
Forsake our folk, nor stand
An alien tongue.
Each doorstep shall a fortress be.'
And when he summoned Wagner for a chorus,
With Siegfried and Bruenhilde at their head,   60
To right a great Teutonic wrong
And quell the rabble discord of this scene,
The Master sent a Nibelung instead –
The scourging Alberich – but Hitler found
Even the thunder of this aria drowned
In the basso roar of a Volga song
Led by the soul of Chaliapin
Before the podium of Stalin.   October 1943

Still Life

To the poets who have fled
To pools where little breezes dusk and shiver,
Who need still life to deliver
Their souls of their songs,
We offer roses blanched of red
In the Orient gardens,
With April lilies to limn
On the Japanese urns –
And time, be it said,
For a casual hymn   10
To be sung for the hundred thousand dead
In the mud of the Yellow River.

And if your metric paragraphs
Incline to Western epitaphs,
Be pleased to return to a plain
Where a million lie
Under a proletarian sky,
Waiting to trouble
Your lines on the scorched Ukrainian stubble.
On the veined marble of their snows   20
Indite a score to tether
The flight of your strain;
Or should you need a rougher grain
That will never corrode with weather,
Let us propose
A stone west of the bend where the Volga flows
To lick her cubs on the Stalingrad rubble.

Hasten, for time may pass you by,
Mildew the reed and rust the lyre;
Look – that Tunisian glow will die   30
As died the Carthaginian fire!
Today the autumn tints are on
The trampled grass at Marathon.
Here are the tales to be retold,
Here are the songs to be resung.
Go, find a cadence for that field-grey mould
Outcropping on the Parthenon.
Invoke, in other than the Latin tongue,
A Mediterranean Muse
To leave her pastoral loves –   40
The murmurs of her soft Theocritean fold,
Mimosa, oleander,
Dovecotes and olive groves,
And court the shadows where the night bedews
A Roman mausoleum hung
Upon the tides from Candia to Syracuse.   1943

Missing: Believed Dead: Returned

Steady, the heart!
Can you not see
You must not break
Incredulously?

The dead has come back,
He is here at the sill;
Try to believe
The miracle.
Give me more breath,
Or I may not withstand   10
The thrill of his voice
And the clasp of his hand.

Be quiet, my heart,
Can you not see
In the beat of my pulse
Mortality?   1943

The Brawler in *Who's Who*

The doctors claimed they never had
A case to handle quite so bad –
A record weight, abnormal girth,
And such disturbance at a birth.
The infant murdered his twin brother
And shortly after that his mother,
To celebrate his debut on the earth.

Defying pedagogic rules,
He made a Bedlam of his schools,
And wrecked them from the floor to rafter,   10
As one by one, with insane laughter,

Harrowed in soul and gaunt in feature,
His nurse, his father, and his teacher
Wasted, and passed into the great Hereafter.

Then came the war! and soon his name
Was but a synonym for fame;
The allied armies and their foes
Alike were stricken by his blows.
And, peace declared, he took the thanks
Of both; returned high in the ranks –   20
Lieutenant-Colonel with two D.S.O.S.

He married and his three young wives
In quick succession lost their lives –
A Gaul, a Teuton, and a Briton.
Just how those marital blooms were smitten,
The colonel never would confess:
They say the tale, now with the Press,
Remains by order of the Court unwritten.

Thence to a fortress – whereupon
He rounded up the garrison,   30
Heading that great historic riot
Concerning roaches in the diet.
A witness swore a brigadier
Gave him the bayonet from the rear
Which laid the brawler flat and strangely quiet.

For one whole day an undertaker
Worked hard upon this mischief-maker
To soften down the muscle twists,
Then called in two evangelists
Who managed somehow to erase   40
The indentations of his face
But failed to straighten out his knotted fists.

They buried him. That very night
With his left hook and lethal right
He put a dozen shades to rout.
The devil refereed the bout
And spread the rumour – so I'm told –
That Death failing to get him cold,
Had fouled him with a technical knock-out.   1943

They Are Returning

Cease Fire! Again the order
Had closed the campaigns of the Western world.
The bugles are silent: the flags are furled.
Only the requiems remain to be sung
And the knells rung
Over the dust of Europe.
And with the order
Ceased, too, those all but animate forms,
Mechanic myths of man's creative act
Transfigured into fact,   10
Endowed with perfect suicidal skill,
With power to fight unbleeding, yet to kill –
The robots that had changed tail-winds
To head-on storms,
Had coasted past the Spitfires
And given the speed of sound a run –
These now to the last one
Have fallen from their lightning thoroughfares,
Or else spoored by the Lancasters
Were caught and smoked out from their Calais lairs.   20

Ceased, too, the official bulletin,
'With deep regrets' sent to the next-of-kin,
The papers' daily pyramid of losses,
The mass production of the wooden crosses –

The story of the unreturning.
These put their bodies
Between us and the flaming skies,
Between us and a night as foul
As ever fell on European eyes,
And more incredible   30
Than any picture lore of fables;
Between us and a fear that tore apart
The deepest instincts of the family ties,
The Nazi deformation of the heart,
The Quisling poison at the household tables,
The son's metallic stare, the start
At the troopers' rap upon the door,
The bullet and the blood upon the floor,
The camps, the pestilential breath
That caught the thousands in the vans of death;   40
Between us and the regimental boot
Upon our altars, the enforced salute,
The lie at the lips, the threat
Of the unknown that kills the mind
Before the body husk, the silhouette
Of helmets on the window-blind,
The laboratory shadow which combined
Cunning of science, terror of the brute,
And running back along the human tree,
Could come up stemming from a simian root   50
To learn how to congeal an infamy
Like Buchenwald or Maidanek or Lidice –
Between us and all that they placed their whole
Economy of body and of soul.

We have known blood to run
Like this before – blood of father, blood of son,
And we had read
That out of blood from hands and feet and side
A faith once came to birth

And found its test of worth,   60
Or were we so misled
And so unprofited,
That in the self-same stream the faith has died,
Lost in the periodic ebb and flow
That left an aftermath upon the earth
Of terror, greed and woe?
And we have seen the way the sons of men
Have passed through Moloch but to pass again
Through Mammon – yet once more
Out of the crumpled gunpits of a War,   70
Faced with the sight of an entire
Continent afire,
We dare in this last phase of the eclipse
To place the morning trumpets to our lips.

They are returning.

Was it five years ago or yesterday
They spent their leisured hours at play,
Were walking through the turnstiles
To watch their heroes of the diamond smash
Their homers, or a bantam flash   80
Hang his opponent on the ropes? The world
Was focused in the hit, the plate, the curled
Pitch, in the yards won in the scrimmage, in the sight
Of a puck flying through the posts.
Then overnight
The game was on another field
With sacrificial gain and yield,
The hedgerow inches grilling into yards
Against the wire and the shrapnel shards.
Five years ago, an age,   90
Or yesterday,
That with heads strained,
Ears cocked, eyes on the sky,

These boys were being trained
To listen to the hum, identify
By cut of wing, tail, fuselage,
The models of the aeroplanes?
So soon they found themselves with wings,
And mingling in free comradeship with star
And cloud and eagles, while far   100
Below in microscopic spaces
Were creeping things
Like slugs and motor cars and trains.

So short a time,
That women too should take their places,
Behind the steering wheel,
In front of the micrometer
Spinning threads as fine as gossamer
For the rifle mountings,
Guiding turret lathes, or welding plates,   110
Spark-testing steel,
Assembling fuses, wires in cables, grinding
Lenses and prisms, or finding
The death-range near the Lines in Italy
Where, standing by a soldier's bed,
They could direct the pale-gold
Drip of the plasma or the *mould*
Into a median vein and see
It re-enact
The Resurrection from the Dead.   120

What brought the change?
The rumble of the panzers into Poland,
The stories of the camps, the latest tale
Of the Gestapo, the *Athenia*, Rotterdam,
That ominous thrust of the arrow-diagram
Upon the maps, Dunkirk, and the fall
Of Paris, following the ram

Of the tanks against the civilian jam
Upon the roads – (Of what avail
The Lines against those fleet   130
Arrows now east and south
Towards Yugoslavia, Greece and Crete?)
Was it but one of these, or all,
The quick contagion of a bugle call,
The highest note in the scale
Of Churchill's voice – 'We shall not fail'?
Or was it something more
That made those children of the first World War,
Scarce come to their majority,
Those heirs of Vimy and of Passchendaele,   140
Gather round to read a legacy
And guard it to the last terms of the will,
Almost, it seemed to us, before
Their fathers' blood was dry upon the codicil?

And so they went, those boys turned into men.

One who had read of ancient Northern France,
And sketched the district known as Normandy,
Knew Carentan, Saint Lô, Rouen, Crécy,
As points within a pageant of Romance,
Of Anglo-Gallic victory and defeat,   150
Where longbows with their grey-goose feathers beat
The crossbows – who knew Bayeux
And its two hundred feet of tapestry
Picturing the record of the Conqueror –
Could he have guessed the fateful chance
That led his steps into an Abbey nave
Where, with survivors of a battered corps,
He would, with dust of Caen upon his tunic,
Survey the Norman's grave?

One who had followed in a Latin book   160
The story of the Second Punic War,
Of Hannibal's descent, and took
As casual names – the Arno, Upper Tiber,
Arezzo and Cassino –
Could he,
Foretell that in two years or three
He would be fighting
On the Tyrrhenian shore,
Or dying at the beach of Trasimeno?

And those whose summer hands had known   170
Only the oars and paddles on a bay,
The rigging of a catboat or a smack,
Turned into leading seamen,
Stemming the winter in Atlantic waters
On the *Swansea* or the *Chilliwack*,
Or, in the *Skeena-Athabascan* way,
Putting the hulls as buffers
Between the convoy and the pack.

And to those youngsters out of school
Came honours higher   180
Than that to which amibition could aspire,
Ribbons and bars and crosses,
In that proud hour of their investiture,
For diving with their Typhoon rocket-fire
Upon the panthers at Esquay,
Pinpointing targets on the Ruhr,
For chasing Messerschmitts,
Conceding odds of three to one,
Under the Malta sun,
Or driving through the North Sea winds to seal   190
The exits to the artery of Kiel.

They have met dangers that outfaced
Homeric myths, gone journeys that outpaced
The farthest-leagued Ulyssean strides.
For they have lodged
In foreign lands with winds and tides
And mountain pines;
Set up their tents under the Apennines;
Or, clothed in ice, were tossed
In the storm pockets of the Himalayas;   200
Climbed over Burma; crossed
The Irrawady; entered Kiska; took the raw
North air on the deck of the *Iroquois*;
Exchanged the *Scharnhorst's* greetings; saw
Murmansk; explored the reaches
Of Scandinavian capes and Arctic seas;
Came back; chugged through the Channel fogs to draw
Around Gibraltar to Calabrian beaches
Fresh lines upon the world's geographies.

They are returning.   210

No dole or bread line must await those hands
That once had clawed at the Ortona sands,
Or held that five-day bridgehead at the Scheldt,
Those feet that raced to join
The *Haida* and *Assiniboine*.
The pilots of the aeroplanes,
Who made the sky their thoroughfare,
Must breathe on earth an unpolluted air
And take the sunlight through the slumless panes,
Their young hearts washed by a great cause   220
Acclaimed at the world's barricades.
Those craftsmen of the arts of flying,
Those foremen of the modes of dying –
They shall come back to new crusades,
To set the red pine to the whirring blades

Along the sky lanes for the marts of peace,
To take the produce of their toil, to say
To the machine, the drills and cranes,
The dynamos and lathes – *Obey!*
To claim the right to reap the autumn stores   230
And the shared yield of the earth's veins,
Masters, not servants, of pre-Cambrian ores,
To own their birthright as the free
Citizens of earth and sky and sea.

They are returning

To write a chapter on the history of beaches.
To trace a line of Trojan spray
Against the dawn of a Norman day;
To draw the eyes that never looked on death,
The frigid muscles and the cancelled breath;   240
To coin the verb and seize the noun
For the first stare as the bow doors opened
And the ramp went down.

To sing the songs for those whose names
Were left unread
In the citations of the hour –
The thousands of unsung amorphous dead,
The sailors of the sweeper-craft,
The ratings of the foc's'les,
The stokers in the holds for whom no bells   250
Tolled when they left their unberibboned toil
Only to try their chances on a raft,
Or plunge beneath the tanker's blazing oil.

To squeeze the crimson from a tube
And mix it with a natural green,
To show how mortars, rockets, tanks,
Could splash the khaki of the ranks –

To paint that scene
On a broken wave of live June corn
Somewhere within the fields between   260
The Odon and the Orne.
To find the way the colour drains
Out of the paratroopers' veins,
The moment at the dropping zone; to catch
The flicker of the pulses at the hatch
Above a rendezvous that lay
Behind the German rim at Carpiquet.

To write a ballad on a crew of eight
In a patrolling Canso flying-boat,
Measure the stresses to relate   270
The curves, the dive, the way they came,
Passed through the storm of the U-boat flak,
With starboard engine dead and wings aflame,
And then came back
To sink her; tell the hours of drift and wait
Of the rubber dinghy with her double freight.

They shall come back to build in stubborn rhyme,
Out of Laurentian rock and Norman lime,
Memorial towers Canadian
Across a continental span;   280
To mix a mortar that shall never crumble
Before the blasts of war or wear of time.
To native tunes
They shall arrange the old-world runes,
Fingering those names keyed to the sound of shells
Above the Benedictine cells –
Foggia, Adriatic, and Ancona,
Ceprano, Florence, Capua, Ortona –
And make them ring new notes in Western steeples.
And from those tonic syllables,   290
Dieppe, Authie, Falaise, and Carpiquet,

Kleve, Emmerich, Antwerp and Groningen,
They shall learn how to wind
Their souls into the reeds and strings
To reach their own *Eroicas*, and find
The *Chorals, Passions, Pathétiques,*
To hymn their Iliad voyagings.   June 1945

Behind the Log

There is a language in a naval log
That rams the grammar down a layman's throat,
Where words unreel in paragraphs, and lines
In chapters. Volumes lie in graphs and codes,
Recording with an algebraic care
The idiom of storms, their lairs and paths;
Or, in the self-same bloodless manner, sorting
The mongrel litters of a battle signal
In victories or defeats or bare survivals,
Flags at half-mast, salutes and guards of honour,   10
Distinguished crosses, burials at sea.

Our navigators trained their astrolabes
And sextants on the skies in lucky weather,
Or added guesses to dead reckoning,
Hauled up their lead, examined mud or shell
Or gravel on the arming – fifty fathoms,
Now forty, thirty, twenty-five, shallowing
Quickly! 'Engines astern, reefs, keep your lead
Going. Have plenty of water under you.'
They did not wait till miracles of science   20
Unstopped the naked ears for supersonics,
Or lifted cataracts from finite vision
To make night and its darkness visible.
How long ago was it since sailors blew
Their sirens at the cliffs while nearing land,

Traversing channels, cocked their ears and waited?
'Where did you hear that echo, mate?'
                                        'Right off
The starboard quarter, Captain. Took ten seconds.'
'That's Gull Rock there a mile away. Where now?'
'Two seconds for the echo from port bow.'   30
'That's Porpoise Head I reckon – Hard a-port!'
With echoes everywhere, stand out to sea.
But when the winds deafened their ears or cloud
And rain blinded their eyes, they were shoved back
Upon their mother wit which either had
To find the exits to the runs and round
The Capes or pile their ships upon the reefs.

And of that lineage are the men today.
They still are calling to the rocks: they get
Their answers in the same hard terms: they call   40
To steel gliding beneath the sea: they pierce
Horizons for the surface hulls: they ping
The sky for the plane's fuselage: even
The moon acknowledged from her crater sills.
But though the radio bursts and vacuum tubes
And electronic beams were miracles
Of yesterday, dismissing cloud and rain
And darkness as illusions of the sense,
Yet always there to watch the colours, note
The V-break in the beam's straight line, to hear   50
The echoes, feel the pain, are eyes, ears, nerves:
Always remains the guess within the judgment
To jump the fine perfection of the physics
And smell mortality behind the log.

As weird a game of ping-pong ever played
Was on the sea – the place, off Cape Farewell,
With the back-curtain of the Greenland ice-cap:
Time – '41 autumnal equinox.

The crisis was the imminence of famine
And the cutting of the ganglia and veins   60
That vitalized the sinews, fed the cells
Of lungs demanding oxygen in air.
The wicks were guttering from want of oil,
And without oil, the bread went with the light,
And without bread, the will could not sustain
The fight, piping its courage to the heart.

Grey predatory fish had pedigreed
With tiger sharks and brought a speed and power
The sharks had never known, for they had been
Committed to the sea under a charter   70
Born of a mania of mind and will
And nurtured by a Messianic slogan.
They were not bounded by the parallels.
They found their habitats wherever there
Was open sea and keels to ride upon it.
Off the North Cape they had outsped the narwhals,
The sawfish of the Rios and the Horn.
They did not kill for food: they killed that food
Should not be used as food. They were the true
Expendables – the flower of their type.   80
They left their mothers for self-immolation,
The penalty the same for being on
Or off the target – for the first to join
Their own combustion to that of the ships,
And for the second, just to go the way
Their victims went – a drunken headlong spiral,
Shunted from an exhausted radius
Down fifteen thousand feet or more of sea,
Engines, propellors, gyros, rudders, dead.

The s.c.42 was being groomed   90
To match a new suspected strategy.
The sleuths till now had surfaced, stabbed and dived

In lone attack. This convoy had to face
The risk of concentrated ambush, meet it
By leaving beaten sea-lanes, east and west,
And in the ambiguity of the wastes
To seek the harsh alliance of the ice
And fog, where Arctic currents were more friendly,
And long nights blanketed the periscopes.

THE CONVOY CONFERENCE

In the Conference room the language dripped with brine.   100
Veterans, who nearly half a century
Ago had flown their flags on battle cruisers,
Were busy grafting some new sprouts of Gaelic
And Newfie-Irish on an English stump.
They had saluted Fisher as cadets,
Heard *Open Fire* under Jellicoe,
Outridden typhoons off the Solomons
And at the Falklands cancelled Coronel.
'Twas time they had a spell of garden peace,
A time to trim their briers and colour Meerschaums.   110
Those old days were the real days – now, by God
They had to tread the decks of merchantmen,
From flagships to dry cargo-ships and tankers.

The Naval Control Service Officer Addresses the Masters:
'Good morning, gentlemen. It is a pleasure
To see familiar faces here today.
To such of you who have commanded ships
In earlier convoys what I have to say
Will be just dishing up the old instructions.
But since to many it is the first adventure,   120
I know you'll pardon me if I should cover
With some precision the important points.
Let me begin by saying that your convoy
Has, in its Commodore, one of the most
Renowned men in the Service. It is not

For me to talk at length about his fine
And honourable record. It is known
To all of you. He has of his free choice
Issued from his well-earned retirement
To place at the disposal of the Allies   130
His knowledge, skill, and practical seamanship.
Here at this table, gentlemen: Rear-Admiral
Sir Francis Horatio Trelawney-Camperdown!

'The Senior Naval Officer will have
Escort and convoy under his command.
An able and distinguished officer,
He is through long and personal experience
Well-versed in enemy tactics, and your safety
Will be the escort's first consideration.

N.C.S.O. Thumbing the Pages of "General Instructions":   140
'Being in all respects ready for sea,
The ships will have steam up and hoist pennants
At daybreak. Note – The Commodore will sound
A prolonged blast. The ships will leave anchorage
In single column and at intervals
Of three minutes, and in the following order,
The Commodore leading...
                        You will shorten cables
XX minutes before you heave up. Note –
You will be making seaward on the ebb.
You start two columns after dropping pilots.   150
Notice in Form A1 all the instructions
Governing matters of sequence, columns and speed.

'May I now draw your most thorough attention
To that important fire page, section B
Of General Instructions (a voice – "regular page
of bumph");   that *complete*
Blackout at night. Only last week reports
Came in of a ship sunk because she showed

A light, and that despite the most emphatic
Warnings at the conference prior to the sailing.   160
Remember – have deadlights and scuttles closed,
The blackout curtains checked, no cigarettes
Or pipes lighted on deck and every measure
To conceal the convoy put into effect.

'And likewise of the first significance,
Page 3 at section D concerning "Smoke."
Advice is being received of ships making
Black smoke which with good visibility
May be observed for many miles at sea,
And I may add for hours after a convoy   170
Has passed a given point. I must repeat
This warning – Do not make black smoke in daylight!

'Again. Your route has with the greatest care
Been chosen by the Admiralty experts.
But may I point out that such care and judgment
Could be offset by so simple a matter
As refuse-dumping over rails. Do not –
(Voices – "Wrap it around the bully beef."
"God, that tomato soup needs body and flavor."
"I'd put it in the kye to take the stink out.")   180
Do NOT throw garbage in the sea in day time.
That's a dead give-away. A crate or carton
Floating astern a convoy might betray
The existence and position of the ships.
That practice must at all cost be avoided.
And most important for internal safety
Of convoy lines is that of station-keeping.
A ship that's not in station is out of control;
The turns in moments of emergency
Cannot successfully be executed,   190
Unless this measure strictly is observed.
I do not need to emphasize this maxim.

'These measures are of front-line urgency.
W/T silence must always be maintained
Along the route. Occasionally it's broken,
Not wilfully indeed but carelessly,
By operators fresh from the radio school,
Whose fingers have not lost the itch to tap
The keys to break the tedium by listening
To crackle on 500 kilocycles.   200
A random da da dit dit dit might be
An invitation to the U-boats ready
To accept it. They are ever listening
In on our frequencies and you know well
The manner the Direction Finder Loop
On a surfaced U-boat will follow a signal.
It's like a human ear alerted, which
Will turn to the source of a sound to get a bearing.
You must remember that the enemy
Will not relax his efforts to pick up   210
Those waves, that German D/F stations even
As far away as Occupied Europe
Are taking bearings, plotting out our ships.

'Now, gentlemen: here is the Commodore.'

Sir Francis Horatio:
'Gentlemen: I shall be very brief and I hope
To be as brief after we get to sea.
I shall keep my signals to a minimum,
But when a hoist *does* go up I shall
Expect immediate acknowledgment.
Many of us have sailed together already,   220
And gone through several trying situations.
But our success, such as it is, has sprung
From absolute obedience to instructions
And from endurance which must be assumed.
While it is true that for the navigation

Of his own ship each master must be held
Responsible, there is but little room
For rugged individualists. Elsewhere
Perhaps the Nelson touch may be applied,
And a captain's intuitions exercised,   230
But not within the stations of a convoy.
(Chuckles amongst the older masters.)

'The N.C.S.O. has referred to the matter
Of showing lights. A match, lit on deck, has
Been spotted by an escort at two miles,
And last crossing, a thoughtless biped left
A port open and failed to notice the signal
From a destroyer. It required a burst
From a machine-gun to close it. I am sure
We shall require no such emphasis   240
In this convoy but I should urge each master
To make the business of lights a top concern,
Particularly at the change of Watch.
Men dropping in to a stuffy galley to make
A mug of tea before going below
Are the principal offenders.
                                   'Do not wait
Till you are deep in fog before you stream
Your fog-buoys. That is generally too late.
Your next astern by that time has lost touch.
Good seamanship and team-play should prevent   250
Avoidable collisions in thick fog.

'If you are new to convoy you may be
Tempted to flash on at full brilliancy
Your navigation lights when another ship
Closes you. DON'T. You are as visible
To him as he to you. Keep closed up. Keep
Lights dimmed except in an emergency.

'I shall say little here about the stragglers.
The record of the losses says it much
More clearly, and the escort cannot help   260
You if you leave the family. They are good;
They can work wonders but not miracles.

'And now if you're uncertain of anything –
Emergency turns, for instance – come and have
A chin with me at the close of the conference.
And to repeat, we're in this business all
Together, and in it up to the neck:
For my part, I am bloody proud of it.
Good morning, gentlemen, and a good voyage.'

N.C.S.O.: 'Questions?'
Chorus: .   'Plenty.'
Harvey Butt: 'I'm in the wrong position.   270
     Too far astern. I have a 12-knot ship.
     I want a place in first or second line
     To save me bumpin' into 6-knot tramps.'

Jim Burdock: 'This convoy got no tramps.'

Butt: 'Well, all I know
     The last one had 'em, and I knocked the sterns
     Off three of them, and I was always goin'
     Full speed astern to save my goddam neck.'

'John Knox' O'Flaherty:
     'I could make 8 knots if I didn't have
     Such lousy coal. The bloody stuff won't steam.
     A half of it is gravel – wouldn't boil   280
     A kettle: looks like salvage from a wreck
     Picked up from sweepings left on Sable Island.'

Charlie Shipside:
   'And I don't like my place – gummed up between
   A couple of tankers. God, if I'm not fished
   I'll be run down.'

Jack Doucette: 'Why should I be back there?
   Never did like the stern of columns. Suppose
   I'm in there just for picking up survivors.
   What do you take me for –an ambulance?'

Jerry Payne:
   '8 knots would tear the guts out of my tub.
   I haven't had a refit for three years.   290
   Can't execute a turn of forty-five degrees.
   We'll be colliding every fifteen seconds.'

Robert Fitzsimmons:
   'My pumps were out of gear when she was built;
   Still out of gear; complained a hundred times,
   But can't get any action.'

Michael Saltaway: 'I have this
   To say. I only got one boiler workin';
   And that one's on half-time – the other half
   Is restin' – and I've only half a crew.'

Norwegian Captain, leaning heavily on native speech:
   'I kan ikke forstaa fordommt ord.
   How in helvete tink dey dat I kan   300
   Faa 8 knots ut of my old vaskelbalja.
   Har ikke hatt fullt mannskap for two year.
   I lar mig fan ikke fortelle what I
   Skal do. You go helvete alle mann.'

N.C.S.O.: 'What did he say?'

'Arry Stubbins: ''E says the bleedin' hinstructions
   Are fine and quite clear to 'is hunderstandin'.'

Robin MacAllister:
   'Nae, nae, he canna' thole thae English turrms.
   He'd ken a' richt, gin you gae him the Gaelic.
   I wad respeckfully suggest the wurrds
   O' the Generral Instructions be convairted   310
   Into a ceevilized tongue so that a chiel
   Micht hae nae doots. Noo, let me spik mi thochts.'

   (Voices: 'Now, what did *he* say?' 'Noo's the day
   and noo's the hour.' 'Is this St. Andrew's Night?'
   'Pipe in the haggis.')

A Danish Captain:
   'No, no. He sess he do not *ikke* know
   One word. His vaskelbalja – tub-tub, washtub,
   Das iss he mean his ship, can't make 8 knots.
   No crew *mannskap* full up for long long time.
   Ship had no refit since she left Bergen
   In 1894. He tol' me dat
   Himself. He not quite clear. He sess ve can   320
   All go to hella. Don't care damn.
                                  I got
   Complaints *also*. Want get dem off my chest.
   Goddam nuisance, I seh, dose para-a-vanes.
   Muss up de vurks. Crew don't like dem damn bit.
   Dey seh put hex on ship – a buncha Jonahs.
   And more *also* I seh. No compass checks.
   Dose D/G coils play hell wid compasses.
   De gear get loose on deck. Dey come adrift.'

Cyrus Bumstead:
   'I don't want anyone to tell me how
   To run my ship – been in the Services,   330
   Merchant and Navy, nigh come forty years.
   I was a Master when the most of them
   Were spottin' patterns on their diapers.'

Mark Knee to Cyrus:
  'I squeezed the Atlantic from my mitts before
  Those Juniors had their birthday buttons on.'

Captain, The Honourable Guy Brimblecombe:
  'Well, sir, you needn't worry about *my* ship.
  She went through this before: she'll go again.
  She's in good trim. I have a splendid crew.
  Signals will be acknowledged to the letter,
  And in the sea tradition, I assure you.'   340

N.C.S.O.: 'Now, gentlemen, since it is quite apparent
  That we are all in utmost harmony
  On the main grounds, it is just left for me
  To wish "good-luck". Never have I attended
  A Conference where there was such fine feeling
  Combined with insight and rare technical grasp
  Of the problems of a convoy operation.
  Let me congratulate you. May I now
  Invite you, on behalf of a great friend
  Of the R.C.N., to the Periwinkle Club   350
  At Lobster Point where you may hoist a couple
  To take the chill from the September fog.'
  . . . . .
In a few hours from the time the blinds
Were drawn upon the jags and the last lisp
Against the universe and things marine
Was but a reminiscence lapsed in rum,
Those men were on the Bridge peering through fog
And moving towards their ordered rendezvous.
  . . . . .
One half a million tons were in the holds,
Cramming to the last precious cubic inch   360

The slow-keeled merchantmen – the sixty-six.
No longer were those ships an industry
Run for peacetime returns upon investment.
They took their line positions for defence.
Against them mainly was the warfare waged –
Bulk cargo carriers with box-like sections,
Ship side to ship side and the main deck to keel,
Carrying their gross of ore and coal and grain;
The ships with 'tween decks running the full length;
Tankers equipped with special pumps for oil;   370
Refrigeration ships, holds insulated
For storage of the perishable goods;
And hybrid types that had their bellies full
Of oranges, aluminum and lint.

How desperate the strait which would commit
A treasure of this price to such a journey!
Where find a steward who would risk his name
To close the page of such accountancy
When every mile along the ocean highway
Was calling for protection, and in calling   380
Demanded life and life's expenditure?
And here the call was answered with a guard
Whose substitute for numbers was its courage –
Four terriers slipped from the Canadian kennel:
But one destroyer, *Skeena*; three corvettes,
Kenogami, *Orillia* and *Alberni*.
Upon their vigil hung the life of all,
Of ships and men. Of sleeker, faster breed,
The *Skeena* ranged a far periphery
At thirty knots, now out of sight and now   390
Closing the convoy as her nose tried out
The dubious scents in narrowing ellipses.
The slower guards kept closer to their broods,
Pushing their way within the column lanes,
Emerged to pace the port and starboard flanks
Or nuzzled with a deep strategic caution

The hulls of those whose tardy engine beats
Brought down the knots of faster ships and made
The gravest risk and worry for the fleet.
They kept a special watch upon the tankers.   400
No ships, no aeroplanes, no jeeps could stir
Without this source of power and lubrication.
Even the merchantmen must flank these ships,
Herded like buffalo young inside the ring.
· · · · ·
Commodore to Signalman:
    'Signal to pennants 73, relay
    To pennants 103, Stop Pouring Smoke!'

Internal murmurings:
    'Look at it tossin' like a Texas twister.
    That smoke is blacker than an Afghan's whiskers.
    I'd like to tell that Captain of the Heads
    He should have stayed at home with the kind of job   410
    That suited him – housebreakin' his Angoras.'

Official:
    'And pennants 114 is out of station.'

Unofficial:
    'That flappin' penguin from the Auckland Islands
    Has been a week on route, yet needs more time
    To get rid of that Newfie-Crowsnest screech.
    He'll lose it when he's doused. Get back in station,
    For if you don't, the canaries will stop singin'.'

The Master's thoughts:
    'I told those sculpins at the conference
    I couldn't make that eight – a half a knot
    Above a six would blow my stinkin' boilers.   420

I haven't had a cleanin' for a year,
And there's a beach of sand inside the gears,
And yet that bargee yells – GET BACK IN STATION!'

Commodore:
   'And pennants 74 by the Diet of Worms!
   He's waddlin' like an old barnyard merganser.
   Another hour by the way he's goin'
   He'll be out on the flanks duckin' his feathers,
   Or lost in fog and stragglin' back to Sydney.
   Keep pumpin' Morse into his ruddy blinkers.'

The Master in question:
   'I've got a twisted rudder – like a corkscrew,   430
   And if that poopin' punk there on the flagship
   Imagines he's Paul Bunyan or the devil,
   Tell him put on his shorts and straighten it.'

P.O. to galley-boy:
   'Gallagher, did your mother tell you nothin'
   On the way home? Stop pitchin' gash in daytime.
   Handin' the convoy on a platter to the subs.
   As bad as smoke to give the trail away.
   Just one more bad tomato over there,
   And all the ships will quit this lovely Service,
   And you'll go with the galley, do you hear?'   440

Gallagher:
   'Why won't that windpipe slitter tell me what
   I got to do with all that mouldy gash?
   'Twas gash when it was brought aboard, 'twas gash
   When it was crated; now it's maggoty.
   Can't eat it and can't burn it and can't dump it.
   I'd like to foul his beak in those tomatoes.'

North of the sixtieth, they had, it seemed,
Found refuge in a sea-berth where the foe,
Finding the chill enter his crop, might seek
More southern fodder. Least of all the hazards   450
Were winds and waves: for these the ships were built.
Their bows could bull the heavier seas head-on.
Their hulls could stand the shock beam-to. The keels
Had learned the way to bite into the troughs:
Such was their native element. The acts
Of God were taken as their daily fare
Received alike with prayers or curses. These
Were as the dice fell – whether luck of devil
Or luck of God spilled on a shifting floor
Close to the steady fringe of the Arctic Circle.   460

For seven days and nights without attack!
The asdic operator in his hut
Had sent his ultra-sounds out and reported
Echoes, but only such as might return
As the dull, soft reverberation notes
From seaweed or low forms of ocean life
Or from a school of porpoises or whales.
His hearing was as vital to the ship
As was the roving sight in a crowsnest.

His ear was as the prism is to light,   470
Unravelling meanings from a skein of tone.
Each sound might hold a threat, a Bremen slur,
An overture to a dementia
Of guns and rockets and torpedo hits
Competing with the orders from the Bridge.
He had to know that threat and not mistake it.
For that his body was a sounding-board.
Even his knees must feel it and his face
Become a score for undetermined notes,
As if a baton in his cortex played   480

Wry movements on his neurones fiddle-taut,
Twitched his reflexes into spasms, narrowed
His pupils, kicked his heart into his throat.

He had an instrument in his control
Attested by the highest signatures of science.
The echoes had traversed wide spans of time: –
Helmholtz and Doppler tapping to each other
Through laboratory walls, and there was Rayleigh
Calling to Langevin, he to Fresnel,
The three hymning Pindarics to Laplace,   490
And all vibrating from their resonators
Salutes to Robert Boyle, halloos to Newton.
And here, his head-phones on, this operator,
Sleeve-rolled mechanic to the theorists,
Was holding in his personal trust, come life,
Come death, their cumulative handiwork.
Occasionally a higher note might hit
The ear-drum like a drill, bristle the chin,
Involving everything from brain to kidneys,
Only to be dismissed as issuing   500
From the submerged foundations of an iceberg,
Or classified as 'mutual interference.'

The hopes were running higher the farther north
The convoy steamed. Would this one get its break?
The Arctic pressed into the human service,
The Circle which had caught the navigators –
The hardiest in the annals of The Search,
Willoughby, Chancellor, Hudson, Bering, Franklin –
Impounded them, twisted and broken them,
Their ships and crews upon its icy spokes: 510
This time through the ironic quirk of War
Changed to an allied *cordon sanitaire*.

The evening of the eighth day and a moon,
High-sailing and impersonal, picked out
The seventy ships, deriding the constrained
Hush of the blackout. Was the latitude
Itself not adequate watch? The sea was calm,
Although with a beam swell the wallowing rate
Was but five knots. The moon illuminated
The *Empire Hudson*, leader of port wing,   520
Loaded with grain, the *Gypsum Queen* with sulphur,
The *Winterswyck*, the *Garm*, the *Scania*,
Muneric (iron ore – sink like a rock
She would if hit), *Bretwalda, Baron Ramsay,*
Gullpool, the *Empire Panther* and *Macgregor,*
The *Lorient, Arosa, Hampton Lodge,*
And others with the same high names and pennants,
Carrying at the load-water line their freight –
Twelve columns of them in their blueprint stations.
A half an hour to dusk the bo'sun's mate   530
Had piped his strictest order – *Darken Ship.*

Thousands of sailors under decks were sealed
As in vast envelopes. They ate and worked
And slept within a world self-quarantined
Against the pestilence of light by bolts,
Bulkheads and battened portholes, for each cell
Was like a tumoured brain, danger within,
Danger without, divided from the world
By an integument of iron bone.
What chance for life the moment when a shell   540
Trepanned the skull? What would release the pressure
Of that stampede to reach the for'ard hatch –
That burial hole in the deckhead – and come up
When the plates buckled in the lower mess?
Danger within? Could not the magazines
By a raffle flirt of fate be made to turn
Against the convoy, striking through the escort,

With final undeliberated measure,
When the oil tanks would join the magazines
To the last ton, to the last gram of blunder?   550
The fires that warmed the galleys could cremate:
For oil and fulminate of mercury,
Nitrated cellulose and T.N.T.
And the constituents of our daily bread,
Fresh water and fresh air, could by a shift,
Sudden and freakish in the molecules,
Be transubstantiated into death.

Added to this might come the blows where friend
Struck friend with utmost shoulder energy –
Blows just as murderous as torpedo hits   560
Where in the darkness, executing turns,
Or in the fog, the convoy ships would find
Their plates as vulnerable as cellophane:
Or from excess of their protective zeal
The fighting units with their double rate
Of convoy speed might plough their sinuous way
Up through the narrow lanes and turn too sharp,
Presenting their full beams across the bows
Of leading merchantmen. Lucky they were
If they escaped with nothing but a blast   570
Of roaring basso from the Commodore's lungs –
'Those lousy, noisy, nattering sons o' badgers,
Where do they think they're going – to Miami,
Harpooning porpoises or flying fish?'

The Silent Service never won its name
With fairer title than it did this night.
Evening at half-past nine and a fresh sound,
An instant octave lift to treble pitch
From the dull datum of 'reverbs' startled
The ear. 'An echo bearing *green four-o*,   580
Range 1500.'

'Hold and classify.'
The *ping-g-g* with its death's head identity!

c.o. to Officer-of-Watch:
'Increase speed 250 revolutions.'

(Officer-of-Watch repeats, calls down voice-pipe to coxswain who
sets engine-room telegraph to speed. The Engineer Officer-of-
Watch acknowledges. His chief e.r.a. swings wheel-throttle-
valve open to make required revolutions. Engine-room telegraph
confirms to wheelhouse and coxswain calls up voice-pipe –
'Wheelhouse-Bridge: 250 revolutions on, sir.' Bridge Officer-of-
Watch repeats to captain.)   590

The *Skeena* heeled to port on 'starboard ten'
To keep the target on the bow. 'Steady
On *two-four-seven*.' (Harry one at the dip.)
'Left cut on two-four-six. ...Right cut
On *two-five-three*.' (Reporting Doppler)
'Echo high and inclination closing.'
The range 1200. 'Target moving right:
Centre bearing, *two-five-five*.'
One thousand yards: 'extent of target – *ten*.'   600

Not ice this time but moving steel submerged –
Two hundred feet of longitudinal plate,
Forged at the Krupp's and tested in the Baltic,
Were answering the taps.
                          'Stand by depth-charges.'

Captain to Chief Yeoman:
     'Take an emergency report to shore:
     "In contact with classified submarine".'

(Chief Yeoman repeats to w.t. office.)
A crackle of Morse, and in bare space of seconds

The warning goes to Admiralty, from there
To allied ships in threatened area, 610
And on the walls in *Operations*, where
The swastikas and shadows of the U-boats
Follow in replica the Atlantic movements,
A red peg moves along the chart to plot
The first of the disease spots that would pock
The body of the s.c.42.

Whatever doubt the eye might have imposed
Upon the ear soon vanished with the signals.
Jedmore reported two torpedoes passed
Ahead, *Muneric*, fourth ship in port column, 620
Attacked, dragged instantly, sank with her iron.
The Commodore – 'Saw U-boat on port bow.'
Kenogami in contact with another,
A third, a fourth. Suspicions which had wormed
Their way along the vine were proved. The first
Wolf-pack engagement of the Atlantic War
Was on! A fifth ... a seventh! They had trailed
The ships to Greenland waters. Moonlight full,
Without the mercy of clouds, had turned
A traitor to the convoy, cancelling 630
The northern length of nights. Like teal not yet
Surprised to wing, the silhouetted ships
Awaited leisured barrels from the hunters,
And the warheads drilled them as from open sights.

Orillia, detailed to sweep astern,
Picked up the few survivors, took in tow
The *S.S. Tachee*, badly hit but still
Afloat: rockets were seen in midst of convoy:
A signal from the flagship – '*Empire Hudson*
Torpedoed on port side.' The triple task – 640
To screen the convoy, counter-attack, and then,
The humane third of rescuing the sailors,

Seemed far beyond the escort's hope or effort.
To save to kill, to kill to save, were means
And ends closely and bloodily allied.
Hundreds of sailors un-lifejacketed
Clawed at the jetsam in the oil and water.
Captains and Commodore were well aware
Of how a lame one in a chase could spatter
With blood the entire herd. High strategy　　　　　650
Demanded of the brain an execution
Protested by the tactics of the heart.
And there was only half an inch or less
Of a steel skin upon the escort's hulls –
Not for self-safety were those ships designed.
Just here the log with its raw elements
Enshrined a saga in a phrase of action.
'The *Empire Hudson* listing badly, crew
And officers were disembarked. Someone
Reported – "Secret papers have not been　　　　　660
Destroyed, mersigs, swept-channels, convoy route,
And codes, the *codes!*" And as there was a chance
The steamer might not sink, *Kenogami*
Was ordered to embark an officer,
Return him to the listed deck to find
And sink the weighted papers – which was done.'
This stark undecorated phrase was just
An interlinear item in the drama,
Three words spelling a deed unadvertised,
When ships announced their wounds by rockets, wrote　　　670
Their own obituaries in flame that soared
Two hundred feet and stabbed the Arctic night
Like some neurotic and untimely sunrise.
Exploding tankers turned the sky to canvas,
Soaked it in orange fire, kindled the sea,
Then carpeted their graves with wreaths of soot.
The sea would tidy up its floor in time,
But not just now – gaskegs and rafts and mops,

Oilskins, sou'westers, sea-boots, duffel coats
Drifted above the night's burnt offerings.   680
Only the names remained uncharred – *Muneric*,
Ulysses, Baron Pentland, Sally Maersk,
The *Empire Crossbill, Empire Hudson, Stargard* –
Merely heroic memories by morning.

The early hours of daylight drove the subs
To cover though the escort knew that eyes,
As sleepless as their own but unobserved
Behind the grey-green mesh of swell and lop,
Were following the convoy's desperate plunge.
All knew that no restrictive rules would hedge   690
This fight: to the last ship, to the last shot,
To the last man, for fair was foul and foul
Was fair in that melee of strength and cunning.
Tirpitz and Fisher thirty years before
Had scanned the riddles in each other's eyes.
What was the argument about the belt
That drained the sophistry of principles
Inside a ring? 'Hit first, hit hard, hit fast!'
Tirpitz had trumped him with – 'Hit anywhere.'
And here today only one point was certain –   700
Sailors above the sea, sailors below,
Drew equally upon a fund of courage.
No one might gamble on the other's fear
Or waning will. Commander Schmidt might flood
His tanks and dive when something on his mirror
Called for discretion, but in his own shrewd time
He could be reckoned on to blow the ballast
And frame that picture on the glass again.
He would come up with Botterschult and Rickert,
Von Braundorff, Niebergall, Schippmann and Fritzsche.   710
They knew their crews would never fail the switches
Or rush the conning towers before the orders,
Though the depth-charges pounded the blood vessels,

Though combing rams just missed them overhead.
In what proportions did the elements
Combine to move those individual pawns
Of power in their massed flesh-and-nerve formation
Across a board? Grit human; bruinine;
Habits that would not heckle a command,
Obedience that sealed the breach of fear,   720
A frenzy that would spurn the slopes of Reason
Under a rhetoric of Will which placed
Before the *herrenvolk* historic choices –
To scramble up a cliff and vandalize
The sunlight or else perish on the ledges.

These were the enemies the convoy fronted:
Metal to metal, though in this arena
The odds lay heavily with the pursuers,
Even by day – for what were periscopes
At distance of three thousand yards, that reared   730
Their tiny heads curved like swamp moccasins?
What was their smothered wake compared with that
Propeller wash, that height and drift of smoke,
Those lines of funnels with their sixty hulls?
And so it was a safe bet on the sub
When at high noon one left her nest and sped
Her charge right at the *S.S. Thistleglen*,
Dead at the waterline and full amidships.
It took three minutes for the merchantman
To dock her pig iron on the ocean floor.   740

'There, there he is!'
          Seven cables from the spot
Where suction swirled above the foundering,
The periscope light-grey – one minute only!
The *Skeena* carried out a pounce attack
Of ten depth-charges fired with shallow settings.
The asdic trailed the sub proceeding north

At three-knot speed. *Kenogami* confirmed
Echoes. Depth-charges with deep settings dropped,
The echoes ceased, and a great patch of oil
Surfaced, and a huge bubble like a blister   750
Broke, close to the position of explosions.
'This time for keeps we pinged his bloody hide, sir:
We've sent him down to join the *Thistleglen.*'

With this by day, what could another night
Not call forth from the cupboard? Afternoon
Wore on till dusk with that dramatic lull
Which acted like narcotics on the heart,
Yet put high-tension circuits in the brain.

'The *Sally Maersk* went down with bread enough
To feed an army for a month.'
                                            'But what   760
A job the corvettes did in rescuing
Them all – the fifty-four under that fire.'
'Most of the *Baron Pentland* too.'
                                            'Her back
Was broken though her lumber kept her floating.'

Could the same chance be taken the next night?

An hour after nightfall and the convoy
Had pierced the sixty-second parallel.
Twelve shortened columns tightened up their gaps,
All ships under instructions – (You will not – repetition –
Not break w.t. silence without deep suspicion of   770
U-boat presence.)   Owing to moon
Rear ships of the port column were instructed
To drop smoke floats should the enemy appear
On the port side. Each minute passed, each mile
Northward were credit items on a ledger.
And now quickening the heart, two friendly shadows,

Corvettes, steamed into shape – *Moose Jaw, Chambly* –
Two added to the four. But still the hope
Was on evasion – on the North – to kick
Them with their wounded heels and merge the spoors   780
Within the Greenland-Iceland ocean tundras.
And so the last night's vigil was repeated,
Although more ominous the silences:
More broken, too, the sleep as the ears buzzed
Still with the dental burr of the point-fives,
And the yellow cordite from the four-point-sevens
Kept up its smart under exhausted eyelids.
The average rate was lowered by three knots.
The *Tachee* was in tow of the *Orillia*,
Fumbling her rudder. From the *Chambly*'s deck,   790
Two miles away, the ships seemed fated targets.
Silent and slow and dark as, clothed with crape,
They journeyed on like mourners, having left
The Saxon burial of their sister ships,
And bearing on themselves the same contagion.
The air was breathing out its prophecy.
So was the water. There was mockery
Within the sea's caress – the way a wave
Would clamber up the bow of the *Moose Jaw*, scout
Around the shadows of the foc's'le,   800
Tattoo the face of the Bridge and lazily
Slither along the deck and then hiss through
The hawse-pipes as the corvette dipped her nose
To the slow anaesthetic of the swell.
Mockery it was on face and lips and fingers,
For, after her reconnaissance, the sea,
As urging death with a forensic fury,
Would shed her velvet syllables, return
With loaded fists to thunder at the gun-shields,
Trying to crack defence before the battle   810
Was joined between the 'patterns' and the 'tubes.'

Eleven-thirty, and the navigator,
His coat and boots on in his bunk, completes
A nightmare with a steady mumbling curse.
He thought the order was *Abandon Ship* –
It was an o.d. calling Middle Watch.
He wakes, turns over, and again turns over,
Yawns, stretches and turns out, proceeds to Bridge,
Peers through the blackout curtains, and in dim
Blue battle-light he squints and notes night orders,　　　　820
The toughest order of the toughest Watch
(Maintain tail sweep from two to four thousand yards).

He focuses binoculars to range
The horizon arcs. 'A lot of whales about
Tonight.' The echoes picked them up. Four hours!
He has to fight that Middle Watch fatigue,
And as the minutes crawl he sucks life-savers,
Or cracks one on his teeth for company.
A line of spray leaps up above the dodger
And like rawhide cuts him across the face.　　　　　　　830
Then, too, that phosphorescence on the sea
Is easily mistaken in its darts,
Flashes and curves for what the lookout fears.
Two hours are gone: another two to go.
(That wrist-watch ticks off hours instead of seconds.)
His eyelids blink to ease the strain that falls
Like mist upon a telescopic lens.
A starboard lookout yell jerks back his senses –
'Torpedo bearing green-four-o.' Lookout
Recoils from an expected blow that does　　　　　　　840
Not strike. 'Damn porpoises: they always home
In on the bow.'

(The navigating officer wipes the sweat from his forehead with his
sleeve, tells the sub-lieutenant to take over for a few minutes as he
wants to go to Heads. Then he calls to a stand-by.)

'Say, Spinney, what about
A mug of kye?'
       'Yes, Sir.'
          Spinney had not
Yet found his legs. Less than six months before
He had been learning Latin and the class-
Room smell had not been kippered from his system.   850
To him the ocean was a place of travel,
A blue-green oriental boulevard
Round unknown continents – up to this year;
And even to last night the illusion stayed,
When for his benefit the Borealis
Staged a rehearsal of the Merry Dancers
Before the blood-red footlights till it paled
The myth upon a tracery of starshell.
He now goes to the galley, fills a jug
With kye, picks up a half a dozen mugs,   860
Stumbles, skates, splashes half of it on deck.
Some drops of rain and sea-foam tincture it.
Along the way a leading-hand of the Watch
And a rheumatic coder cadge a drink,
And by the time that Spinney finds his balance
On the bridge only a soapy seawash greets
The navigator's throat. 'What in the name
Of all buck goats is this? Where did you get
This swill?' (He hands it to the sub to drink.)
      'Go back and fill her up again,
And keep her clean.'   870
          Spinney steps down from bridge,
Staggers, makes for the ladder, cracks the jug
Against the signal-box before he slides,
Reaches the galley and returns, tries hard
To wean his legs from the quadrangle walk,
Does a Blue Danube on the deck, and then
Revokes his quondam heroes (what a bunch
Of fools those ancients were to travel,

Aeneas was the biggest ass on earth!)
And flinging out his last accusative   880
At what is limned on the horizon, he
Remeasures his Virgilian cadences
In terms of stresses gliding queasily
Along the black ramps of the North Atlantic.

At ten to four Lieutenant Snell takes over,
And the two victims of the Watch slope down
With brains of fog and eyes of fractured glass.
Their legs go aft by instinct to their bunks,
Their minds well in advance entering a coma
Beyond gun-cotton shock or Gabriel's horn.   890

'Twas only in a stupor that O'Leary
Recalled his reprimand. When did it happen?
'Yeoman, you dropped no markers with that pattern.
That's standing orders now – smoke-floats to mark
Areas attacked. Ever heard it? Don't you know
Your drill? You'll be in my report in the morning.'
O'Leary gagged upon his chewing quid,
Hiccupped, sending a spurt of nicotine
And hydrochloric acid on the sea.
'He said to me, said he, "O'Leary, don't   900
You know your drill?" –Say, how the hell would I know?
Nobody tells me nothing in this Navy.'

A bo'sun caught the Peggy with a fag.
'Cripes, do you want to bitch this midnight show?
That lighted butt is visible for miles,
And on the starboard wing, too. Don't you know
The one and only moral law of Moses
Is never light a fag on deck at night?
A law you got to learn while in the Service.
A light can be machine-gunned by the escort.   910
They'd ping your fag and teeth at the same time.'

Peggy, out of earshot:
'I didn't light it on the deck. I cupped
My hands and took three drags and that was all.
That jockey groomed for donkeys thinks he's got
The whole world by the tail in a down pull.
When I get back to Civvy Street, I'll call him.'

O'Meara, Steele and Casey had a lot
To say. They'd gab it when the day came round –
The day the *Stargard* reached her port – but somehow
The water and the salt got in their throats   920
The moment when the *Stargard* took them under.

The dark was sedative and irritant.
How easy was it for an interval
To muffle the senses with a hushed blackout,
And the diminuendo of the run
Could well delude the reason. This was not
The rate that marked the fever of pursuit,
And nothing from the decks was visible
To show the way the trimmest escort unit
Could be in shackles to a lubber keel,   930
And have to be replaced in precious moments;
Nothing to show how gyros and magnetics
Could be ungeared by submarine explosions.
For this was information undiffused
Among the crew or countered by illusions,
Or by resumption of the normal tasks.
No one from the *Ulysses* lived to cite
The witness of the E.R.A.s and firemen,
Pounding the steel rungs in that inner trap
When the torpedo struck her gas and oil.   940

The drama of the night before was over.
No headlines would record as news the toil,
As stokers every hour took temperatures
Of bearings, scribbled them on pads, transferred
Them to the logs and then resumed their rounds
To watch for popping valves, to check the flow
By turning wheels when the full head of steam
Was hitting the square inches of the boilers.
There was no spotlight on the items when
A leading seaman of the watch reported   950
'The temperature of the sea forty degrees,
The lowering falls are clear, boats off the pins,
The watertight compartments are all closed.'
No one would mould the linotype for such
A mass that might survive or not survive
Their tedium of watches in the holds –
The men with surnames blotted by their jobs
Into a scrawl of anonymity.
A body blow at the boilers would untype
All differentiations in the blood   960
Of pumpmen, wipers, messmen, galley boys
Who had become incorporate with the cogs
On ships that carried pulp and scrap to Europe.

Desire invoking for the memory
Amnesia for the nightmare that had passed,
It might have been a run in peaceful times.
The sounds seemed casual enough – lookouts
Reporting to the officers on watch,
Got back the usual laconic answers.
The turbine notes ran up from C to G   970
And down according to the scale of speed.
The scraps of speech from duffel-coated forms,
Huddled beneath the after-canopy,
Had by tacit agreement in the eyes
Nothing to do with present urgencies.

A rating 'in the rattle' salved his mind
By giving his opinion of a buffer,
Casting suspicion on the buffer's birth
And pedigree. His *b*'s and *g*'s and *s*'s,
Delivered through his teeth in confidence   980
To the high winds and seas from A-gun deck,
Had all the symptoms of a normal trip.
Only the action-station gongs could jar
That gentle wishful thinking – and they did.

Horse-power to the limit on the engines,
Levied for scout assault and close defence,
Was routed quickly to defence, for short
Beyond believing was the interval
Between the echoes and torpedo hits,
Between them and the spotted periscopes.   990
The Commodore reported, '*Gypsum Queen*
Torpedoed and sunk.' *Alberni* gets an echo,
Five hundred yards, *Kenogami* confirming.
Chambly and *Moose Jaw* get a definite kill
With prisoners, and then a 'probable'.
The peril of the night before was doubled.
This time the subs had dived within the convoy,
'Attacking from within the lines' – the fear
Above all fears, for, out to sea, the lairs
Might be discerned and the protective screens   1000
Be interposed between them and the convoy.
But now the hazards of the fight were weighted
In favor of the foe. Seven or eight
Out of the estimated twelve were there
Inside or hanging on to flank or rear.
Even blindly they could not miss – on port
And starboard bow, amidships, on the quarter.

Upon the *Skeena*'s Bridge the judgment fought
With chaos. Blindness, deafness visited
The brain. Through a wild paradox of sight   1010
And sound, the asdic echoes would not fall
Within their ribbon-tidy categories.
They bounded in confusion from the hulls
Of tankers and corvettes: the ash-can sounds
Were like those of explosions from torpedoes.
Wake-echoes and reverbs, and *quenching* caused
By pitch and roll of a heavy following sea,
Had blended with the sharper pings from steel
To give the effect of a babel and a brawl.

But blindness was the worst. To find the foe   1020
By starshell served indeed to spot the target,
But carved in white the escort's silhouette.
The need called for the risk. A megaphone
Informed the *Skeena* that a sub was seen
Between the columns seven and eight, its course
Marked by a steady hail of tracer bullets.
The *Skeena* tried to ram; the sub escaped
To an adjacent lane and turned right angles
In opposite direction to destroyer.
The shelter of the dark was now a threat   1030
Holding collision as the convoy ships
Made their sharp turn of forty-five degrees.
Her fighting and her navigating lights
Were switched on to identify the *Skeena*,
Scratching the paint upon the merchant hulls,
As orders pelted down the voice-pipe, helm
And engines answering – 'Full speed ahead ...
Starboard twenty ... Stop both ... Half-ahead port ...
Half-astern starboard ... Stop starboard ...
Half-ahead starboard ... Full ahead both. ...'   1040

This was infighting at its grisly worst.
The issue grew more leaden as the night
Advanced, and what relief could daylight offer
Against the weary arithmetic count?
The *Winterswyck* blown up, sunk with her phosphate;
Stonepool torpedoed on both sides, gone down
With general cargo and a fleet of trucks.
And matching the confusion on the decks
Was the confusion in the ether, ships
Torpedoed, burning, sinking, hammering out   1050
Their cryptocodes. What listeners could sort them,
Solve those recurring decimals of dots
And those long dashes when the operators
Screwed down the keys – their last official acts –
To give the drowning wails of instruments?
What rescuers could hurry to position?
Only the fighting ships – and they were fighting.

'Which one was that?'
                              'A tanker bad enough,
But not as bad as that; a flame that would
Frizzle a glacier.'
                              'Aviation gas?'   1060
'It could create that light but not that roar,
'Twould cause stokehold concussion miles away,
And wake up Julianehaab.'
                              ''Twas ammunition.'

The *Garm* and *Scania* with their lumber lost!
Rockets observed from *Randa* and *Benury* –
The signals ceased – both missing in the morning!

The fourteen sunk and others just afloat,
The remnant staggered on still north-by-east.
· · · · ·

Last night, the second night, and must there come
A third? The ratio of loss had climbed   1070
Beyond all normal fears. The logs themselves
Might not be legible on that third morning.
So far the tale was grim enough – but six
Saved of the *Jedmore*'s crew; eight from the *Stonepool*;
Less than half from the *Garm*; six from the *Stargard*;
Two from the *Winterswyck*; and a great blank –
The fate of crew unknown – was logged for *Scania*,
The *Empire Springbuck, Crossbill, Thistleglen,
Muneric* and *Ulysses*. The third night
To come! Those hammerheads were off there still,   1080
Hiding, biding. How many? How those freighters
Foundered! How fast? Minutes or seconds?

                                        'Did
You see the way the *Crossbill* took her dive?
Her cargo steel, she went down like a gannet.'

'The *Muneric* beat her to it. A life-belt
Would have no chances in that suction-hole,
Say nothing of a man. I saw her blades
Rise, edge themselves against the *Alberni* gunfire.'

Why should those phobias of speed, colour
And shape belonging to the night alone   1090
Return to plague the mind in open daylight?
Would those fires start again? A chemistry
That would incinerate its own retort
Raged round the *Stonepool* when she sank. Water
And fire, water and oil, blood, fire and salt
Had agonized their journey through nerve-endings
To char themselves upon a graphite-grey
Precipitate. Survivors from the *Stargard*,
Who would for life carry their facial grafts,
Told of the scramble from the boiler rooms,   1100

Up canted ladders and the reeling catwalks,
Only to find their exit was the sea,
And there to find their only exit from
Its cauldron surface was its drowning depth.
Where find the straws to grasp at in this sea?
Where was the cause which once had made a man
Disclaim the sting of death? What ecstasy
Could neutralize this salt and quench this heat
Or open up in victory this grave?
But oil and blood were prices paid for blood   1110
And oil. However variable the time,
The commerce ever was in barter. Oil
Propelled the ships. It blew them up. The men
Died oil-annointed as it choked the 'Christ!'
That stuttered on their lips before the sea
Paraded them as crisps upon her salver.
This was the payment for the oil designed
To sleek the gears and punch the pistons in
And over Alamein and Normandy.
And blood mixed with the sea-foam was the cost   1120
Of plasma safely carried in the holds
Across an ocean to a continent,
There to unblanch the faces on the fields,
There to revein the vines for fresher fruits
In a new harvest on a hoped tomorrow;
And over all, the purchase of the blood
Was that an old dishonoured postulate,
Scrubbed of its rust, might shine again – *Granted*
That what the mind may think, the tongue may utter.
. . . . .

Three morning hours were gone and no attack.   1130
Were the U-boats destroyed or shaken off
Or still awaiting night? What mattered it?
What mattered the rotation of the earth?
The clock had struck in seasons those two nights,

And Time was but a fiddler off his key,
Treading the youth through middle age towards death.

From the lookout a signal – *Smoke ahead!*
Was it a surface raider? This would mean
Extinction, still another word for sleep.
The smoke took shape – five funnels pouring it.   1140
Binoculars from the crowsnests and bridges
Of all the ships, escort and convoy, swept
The horizon: dots turned into lines, the lines
To hulls and decks and guns and turrets – five
British destroyers making thirty knots.
This was the restoration for the hearts
Of fifty ships – the maimed, the blind, the whole.
Around them raced the fighters, plotting out
Suspicious zones whenever asdic sweeps
Reported doubtful contacts, searching far   1150
Afield, then closing to resume position
On screen. And so the s.c.42,
With mutilated but with fashioned columns,
Covered the lap across the Denmark Strait
With that same chivalry of knots which meant
Rescue for hundreds in the Greenland battle.
For with the battered *Tachee* still in tow
Of the *Orillia*, they reached the two
Most northern outposts of the Old World havens,
Rock-armoured Hvalfjord and Reykjavik,   1160
Then took their southern stretch until the convoy
Sighted Inishtrahull and there dispersed.
And the fighting ships, miraculously unscathed,
Proceeded to Molville, to Lishahally,
Thence up the winding Foyle to seek their berths
Around the crowded docks of Londonderry.   1947

Summit Meetings

Why hurry? Stow your jackets in the lockers!
A bloodless argument could dry its rage
Upon an igneous or a glacial page.
Some day the pterodactyls may return.
What warden whispered that a lizard dwells
In the green suburbs of your syllables?

Caesar aut nihil. Deserts lie between.
Covet the lulls in your penultimates
Made up of aspirates and carbonates.
The sand drifts round the black and white, the *Yes*   10
And *No.* Check well before you leave your chairs
The journey straps between those camel pairs.

Delay decisions. Visit the museums,
The markets, public squares, the parks and beaches
For convalescent moments after speeches.
Observe all signals – *green, red, stop, go.*
Note last – 'This way to the memorial plaques
To find the exits to your *cul-de-sacs.*'

Rumble your bellyfuls and crack your chins;
But let the thunder like a thousand Babels   20
Bark its black knuckles on the oak of tables.
This is the *summum* that the dead may wish –
That these, their broods not yet entombed, may snatch
A loaf of life before their canines hatch.   Summer 1948

Newfoundland Calling

Out of the fog along a strip of shore,
Out of the surf from some uncharted rock,
The coastline from Cape Race to Labrador

Has traced the sagas of their life and stock.
Where human hands and the storm sinews met
Ballads have built their salty alphabet.

From the sea's font their births were solemnized –
Random, Seldom-Come-By and Come-By-Chance –
The names caressed, rebuked, warned or chastized
With the drum's beat or hiss of sibilance.   10
The labials and the dentals worked to cut
The Topsails, Joe Batt's Arm, Bay Bulls, Turk's Gut.

But when two months from the last anchor hold
The landfalls blessed the navigators' eyes,
When bluffs and promontories enclosed a fold
And harbour ripples strung their lullabies –
'Twas then the words in a high ritual fell
Like music cradled in a syllable.

'Cape Bonavista' – Cabot's hail! Secure
The *Matthew* would ride out the gale that night.   20
This chiming name was just the overture
To Heart's Content, Bonne Bay and Heart's Delight.
What psalm made luminous the captain's face
When double-reefed his ship made Harbour Grace?

Who did the christening at those hallowed spots
Under the sunset's rose and purple changes –
Spread Eagle Peak, Blue Hills and Butter Pots,
Transfiguring the Avalonian Ranges?
What magic stopped the breath of boatmen rowing
With Gander-Gambo-Terra Nova flowing?   30

The names will know their cousins when they see
Them, greet them with the same sonorous hail:
Red Indian Lake will call Timagami;
The Humber, Restigouche; Codroy won't fail
The Saguenay; nor will that Avalonian
Be outsung by Laurentian or Huronian.

Nor will the consonants refuse to mix
Their lusty breeds and march with cymbal and fife –
Pugwash, Tignish, Flin Flon, Medonegonix,
Exploits, Whitehorse, Chinook and Yellowknife,   40
Twin Butte – tapped by the same baptismal quirk
That spattered adult drops on 'Mother Burke.'

By birth certificates of race or weather,
Bare Need and Empty Basket, Joliette
And Annieopsquotch howled or laughed together
With Skookumschuck, Ha Ha Bay, Lillooet,
While Bumble Bee Bight and Pinch Gut Tickle cried
With God Almighty Cove and Stepaside.

They have survived through strains of genes and blood
Storms, fishing admirals and dust-bowls; rolled   50
On decks and log-jams; watched pitheads; withstood
The prairies' drought, blizzard and rust, and told
The explorers' yarns through a long Arctic night
Till dawn broke with a soft Pacific light.

Listen – across the Rockies, tunnel and gorge,
Sir Humphrey Gilbert calls to Captain George!   31 March 1949

Newfoundland Seamen

This is their culture, this – their master passion
Of giving shelter and of sharing bread,
Of answering rocket signals in the fashion
Of losing life to save it. In the spread
Of time – the Gilbert-Grenfell-Bartlett span –
The headlines cannot dim their daily story,
Nor calls like London! Gander! Teheran!
Outplay the drama of the sled and dory.

The wonders fade. There overhead a mile,
Planes bank like gulls: like curlews scream the jets.   10
The caravans move on in radar file
Scarce noticed by the sailors at their nets,
Bracing their bodies to their tasks, as when,
Centuries before Argentia's smoking funnels,
That small ancestral band of Devon men
Red-boned their knuckles on the *Squirrel* gunwales.

As old as it is new, as new as old,
Enduring as a cape, as fresh as dulse,
This is the Terra Nova record told
Of uncontractual blood behind the pulse   20
On sea or land. Was it but yesterday
That without terms and without drill commands,
A rescue squad found Banting where he lay
With the torn tissues of his healing hands?   31 March 1949

The Last Watch

The sea had opened up its bag of tricks
To dispossess a property of earth –
To him the room was as a reeling berth:
To us as steady as a crucifix.

His hands were fumbling something in the dark,
Tracing a chart, it seemed, or logging knots.
The pupils of his eyes like codein dots
Roved with a lantern measuring its arc.

His head was bowed as to a sudden gale,
Though not a jib could stir in that night air,   10
And though the aneroid was pointing *Fair*,
We listened to an order – 'Shorten Sail!'

We waited for a token. We could feel
A swallow's wing brushing the window-pane:
Something had hammered at the weather-vane,
A master's voice had called – 'Hard-down the wheel!'

Summer 1949

Displaced

It is not *sadness* that invades you now –
Romantic figure for a creed fixation –
A tougher noun is needed for the sough
Of surf on limestone at your embarkation.

A jumpy needle just points 'outward-bound,'
Uncertain of its adjectival use:
From roots and rubble let the word be ground
And mixed with ashes from the hemlock spruce.

Watchman! We cannot hear your voice or bell,
Stationed so far away on the world's ledges: 10
How can we sift your midnight's 'All is well'
From faiths confronting faiths with slit-throat edges?

Sailor! Can you forecast the day? Tell what
Those lava-troughs and peaks like Everest
Mean by scotching the sunset? You can not
Decipher black-and-scarlet palimpsest.

To *you* with wisdom culled from Board Room sessions,
Who curved the cycles, carved their epitaphs –
Are these the tidal booms and their depressions
Mirrored in driftwood polish of your graphs?   20

Woman! The limit of your husbandry
May be exacted by yon myrmidons:
Go, gather up the children's crumbs and free
Those tapered fingers for your orisons.

Perhaps an ancient God who dealt in wonders –
Trading a heart of flesh for one of stone –
Will offer benedictions, not his thunders,
Bending his ear to catch a cradle moan.   June 1949

Blind from Singapore
('Our orders are to burn the city')

Only in memory is petroleum burning:
Why do you keep your lids turning
Upward as though you feared light from the sun?

There was economy
In what was said, in what was done: –
A second just to read
The signal, just an hour for the deed.
As for your memory,
Was not six years enough to have consumed the city?
The physical fear has gone   10
A substitute has come:
You find it hard to take our pity,
This the hardest of all – better the dumb
Gestures you cannot see.

Your enemy
Is light,
Although withdrawn
In ambush through the stars.

Your friend is Night.
Wise to the clock in candid ambiguity,   20
She sidles to your bed at dawn,
Carries no mirror for your scars
And stays with you till dewfall. We
Alone can read those figures on the page
That multiplied your age.   December–January 1949–50

A Call

So quiet was the place, it teemed
With peace invasions of the shore –
The sky and sea were undisturbed
By ruffle of wing or riffle of oar.

Only the chatter of surprise
Of children gathering ear-lobed shells
Was teasing silence when the foam
Let go the handrope of its bells.

The air grew morbid with a load
Of clam and balsam smells like musk: 10
Veils of chiffon hung in the west
While afternoon was threading dusk.

I hastened to the shore and called,
Their blue eyes wondering – 'Why, come home!
There is no danger in the tide,
There is no threat of rain or foam.'

'Come home!' There was no reason given.
Nor could I give it. I alone   20
Could penetrate that sign of rain,
The stalking thunder in that drone.

Despite the Sandman's aid, I knew
No barbiturates in those skies
Would join the solvent of the musk
To wash the daylight from their eyes.
· · · · ·
I have forgotten now the peace
That held the tides without a foam:
All I remember is the cry,
Unanswered still – 'Come home, come home!'

December–January 1949–50

The Good Earth

Let the mind rest awhile, lower the eyes,
Relieve the spirit of its Faustian clamour:
An atom holds more secrets than the skies;
Be patient with the earth and do not cram her

With seed beyond the wisdom of her soil.
She knows the foot and hoof of man and ox,
She learned the variations of their toil –
The ploughshare's sensitivity to rocks.

Gather the stones for field and garden walls,
Build cellars for your vegetable stores,   10
Forgo the architecture of your halls,
Until your hands have fashioned stable doors.

She likes the smell of nitrates from the stalls,
She hates a disciplined tread, the scorching roar
At the grain's roots: she is nervous at the calls
Of men in panic at a strike of ore.

Patient she is in her flesh servitude,
Tolerant to curry ticklings of the harrow,
But do not scratch past her agrarian mood
To cut the calcium in her bone and marrow.   20

Hold that synthetic seed, for underneath
Deep down she'll answer to your horticulture:
She has a way of germinating teeth
And yielding crops of carrion for the vulture.   Summer 1950

Myth and Fact

We used to wake our children when they screamed;
We felt no fever, found no pain,
And casually we told them that they dreamed
And settled them in sleep again.

So easy was it thus to exorcise
The midnight fears the morning after.
We sought to prove they could not literalize
Jack, though the giant shook with laughter.

We showed them pictures in a book and smiled
At red-shawled wolves and chasing bruins –   10
Was not the race just an incarnate child
That sat at wells and haunted ruins?

We had outgrown the dreams, outrung the knells
Through voodoo, amulet and prayer,
But knew that daylight fastened on us spells
More fearful than Medusa's hair.

We saw the bat-companioned dead arise
From shafts and pipes, and nose like beagles
The spoors of outlaw quarry in the skies
Whose speed and spread made fools of eagles.   20

We shut our eyes and plugged our ears, though sound
And sight were our front-line defences,
The mind came with its folly to confound
The crystal logic of the senses.

Then turned we to the story-books again
To see that Cyclopean stare.
'Twas out of focus for the beast was slain
While we were on our knees in prayer.

Who were those giants in their climbing strength?
No reason bade us calibrate   30
These flying lizards in their scaly length
Or plumb a mesozoic hate.

The leaves released a genie to unbind
Our feet along a pilgrimage:
The make-believe had furnished to the mind
Asylum in the foliage.

Draw down the blinds and lock the doors tonight:
We would be safe from that which hovers
Above the eaves. God send us no more light
Than falls between our picture covers.   40

For what the monsters of the long-ago
Had done were nursery peccadilloes
To what those solar hounds in tally-ho
Could do when once they sniffed the pillows.   Spring 1951

Cycles

There was a time we knew our foes,
Could recognize their features well,
Name them before we bartered blows;
So in our challenges could tell
What the damned quarrel was about,
As with our fists we slugged it out.

When distance intervened, the call
Of trumpets sped the spear and arrow;
From stone and sling to musket ball
The path was blasted to the marrow;   10
But still we kept our foes in sight,
Dusk waiting for the morning light.

We need no more that light of day,
No need of faces to be seen;
The squadrons in the skies we slay
Through moving shadows on a screen:
By nailing echoes under sea
We kill with like geometry.

Now since the Lord of Love is late
In being summoned to the ring   20
To keep in bounds the range of hate,
The Lord of Hosts to whom we sing
As Marshal of both man and brute
May be invoked as substitute.

Whether from heaven or from hell,
May he return as referee,
And, keen-eared to an honest bell,
Splitting the foul from fair, feel free
To send us forth into the lists,
Armed only with our naked fists.   30

And then before our voice is dumb,
Before our blood-shot eyes go blind,
The Lord of Love and Life may come
To lead our ebbing veins to find
Enough for their recovery
Of plasma from Gethsemane.   Fall 1951

The Deed

Where are the roadside minstrels gone who strung
Their fiddles to the stirrup cavalcades?
What happened to the roses oversung
By orchard lovers in their serenades?

A feudal dust that draggle-tailed the plumes
Blinded the minstrels chasing cavaliers:
Moonlight that sucked the colour from the blooms
Had soaked the lyrists and the sonneteers.

Where is the beauty still inspired by rhyme,
Competing with those garden miracles,   10
When the first ray conspires with wind to chime
The matins of the Canterbury bells?

Not in the fruit or flower nor in the whir
Of linnet's wings or plaint of nightingales,
Nor in the moonstruck latticed face of her
Who cracked the tenor sliding up his scales.

We saw that beauty once – an instant run
Along a ledge of rock, a curve, a dive;
Nor did he count the odds of ten to one
Against his bringing up that boy alive.   20

This was an arch beyond the salmon's lunge,
There was a rainbow in the rising mists:
Sea-lapidaries started at the plunge
To cut the facets of their amethysts.

But this we scarcely noticed, since the deed
Had power to cleanse a grapnel's rust, transfigure
The blueness of the lips, unmat the weed
And sanctify the unambiguous rigour.

For that embrace had trapped the evening's light,
Racing to glean the red foam's harvestings: 30
Even the seagulls vanished from our sight,
Though settling with their pentecostal wings.   Summer 1952

Magic in Everything

How freely came belief when we were young!
Unruffled by an argument, the tongue
Had left the mind a garden where the seeds
Sprouted and grew and blossomed without weeds.

From parents who were wise and old
We simply took what we were told.
That Santa with his reindeer should arrive
From his far northern drive,
Seek out our very house and come
Down through the chimney and deposit   10
Around the hearth or in the bedroom closet
His gifts that left us saucer-eyed and dumb –
But miracles had happened on this earth
And we had thrived on wonders from our birth.
And here was one, for we regarded him,
His ruddy-apple cheeks and snowy beard,
With the same sanctity that we revered
The chubby pictures of the cherubim.
'Twas true that those who matched their faith with wit,
And wanted legends proved,   20
Looked at the fire-place and measured it.
To ease the downward journey they removed
The ashes and the logs,
Cleared out the soot and shoved away the 'dogs.'
'Santa must come down clean' – *that* we could follow –
And clean must be the presents that he brought.
We felt the reindeer story hard to swallow,
Yet to *our* minds there was no need for *proofs*:
Twelve months ago that night our ears had caught
The 'hail!' of Santa and the thud of hoofs.   30

A few years passed and we began
Half furtively to question one another,
And still more warily our dad and mother:
And this is how our questions ran –
How did the old man stand that polar race,
Enter a house that with no fire-place
Had but a kitchen stove? This point was hard.
Only the Lord could push a body through
A passage narrow as the kitchen flue.

Were windows open? Was the door unbarred?   40
This sacrilege of doubt assailed
The toughening spirit of our thought.
Those letters we had written, sealed and mailed
A week or month before – what post had brought
Them to the north? Was it the right address?
Had Santa seen them? Yes,
He must; for there upon the tree or floor
Were the crammed stockings, trains that ran
On tracks, a Jack-in-the-box: outside the door
A pair of snow-shoes and a catamaran –   50
Just what we asked. Yes, these were real, but why
Did other things escape his eye –
Gifts we had pondered on for many a day?
Was there a limit to his Christmas sleigh?
And when our parents could not satisfy
The older sceptics with a sane reply,
They winked and smiled, grew restless or were bored,
Or ended with one answer long prepared,
An answer which we dared
Not question – 'Back of Santa was the Lord.'   60

The Lord! He knew all wherefores, all the whys.
Was He not Lord of earth and skies?
In some strange way
He was related to the Christmas day.
For early on that morn
The steeple chimes were ringing
And choirs were singing
'Unto us a child is born.'
Under the charm of that celestial sound,
Within the story of his life we found
The riddles of our youth   70
Were tongued from higher ground
And solved by proclamation of an Act.
A myth took refuge in a fact,

A fairy tale into a truth.
For painlessly the changes came
Though Santa Claus was still allowed his name.
We banished reindeer with our smiles,
Their voyage through those northern miles.
We closed the argument   80
About the way the gifts were sent.
No longer did we measure
The chimney width for fear he might be burned
Or ashes smother up the Christmas treasure.
And so completely vanished all our doubt
That we forgot to put the fire out.
What mattered it when in due time we learned
The givers were our parents who, as wise
As Santa, offered to our dawning eyes
That spruce tree with its gay surprise.   90
Nor did we bother much to reconcile
The ancient fable with a father's smile.
And even if the youngest of us tried
To get a smattering of sense
Out of the Santa Claus 'pretence,'
It wasn't long before his tears were dried
By what he saw: the gifts were real as bread,
Something to touch and taste and eat.
No apples were more fresh and red,
No candy was more sweet;   100
The wooden horse was there to ride,
And magic was in everything –
The Jacks popped with the spring,
And there were shining runners on the slide.

So, when we found ourselves bereft
Of childhood fantasies we still had left
The memories that years could not corrode –
Behind the celebration of the Day
Were living hands that had bestowed

The gifts, and love behind the hands, and then   110
Something our reasons could not rub away –
The story of a Birth bequeathed to men.
How could we question that under the spells
Woven around us by the Christmas bells?   December 1952

Towards the Last Spike

It was the same world then as now – the same,
Except for little differences of speed
And power, and means to treat myopia
To show an axe-blade infinitely sharp
Splitting things infinitely small, or else
Provide the telescopic sight to roam
Through curved dominions never found in fables.
The same, but for new particles of speech –
Those algebraic substitutes for nouns
That sky cartographers would hang like signboards   10
Along the trespass of our thoughts to stop
The stutters of our tongues with their equations.

As now, so then, blood kept its ancient colour,
And smoothly, roughly, paced its banks; in calm
Preserving them, in riot rupturing them.
Wounds needed bandages and stomachs food:
The hands outstretched had joined the lips in prayer –
'Give us our daily bread, give us our pay.'
The past flushed in the present and tomorrow
Would dawn upon today: only the rate   20
To sensitize or numb a nerve would change;
Only the quickening of a measuring skill
To gauge the onset of a birth or death
With the precision of micrometers.
Men spoke of acres then and miles and masses,
Velocity and steam, cables that moored

Not ships but continents, world granaries,
The east-west cousinship, a nation's rise,
Hail of identity, a world expanding,
If not the universe: the feel of it   3
Was in the air – 'Union required the Line.'
The theme was current at the banquet tables,
And arguments profane and sacred rent
God-fearing families into partisans.
Pulpit, platform and floor were sounding-boards;
Cushions beneath the pounding fists assumed
The hues of western sunsets; nostrils sniffed
The prairie tang; the tongue rolled over texts:
Even St Paul was being invoked to wring
The neck of Thomas in this war of faith   4
With unbelief. Was ever an adventure
Without its cost? Analogies were found
On every page of history or science.
A nation, like the world, could not stand still.
What was the use of records but to break them?
The tougher armour followed the new shell;
The newer shell the armour; lighthouse rockets
Sprinkled their stars over the wake of wrecks.
Were not the engineers at work to close
The lag between the pressures and the valves?   5
The same world then as now thirsting for power
To crack those records open, extra pounds
Upon the inches, extra miles per hour.
The mildewed static schedules which before
Had like asbestos been immune to wood
Now curled and blackened in the furnace coal.
This power lay in the custody of men
From down-and-outers needing roofs, whose hands
Were moulded by their fists, whose skins could feel
At home incorporate with dolomite,   6
To men who with the marshal instincts in them,
Deriving their authority from wallets,
Directed their battalions from the trestles.

THE GATHERING

('Oats – a grain which in England is generally given to horses, but
in Scotland supports the people.' –Dr Samuel Johnson. 'True,
but where will you find such horses, where such men?' –Lord
Elibank's reply as recorded by Sir Walter Scott.)

Oatmeal was in their blood and in their names.
Thrift was the title of their catechism.
It governed all things but their mess of porridge
Which, when it struck the hydrochloric acid
With treacle and skim-milk, became a mash.
Entering the duodenum, it broke up
Into amino acids: then the liver   70
Took on its natural job as carpenter:
Foreheads grew into cliffs, jaws into juts.
The meal, so changed, engaged the follicles:
Eyebrows came out as gorse, the beards as thistles,
And the chest-hair the fell of Grampian rams.
It stretched and vulcanized the human span:
Nonagenarians worked and thrived upon it.
Out of such chemistry run through by genes,
The food released its fearsome racial products: –
The power to strike a bargain like a foe,   80
To win an argument upon a burr,
Invest the language with a Bannockburn,
Culloden or the warnings of Lochiel,
Weave loyalties and rivalries in tartans,
Present for the amazement of the world
Kilts and the civilized barbaric Fling,
And pipes which, when they acted on the mash,
Fermented lullabies to *Scots wha hae*.

Their names were like a battle muster – Angus
(He of the Shops) and Fleming (of the Transit),   90
Hector (of the *Kicking Horse*), Dawson,
'Cromarty' Ross, and Beatty (Ulster Scot),

Bruce, Allan, Galt and Douglas, and the 'twa' –
Stephen (Craigellachie) and Smith (Strathcona) –
Who would one day climb from their Gaelic hide-outs,
Take off their plaids and wrap them round the mountains.
And then the everlasting tread of the Macs,
Vanguard, centre and rear, their roving eyes
On summits, rivers, contracts, beaver, ledgers;
Their ears cocked to the skirl of Sir John A.,   100
The general of the patronymic march.

(*Sir John revolving round the Terms of Union with British Columbia.
Time, late at night.*)

Insomnia had ripped the bed-sheets from him
Night after night. How long was this to last?
Confederation had not played this kind
Of trickery on him. That was rough indeed,
So gravelled, that a man might call for rest
And take it for a life accomplishment.
It was his laurel though some of the leaves
Had dried. But this would be a longer tug
Of war which needed for his team thick wrists   110
And calloused fingers, heavy heels to dig
Into the earth and hold – men with bull's beef
Upon their ribs. Had he himself the wind,
The anchor-waist to peg at the rope's end?
'Twas bad enough to have these questions hit
The waking mind: 'twas much worse when he dozed;
For goblins had a way of pinching him,
Slapping a nightmare on to dwindling snoozes.
They put him and his team into a tug
More real than life. He heard a judge call out –   120
'Teams settle on the ropes and take the strain!'
And with the coaches' *heave*, the running welts
Reddened his palms, and then the gruelling *backlock*
Inscribed its indentations on his shoulders.

This kind of burn he knew he had to stand;
It was the game's routine; the other fire
Was what he feared the most for it could bake him –
That white dividing rag tied to the rope
Above the centre pole had with each heave
Wavered with chances equal. With the backlock,   130
Despite the legs of Tupper and Cartier,
The western anchor dragged; the other side
Remorselessly was gaining, holding, gaining.
No sleep could stand this strain and, with the nightmare
Delivered of its colt, Macdonald woke.

Tired with the midnight toss, lock-jawed with yawns,
He left the bed and, shuffling to the window,
He opened it. The air would cool him off
And soothe his shoulder burns. He felt his ribs:
Strange, nothing broken – how those crazy drowses   140
Had made the fictions tangle with the facts!
He must unscramble them with steady hands.
Those Ranges pirouetting in his dreams
Had their own knack of standing still in light,
Revealing peaks whose known triangulation
Had to be read in prose severity.
Seizing a telescope, he swept the skies,
The north-south drift, a self-illumined chart.
Under Polaris was the Arctic Sea
And the sub-Arctic gates well stocked with names: 150
Hudson, Davis, Baffin, Frobisher;
And in his own day Franklin, Ross and Parry
Of the Canadian Archipelago;
Kellett, McClure, McClintock, of *The Search*.
Those straits and bays had long been kicked by keels,
And flags had fluttered on the Capes that fired
His youth, making familiar the unknown.
What though the odds were nine to one against,
And the Dead March was undertoning trumpets,

There was enough of strychnine in the names   160
To make him flip a penny for the risk,
Though he had palmed the coin reflectively
Before he threw and watched it come down *heads*.
That stellar path looked too much like a road map
Upon his wall – the roads all led to market –
The north-south route. He lit a candle, held
It to a second map full of blank spaces
And arrows pointing west. Disturbed, he turned
The lens up to the zenith, followed the course
Tracked by a cloud of stars that would not keep   170
Their posts – Capella, Perseus, were reeling;
Low in the north-west, Cassiopeia
Was qualmish, leaning on her starboard arm-rest,
And Aries was chasing, butting Cygnus,
Just diving. Doubts and hopes struck at each other.
Why did those constellations look so much
Like blizzards? And what lay beyond the blizzards?

'Twas chilly at the window. He returned
To bed and savoured soporific terms:
Superior, the *Red River*, *Selkirk*, *Prairie*,   180
Port Moody and *Pacific*. Chewing them,
He spat out *Rocky* grit before he swallowed.
Selkirk! This had the sweetest taste. Ten years
Before, the Highland crofters had subscribed
Their names in a memorial for the Rails.
Sir John reviewed the story of the struggle,
That four months' journey from their native land –
The Atlantic through the Straits to Hudson Bay,
Then the Hayes River to Lake Winnipeg
Up to the Forks of the Assiniboine.   190
He could make use of that – just what he needed,
A Western version of the Arctic daring,
Romance and realism, double dose.
How long ago? Why, this is '71.

Those fellows came the time Napoleon
Was on the steppes. For sixty years they fought
The seasons, 'hoppers, drought, hail, wind and snow;
Survived the massacre at Seven Oaks,
The 'Pemmican War' and the Red River floods.
They wanted now the Road – those pioneers   200
Who lived by spades instead of beaver traps.
Most excellent word that, pioneers! Sir John
Snuggled himself into his sheets, rolling
The word around his tongue, a theme for song,
Or for a peroration to a speech.

THE HANGOVER AT DAWN

He knew the points that had their own appeal.
These did not bother him: the patriot touch,
The Flag, the magnetism of explorers,
The national unity. These could burn up
The phlegm in most of the provincial throats.   210
But there was one tale central to his plan
(The focus of his headache at this moment),
Which would demand the limit of his art –
The ballad of his courtship in the West:
Better reveal it soon without reserve.

THE LADY OF BRITISH COLUMBIA

Port Moody and Pacific! He had pledged
His word the Line should run from sea to sea.
'From sea to sea,' a hallowed phrase. Music
Was in that text if the right key were struck,
And he must strike it first, for, as he fingered   220
The clauses of the pledge, rough notes were rasping –
'No Road, No Union,' and the converse true.
East-west against the north-south run of trade,
For California like a sailor-lover

Was wooing over-time. He knew the ports.
His speech was as persuasive as his arms,
As sinuous as Spanish arias –
Tamales, Cazadero, Mendecino,
Curling their baritones around the Lady.
Then Santa Rosa, Santa Monica,   230
Held absolution in their syllables.
But when he saw her stock of British temper
Starch at ironic sainthood in the whispers –
'Rio de nuestra senora de buena guia,'
He had the tact to gutturalize the liquids,
Steeping the tunes to drinking songs, then take
Her on a holiday where she could watch
A roving sea-born Californian pound
A downy chest and swear by San Diego.

Sir John, wise to the tricks, was studying hard   240
A fresh proposal for a marriage contract.
He knew a game was in the ceremony.
That southern fellow had a healthy bronze
Complexion, had a vast estate, was slick
Of manner. In his ardour he could tether
Sea-roses to the blossoms of his orchards,
And for his confidence he had the prime
Advantage of his rival – *he was there.*

THE LONG-DISTANCE PROPOSAL

A game it was, and the Pacific lass
Had poker wisdom on her face. Her name   250
Was rich in values – *British*; this alone
Could raise Macdonald's temperature: so could
Columbia with a different kind of fever,
And in between the two, *Victoria.*
So the *Pacific* with its wash of letters
Could push the Fahrenheit another notch.

She watched for bluff on those Disraeli features,
Impassive but for arrowy chipmunk eyes,
Engaged in fathoming a contract time.
With such a dowry she could well afford   260
To take the risk of tightening the terms –
'Begin the Road in two years, end in ten' –
Sir John, a moment letting down his guard,
Frowned at the Rocky skyline, but agreed.

(*The Terms ratified by Parliament, British Columbia enters Confedera-
tion July 1871, Sandford Fleming being appointed engineer-in-chief of the
proposed Railway, Walter Moberly to co-operate with him in the loca-
tion of routes. 'Of course, I don't know how many millions you have, but
it is going to cost you money to get through those canyons.' – Moberly
to Macdonald.*)

THE PACIFIC SCANDAL

(*Huntingdon's charges of political corruption based on correspondence
and telegrams rifled from the offices of the solicitor of Sir Hugh Allan,
Head of the Canada Pacific Company; Sir John's defence; and the ap-
pearance of the Honourable Edward Blake who rises to reply to Sir John
at 2 a.m.*)

BLAKE IN MOOD

Of all the subjects for debate here was
His element. His soul as clean as surf,
No one could equal him in probing cupboards
Or sweeping floors and dusting shelves, finding
A skeleton inside an overcoat;
Or shaking golden eagles from a pocket   270
To show the copper plugs within the coins.
Rumours he heard had gangrened into facts –
Gifts nuzzling at two-hundred-thousand dollars,
Elections on, and with a contract pending.

The odour of the bills had blown his gorge.
His appetite, edged by a moral hone,
Could surfeit only on the Verities.

November 3, 1873

A Fury rode him to the House. He took
His seat, and with a stoic gloom he heard
The Chieftain's great defence and noted well   280
The punctuation of the cheers. He needed all
The balance of his mind to counterpoise
The movements of Macdonald as he flung
Himself upon the House, upon the Country,
Upon posterity, upon his conscience.
That plunging played the devil with Blake's tiller,
Threatened the set of his sail. To save the course,
To save himself, in that five hours of gale,
He had to jettison his meditation,
His brooding on the follies of mankind,   290
Clean out the wadding from his tortured ears:
That roaring mob before him could be quelled
Only by action; so when the last round
Of the applause following the peroration
Was over, slowly, weightily, Blake rose.

A statesman-chancellor now held the Floor.
He told the sniffing Commons that a sense
Keener than smell or taste must be invoked
To get the odour. Leading them from facts
Like telegrams and stolen private letters,   300
He soared into the realm of principles
To find his scourge; and then the men involved,
Robed like the Knights of Malta, Blake undressed,
Their cloaks inverted to reveal the shoddy,
The tattered lining and bare-threaded seams.
He ripped the last stitch from them – by the time

Recess was called, he had them in the dock
As brigands in the Ministry of Smells,
Naked before the majesty of Heaven.

For Blake recesses were but sandwiches
Provided merely for cerebral luncheons –
No time to spread the legs under the table,
To chat and chaff a while, to let the mind
Roam, like a goblet up before the light
To bask in natural colour, or by whim
Of its own choice to sway luxuriously
In tantalizing arcs before the nostrils.
A meal was meant by Nature for nutrition –
A sorry farinaceous business scaled
Exactly to caloric grains and grams
Designed for intellectual combustion,
For energy directed into words
Towards proof. Abuse was overweight. He saw
No need for it; no need for caricature,
And if a villainous word had to be used,
'Twas for a villain – keen upon the target.
Irrelevance was like a moral lesion
No less within a speech than in a statute.
What mattered it who opened up the files,
Sold for a bid the damning correspondence –
That Montreal-Chicago understanding?
A dirty dodge, so let it be conceded.
But *here* the method was irrelevant.
Whether by legal process or by theft,
The evidence was there unalterable.
So with the House assembled, he resumed
Imperial indictment of the bandits.
The logic left no loopholes in the facts.
Figures that ran into the hundred-thousands
Were counted up in pennies, each one shown
To bear the superscription of debasement.

310

320

330

340

Again recess, again the sandwiches,
Again the invocation of the gods:
Each word, each phrase, each clause went to position,
Each sentence regimented like a lockstep.
The only thing that would not pace was time;
The hours dragged by until the thrushes woke –
Two days, two nights – someone opened a window,
And members of the House who still were conscious
Uncreaked their necks to note that even Sir John   350
Himself had put his fingers to his nose.

(*The appeal to the country: Macdonald defeated: Mackenzie assumes power, 1874.*)

A change of air, a drop in temperature!
The House had rarely known sobriety
Like this. No longer clanged the 'Westward Ho!'
And quiet were the horns upon the hills.
Hard times ahead. The years were rendering up
Their fat. Measured and rationed was the language
Directed to the stringency of pockets.
The eye must be convinced before the *vision.*
'But one step at a time,' exclaimed the feet.   360
It was the story of the hen or egg;
Which came before the other? ' 'Twas the hen,'
Cried one; 'undoubtedly the hen must lay
The egg, hatch it and mother it.' 'No so,'
Another shouted, ' 'Twas the egg or whence
The hen?' For every one who cleared his throat
And called across the House with Scriptural passion –
'The Line is meant to bring the loaves and fishes,'
A voting three had countered with the question –
'Where are the multitudes that thirst and hunger?'   370
Passion became displaced by argument.
Till now the axles justified their grease,
Taught coal a lesson in economy.
All doubts here could be blanketed with facts,
With phrases smooth as actuarial velvet.

For forty years in towns and cities men
Had watched the Lines baptized with charters, seen
Them grow, marry and bring forth children.
Parades and powder had their uses then
For gala days; and bands announced arrivals,   380
Betrothals, weddings and again arrivals.
Champagne brimmed in the font as they were named
With titles drawn from explorers' routes,
From Saints and Governors, from space and seas
And compass-points – Saints Andrew, Lawrence, Thomas,
Louis and John; Champlain, Simcoe; Grand Trunk,
Intercolonial, the Canadian Southern,
Dominion-Atlantic, the Great Western – names
That caught a continental note and tried
To answer it. Half-gambles though they were,   390
Directors built those Roads and heard them run
To the sweet silver jingle in their minds.

The airs had long been mastered like old songs
The feet could tap to in the galleries.
But would they tap to a new rhapsody,
A harder one to learn and left unfinished?
What ear could be assured of absolute pitch
To catch this kind of music in the West?
The far West? Men had used this flattering name
For East or but encroachment on the West.   400
And was not Lake Superior still the East,
A natural highway which ice-ages left,
An unappropriated legacy?
There was no discord in the piston-throbs
Along this Road. This was old music too.
That northern spine of rock, those western mountains,
Were barriers built of God and cursed of Blake.
Mild in his oaths, Mackenzie would avoid them.
He would let contracts for the south and west,
Push out from settlement to settlement.   410
This was economy, just plain horse-sense.

The Western Lines were there – American.
He would link up with them, could reach the Coast.
The Eagle and the Lion were good friends:
At least the two could meet on sovereign terms
Without a sign of fur and feathers flying.
As yet, but who could tell? So far, so good.
Spikes had been driven at the boundary line,
From Emerson across the Red to Selkirk,
And then to Thunder Bay – to Lake Superior;   420
Across the prairies in God's own good time,
His plodding, patient, planetary time.

Five years' delay: surveys without construction;
Short lines suspended, discord in the Party.
The West defrauded of its glittering peaks,
The public blood was stirring and protesting
At this continuous dusk upon the mountains.
The old conductor off the podium,
The orchestra disbanded at the time
The daring symphony was on the score,   430
The audience cupped their ears to catch a strain:
They heard a plaintive thinning oboe-A
That kept on thinning while slow feeble steps
Approached the stand. Was this the substitute
For what the auditorium once knew –
The maestro who with tread of stallion hoofs
Came forward shaking platforms and the rafters,
And followed up the concert pitch with sound
Of drums and trumpets and the organ blasts
That had the power to toll out apathy   440
And make snow peaks ring like Cathedral steeples?
Besides, accompanying those bars of music,
There was an image men had not forgotten,
The shaggy chieftain standing at his desk,
That last-ditch fight when he was overthrown,
That desperate five hours. At least they knew

His personal pockets were not lined with pelf,
Whatever loot the others grabbed. The words
British, the West instead of South, the Nation,
The all-Canadian route –these terms were singing   450
Fresher than ever while the grating tones
Under the stress of argument had faded
Within the shroud of their monotony.

(*Sir John returns to power in 1878 with a National Policy of
Protective Tariff and the Transcontinental.*)

Two years of tuning up: it needed that
To counterpoint Blake's eloquence or lift
Mackenzie's non-adventurous common sense
To the ignition of an enterprise.
The pace had to be slow at first, a tempo
Cautious, simple to follow. Sections strewn
Like amputated limbs along the route   460
Were sutured. This appealed to sanity.
No argument could work itself to sweat
Against a prudent case, for the terrain
Looked easy from the Lake to the Red River.
To stop with those suspensions was a waste
Of cash and time. But the huge task announced
Ten years before had now to start afresh –
The moulding of men's minds was harder far
Than moulding of the steel and prior to it.
It was the battle of ideas and words   470
And kindred images called by the same name,
Like brothers who with temperamental blood
Went to it with their fists. Canyons and cliffs
Were precipices down which men were hurled,
Or something to be bridged and sheared and scaled.
Likewise the Pass had its ambiguous meaning.
The leaders of the factions in the House
And through the country spelled the word the same:

The way they got their tongue around the word
Was different, for some could make it hiss   480
With sound of blizzards screaming over ramparts:
The Pass – the Yellowhead, the Kicking Horse –
Or jam it with *coureur-de-bois* romance,
Or join it to the empyrean. Eagles,
In flight banking their wings above a fish-stream,
Had guided the explorers to a route
And given the Pass the title of their wings.
The stories lured men's minds up to the mountains
And down along the sandbars of the rivers.
Rivalling the 'brown and barren' on the maps,   490
Officially 'not fit for human life,'
Were vivid yellows flashing in the news –
'Gold in the Cariboo,' 'Gold in the Fraser.'
The swish of gravel in the placer-cradles
Would soon be followed by the spluttering fuses,
By thunder echoing thunder; for one month
After Blake's Ottawa roar would Onderdonk
Roar back from Yale by ripping canyon walls
To crash the tons by millions in the gorges.

The farther off, as by a paradox   500
Of magnets, was the golden lure the stronger:
Two thousand miles away, imagined peaks
Had the vacation pull of mountaineering,
But with the closer vision would the legs
Follow the mind? 'Twas Blake who raised the question
And answered it. Though with his natural eyes
Up to this time he had not sighted mountains,
He was an expert with the telescope.

THE ATTACK

Sir John was worried. The first hour of Blake
Was dangerous, granted the theme. Eight years   510

Before, he had the theme combined with language.
Impeachment – word with an historic ring,
Reserved for the High Courts of Parliament,
Uttered only when men were breathing hard
And when the vertebrae were musket-stiff:
High ground was that for his artillery,
And *there*, despite the hours the salvos lasted.

But *here* this was a theme less vulnerable
To fire, Macdonald thought, to Blake's gunfire,
And yet he wondered what the orator   520
Might spring in that first hour, what strategy
Was on the Bench. He did not mind the close
Mosaic of the words – too intricate,
Too massive in design. Men might admire
The speech and talk about it, then forget it.
But few possessed the patience or the mind
To tread the mazes of the labyrinth.
Once in a while, however, would Blake's logic
Stumble upon stray figures that would leap
Over the walls of other folds and catch   530
The herdsmen in their growing somnolence.
The waking sound was not – 'It can't be done';
That was a dogma, anyone might say it.
It was the following burning corollary:
'To build a Road over that sea of mountains.'
This carried more than argument. It was
A flash of fire which might with proper kindling
Consume its way into the public mind.
The House clicked to the ready and Sir John,
Burying his finger-nails into his palms,   540
Muttered – 'God send us no more metaphors
Like that – except from Tory factories.'

Had Blake the lift of Chatham as he had
Burke's wind and almost that sierra span
Of mind, he might have carried the whole House
With him and posted it upon that sea
Of mountains with sub-zeros on their scalps,
Their glacial ribs waiting for warmth of season
To spring an avalanche. Such similes
Might easily glue the members to their seats   550
With frost in preparation for their ride.
Sir John's 'from sea to sea' was Biblical;
It had the stamp of reverent approval;
But Blake's was pagan, frightening, congealing.
The chieftain's lips continued as in prayer,
A fiercely secular and torrid prayer –
'May Heaven intervene to stop the flow
Of such unnatural images and send
The rhetorician back to decimals,
Back to his tessellated subtleties.'   560
The prayer was answered for High Heaven did it.
The second hour entered and passed by,
A third, a fourth. Sir John looked round the House,
Noticed the growing shuffle of the feet,
The agony of legs, the yawn's contagion.
Was that a snore? Who was it that went out?
He glanced at the Press Gallery. The pens
Were scratching through the langour of the ink
To match the words with shorthand and were failing.
He hoped the speech would last another hour,   570
And still another. Well within the law,
This homicidal master of the opiates
Loosened the hinges of the Opposition:
The minds went first; the bodies sagged; the necks
Curved on the benches and the legs sprawled out.
And when the Fundy Tide had ebbed, Sir John,
Smiling, watched the debris upon the banks,
For what were yesterday grey human brains

Had with decomposition taken on
The texture and complexion of red clay.   580

(*In 1880 Tupper lets contract to Onderdonk for survey and
construction through the Pacific Section of the mountains. Sir
John, Tupper, Pope, and McIntyre go to London to interest capital
but return without a penny.*)

Failing to make a dent in London dams,
Sir John set out to plumb a reservoir
Closer in reach. He knew its area,
Its ownership, the thickness of its banks,
Its conduits – if he could get his hands
Upon the local stopcocks, could he turn them?
The reservoir was deep. Two centuries
Ago it started filling when a king
Had in a furry moment scratched a quill
Across the bottom of His Royal Charter –   590
'Granting the Governor and His Company
Of Gentlemen Adventurers the right
Exclusive to one-third a continent.'
Was it so easy then? A scratch, a seal,
A pinch of snuff tickling the sacred nostrils,
A puff of powder and the ink was dry.
Sir John twisted his lips: he thought of London.
Empire and wealth were in that signature
For royal, princely, ducal absentees,
For courtiers to whom the parallels   600
Were nothing but chalk scratches on a slate.
For them wild animals were held in game
Preserves, foxes as quarry in a chase,
And hills were hedges, river banks were fences,
And cataracts but fountains in a garden
Tumbling their bubbles into marble basins.
Where was this place called Hudson Bay? Some place
In the Antipodes? Explorers, traders,

Would bring their revenues over that signet.
Two centuries – the new empire advanced, 610
Was broken, reunited, torn again.
The *fleur-de-lis* went to half-mast, the *Jack*
To the mast-head, but fresher rivalries
Broke out – Nor'-Westers at the Hudson's throat
Over the pelts, over the pemmican;
No matter what – the dividends flowed in
As rum flowed out like the Saskatchewan.

The twist left Sir John's lips and he was smiling.
Though English in ambition and design,
This reservoir, he saw there in control 620
Upon the floodgates not a Londoner
In riding breeches but, red-flannel-shirted,
Trousered in homespun, streaked and blobbed with seal-oil,
A Scot with smoke of peat fire on his breath –
Smith? Yes: but christened Donald Alexander
And loined through issue from the Grants and Stuarts.

To smite the rock and bring forth living water,
Take lead or tin and transmute both to silver,
Copper to gold, betray a piece of glass
To diamonds, fabulize a continent, 630
Were wonders once believed, scrapped and revived;
For Moses, Marco Polo, Paracelsus,
Fell in the same retort and came out *Smith.*
A miracle on legs, the lad had left
Forres and Aberdeen, gone to Lachine –
'Tell Mr Smith to count and sort the rat-skins.'
Thence Tadoussac and Posts off Anticosti;
From there to Rigolet in Labrador,
A thousand miles by foot, snowshoe and dog-sled.
He fought the climate like a weathered yak, 640
And conquered it, ripping the stalactites
From his red beard, thawing his feet, and wringing

Salt water from his mitts; but most of all
He learned the art of making change. Blankets,
Ribbons and beads, tobacco, guns and knives,
Were swapped for muskrat, marten, fox and beaver.
And when the fur trade thinned, he trapped the salmon,
Canned it; hunted the seal, traded its oil
And fertilized the gardens with the carcass.
Even the melons grew in Labrador.   650
What could resist this touch? Water from rock!
Why not? No more a myth than pelts should be
Thus fabricated into bricks of gold.

If rat-skins, why not tweeds? If looms could take
Raw wool and twill it into selling shape,
They could under the draper's weaving mind
Be patterning gold braid:
                    So thought George Stephen.

His legs less sturdy than his cousin Donald's,
His eyes were just as furiously alert.
His line of vision ran from the north-west   660
To the Dutch-held St Paul-Pacific Railway.
Allied with Smith, Kitson and Kennedy,
Angus, Jim Hill and Duncan McIntyre,
Could he buy up this semi-bankrupt Road
And turn the northern traffic into it?
Chief bricklayer of all the Scotian clans,
And foremost as a banking metallurgist,
He took the parchments at their lowest level
And mineralized them, roasted them to shape,
Then mortared them into the pyramid,   670
Till with the trowel-stretching exercise
He grew so Atlas-strong that he could carry
A mountain like a namesake on his shoulders.

(*The Charter granted to The Canadian Pacific Railway, February 17,
1881, with George Stephen as first President ... One William Corne-
lius Van Horne arrives in Winnipeg, December 31, 1881, and there late
at night, forty below zero, gives vent to a soliloquy.*)

Stephen had laid his raw hands on Van Horne,
Pulled him across the border, sent him up
To get the feel of northern temperatures.
He knew through Hill the story of his life
And found him made to order. Nothing less
Than geologic space his field of work,
He had in Illinois explored the creeks   680
And valleys, brooded on the rocks and quarries.
Using slate fragments, he became a draughtsman,
Bringing to life a landscape or a cloud,
Turning a tree into a beard, a cliff
Into a jaw, a creek into a mouth
With banks for lips. He loved to work on shadows.
Just now the man was forcing the boy's stature,
The while the youth tickled the man within.
Companioned by the shade of Agassiz,
He would come home, his pockets stuffed with fossils –   690
Crinoids and fish-teeth – and his tongue jabbering
Of the earth's crust before the birth of life,
Prophetic of the days when he would dig
Into Laurentian rock. The morse-key tick
And tape were things mesmeric – space and time
Had found a junction. Electricity
And rock, one novel to the coiling hand,
The other frozen in the lap of age,
Were playthings for the boy, work for the man.
As man he was the State's first operator;   700
As boy he played a trick upon his boss
Who, cramped with current, fired him on the instant;
As man at school, escaping Latin grammar,
He tore the fly-leaf from the text to draw

The contour of a hill; as boy he sketched
The principal, gave him flapdoodle ears,
Bristled his hair, turned eyebrows into quills,
His whiskers into flying buttresses,
His eye-tusks into rusted railroad spikes,
And made a truss between his nose and chin.   710
Expelled again, he went back to the keys,
To bush and rock and found companionship
With quarry-men, stokers and station-masters,
Switchmen and locomotive engineers.

Now he was transferred to Winnipeg.
Of all the places in an unknown land
Chosen by Stephen for Van Horne, this was
The pivot on which he could turn his mind.
Here he could clap the future on the shoulder
And order Fate about as his lieutenant,   720
For he would take no nonsense from a thing
Called Destiny – the stars had to be with him.
He spent the first night in soliloquy,
Like Sir John A. but with a difference.
Sir John wanted to sleep but couldn't do it:
Van Horne could sleep but never wanted to.
It was a waste of time, his bed a place
Only to think or dream with eyes awake.
Opening a jack-knife, he went to the window,
Scraped off the frost. Great treks ran through his mind,   730
East-west. Two centuries and a half gone by,
One trek had started from the Zuyder Zee
To the new Amsterdam. 'Twas smooth by now,
Too smooth. His line of grandsires and their cousins
Had built a city from Manhattan dirt.
Another trek to Illinois; it too
Was smooth, but this new one it was his job
To lead, then build a highway which men claimed
Could not be built. Statesmen and engineers

Had blown their faces blue with their denials: 740
The men who thought so were asylum cases
Whose monomanias harmless up to now
Had not swept into cells. His bearded chin
Pressed to the pane, his eyes roved through the west.
He saw the illusion at its worst – the frost,
The steel precision of the studded heavens,
Relentless mirror of a covered earth.
His breath froze on the scrape: he cut again
And glanced at the direction west-by-south.
That westward trek was the American,   750
Union-Pacific – easy so he thought,
Their forty million stacked against his four.
Lonely and desolate this. He stocked his mind
With items of his task: the simplest first,
Though hard enough, the Prairies, then the Shore
North of the Lake – a quantity half-guessed.
Mackenzie like a balky horse had shied
And stopped at this. Van Horne knew well the reason,
But it was vital for the all-land route.
He peered through at the South. Down there Jim Hill   760
Was whipping up his horses on a road
Already paved. The stations offered rest
With food and warmth, and their well-rounded names
Were tossed like apples to the public taste.

He made a mental note of his three items.
He underlined the Prairies, double-lined
The Shore and triple-lined *Beyond the Prairies*,
Began counting the ranges – first the Rockies;
The Kicking Horse ran through them, this he knew;
The Selkirks? Not so sure. Some years before   770
Had Moberly and Perry tagged a route
Across the lariat loop of the Columbia.
Now Rogers was traversing it on foot,
Reading an aneroid and compass, chewing

Sea-biscuit and tobacco. Would the steel
Follow this trail? Van Horne looked farther west.
There was the Gold Range, there the Coastal Mountains.
He stopped, putting a period to the note,
As rivers troubled nocturnes in his ears.
His plans must not seep into introspection –   780
Call it a night, for morning was at hand,
And every hour of daylight was for work.

(*Van Horne goes to Montreal to meet the Directors.*)

He had agenda staggering enough
To bring the sweat even from Stephen's face.
As daring as his plans, so daring were
His promises. To build five hundred miles
Upon the prairies in one season: this
Was but a cushion for the jars ahead.
The Shore – he had to argue, stamp and fight
For this. The watercourses had been favoured,   790
The nation schooled to that economy.
He saw that Stephen, after wiping beads
From face and forehead, had put both his hands
Deep in his pockets – just a habit merely
Of fingering change – but still Van Horne went on
To clinch his case: the north shore could avoid
The over-border route – a national point
If ever there was one. He promised this
As soon as he was through with buffalo-grass.
And then the little matter of the Rockies: 800
This must be swallowed without argument,
As obvious as space, clear as a charter.
But why the change in Fleming's survey? Why
The Kicking Horse and not the Yellowhead?
The national point again. The Kicking Horse
Was shorter, closer to the boundary line;
No rival road would build between the two.

He did not dwell upon the other Passes.
He promised all with surety of schedule,
And with a self-imposed serenity   810
That dried the sweat upon the Board Room faces.

NUMBER ONE

Oak Lake to Calgary. Van Horne took off
His coat. The North must wait, for that would mean
His shirt as well. First and immediate
This prairie pledge – five hundred miles, and it
Was winter. Failure of this trial promise
Would mean – no, it must not be there for meaning.
An order from him carried no repeal:
It was as final as an execution.
A cable started rolling mills in Europe: 820
A tap of Morse sent hundreds to the bush,
Where axes swung on spruce and the saws sang,
Changing the timber into pyramids
Of poles and sleepers. Clicks, despatches, words,
Like lanterns in a night conductor's hands,
Signalled the wheels: a nod put Shaughnessy
In Montreal: supplies moved on the minute.
Thousands of men and mules and horses slipped
Into their togs and harness night and day.
The grass that fed the buffalo was turned over,   830
The black alluvial mould laid bare, the bed
Levelled and scraped. As individuals
The men lost their identity; as groups,
As gangs, they massed, divided, subdivided,
Like numerals only – sub-contractors, gangs
Of engineers, and shovel gangs for bridges,
Culverts, gangs of mechanics stringing wires,
Loading, unloading and reloading gangs,
Gangs for the fish-plates and the spiking gangs,
Putting a silver polish on the nails.   840

But neither men nor horses ganged like mules:
Wiser than both they learned to unionize.
Some instinct in their racial nether regions
Had taught them how to sniff the five-hour stretch
Down to the fine arithmetic of seconds.
They tired out their rivals and they knew it.
They'd stand for overwork, not overtime.
Faster than workmen could fling down their shovels,
They could unhinge their joints, unhitch their tendons;
Jumping the foreman's call, they brayed 'Unhook'   850
With a defiant, corporate instancy.
The promise which looked first without redemption
Was being redeemed. From three to seven miles
A day the parallels were being laid,
Though Eastern throats were hoarse with the old question –
Where are the settlements? And whence the gift
Of tongues which could pronounce place-names that purred
Like cats in relaxation after kittens?
Was it part of the same pledge to turn
A shack into a bank for notes renewed;   860
To call a site a city when men saw
Only a water-tank? This was an act
Of faith indeed – substance of things unseen –
Which would convert preachers to miracles,
Lure teachers into lean-to's for their classes.
And yet it happened that while labourers
Were swearing at their blisters in the evening
And straightening out their spinal kinks at dawn,
The tracks joined up Oak Lake to Calgary.

NUMBER TWO

On the North Shore a reptile lay asleep –   870
A hybrid that the myths might have conceived,
But not delivered, as progenitor
Of crawling, gliding things upon the earth.

228

She lay snug in the folds of a huge boa
Whose tail had covered Labrador and swished
Atlantic tides, whose body coiled itself
Around the Hudson Bay, then curled up north
Through Manitoba and Saskatchewan
To Great Slave Lake. In continental reach
The neck went past the Great Bear Lake until   880
Its head was hidden in the Arctic Seas.
This folded reptile was asleep or dead:
So motionless, she seemed stone dead – just seemed:
She was too old for death, too old for life,
For as if jealous of all living forms
She had lain there before bivalves began
To catacomb their shells on western mountains.
Somewhere within this life-death zone she sprawled,
Torpid upon a rock-and-mineral mattress.
Ice-ages had passed by and over her,   890
But these, for all their motion, had but sheared
Her spotty carboniferous hair or made
Her ridges stand out like the spikes of molochs.
Her back grown stronger every million years,
She had shed water by the longer rivers
To Hudson Bay and by the shorter streams
To the great basins to the south, had filled
Them up, would keep them filled until the end
Of Time.

          Was this the thing Van Horne set out
To conquer? When Superior lay there   900
With its inviting levels? Blake, Mackenzie,
Offered this water like a postulate.
'Why those twelve thousand men sent to the North?
Nonsense and waste with utter bankruptcy.'
And the Laurentian monster at the first
Was undisturbed, presenting but her bulk
To the invasion. All she had to do

Was lie there neither yielding nor resisting.
Top-heavy with accumulated power
And overgrown survival without function,   910
She changed her spots as though brute rudiments
Of feeling foreign to her native hour
Surprised her with a sense of violation
From an existence other than her own –
Or why take notice of this unknown breed,
This horde of bipeds that could toil like ants,
Could wake her up and keep her irritated?
They tickled her with shovels, dug pickaxes
Into her scales and got under her skin,
And potted holes in her with drills and filled   920
Them up with what looked like fine grains of sand,
Black sand. It wasn't noise that bothered her,
For thunder she was used to from her cradle –
The head-push and nose-blowing of the ice,
The height and pressure of its body: these
Like winds native to clime and habitat
Had served only to lull her drowsing coils.
It was not size or numbers that concerned her.
It was their foreign build, their gait of movement.
They did not crawl – nor were they born with wings.   930
They stood upright and walked, shouted and sang;
They needed air – that much was true – their mouths
Were open but the tongue was alien.
The sounds were not the voice of winds and waters,
Nor that of any beasts upon the earth.
She took them first with lethargy, suffered
The rubbing of her back – those little jabs
Of steel were like the burrowing of ticks
In an elk's hide needing an antler point,
Or else left in a numb monotony.   940
These she could stand but when the breed
Advanced west on her higher vertebrae,
Kicking most insolently at her ribs,

Pouring black powder in her cavities,
And making not the clouds but her insides
The home of fire and thunder, then she gave
Them trial of her strength: the trestles tottered;
Abutments, bridges broke; her rivers flooded:
She summoned snow and ice, and then fell back
On the last weapon in her armoury –   950
The first and last – her passive corporal bulk,
To stay or wreck the schedule of Van Horne.

NUMBER THREE

The big one was the mountains – seas indeed!
With crests whiter than foam: they poured like seas,
Fluting the green banks of the pines and spruces.
An eagle-flight above they hid themselves
In clouds. They carried space upon their ledges.
Could these be overridden frontally,
Or like typhoons outsmarted on the flanks?
And what were on the flanks? The troughs and canyons,   960
Passes more dangerous to the navigator
Than to Magellan when he tried to read
The barbarous language of his Strait by calling
For echoes from the rocky hieroglyphs
Playing their pranks of hide-and-seek in fog:
As stubborn too as the old North-West Passage,
More difficult, for ice-packs could break up;
And as for bergs, what polar architect
Could stretch his compass points to draught such peaks
As kept on rising there beyond the foothills?   970
And should the bastions of the Rockies yield
To this new human and unnatural foe,
Would not the Selkirks stand? This was a range
That looked like some strange dread outside a door
Which gave its name but would not show its features,
Leaving them to the mind to guess at. This

Meant tunnels – would there be no end to boring?
There must be some day. Fleming and his men
Had nosed their paths like hounds; but paths and trails,
Measured in every inch by chain and transit,   980
Looked easy and seductive on a chart.
The rivers out there did not flow: they tumbled.
The cataracts were fed by glaciers;
Eddies were thought as whirlpools in the Gorges,
And gradients had paws that tore up tracks.

Terror and beauty like twin signal flags
Flew on the peaks for men to keep their distance.
The two combined as in a storm at sea –
'Stay on the shore and take your fill of breathing,
But come not to the decks and climb the rigging.'   990
The Ranges could put cramps in hands and feet
Merely by the suggestion of the venture.
They needed miles to render up their beauty,
As if the gods in high aesthetic moments,
Resenting the profanity of touch,
Chiselled this sculpture for the eye alone.

(*Van Horne in momentary meditation at the Foothills.*)

His name was now a legend. The North Shore,
Though not yet conquered, yet had proved that he
Could straighten crooked roads by pulling at them,
Shear down a hill and drain a bog or fill   1000
A valley overnight. Fast as a bobcat,
He'd climb and run across the shakiest trestle
Or, with a locomotive short of coal,
He could supply the head of steam himself.
He breakfasted on bridges, lunched on ties;
Drinking from gallon pails, he dined on moose.
He could tire out the lumberjacks; beat hell
From workers but no more than from himself.

Only the devil or Paul Bunyan shared
With him the secret of perpetual motion, 1010
And when he moved among his men they looked
For shoulder sprouts upon the Flying Dutchman.

But would his legend crack upon the mountains?
There must be no retreat: his bugles knew
Only one call – the summons to advance
Against two fortresses: the mind, the rock.
To prove the first defence was vulnerable,
To tap the treasury at home and then
Untie the purse-strings of the Londoners,
As hard to loosen as salt-water knots – 1020
That job was Stephen's, Smith's, Tupper's, Macdonald's.
He knew its weight: had heard, as well as they,
Blake pumping at his pulmonary bellows,
And if the speeches made the House shock-proof
Before they ended, they could still peal forth
From print more durable than spoken tones.
Blake had returned to the attack and given
Sir John the ague with another phrase
As round and as melodious as the first:
'The Country's wealth, its millions after millions 1030
Squandered – LOST IN THE GORGES OF THE FRASER':
A beautiful but ruinous piece of music
That could only be drowned with drums and fifes.
Tupper, fighting with fists and nails and toes,
Had taken the word *scandal* which had cut
His master's ballots, and had turned the edge
With his word *slander*, but Blake's *sea*, how turn
That edge? Now this last devastating phrase!
But let Sir John and Stephen answer this
Their way. Van Horne must answer it in his. 1040

INTERNECINE STRIFE

The men were fighting foes which had themselves
Waged elemental civil wars and still
Were hammering one another at this moment.
The peaks and ranges flung from ocean beds
Had wakened up one geologic morning
To find their scalps raked off, their lips punched in,
The colour of their skins charged with new dyes.
Some of them did not wake or but half-woke;
Prone or recumbent with the eerie shapes
Of creatures that would follow them. Weather   1050
Had acted on their spines and frozen them
To stegosaurs or, taking longer cycles,
Divining human features, had blown back
Their hair and, pressing on their cheeks and temples,
Bestowed on them the gravity of mummies.
But there was life and power which belied
The tombs. Guerrilla evergreens were climbing
In military order: at the base
The *ponderosa* pine; the fir backed up
The spruce; and it the Stoney Indian lodge-poles;   1060
And these the white-barks; then, deciduous,
The outpost suicidal Lyell larches
Aiming at summits, digging scraggy roots
Around the boulders in the thinning soil,
Till they were stopped dead at the timber limit –
Rock *versus* forest with the rock prevailing.
Or with the summer warmth it was the ice,
In treaty with the rock to hold a line
As stubborn as a Balkan boundary,
That left its caves to score the Douglases,   1070
And smother them with half a mile of dirt,
And making snow-sheds, covering the camps,
Futile as parasols in polar storms.
One enemy alone had battled rock

And triumphed: searching levels like lost broods,
Keen on their ocean scent, the rivers cut
The quartzite, licked the slate and softened it,
Till mud solidified was mud again,
And then, digesting it like earthworms, squirmed
Along the furrows with one steering urge –   1080
To navigate the mountains in due time
Back to their home in worm-casts on the tides.

Into this scrimmage came the fighting men,
And all but rivers were their enemies.
Whether alive or dead the bush resisted:
Alive, it must be slain with axe and saw,
If dead, it was in tangle at their feet.
The ice could hit men as it hit the spruces.
Even the rivers had betraying tricks,
Watched like professed allies across a border.   1090
They smiled from fertile plains and easy runs
Of valley gradients: their eyes got narrow,
Full of suspicion at the gorges where
They leaped and put the rickets in the trestles.
Though natively in conflict with the rock,
Both leagued against invasion. At Hell's Gate
A mountain laboured and brought forth a bull
Which, stranded in mid-stream, was fighting back
The river, and the fight turned on the men,
Demanding from this route their bread and steel.   1100
And there below the Gate was the Black Canyon
With twenty-miles-an-hour burst of speed.

(*Onderdonk builds the 'Skuzzy' to force the passage.*)

'Twas more than navigation: only eagles
Might follow up this run; the spawning salmon
Gulled by the mill-race had returned to rot
Their upturned bellies in the canyon eddies.

Two engines at the stern, a forrard winch,
Steam-powered, failed to stem the cataract.
The last resource was shoulders, arms and hands.
Fifteen men at the capstan, creaking hawsers,　　　　　　　1110
Two hundred Chinese tugging at shore ropes
To keep her bow-on from the broadside drift,
The *Skuzzy* under steam and muscle took
The shoals and rapids, and warped through the Gate,
Until she reached the navigable water –
The adventure was not sailing: it was climbing.

As hard a challenge were the precipices
Worn water-smooth and sheer a thousand feet.
Surveyors from the edges looked for footholds,
But, finding none, they tried marine manoeuvres.　　　　　　1120
Out of a hundred men they drafted sailors
Whose toes as supple as their fingers knew
The wash of reeling decks, whose knees were hardened
Through tying gaskets at the royal yards:
They lowered them with knotted ropes and drew them
Along the face until the lines were strung
Between the juts. Barefooted, dynamite
Strapped to their waists, the sappers followed, treading
The spider films and chipping holes for blasts,
Until the cliffs delivered up their features　　　　　　　　1130
Under the civil discipline of roads.

RING, RING THE BELLS

Ring, ring the bells, but not the engine bells:
Today only the ritual of the steeple
Chanted to the dull tempo of the toll.
Sorrow is stalking through the camps, speaking
A common mother-tongue. 'Twill leave tomorrow
To turn that language on a Blackfoot tepee,
Then take its leisurely Pacific time

To tap its fingers on a coolie's door.
Ring, ring the bells but not the engine bells: 1140
Today only that universal toll,
For granite, mixing dust with human lime,
Had so compounded bodies into boulders
As to untype the blood, and, then, the Fraser,
Catching the fragments from the dynamite,
Had bleached all birthmarks from her swirling dead.

Tomorrow and the engine bells again!

THE LAKE OF MONEY

(The appeal to the Government for a loan of twenty-two-and-a-half
million, 1883.)

Sir John began to muse on his excuses.
Was there no bottom to this lake? One mile
Along that northern strip had cost – how much? 1150
Eleven dollars to the inch. The Road
In all would measure up to ninety millions,
And diverse hands were plucking at his elbow.
The Irish and the Dutch he could outface,
Outquip. He knew Van Horne and Shaughnessy
Had little time for speeches – one was busy
In grinding out two thousand miles; the other
Was working wizardry on creditors,
Pulling rabbits from hats, gold coins from sleeves
In Montreal. As for his foes like Blake, 1160
He thanked his household gods the Irishman
Could claim only a viscous brand of humour,
Heavy, impenetrable till the hour
To laugh had taken on a chestnut colour.
But Stephen was his friend, hard to resist.
And there was Smith. He knew that both had pledged
Their private fortunes as security

For the construction of the Road. But that
Was not enough. Sir John had yet to dip
And scrape further into the public pocket,   1170
Explore its linings: his, the greater task;
His, to commit a nation to the risk.
How could he face the House with pauper hands?
He had to deal with Stephen first – a man
Laconic, nailing points and clinching them.
Oratory, the weapon of the massed assemblies
Was not the weapon here – Scot meeting Scot.
The burr was hard to take; and Stephen had
A Banffshire-cradled *r*. Drilling the ear,
It paralysed the nerves, hit the red cells.   1180
The logic in the sound, escaping print,
Would seep through channels and befog the cortex.

Sir John counted the exits of discretion:
Disguise himself? A tailor might do much;
A barber might trim down his mane, brush back
The forelock, but no artist of massage,
Kneading that face from brow to nasal tip,
Could change a chunk of granite into talc.
His rheumatism? Yet he still could walk.
Neuralgia did not interfere with speech.   1190
The bronchial tubing needed softer air?
Vacations could not cancel all appointments.
Men saw him in the flesh at Ottawa.
He had to speak this week, wheedling committees,
Much easier than to face a draper's clerk,
Tongue-trained on Aberdonian bargain-counters.
He raised his closed left hand to straighten out
His fingers one by one – four million people.
He had to pull a trifle on that fourth,
Not so resilient as the other three.   1200
Only a wrench could stir the little finger
Which answered with a vicious backward jerk.

The dollar fringes of one hundred million
Were smirching up the blackboard of his mind.
But curving round and through them was the thought
He could not sponge away. Had he not fathered
The Union? Prodigy indeed it was
From Coast to Coast. Was not the Line essential?
What was this fungus sprouting from his rind
That left him at the root less clear a growth   1210
Than this Dutch immigrant, William Van Horne?
The name suggested artificial land
Rescued from swamp by bulging dikes and ditches;
And added now to that were bogs and sloughs
And that most cursèd diabase which God
Had left from the explosions of his wrath.
And yet this man was challenging his pride.
North-Sea ancestral moisture on his beard,
Van Horne was now the spokesman for the West,
The champion of an all-Canadian route,   1220
The Yankee who had come straight over, linked
His name and life with the Canadian nation.
Besides, he had infected the whole camp.
Whether acquired or natural, the stamp
Of faith had never left his face. Was it
The artist's instinct which had made the Rockies
And thence the Selkirks, scenes of tourist lure,
As easy for the passage of an engine
As for the flight of eagles? Miracles
Became his thought: the others took their cue   1230
From him. They read the lines upon his lips.
But miracles did not spring out of air.
Under the driving will and sweltering flesh
They came from pay-cars loaded with the cash.
So that was why Stephen had called so often –
Money – that lake of money, bonds, more bonds.

(*The Bill authorizing the loan stubbornly carries
the House.*)

DYNAMITE ON THE NORTH SHORE

The lizard was in sanguinary mood.
She had been waked again: she felt her sleep
Had lasted a few seconds of her time.
The insects had come back – the ants, if ants   1240
They were – dragging *those* trees, *those* logs athwart
Her levels, driving in *those* spikes; and how
The long grey snakes unknown within her region
Wormed from the east, unstriped, sunning themselves
Uncoiled upon the logs and then moved on,
Growing each day, ever keeping abreast!
She watched them, waiting for a bloody moment,
Until the borers halted at a spot,
The most invulnerable of her whole column,
Drove in that iron, wrenched it in the holes,   1250
Hitting, digging, twisting. Why that spot?
Not this the former itch. That sharp proboscis
Was out for more than self-sufficing blood
About the cuticle: 'twas out for business
In the deep layers and the arteries.
And this consistent punching at her belly
With fire and thunder slapped her like an insult,
As with the blasts the caches of her broods
Broke –nickel, copper, silver and fool's gold,
Burst from their immemorial dormitories   1260
To sprawl indecent in the light of day.
Another warning – this time different.

Westward above her webs she had a trap –
A thing called muskeg, easy on the eyes
Stung with the dust of gravel. Cotton grass,
Its white spires blending with the orchids,
Peeked through the green table-cloths of sphagnum moss.
Carnivorous bladder-wort studded the acres,
Passing the water-fleas through their digestion.
Sweet-gale and sundew edged the dwarf black spruce;   1270

And herds of cariboo had left their hoof-marks,
Betraying visual solidity,
But like the thousands of the pitcher plants,
Their downward-pointing hairs alluring insects,
Deceptive – and the men were moving west!
Now was her time. She took three engines, sank them
With seven tracks down through the hidden lake
To the rock bed, then over them she spread
A counterpane of leather-leaf and slime.
A warning, that was all for now. 'Twas sleep   1280
She wanted, sleep, for drowsing was her pastime
And waiting through eternities of seasons.
As for intruders bred for skeletons –
Some day perhaps when ice began to move,
Or some convulsion ran fires through her tombs,
She might stir in her sleep and far below
The reach of steel and blast of dynamite,
She'd claim their bones as her possessive right
And wrap them cold in her pre-Cambrian folds.

THREATS OF SECESSION

The Lady's face was flushed. Thirteen years now   1290
Since that engagement ring adorned her finger!
Adorned? Betrayed. She often took it off
And flung it angrily upon the dresser,
Then took excursions with her sailor-lover.
Had that man with a throat like Ottawa,
That tailored suitor in a cut-away,
Presumed compliance on her part? High time
To snub him for delay – for was not time
The marrrow of agreement? At the mirror
She tried to cream a wrinkle from her forehead,   1300
Toyed with the ring, replaced it and removed it.
Harder, she thought, to get it on and off –
This like the wrinkle meant but one thing, age.

So not too fast; play safe. Perhaps the man
Was not the master of his choice. Someone
Within the family group might well contest
Exotic marriage. Still, her plumes were ruffled
By Blake's two-nights' address before the Commons:
Three lines inside the twenty thousand words
Had maddened her. She searched for hidden meanings –   1310
'Should she insist on those preposterous terms
And threaten to secede, then let her go,
Better than ruin the country.' 'Let her go,'
And 'ruin' – language this to shake her bodice.
Was this indictment of her character,
Or worse, her charm? Or was it just plain dowry?
For this last one at least she had an answer.
Pay now or separation – this the threat.
Dipping the ring into a soapy lather,
She pushed it to the second knuckle, twirled   1320
It past. Although the diamond was off-colour,
She would await its partner ring of gold –
The finest carat; yes, by San Francisco!

BACK TO THE MOUNTAINS

As grim an enemy as rock was time.
The little men from five-to-six feet high,
From three-to-four score years in lease of breath,
Were flung in double-front against them both
In years a billion strong; so long was it
Since brachiapods in mollusc habitats
Were clamping shells on weed in ocean mud.   1330
Now only yesterday had Fleming's men,
Searching for toeholds on the sides of cliffs,
Five thousand feet above sea-level, set
A tripod's leg upon a trilobite.
And age meant pressure, density. Sullen
With aeons, mountains would not stand aside;

Just block the path – morose but without anger,
No feeling in the menace of their frowns,
Immobile for they had no need of motion;
Their veins possessed no blood – they carried quartzite.   1340
Frontal assault! To go through them direct
Seemed just as inconceivable as ride
Over their peaks. But go through them the men
Were ordered and their weapons were their hands
And backs, pickaxes, shovels, hammers, drills
And dynamite – against the rock and time;
For here the labour must be counted up
In months subject to clauses of a contract
Distinguished from the mortgage-run an age
Conceded to the trickle of the rain   1350
In building river-homes. The men bored in,
The mesozoic rock arguing the inches.

This was a kind of surgery unknown
To mountains or the mothers of the myths.
These had a chloroform in leisured time,
Squeezing a swollen handful of light-seconds,
When water like a wriggling casuist
Had probed and found the areas for incision.
Now time was rushing labour – inches grew
To feet, to yards: the drills – the single jacks,   1360
The double jacks – drove in and down; the holes
Gave way to excavations, these to tunnels,
Till men sodden with mud and roof-drip steamed
From sunlight through the tar-black to the sunlight.

HOLLOW ECHOES FROM THE TREASURY VAULT

Sir John was tired as to the point of death.
His chin was anchored to his chest. Was Blake
Right after all? And was Mackenzie right?
Superior could be travelled on. Besides,

It had a bottom, but those northern bogs
Like quicksands could go down to the earth's core.   1370
Compared with them, quagmires of ancient legend
Were backyard puddles for old ducks. To sink
Those added millions down that wallowing hole!
He thought now through his feet. Many a time
When argument cemented opposition,
And hopeless seemed his case, he could think up
A tale to laugh the benches to accord.
No one knew better, when a point had failed
The brain, how to divert it through the ribs.
But now his stock of stories had run out.   1380
This was exhaustion at its coma level.
Or was he sick? Never had spots like these
Assailed his eyes. He could not rub them out –
Those shifting images – was it the sunset
Refracted through the bevelled window edges?
He shambled over and drew down the blind;
Returned and slumped; it was no use; the spots
Were there. No light could ever shoot this kind
Of orange through a prism, or this blue,
And what a green! The spectrum was ruled out;   1390
Its bands were too inviolate. He rubbed
The lids again – a brilliant gold appeared
Upon a silken backdrop of pure white,
And in the centre, red – a scarlet red,
A dancing, rampant and rebellious red
That like a stain spread outward covering
The vision field. He closed his eyes and listened:
Why, what was that? 'Twas bad enough that light
Should play such pranks upon him, but must sound
Crash the Satanic game, reverberate   1400
A shot fifteen years after it was fired,
And culminate its echoes with the thud
Of marching choruses outside his window:

'We'll hang Riel up the Red River,
And he'll roast in hell forever,
We'll hang him up the River
With a yah-yah-yah.'

The noose was for the shot: 'twas blood for blood;
The death of Riel for the death of Scott.
What could not Blake do with that on the Floor,   1410
Or that young, tall, bilingual advocate
Who with the carriage of his syllables
Could bid an audience like an orchestra
Answer his body swaying like a reed?
Colours and sounds made riot of his mind –
White horses in July processional prance,
The blackrobe's swish, the Métis' sullen tread,
And out there in the rear the treaty-wise
Full-breeds with buffalo wallows on their foreheads.

This he could stand no longer, sick indeed: 1420
Send for his doctor, the first thought, then No;
The doctor would advise an oculist,
The oculist return him to the doctor,
The doctor would see-saw him to another –
A specialist on tumours of the brain,
And he might recommend close-guarded rest
In some asylum – Devil take them all,
He had his work to do. He glanced about
And spied his medicine upon the sideboard;
Amber it was, distilled from Highland springs,   1430
That often had translated age to youth
And boiled his blood on a victorious rostrum.
Conviction seized him as he stood, for here
At least he was not cut for compromise,
Nor curried to his nickname Old Tomorrow.
Deliberation in his open stance,
He trenched a deep one, gurgled and sat down.

What were those paltry millions after all?
They stood between completion of the Road
And bankruptcy of both Road and Nation.   1440
Those north-shore gaps must be closed in by steel.
It did not need exhilarated judgment
To see the sense of that. To send the men
Hop-skip-and-jump upon lake ice to board
The flatcars was a revelry for imps.
And all that cutting through the mountain rock,
Four years of it and more, and all for nothing,
Unless those gaps were spanned, bedded and railed.
To quit the Road, to have the Union broken
Was irredeemable. He rose, this time   1450
Invincibility carved on his features,
Hoisted a second, then drew up the blind.
He never saw a sunset just like this.
He lingered in the posture of devotion:
That sun for sure was in the west, or was it?
Soon it would be upholstering the clouds
Upon the Prairies, Rockies and the Coast:
He turned and sailed back under double-reef,
Cabined himself inside an armchair, stretched
His legs to their full length under the table.   1460
Something miraculous had changed the air –
A chemistry that knew how to extract
The iron from the will: the spots had vanished
And in their place an unterrestrial nimbus
Circled his hair: the jerks had left his nerves:
The millions kept on shrinking or were running
From right to left: the fourth arthritic digit
Was straight, and yes, by heaven, the little fifth
Which up to now was just a calcium hook
Was suppling in the Hebridean warmth.   1470
A blessèd peace fell like a dew upon him,
And soon, in trance, drenched in conciliation,
He hiccuped gently – 'Now let S-S-Stephen come!'

(*The Government grants the Directors the right to issue $35,000,000,
guarantees $20,000,000, the rest to be issued by the Railway Directors.
Stephen goes to London, and Lord Revelstoke, speaking for the House of
Baring, takes over the issue.*)

SUSPENSE IN THE MONTREAL BOARD ROOM

Evening had settled hours before its time
Within the Room and on the face of Angus.
Dejection overlaid his social fur,
Rumpled his side-burns, left moustache untrimmed.
The vision of his Bank, his future Shops,
Was like his outlook for the London visit.
Van Horne was fronting him with a like visage   1480
Except for two spots glowing on his cheeks –
Dismay and anger at those empty pay-cars.
His mutterings were indistinct but final
As though he were reciting to himself
The Athanasian damnatory clauses.
He felt the Receiver's breath upon his neck:
To come so near the end, and then this hurdle!

Only one thing could penetrate that murk –
A cable pledge from London, would it come?
Till now refusal or indifference   1490
Had met the overtures. Would Stephen turn
The trick?
              A door-knock and a telegram
With Stephen's signature! Van Horne ripped it
Apart. Articulation failed his tongue,
But Angus got the meaning from his face
And from a noisy sequence of deductions: –
An inkstand coasted through the office window,
Followed by shredded maps and blotting-pads,
Fluttering like shad-flies in a summer gale;
A bookshelf smitten by a fist collapsed;   1500

Two chairs flew to the ceiling – one retired,
The other roosted on the chandelier.
Some thirty years erased like blackboard chalk,
Van Horne was in a school at Illinois.
Triumphant over his two-hundred weight,
He leaped and turned a cartwheel on the table,
Driving heel sparables into the oak,
Came down to teach his partner a Dutch dance;
And in the presence of the messenger,
Who stared immobilized at what he thought   1510
New colours in the managerial picture,
Van Horne took hold of Angus bodily,
Tore off his tie and collar, mauled his shirt,
And stuffed a Grand Trunk folder down his breeches.

(*The last gap in the mountains – between the Selkirks and Savona's
Ferry – is closed.*)

The Road itself was like a stream that men
Had coaxed and teased or bullied out of Nature.
As if watching for weak spots in her codes,
It sought for levels like the watercourses.
It sinuously took the bends, rejoiced
In plains and easy grades, found gaps, poured through them, 1520
But hating steep descents avoided them.
Unlike the rivers which in full rebellion
Against the canyons' hydrophobic slaver
Went to the limit of their argument:
Unlike again, the stream of steel had found
A way to climb, became a mountaineer.
From the Alberta plains it reached the Summit,
And where it could not climb, it cut and curved,
Till from the Rockies to the Coastal Range
It had accomplished what the Rivers had,   1530
Making a hundred clean Caesarian cuts,
And bringing to delivery in their time
Their smoky, lusty-screaming locomotives.

THE SPIKE

Silver or gold? Van Horne had rumbled 'Iron.'
No flags or bands announced this ceremony,
No Morse in circulation through the world,
And though the vital words like Eagle Pass,
Craigellachie, were trembling in their belfries,
No hands were at the ropes. The air was taut
With silences as rigid as the spruces   1540
Forming the background in November mist.
More casual than camera-wise, the men
Could have been properties upon a stage,
Except for road maps furrowing their faces.

Rogers, his both feet planted on a tie,
Stood motionless as ballast. In the rear,
Covering the scene with spirit-level eyes,
Predestination on his chin, was Fleming.
The only one groomed for the ritual
From smooth silk hat and well-cut square-rig beard   1550
Down through his Caledonian longitude,
He was outstaturing others by a foot,
And upright as the mainmast of a brig.
Beside him, barely reaching to his waist,
A water-boy had wormed his way in front
To touch this last rail with his foot, his face
Upturned to see the cheek-bone crags of Rogers.
The other side of Fleming, hands in pockets,
Eyes leaden-lidded under square-crowned hat,
And puncheon-bellied under overcoat,   1560
Unsmiling at the focused lens – Van Horne.
Whatever ecstasy played round that rail
Did not leap to his face. Five years had passed,
Less than five years – so well within the pledge.

The job was done. Was this the slouch of rest?
Not to the men he drove through walls of granite.
The embers from the past were in his soul,
Banked for the moment at the rail and smoking,
Just waiting for the future to be blown.

At last the spike and Donald with the hammer!   1570
His hair like frozen moss from Labrador
Poked out under his hat, ran down his face
To merge with streaks of rust in a white cloud.
What made him fumble the first stroke? Not age:
The snow belied his middle sixties. Was
It lapse of caution or his sense of thrift,
That elemental stuff which through his life
Never pockmarked his daring but had made
The man the canniest trader of his time,
Who never missed a rat-count, never failed   1580
To gauge the size and texture of a pelt?
Now here he was caught by the camera,
Back bent, head bowed, and staring at a sledge,
Outwitted by an idiotic nail.
Though from the crowd no laughter, yet the spike
With its slewed neck was grinning up at Smith.
Wrenched out, it was replaced. This time the hammer
Gave a first tap as with apology,
Another one, another, till the spike
Was safely stationed in the tie and then   1590
The Scot, invoking his ancestral clan,
Using the hammer like a battle-axe,
His eyes bloodshot with memories of Flodden,
Descended on it, rammed it to its home.
. . . . .
The stroke released a trigger for a burst
Of sound that stretched the gamut of the air.
The shouts of engineers and dynamiters,

Of locomotive-workers and explorers,
Flanking the rails, were but a tuning-up
For a massed continental chorus. Led   1600
By Moberly (of the Eagles and *this* Pass)
And Rogers (of *his own*), followed by Wilson,
And Ross (charged with the Rocky Mountain Section),
By Egan (general of the Western Lines),
Cambie and Marcus Smith, Harris of Boston,
The roar was deepened by the bass of Fleming,
And heightened by the laryngeal fifes
Of Dug McKenzie and John H. McTavish.
It ended when Van Horne spat out some phlegm
To ratify the tumult with 'Well Done'   1610
Tied in a knot of monosyllables.

Merely the tuning up! For on the morrow
The last blow on the spike would stir the mould
Under the drumming of the prairie wheels,
And make the whistles from the steam out-crow
The Fraser. Like a gavel it would close
Debate, making Macdonald's 'sea to sea'
Pour through two oceanic megaphones –
Three thousand miles of *Hail* from port to port;
And somewhere in the middle of the line   1620
Of steel, even the lizard heard the stroke.
The breed had triumphed after all. To drown
The traffic chorus, she must blend the sound
With those inaugural, narcotic notes
Of storm and thunder which would send her back
Deeper than ever in Laurentian sleep.   1952

The Unromantic Moon

The radar pinged the moon one starlit night –
'Good evening!' the operator meant.
Less than 'good evening' did the satellite
Reply – its echo quite indifferent.

Only the echo! Could it be that she
Had never trod the court of our conventions?
And learned the art in her simplicity
To ask – 'My lord, just what are your intentions?'

Oho, ye lovers! Many centuries
Have written the inscriptions of your tender   10
Pledges – the cardiograms of your disease –
To that pale maiden with a neuter gender.

And so nocturnes might have been sung forever
By swains and courtiers equally dejected,
Had not a new Minerva chanted – 'Never
Have lover-lunar orbits intersected.'

Take up your lyres, but tune your orchard trills
To other ears than those of Heaven's queen:
Dead Letter Offices are crater sills
Surrendering to the prose of a machine.   June 1953

Textual Variants and Emendations

This list is a record of all *substantive variants* between the poem chosen as copy-text (designated with an asterisk) and all other authoritative printed versions; it also makes reference to all emendations made by the editors and may, at times, offer interesting variants from manuscript sources. Not accepted as authoritative versions are poems included in minor anthologies, unless they occur nowhere else or are first versions; and not included in this list of variants are the accidentals – the typographical errors and minor punctuation changes (of which there are very few). If titles are missing from this list, the reader is to understand that no variants exist (ie, no major errors have occurred in previous printings or revisions been made by the author after the first printing), and no emendations have made to the copy-text. A detailed bibliographical description and textual transmission of all poems can be found in the descriptive bibliography included in this volume.

ABBREVIATIONS

CF	Canadian Forum	NP	New Provinces
CP	Collected Poems (1944 & 1958)	NW	New World
CPM	Canadian Poetry Magazine	QQ	Queen's Quarterly
FG	Fable of the Goats	SL	Still Life
HTF	Here the Tides Flow,	SW	Star Weekly
	ed. D.G. Pitt	TSP	Ten Selected Poems
NF	New Frontier	VV	Voice of Victory

Silences
CF (1936), FG (1937), CP (1944), CP* (1958), HTF (1962)

5 growth] worth, *CP* (44)
24 pairs] pair, *CF*

Seen on the Road
NF (1936), *NP* (1936), *FG* (1937), *CP* (1944), *CP** (1958)
2 spring-time] springtime, *CF* & *FG*
6 a road] the road, *NP*
11 planet-eyed] planet-wise, *CF* & *FG*

The Baritone
CF (1936), *FG* (1937), *CP* (1944), *CP**(1958)
Alternate title: 'Dictator (Baritone),' *CF*

Puck Reports Back
CPM (1937), *FG**(1937)
30 This line omitted from *CPM*
48 but when] and when, *CPM*
52 caparison] comparison, *FG*
125 tautness] tartness, *FG*; the latter is an obvious error

The Fable of the Goats
FG (1937), *CP**(1944)
71 corporate enterprise] a state enterprise, *FG*
119 His stroke] This stroke, *FG*
119 His *coup d'état*] This *coup d'état*, *FG*
143 mangage to domesticate] Learn so to domesticate, *FG*
144 and] to, *FG*
176 One had appeared like this to show] Had not one just appeared to show, *FG*
194 Moreover, Nature – quirky dame –] Moreover, had this quirky dame, *FG*
195 Had planted] Implanted, *FG*
306 His sires – grands and great-grands – fall] His sires, grandsires, and great-grands fall, *FG*
376 A steadying] That steadying, *FG*

The Illusion
FG (1937), *CP**(1958)
Alternate title: 'The Drowning,' *FG*

The Dying Eagle
QQ (1939), *SL* (1943), *CP* (1944), *TSP* (1947), *CP**(1958)
Alternate title: 'The Old Eagle,' *QQ* & *TSP*. Pratt considered 'The Dying
Eagle' to be in error. See Gingell, *On His Life and Poetry*, 113.
43 Andes] Rockies, *TSP*
71 sloven] slattern, *QQ*

The Radio in the Ivory Tower
CF (1939), *SL* (1943), *CP* (1944), *CP**(1958)
90 cobbles] rubble, *CF*
98–9 (September 1939)] omitted from *CF*
118 mortar] rubble, *CF*

Dunkirk
Maclean's* (1940), *CPM* (1940), *NW* (1941), *VV* (1941)
13 Attending] Desperate, *VV*

Brébeuf and His Brethren
Distinct first edition (Toronto: Macmillan), 1940; distinct second edition
(Toronto: Macmillan), 1940; 2nd ed. rpt, 1941; distinct edition (Detroit:
Basilian), 1942; *CP* (1944), *CP**(1958)
2071 In the first edition only (Toronto: Macmillan 1940), the poem ended
in this fashion:
The wheel had come full circle with the visions
In France of Brébeuf poured through the mould of St Ignace.
Lalemant died in the morning at nine, in the flame
Of the pitch belts. Flushed with the sight of the bodies, the foes
Gathered their clans and moved back to the north and west
To join the the fight against the tribes of the Petuns,
And, with the attack to be made on Sainte Marie,
Secure no less than the death of the Huron tribes.

Garnier was at the mission of St Jean,
Covering again the ground which he and Jogues
Had pioneered nine years before. The town
Under the impact of the Iroquois
Broke like St Joseph and the fate of Daniel
The fate of Garnier. Chabanel,
Ordered by his Superior to return

From St Matthias was the last to add
His name to the great roll when in the woods,
Exhausted on his knees, he was discovered
And murdered through the treachery of a Huron.

Within a year dispersion was complete.
The nation perished with its priests. Ragueneau,
To avoid the capture of the fort, applied
The torch himself. 'Inside an hour,' he wrote,
'We saw the fruit of ten years' labour end
In smoke. We took a last look at the fields,
Put our belongings on a raft of logs,
And made our way to the Island of St Joseph.'
But even there the old tale was retold –
Of hunger and the search for roots and acorns,
Of cold, of persecution unto death
By Iroquois, of Jesuit will and courage
As Ragueneau and Chaumonot led back
The remnant of a nation to Quebec.

. . . . .

Three hundred years have gone, but the voices that led
The martyrs through death unto life are heard again
In the pines and elms by the great Fresh Water Sea.
The Mission sites have returned to the fold of the Order.
Near to the ground where the cross broke under the hatchet,
And went with it into the soil to come back at the turn
Of the spade with the carbon and calcium char of the bodies,
The shrines and altars are built anew; the *Aves*
And prayers ascend and the Holy Bread is broken.

Dunkirk

Distinct edition (Toronto: Macmillan), 1941; *CP* (1944), *TSP* (1947), *CP**
(1958)
46–7 The following extra lines were included in the 1941 edition:
It reasoned well –
Brutality, an art which had been bogged
In some stray corner of the field

In that Gallic-Anglo-Saxon fumble of the game.
212 Very] Verey, 1941, *CP* (44) and *TSP*
295 sheering] shearing, *TSP*. The *TSP* reading seems to make better
    sense, but since 'sheer' is a well-known nautical term, meaning to
    deviate from course, it is possible that Pratt intended this word.
315 scoots] skoots, 1941 & *CP* (44)

The Truant
CF (1942), *Voices* (1943), *SL* (1943), *CP* (1944), *CP**(1958)
6 forcibly] universally, *CF, Voices*
7 This line omitted from *CF* and *Voices*
122 mileage] *mumu's, CF, Voices, SL, CP* (44)

Autopsy on a Sadist
Voices (1943), *SL* (1943), *CP* (1944), *CP** (1958)
Subtitle omitted from *Voices*

Still Life
SL (1943), *CP* (1944), *CP** (1958)
This poem first appeared as a single stanza in *SN*, 54 (28 October 1939).
    It reads as follows:
    To the poets who have fled
    To pools where little breezes dusk and shiver,
    Who need still life to deliver
    Their souls of their songs –
    There are roses blanched of red
    In the Orient gardens, Japanese urns to limn
    With delicate words, and enough wrongs
    To exhaust an Olympian quiver,
    And time, be it said,
    For a casual hymn
    To be sung for the hundred thousand dead
    In the mud of the Yellow River.
Pratt subsequently revised the stanza, and added others, for the *Still Life*
    (1943) publication.

The Brawler in *Who's Who*
SL (1943), *CP* (1944), *CP** (1958)
32 concerning roaches] touching cockroaches, *SL*

They Are Returning
Maclean's (1945), distinct edition (Macmillan), 1945
41 regimental] Prussian, *Maclean's*
51 congeal] refine, *Maclean's*
52 Like Buchenwald or Maidanek or Lidice] Like Oradour, Distomo, Lidice –, *Maclean's*
104–44 Omitted from *Maclean's*
177 Or, in the *Skeena-Athabascan* way] Or, in the Athabascan way, *Maclean's*
236–76 Omitted from *Maclean's*
292 Kleve, Emmerich, Antwerp and Groningen] Kleve, Emmerich, Xanten, Antwerp, Groningen, *Maclean's*

Behind the Log
CPM (1947), distinct edition (Macmillan), 1947, *CP** (1958)
2 the] omitted from 1947
3 unreel] unwind, *CPM*
6 The idiom of storms, their lairs and paths] The ways of storms, their lairs, habits and paths, *CPM*
15–19 Omitted from *CPM*
31 Hard a-port] Hard-a-starboard, *CPM*
35 mother] native, *CPM*
42 ping] hail, *CPM*
43 The sky for the plane's fuselage] The sky at night for the plane's fuselage, *CPM*
43–4 'even / The moon acknowledged from her crater sills,' omitted from *CPM*
53 fine] fire, 1947; an obvious error.
57–8
   'Back-curtained by the Greenland ice-cap – time,
   The '41 autumnal equinox,' *CPM*
90–6 In the *CPM* version this is abbreviated to:
   'The convoy s.c. 42 had tried
   To circumvent the foe's new strategy –
   The concentrated ambush of the pack –
   By leaving beaten sea-lanes, east and west.'
100–358 Omitted from *CPM*
362–74 Omitted from *CPM*
400–46 Omitted from *CPM*

449 crop] guts, *CPM*
463 Had sent his ultra-sounds out and reported] Had sent his sound
 waves out and had reported, *CPM*
469 crowsnest] crow's nest, *CPM*
472–5
 'Each sound might hold a threat, an overture
 To a dementia of guns and rockets,
 Torpedo hits, cries of distress, and all
 Competing with the orders from the Bridge,' *CPM*
476–83 Omitted from *CPM*
489–90
 'Calling to Tyndale, Tyndale answering Kelvin,
 And all vibrating from their resonators,' *CPM*
497–512 Omitted from *CPM*
519 five] six, *CPM*
522–31 Condensed in *CPM* to:
 The *Winterswyck* with phosphate; *Garm*
 And *Scania* with lumber; the *Muneric*
 Loaded with iron ore (sink like a rock
 She would if hit); and others with deep freight,
 Twelve columns of them in their ordered stations.
547 Against the convoy, striking through the escort] Against the convoy
 as against the foe, *CPM*
558–76 Omitted from *CPM*
584–93 Omitted from *CPM*
600–1 These lines omitted from 1947 and *CP*:
 'Centre bearing, two-five-o'
 'Starboard ten. Steady on two-five-o'
607–18 Omitted from *CPM*
623–4 These lines omitted from 1947 and *CP*:
 Whatever hope had lingered in the brain
 That one alone was on the prowl was gone.
626–30 Condensed in *CPM* to:
 A third, a fourth. The pack had trailed and found
 Them in the Greenland waters. Moonlight full,
637 *Tachee*] *Tascee*, *CPM*; spelled that way through the *CPM* version
658–71 Omitted from *CPM*
670 When] The, *CPM*
679–82 Omitted from *CPM*

691–729 Omitted from *CPM*

743–5 Condensed in *CPM* to:
But seven cables from the foundered ships,
The killer's light-grey periscope was sighted,
Remaining visible one minute only.

761–7 Omitted from *CPM*

783 Within the Greenland-Iceland ocean tundras] Within the rolling
Greenland-Iceland tundras, *CPM*

792–8 The section from 'From the *Chambly's* deck' to 'So was the water'
omitted from *CPM*

813–923 Omitted from *CPM*

985 Horse-power to the limit on the engines] Horse-power to the limit on
the engines, *CPM*

1008 Upon the *Skeena's* Bridge the judgment fought] Within the captain's
brain the judgment fought, *CPM*

1010 brain] Bridge, *CPM*

1050–65 Omitted from *CPM*

1072–82 The section from 'The ratio...' to '...to come!' omitted from *CPM*

1087–92 Condensed in *CPM* to
I saw the blades of the *Muneric* rise
And edge themselves against the Alberni *gunfire*.

1107–11 Omitted from *CPM*

1134–8 Omitted from *CPM*

1167 'From there up the Loch Foyle to seek their berths,' *CPM*

Summit Meetings
Outposts (1948), *CP** (1958)
Alternate title: 'Lake Success,' *Outposts*

3 a] omitted from *Outposts*

12 The journey straps between those camel pairs] The straps between
those dromedary pairs, *Outposts*

18–19 In the *Outposts* version there was an extra stanza between three
and four:
But keep the rivals from the garden where,
Upon the latch click as each session closes,
They could stroll in to pollinate the roses.
For be the years one hundred, seven or thirty,
A howling larynx can endure this strain
Of effluent more readily than a vein.

19 bellyfuls] hulls, *Outposts*

Newfoundland Calling
*SW** (1949), *HTF* (1962)
Stanzas two, three, six, seven, eight, and nine omitted from *HTF*
The final stanza in *HTF* is as follows:
> The Eastern Maritimes will learn anew
> The silver rise in the barometer.
> What power in the heavens could so subdue
> St. Lawrence, Gulf and River, or defer
> The hurricane speed? – only the Island's door
> Is latched against the North Atlantic's roar.

Newfoundland Seamen
Winnipeg Free Press (1949), *CP** (1958), *HTF* (1962)
The holograph version of this poem, now in the Lorne Pierce Collection
    at Queen's, was published as the frontispiece to *This is Newfoundland*,
    ed. Ewart Young (Toronto: Ryerson Press 1949). The title of that
    version was 'Newfoundland Sailors.'

Annotations

Sandra Djwa, Robert Gibbs,
David Savage

The notes, which are intended to provide a general guide for the student of Pratt's poetry, include explanations of archaic words, some proper names, nautical terms, and Newfoundland dialect words as well as brief references to biblical, literary, mythological, and historical allusions.

ABBREVIATIONS

EJP: EV	*E.J. Pratt: The Evolutionary Vision*, by Sandra Djwa
EJP: MY	*E.J. Pratt: The Master Years 1927–1964*, by David G. Pitt
EJP: TY	*E.J. Pratt: The Truant Years 1882–1964*, by David G. Pitt
NV	*Newfoundland Verse*
OHLP	*E.J. Pratt: On His Life and Poetry*, ed. Susan Gingell
TSP	*Ten Selected Poems*, ed. E.J. Pratt
UTQ	*University of Toronto Quarterly*

Silences
For Pratt's explanations of the poem, see *OHLP* 108–9. See also Charles
G.D. Roberts' *The Haunters of the Silences* (Boston: Page 1907), 202,
299. 'It was a life of noiseless but terrific activity, of unrelenting and
incessant death, in a darkness streaked fitfully with phosphorescent
gleams from the bodies of the darting, writhing, or pouncing
creatures that slew and were slain in the stupendous silence.'
4 'milt': roe of male fish
4 'spawn': in this context, eggs of female fish
6 'bonitoes': predatory fish about two feet long
9 'molluscs': series of invertebrate animals that includes such varied
    creatures as snails, oysters, and cuttle-fish. Giant squids are a
    species of cuttle-fish.

Seen on the Road

10 'tumbril': type of cart that had acquired an ominous connotation from Charles Dickens's use of it in describing transportation of the condemned to the guillotine in *A Tale of Two Cities*

The Baritone

Title: alludes to Benito Mussolini (1883–1945), Italian dictator and leader of the fascist movement

18 'the *Marseillaise*': French national anthem, sung by the volunteers of Marseilles when they entered Paris to support the French Revolution

19 'The *Giovanezza*' (usual spelling 'Giovinezza'): 'Giovinezza' is Italian for 'youthfulness,' but the usual English title for this song is 'Song of the Blackshirts.'

20 'The *Deutschlandlied*': 'Deutschland über Alles,' or 'Germany Over All,' national anthem of the Third Reich. An abridged version is now the national anthem of West Germany.

21 'stretto': portion of a fugue in which one voice follows closely on the preceding one

22 'the *Dead March*': from Handel's oratorio *Saul*

25 'codetta': short coda. A coda is a passage introduced at the end of a musical composition to bring the latter to a satisfactory conclusion.

31 'Orion': In the signs of the zodiac, the constellation Orion is pictured as a hunter with a belt and sword.

Puck Reports Back

Title 'Puck': merry sprite in Shakespeare's *A Midsummer Night's Dream*
Oberon: king of the fairies in *A Midsummer Night's Dream*

7 'Lysander and Hermia': lovers in *A Midsummer Night's Dream*

8 'Bottom': conceited weaver in *A Midsummer Night's Dream*

20 'Hyrcanian': of Hyrcania, province of ancient Persia on the shores of the Caspian Sea

21 'scrip': traveller's satchel or an alternate word for 'scrap' and associated with the word 'script.' It means a small scrap of paper or, in this instance, a small scrap of writing.

24 'love-juice of a herb': See *A Midsummer Night's Dream* ii, i, 166–8, 176–8. Oberon quarrels with his wife Titania and, when she is asleep, anoints her eyelids with 'Love-in-Idleness,' a potion which causes the recipient to fall in love with the first person seen on waking.

52 'caparison': horse's harness

56 'beavers': In this context, a beaver is the lower face-guard of a helmet.

119 'Hallowtide': season encompassing All Saints' Day
125 'Parthian': Parthia was an ancient kingdom in western Asia. The
Parthians fought on horseback with bow and arrow, and after each
shot turned their horses as if fleeing. Thus 'Parthian shot' became a
phrase meaning a cutting or telling remark made as one left.
130 'county's': count's
137 'Zounds': archaic oath, short for 'God's wounds,' meaning the
wounds of Christ upon the cross
140 'Olympian': Mount Olympus was the home of the ancient Greek
gods; thus the term implies that someone is superior or superhuman.
170 'Nestor': In Greek legend, Nestor was the king of Pylos in Greece, and
the oldest and most experienced chieftain involved in the siege of Troy.
174 'distaff': cleft stick on which wool or flax is wound for spinning. It
came to denote women's work or women.

The Fable of the Goats
For Pratt's account of the poem's sources and composition, see *OHLP*,
109–12. There he mistakenly attributes authorship of 'Les deux
chèvres' to Aesop when, in fact, the author is La Fontaine. D.G. Pitt
speculates that Pratt first read this fable in translation in a school text,
where it was printed anonymously.
2 'Aralasian' – 8. 'Carolonian' – 99. 'Fallopian' – 99. 'Ovidian' – 100:
'The geographical names are fictitious but euphonic, suggesting
central Europe.' *OHLP* 108
30 'Dolomites': mountain range in northern Italy
46 'Kyber Route' (usual spelling 'Khyber'): Khyber Pass, a narrow
gorge between northwest India and Afghanistan
47 'Thermopylae': narrow pass in northern Greece. In 480 B.C.
Leonidas and his 300 Spartans made their last stand at Thermopylae
against invading Persians.
53 'argalis': An argali is a wild sheep of Asia.
73 'Cyrus': The head of the goats perhaps was named Cyrus after King
Cyrus of Persia, who founded the Persian empire in the sixth
century B.C.
113 'Caliphate': rank or government of a caliph, who is a Mohammedan
ruler
124–5 'Ipomoea Purga': species of creeping plant
128 'Croton Tiglium': castor oil tree
131 'ballista': ancient military engine for hurling stones
139 'Abimelech': king of Gerar. See Genesis 20:2ff.

182 'jerboa': rodent of the African deserts

185 'fourteenth point': 'Point' is here used to mean a characteristic in appraising the qualities of an animal, as in a show.

269 '*Excelsior!*': (L.) 'Higher!'

297 'Carthaginian rams': Carthage was an ancient African city whose power threatened Rome. A ram was a projecting beak beyond the bows of a war vessel that enabled it to ram and batter the side of an opposing ship.

300 'milcher dams': in this context, milk-giving female goats with young

324 'witenagemot': Old English national council

370 'Irish Moss and carrageen': two names for the same object, a kind of purplish seaweed from which is extracted a jelly used in food and medicine

376 'digitalis': medicine derived from the foxglove, used as in treating the heart

414 'phagocyte': type of leucocyte, a colourless corpuscle of blood that guards the system by absorbing disease-producing microbes

Under the Lens

10 'hamadryads': in this context, venomous Indian serpents

The Old Organon (1225 A.D.)

Title 'Organon': system of logic or a treatise on logic. *Organon* was the title of Aristotle's logical treatises. In 1620, English philosopher Francis Bacon wrote *Novum Organum* (*The New Organon*).

1225 A.D.: The empire of Genghis Khan reached its height then with the conquest of southeastern Europe.

3-4 Bokhara, Otrar, and Samarcand fell to the Mongols in 1220, and Herat in 1221.

9 'Mohammed': Shah Muhammad II (?-1221), Turkish ruler of the Khwarismian Empire, which included much of the present-day Iran, Afghanistan, and Pakistan

9 'Jehal-ud-Din': son of Shah Muhammad II. In 1221 he made a successful stand against the Mongols in Afghanistan, but in 1222, with the Indus behind him and after a violent struggle, he was forced to flee into India. In 1230 he fled westward before a horde of 30,000 Mongols.

The New (1937 A.D.)

The meeting described in the poem refers generally to contemporary international conferences. Pratt may have had in mind the assemblies of the League of Nations, the seventeenth of which in

1937, by accepting the credentials of an Ethiopian delegation, led to Italy's withdrawing from the League. Ironically, however, despite sanctions from the League of Nations, oil continued to be supplied to Italy by the international cartels controlled by England and France. See also 'The Prize Cat.'

The Impatient Earth
16 'blood-root': popular name for various plants, especially tormentil, a low-growing herb

The Submarine
For Pratt's accounts of the poem, see *OHLP* 112–13.

Old Harry
See *OHLP* 113: 'Old Harry is a name given to a rock, responsible for a number of shipwrecks.'

The Dying Eagle
See *OHLP* 113: 'The next is called "The Old Eagle": It is entitled in the collection 'The Dying Eagle' but that is an error. It might have been more properly called "The Old Eagle Has His First Sight of an Aeroplane".'
41 'pterodactyls': extinct flying reptiles

The Radio in the Ivory Tower
For Pratt's comments on the poem, see *OHLP* 113.
10 'this Rock': The hermit persona of this poem, like Robinson Jeffers, builds himself a castle on the Californian coast (*OHLP* 113). In addition, the island of Newfoundland is sometimes called 'the rock.'
12 'Lord of Misrule': Master of the Revels at Twelfth Night, or the officer in charge of entertainment at the court. See Alfred Noyes's poem, 'Lord of Misrule.'
116 'Gotterdammerung': in Germanic mythology, the apocalyptic 'twilight of the gods.' *Gotterdammerung* is also the title of Wagner's 1876 opera, one of four in the cycle called *The Ring of the Nibelung*.
143 'Apollyon': Greek word meaning 'destroyer.' Apollyon was the angel of the bottomless pit; see Revelation 9:11.

Dunkirk
14 'Corunna': La Coruna, port in northwest Spain from which the Spanish Armada sailed in 1588. It was sacked by the British fleet under Drake in 1589.

14 'Verdun': garrison town in northwest France, site of a protracted battle in World War I. The area around it contains 70 Allied and German military cemeteries.

Brébeuf and His Brethren

For Pratt's five accounts of the poem's background and composition, see *OHLP* 114–26.

Brébeuf, Jean de (1593–1649)

10 'St Francis of Assisi': St Francis (1182–1226) founded the Franciscan order, based on vows of poverty, chastity, and obedience. Assisi is a city in Umbria, Italy.

12 'plague-infested towns': Epidemics of bubonic plague occurred in Europe from the sixth to the twelfth centuries.

16 'Vincent de Paul': St Vincent de Paul (1581–1660), founder of the Congregation of the Mission and the Sisters of Charity

17 'Francis de Sales': St Francis of Sales (1567–1622), who founded the Order of the Visitation in 1610. He wrote the widely read *Introduction à la vie dévote* in 1608.

20 'The architect of the palaces': St Augustine

24 'Kempis through the *Imitatio*': St Thomas Kempis was a fifteenth-century German ecclesiastic who wrote *Imitatio Christi* (*The Imitation of Christ*) in 1417–21.

28 'Theresa': sixteenth-century Sp. nun known for religious visions

29 'Carmelites': members of a religious order founded in the twelfth century at Mt Carmel, Palestine

30 'John of the Cross': sixteenth-century Spanish religious reformer. With St Theresa he founded the order of the discalced (meaning barefooted or wearing sandals) Carmelites and was imprisoned by the older order of Carmelites.

33 'Xavier': St Francis Xavier, sixteenth-century missionary who helped St Ignatius Loyola (l. 35 below) establish the Society of Jesus in 1534.

36 'Pampeluna': St Ignatius Loyola, a Spaniard, was severely wounded in the Spanish siege of Napoleonic forces in Pampeluna, the old name for Pamplona, Spain.

37 'Montserrata': Montserrat is an island of the Leeward Group, in the West Indies federation.

39 '*Company of Jesus*': Jesuits

58 'Bayeux': near the coast of Normandy

62 'Via Dolorosa': the mile Jesus walked from the Mount of Olives to Golgotha

68 *'per ignem et per aquam'*: through fire and water
74 'Brulé': Etienne Brulé (c1592–1633), adventurer and explorer, probably the first white man to enter Huron territory. He lived among the Hurons from 1610 until his death and became an interpreter of their language.
74 'Viel': Fr Nicolas Viel (?–1625), Recollet priest, missionary to the Hurons, 1623–5, assassinated by them at Rivière des Prairies
75 'Sagard': Fr Gabriel, Recollet friar, missionary to the Hurons 1623–4, author of *Le grand voyage au pays des Hurons* (1632) and *L'histoire du Canada* (1636)
75 'Le Caron': Fr Joseph (c1586–1632), Recollet priest, first missionary among the Hurons
104 'the Crusades': The Crusades, also known as the Wars of the Cross, were a series of religious wars between the Christians of the West and the Mohammedans of the East in an attempt by the Christians to guarantee safe passage for Christian pilgrims to Jerusalem. There were nine crusades, the first starting in 1097 and the last in 1271.
104 'Hastings': Battle of Hastings, 1066
105 'Howards': family name of the Dukes of Norfolk. The family's earlier name was Hereward. Hereward the Wake held out against William the Conqueror after the Battle of Hastings.
117 'Mass': Fr Enemond Massé (1575–1646), Jesuit priest and missionary to Acadia, 1611–13, and to Quebec from 1625 until his death
117 'Charles Lalemant': (1587–1674). First superior of the Jesuits in Quebec and responsible for setting up a Jesuit mission in Canada, he came to Quebec with Fathers Massé and Brébeuf in 1625.
121 'Daillon': Fr Joseph de la Roche Daillon (?–1656), Recollet priest who came to New France in 1625 to assist Fr Viel in his mission to the Hurons
150 'sagamite': kind of gruel made from coarse hominy, which is hulled corn.
153 'Turk's cap': flower, commonly called the American swamp lily
161 'de Noué': Fr Anne de Noué (1587–1646), Jesuit priest and missionary to the Hurons, 1626–7
251 'Arendiwans': Huron medicine men
266 'Kirke': Sir David Kirke (1597–1654), British adventurer who with his four brothers seized Tadoussac in 1627 and in 1629 forced the surrender of Quebec
306 'La Rochelle': French seaport which during the Reformation became a centre of Protestantism. In 1628 it was besieged and taken by Richelieu's forces.

306 'Fribourg': city now in Switzerland that during the Thirty Years War was on the French-German border

308 'Richelieu': Cardinal Armand Jean du Plessis Richelieu (1585–1642)

308 'Mazarin': Cardinal Jules Mazarin (1602–61)

308 'Condé': Louis II de Bourbon Condé (1621–86), French general during the Thirty Years War

309 'Turenne': Henri De La Tour D'Auvergne, Vicompte de Turenne (1611–75), French general during the Thirty Years War

314 'Le Jeune': Fr Paul Le Jeune (1591–1664), Jesuit priest and missionary to the Hurons, 1639–49

314 'Biard': Pierre Biard (1567–1622), Roman Catholic missionary who went to Acadia in 1611

319 'Chastellain': Fr Pierre Chastellain (1606–84), Jesuit priest and missionary to the Hurons, 1639–49

320 'Pijart': Fr Claude Pijart (1600–83), Jesuit priest and missionary to the Nipissings and Algonkins, 1637–44

320 'Le Mercier': Fr François-Joseph Le Mercier (1604–90), Jesuit priest and missionary to the Hurons, 1635–50

320 'Isaac Jogues': (1607–46), Jesuit priest, missionary among the Hurons, 1637–42, and among the Iroquois from 1646 until his death at their hands

321 'The Lalemants': Jérôme and Gabriel, brothers of Charles Lalemant. Fr Jérôme Lalemant (1593–1673), a Jesuit priest, succeeded Brébeuf as superior of the Huron mission and served in that capacity until 1645. Fr Gabriel Lalemant (1610–49), also a Jesuit priest, was a missionary to the Hurons from 1648 until his death at the hands of the Iroquois.

323 'Ragueneau': Fr Paul Ragueneau (1608–80), Jesuit priest, superior of the mission to the Hurons 1645–50, and of the Jesuits in Canada 1650–3

333 'Garnier': Fr Charles Garnier (c1605–49), Jesuit priest, missionary to the Hurons from 1636 until his death at the hands of the Iroquois

342 'Chabanel': Fr Noell Chabanel (1613–49), Jesuit priest, missionary to the Hurons from 1644 until his death at their hands

370 'Chaumonot': Fr Pierre Joseph-Marie Chaumonot (1611–93), Jesuit priest and missionary to the Hurons, 1639–50

375 'the Lady of Loretto' (usual spelling 'Loreto'): the Virgin Mary. Santa Casa, a famous chapel of the Virgin in Loreto, Italy, is a place of pilgrimage.

384 'Davost': Fr Amboise Davost (1586–1643), Jesuit priest and missionary to the Hurons, 1634–6

384 'Daniel': Fr Antoine Daniel (1601–48), Jesuit priest, missionary to the Hurons from 1634 until his death at the hands of the Iroquois

430 'Martin': presumably a donn, or lay assistant, pledged to serve the Jesuit order, identified in the *Relations* only as 'little Martin,' who was 'very roughly treated, and at last left behind with the Bissiriniens.' *The Jesuit Relations and Allied Documents* ed. R.G. Thwaites et al. (Cleveland: Barrows Bros. 1897) VIII, 81

431 'Baron': Simon Baron, a Jesuit donn, who served in Huronia 1634–7

453 'arquebuses': early type of portable gun

457 '*Echon*': name given to Brébeuf by the Hurons, signifying one who pulls a heavy load

463–74 'No Louvre ... vessels of the Mass': verse paraphrase of parts of a letter from Brébeuf to Fr Le Jeune. See *The Jesuit Relations* VIII, 105–9.

500 'Uoki': Huron spirit or demon

513 'A moon eclipse was due ...': See *OHLP* 118.

568–84 'Brébeuf prepared a sermon ... "dirty"': paraphrased from 'Instructions for the Fathers of Our Society Who Shall Be Sent to the Hurons.' See *The Jesuit Relations and Allied Documents* XII, 115–23.

609 'How often ... written story': suggests Wilhelm Wundt's stimulus-response theory

623 'kibes': chilblains

737–813 '"Herein I show you" ... "Enough, O Lord!"': See *The Jesuit Relations and Allied Documents* X, 88–115.

756 'Saint Thomas': St Thomas Aquinas, thirteenth-century theologian and teacher

823 'Du Peron': Fr François Du Peron (1610–65), Jesuit priest and missionary to the Hurons, 1639–49

828 'Patmos': See Revelation 1:9.

905 'Saracen': Arab or Moslem nomad who attacked Christians during the Crusades

969 'Poncet': Fr Joseph-Antoine Poncet De La Rivière (1610–75), Jesuit priest and missionary to the Hurons, 1639–40

970 'Le Moyne': Fr Simon Le Moyne (1604–65), Jesuit priest and missionary to the Hurons, 1638–49

970 'Charles Raymbault': (1602–42), Jesuit priest and missionary to the Hurons, 1637–40

970 'René Menard': (1605–61), Jesuit priest and missionary to the Hurons, Algonkins, Nipissings, and Iroquois from 1641 until his disappearance in 1661

972 'Le Coq': (?–1650), donn of the Jesuits, who was supervisor of buildings and equipment at Sainte-Marie-des-Hurons from 1634 to 1649

972 'Christophe Reynaut': Jesuit donn, who assisted in building the fort

972 'Charles Boivin': one of three brothers who came as donns of the Jesuits to assist in building the fort in 1640

973 'Couture': Guillaume Couture (?–1701), donn who served in Huronia from 1641 to 1642. Captured by the Iroquois in 1642, he later became an ambassador to the Mohawks.

973 'Jean Gurin': donn who assisted in building the fort

1225 'Goupil': René Goupil (1608–42), surgeon, possibly a Jesuit donn, who accompanied Isaac Jogues into Huron country in 1642, where he was captured and killed by the Iroquois

1230 'Eustache': Ahatsistari Eustache (1602–42), Huron warrior, baptized Eustache in 1642. A resident of Saint-Joseph II, he was killed by the Iroquois while accompanying Fr Jogues back to Huronia.

1439 'Montmagny': Charles Huault De Montmagny (c1583–1653), first governor of New France from 1636 to 1648

Before 1461 '*Bressani*': Fr François-Joseph Bressani (1612–72), Jesuit priest and missionary to the Hurons, 1644–50

1548 'Garreau': Fr Leonard Garreau (c1609–56), Jesuit priest and missionary to the Hurons, 1644–54

1661 'astrolabe': instrument formerly used for measuring altitude

1679 'Bonin': Fr Jacques Bonin (1617-?), Jesuit priest and missionary to the Hurons, 1648–50

1679 'Daran': Fr Adrien D'Aran (1615–70), Jesuit priest and missionary to the Hurons, 1648–50

1679 'Greslon': Fr Adrien Greslon (1617–97), Jesuit priest and missionary to the Hurons, 1648–50

1925 'maniple': vestment worn hanging from the left arm

1933 'Palestrina': Giovanni Palestrina, sixteenth-century Italian composer

1997 '*cidreries*': French for cider-houses

2124 '… the ashes of St Ignace are glowing afresh': For Pratt's account of the excavations at Huronia, see *OHLP* 120–1.

Come Away, Death

Title: The song, 'Come away, come away, death,' is sung by Feste, a clown in Shakespeare's *Twelfth Night*, 2.1.52–68.

1 'Willy-nilly, he comes or goes,': See the chop-logic of the First Clown, the gravedigger, in *Hamlet*, 5.1.17–19 and also his song, 5.1.69–105.

2 'Comic in epitaph, tragic in epithalamium,': See *Hamlet*, 5.1.236–9 and 267–9.

3 'muséd rhyme': See Keats's 'Ode To a Nightingale' 53.

5–6 'Whatever the course of the garden variables / ... the constant': In mathematics it is possible to construct a grid to determine the occurrence of irrational factors. Human reason considers life a constant and death an irrational interruption, but the argument of the first stanza is that such a grid would demonstrate the reverse: that death rather than generation, or life, is the constant factor.

7 'poppy seeds': The narcotic properties of the poppy have been associated with death since ancient times. In Canada the poppy is particularly associated with the war dead; see Colonel John McCrae's 'In Flanders Fields.'

8 'he came in formal dress': allusion to Death knocking on man's door, possibly the medieval figure of 'The Dance of Death'

12 'sacramental wine': as in the last rites of the Catholic Church or in Methodist communion

17 'cool longitudes': distance east or west on the earth's surface, measured by the angle which the meridian of a particular place makes with a standard meridian, as that of Greenwich; by extension, a gravepit

20 'the flame of the capitals': Capital letters were illuminated in medieval manuscripts. Pratt also may have intended to make a secondary pun on the medieval sacking of capital cities.

21 'turn of the thumb': literally, turning of a page, but also, perhaps, reference to the thumbscrew, an instrument of torture sometimes used by the medieval church

24 'Venetian mosaics': A revival of Byzantine mosaic art in the eleventh, twelfth, and thirteenth centuries A.D. in Italy produced many fine examples of the art; among the best known are those in the Basilica of St Mark, Venice.

28 'clay to clay': This phrase parallels the burial service, 'ashes to ashes, dust to dust,' but may also refer to God's modelling man from clay.

See Isaiah 46:9, 64:8, and Job 10:9. See also Pratt's verse drama 'Clay.'

30 'the gride of his traction tread': With World Wars I and II death came in a new and mechanical form – the tank.

31 'one September night': possibly a double allusion: World War II began on 3 September 1939 with the bombing, by Germany, of Poland. However, the poem was prompted by the Battle of Britain of August and September 1940. On 7 September, the date of the heavier raid, 400 bombers struck London.

41 'the sound of the motor drone': This suggests the V2 buzz bombs of World War II; when the sound of the motor stopped, the bomb had begun its descent.

52 'Piltdown': At Piltdown, England, 1911–15, parts of a fossilized skull were found and claimed to be the remains of the oldest known human in Europe. But in 1953, 12 years after this poem was written, the skull was discredited.

53 'Java': Java ape man, discovered in 1891, the remains of what was thought to be one of the earliest humans

56 'stylus': ancient writing instrument for use on clay or papyrus

57 'Apocalypse': generally refers to a revelation, and here alludes to one of the Four Horsemen of the Apocalypse (conquest, war, famine, and death) as described in Revelation 6:1–8

Date 'April, 1941': exceedingly bleak point in the war. In this month there were heightened air attacks by Germany on London and other British cities, resulting in heavy civilian casualties. Simultaneously, German forces overran Greece while British forces in North Africa lost Derna and Bardia.

Dunkirk

For Pratt's accounts of the events and of the intent of his poem, see *OHLP* 126–32.

On 10 May 1940, Germany invaded Belgium, Holland, and Luxembourg. British and other forces were soon trapped in Dunkirk, France, on the Strait of Dover. Between 28 May and 3 June, 222 ships of the Royal Navy, aided by 665 yachts and other small civilian boats, under heavy air attack evacuated 224,585 British soldiers and 112,546 French and Belgian troops to Britain.

6 'nightingales' throats': The nightingale is traditionally a symbol of natural art; in addition, one of the best-known English

songs of World War II was 'A Nightingale Sang in Berkeley Square.'

11 'Churchill and Bevin': In 1940 Winston Churchill, a Conservative, became Prime Minister and Defence Minister of Britain's wartime Coalition government, which included Labour MP Ernest Bevin as Minister of Labour and National Service.

14 *'adversatives'*: words such as 'but,' 'yet,' 'however' which introduce debate

50 'Stonehenge': prehistoric stone circle or solar temple in England

57 'Caractacus': British chieftain who led the struggle against the Romans around 50 A.D.

60 'Boadicea': (?–62 A.D.), British queen of the Icenti who led a revolt against the Romans

63 'Alban': Saint Alban (*c*300), British martyr

63 'Alfred': King Alfred (849–99)

63 'Athelney': King Alfred's stronghold, in 878 his hiding place from the Danes

63 'Edington': in Wiltshire, site of Alfred's decisive victory over the Danes

66 'Ball' and 'Tyler': John Ball (?–1381) was an instigator of the Peasants' Revolt, which was led by Wat Tyler (?–1381).

67 'Enclosures': enclosing of common land, formerly used by peasants, for private use in the twelfth to seventeenth centuries in England

70 'Hawkins': Sir John (1532–95), British mariner who fought with Drake against the Spanish Armada, 1588

71 'Morgan-mouthed': Sir Henry Morgan (1635–88), British buccaneer and leader of the Barbados pirates, was known for his strong language.

75 'Frobisher': Sir Martin (1535?–94), English mariner, associated with Sir Francis Drake in the defeat of the Spanish Armada

77 'Marne': Marne River in France, site of two major battles in World War I

81 'Charters': In England a charter is an instrument granted by the Crown and conferring certain privileges or immunities. Magna Carta (Great Charter), granted by King John at Runnymede in 1215, established the fundamental principles of English law.

84 'Royal Yacht squadrons': Royal Yacht Squadron, Cowes, Isle of Wight, and any other yachting group granted the royal appointment

85 *'wave-line theory'*: theory held by some naval architects that a certain type of hull facilitates movement through the waves

87 *'Genesta* and the *Galatea'*: British yachts, famous on both sides of the Atlantic. The *Galatea*, a large cutter, raced for the America's Cup in 1865. The *Genesta* lost her bowsprit in a race for General Paine's Cup in 1885.

88 'racing spinnakers': large three-cornered sails carried by racing yachts and used in running before the wind

90 'Cutters': small single-masted sailing vessels

91 'press balloon-jibs': triangular staysail that balloons out in a press (strong push) of wind

99 'luggers': small ships with four-cornered sails set fore and aft

101 'Deal': port on the east coast of Kent

102 'Smacks': small one-masted vessels often used for fishing

102 'Grimsby': port on the coast of Lincolnshire, and England's chief fishing port

103 'Yawls': two-masted fore and aft sailing boats, with a mizzenmast stepped abaft the rudder post

105 'spritsail-rigged with jigger booms': A spritsail is a sail extended by a sprit (a small boom that crosses the fore and aft sail diagonally from the mast to the upper hindmost corner of the sail, which it extends and elevates). A boom is a spar run out to extend the foot of a sail. A jigger boom is one fitted with a jigger, which is a type of rigging.

106 'Bluff-blowed billyboys': billyboy, or river barge, presenting a broad flattened front; echoes phrase from Trelawney's book (l. 115)

106 'wherries': light shallow rowboats

108 'scoots' (or 'scouts'): flat-bottomed boats used in the river trade of Holland

108 'bawleys' (or bauleys'): south coast of England dialect word for small fishing smacks

114 'Collingwood': Admiral Cuthbert Lord Collingwood, 1750–1810, second in command under Admiral Lord Nelson at Trafalgar

115 'Trelawny': Edward John Trelawny, 1792–1881, English sailor and adventurer, author of *Recollections of the Last Days of Shelley and Byron*, 1858

115 'Grenville': Sir Richard Grenville, ?1541–91. Off Flores in the Azores in 1591 he commanded the British ship *Revenge*, which battled alone against a number of Spanish ships. He was captured

and died of his wounds. The battle inspired Tennyson's poem, 'The "Revenge".'
133 'Boodles': famous club in London
140 'Harrow': English public school, founded 1541
172 'mesen': variant of 'myself'
174 'Dardanelles': strait between Europe and Asiatic Turkey, scene of an Allied defeat in World War I
179 'Bapaume': in Northern France, scene of fighting in World War I
185 'Armenteers': British slang name for Armentières, northern France, scene of fighting in World War I
192 '"Yde Park"': Cockney for Hyde Park, London
201 'costermonger': seller of fruit and other food from a barrow in the street
201 'Petticoat Lane': street in London
206 'Ilissus': river in ancient Greece, flowing east and south of Athens
216 'the Rand': region of Transvaal in South Africa where a third of the world's gold is produced
219 'the single Mole': pier at Dunkirk
252 'Tamburlaine' (or 'Tamerlane'): Tartar, 1336?–1405, who conquered vast parts of Asia and India
288 'Stukas': German dive bombers
308 'leadlines': lines with lead attached to measure the depth of the water
353 'The peace that passes understanding': See Philippians 4:7.
359 'Medway': the Medway river in Kent

Heydrich
Title: Reinhard Heydrich (1904–42) was a German Nazi official and chief deputy to Heinrich Himmler. As Nazi 'protector' of Czechoslovakia he was assassinated by Czech patriots on 27 May 1942.
20 'Lidice': a village in Czechoslovakia razed by the Germans on 10 June 1942 in retaliation for the assassination of Heydrich

The Truant
For Pratt's summary of the poem's theme, see *OHLP* 132–3.
See also W.H.D. Rowse's introduction to and translation of *Lucretius: De Rerum Natura* (Cambridge, MA: Harvard University Press, and London: William Heinemann 1924, 3rd ed., 1966) and T.H. Huxley and Julian Huxley, *Evolution and Ethics 1893–1943* (London: Pilot Press 1947) 68. Compare notes to *The Iron Door*.

1 'Panjandrum': See Brian Traherne, 'A Possible Source for "The Truant"' *Canadian Poetry* 7 (1980) 73–9, where he argues that the concept of the truant and the name Panjandrum may well be derived from the British comic strip 'The Noah Family.'

20–9 'Pedigree': compare discussion of the elements of man in Lord Byron's *Manfred* I, ii, 39–44

43 'thaumaturge': worker of miracles

54 'coprophagite': eater of dung

58 'troglodyte': prehistoric caveman

107 'anserine': stupid as a goose

127–8 'your rings / Of *pure and endless light*': See Henry Vaughan's 'The World.'

143 'eolith': stone tool from the earliest age of man

150 'caves of death': See Byron's *Manfred* II.ii.80.

155 'Lucretian atoms': See *De Rerum Natura*.

159 'chaos and Old Night': See John Milton, *Paradise Lost*.

180 'cat-and-truncheon bastinades': 'cat' is short for 'cat-o'-nine-tails,' a rope whip with nine knotted lashes, once used for flogging. A 'bastinade' is a blow with a stick or whip, especially on the soles of the feet.

The Stoics

For Pratt's comment on this poem, see *OHLP* 133.

5 'pyrites': sulphide of iron, sometimes called 'fool's gold' because it is mistaken for gold

9 '*gravitas*': Latin for gravity or sober dignity

11 'Aurelius': Marcus Aurelius Antoninus, 121–80, a Roman emperor and disciple of the Stoics (l. 27 below). Stoicism was a branch of Greek philosophy founded about 308 B.C. Of this poem Northrop Frye writes: 'the stoic is the most impressive example of a man who tries to find some kind of moral order behind nature, and so tries to keep neutral in the struggle of human heroism and natural indifference: a neutrality always dubious and in the twentieth century entirely impossible.' (*Silence in the Sea*, The Pratt Lecture, St John's, Memorial University of Newfoundland, 1969)

23 'panzers': German word for 'armour,' used in World War II to describe armoured divisions. The most important panzer vehicle was the tank, hence Pratt's reference to 'the traction of the panzers.'

Father Time

22 'gneiss': layered rock of quartz, feldspar, and mica

40 'SEBASTOPOL': The Black Sea port of Sebastopol resisted British, French, and Turkish forces for eleven months during the Crimean War and resisted German forces for eight months during World War II. It fell on 3 July 1942, and was recaptured in May 1944.

Autopsy on a Sadist

Subtitle: 'after Lidice' suggests the sadist was modelled after Reinhard Heydrich. See notes to 'Heydrich.'

Niemoeller

Title: Martin Niemoeller (1892–1984), a German Protestant churchman, was imprisoned in 1938 for his anti-Hitler views, and was liberated by the Allies in 1945.

6 'Essen': centre of the German steel industry of the Ruhr, and site of the Krupp armament works

8 'Procurator': officer or attorney. See Matthew 26:57ff.

Der Fuehrer's Pot-Pourri

17 'Drug Tito': Comrade Tito (1892–1980). Born Josip Broz, Tito led the Yugoslavian partisans' resistance to the Germans during World War II. He became head of state in 1943 and was Yugoslavia's first elected president from 1953 to 1980.

17 'Mikhailovitch': Dragoljub Mihajlovic (1893–1946), leader of a rival underground resistance movement in Yugoslavia during World War II and committed to restoring the Serbian dynasty. Captured in 1946 by Tito's partisans, Mihajlovic was sentenced to death by hanging.

28 'Die Wacht am Rhein': 'The Watch on the Rhine,' German national song

29 '"Allons enfants de la patrie"': first line of 'La Marseillaise'

30 'Horst Wessel melody': Horst Wessel (1907–30), a German student composer and member of the Nazi party, wrote the song known as 'Horst-Wessel-Lied,' which with 'Deutschland ueber Alles' was accepted as a national song of the Nazi ss

31–2 '"Sprung from the soil ... Liberty"': from the Greek national anthem

37–8 '"I'm William ... in my veins"': from 'Wilhelmus von Nassouwe,' The Netherlands national anthem

39–40 '"King Christian stood ... swinging fast"': from 'Kong Kristian,' Danish national anthem

42 'O Tannenbaum': 'O Fir Tree,' German Christmas song

43 'O Lebensraum': 'O Living Space.' Lebensraum was a slogan adopted by Hitler from the German geographer Friedrich Ratzel (1844–1904). Pratt is obviously punning here on Liszt's Liebenstraum.

47 '"The waters ... homes"': from Norway's national anthem

49 'Starzynski': Stefan Starzynski (1893–1940), mayor of Warsaw from 1937 to 1939. For his stand against the German invasion he became known as 'stubborn Stefan.' After the fall of his city, he was captured by the Germans and executed at Dachau in 1940.

50 'Benes': Eduard Benes (1887–1948), president of Czechoslovakia, 1935–8 and 1945–8. Exiled after the Munich Pact, he headed the Czech provisional government in London during the war. Re-elected following the war, he resigned after the Communist coup in 1948.

53 '"But we shall be free"': from the Czech national song

54 'rota': round

55–8 '"We shall not leave ... a fortress be"': from a Polish national song

64 'Alberich': King of the Dwarfs in the Nibelungenleid. In Wagner's Ring he is the ugly gnome who steals the Rheingold

67 'Chaliapin': Fyodor Ivanovic Chaliapin (1873–1938), renowned Russian basso, known particularly for his role as Boris Godunov in the Modest Moussorgsky opera

Still Life

2 'little breezes dusk and shiver': from Tennyson's 'The Lady of Shalott,' l. 11

30 'that Tunisian glow': refers to the fighting in Tunis during the North African campaign in World War II

31 'Carthaginian fire': Carthage was destroyed by the Romans in 146 B.C.

41 'Theocritean': of Theocritus, Greek pastoral poet of the third century B.C.

They Are Returning

Poem commissioned by Maclean's Magazine in honour of the returning Canadian servicemen

35 'Quisling': term created in World War II to mean a traitor or collaborator. Vidkun Quisling became head of the puppet government of Norway after the German invasion of 1940.

52 'Maidanek': town in Poland, site of Jewish labour camp in World War II

52 'Lidice': See 'Heydrich,' l. 20.

68 'Moloch': god of the Ammonites, who sacrificed children to him. Thus, any influence which demands sacrifice of what we hold most dear. See 2 Kings 23:10 and Milton, *Paradise Lost* 1, 392–8.

117 'the *mould*': penicillin

124 '*Athenia*': British passenger ship sunk by a German U-boat 3 September 1939

124 'Rotterdam': heavily bombed by the Germans in their invasion of Holland in World War II

140 'Vimy ... Passchendaele': sites of major battles in World War I

148 'Carentan': ancient town in the canton of La Manche in Normandy

148 'Saint Lô': town in Normandy almost completely destroyed by Allied bombings in World War II. It was taken by U.S. forces in June 1944.

148 'Rouen': ancient port in Normandy, part of which was completely destroyed in World War II

148 'Crécy': ancient town in Normandy, site of the battle between the French and the English in 1346

156–9 'an Abbey nave ... the Norman's grave': Abbeye aux Hommes in Caen, site of William the Conqueror's tomb

162 'Hannibal's descent': Hannibal (247–c182 B.C.), Carthaginian general who descended into Italy to invade in 217 B.C.

163 'the Arno': river in northern Italy, scene of fighting in World War II

163 'Upper Tiber': river flowing into the Tyrrhenian Sea on Italy's west coast

164 'Arezzo': in Italy, south of Rome

164 'Cassino': The Benedictine abbey of Monte Cassino, southeast of Rome, was destroyed by Allied air attack on 14 February 1944, as it was an important observation post for the Germans. But the German defenders held the ruins until 18 May 1944, when Polish forces occupied the hill.

169 'Trasimeno': large lake in northern Italy

175 '*Swansea*': HMCS Swansea, frigate

175 '*Chilliwack*': HMCS *Chilliwack*, a corvette

176 'the *Skeena-Athabascan*' (usual spelling 'Athabaskan'): HMCS Skeena, destroyer sunk by torpedo 26 April 1944, and HMCS *Athabaskan*, also a destroyer, were both convoy escorts on the Atlantic.

184 'Typhoon rocket-fire': The Hawker Typhoon was a British fighter-bomber, late models of which each carried eight rockets.

185 'panthers at Esquay': The Panther was a German medium-heavy tank. Esquay, short for Esquay-sur-Seulles, is a small town near Le Havre, a French port on the English Channel.

187 'Messerschmitts': various series of German fighter planes, of which the ME109 was produced in greater numbers than was any other warplane in World War II

189 'Malta': Malta was under such heavy and frequent bombardment by German aircraft that King George VI awarded the George Cross, Britain's highest decoration for civilian valour, to 'the island and people of Malta.'

191 'the artery of Kiel': The Germans built submarines at the Baltic port of Kiel. The 'artery' was the Kaiser Wilhelm Canal, which ends at Kiel.

198 'Appenines': principal mountain range of Italy

202 'Irrawady' (usual spelling 'Irrawaddy'): chief river in Burma

203 'Iroquois': HMCS Iroquois, destroyer. Because the ship served as a convoy escort on the run to Russia's northern port of Murmansk, it encountered the extreme cold of 'the North air' mentioned in this line.

204 'Scharnhorst's greetings': The German light battle cruiser Scharnhorst exchanged 'Greetings' in the form of gunfire with Canadians operating motor torpedo boats (MTB's) in the English Channel in 1942. The Scharnhorst was sunk on 26 December 1943.

208 'Calabrian beaches': Calabria is the southernmost province of Italy.

212 'Ortona': Italian port on the Adriatic. In August 1943, Canadian troops participating in the assault on Italy. They entered Ortona at the end of that year.

213 'Scheldt': The estuary of the Scheldt River in Belgium gave access to Antwerp, 55 miles inland. In 1944, Allied troops captured Antwerp from the Germans, but then had to clear the enemy from the banks of the Scheldt estuary. This was accomplished after fierce fighting in which the Allies, mainly Canadians, suffered 13,000 casualties.

215 'Haida': HMCS Haida, destroyer

261 'Odon,' 'Orne': French rivers, scenes of fighting in the invasion of Normandy

267 'Carpiquet': town west of Caen in Normandy and scene of fighting in the summer of 1944

287 'Foggia': capital of the Italian province of that name
287 'Ancona': northern Italian port on the Adriatic
288 'Ceprano': in Italy, south of Rome
288 'Capua': in Italy, south of Rome
291 'Dieppe': French port on the English Channel. Allied forces, mainly
Canadian, raided Dieppe on 19 August 1942. Three-quarters of
the 5,100 Canadians were killed or wounded.
291 'Authie': river in Flanders, on the boundary between France and
Belgium, that empties into the North Sea
291 'Falaise': city in Normandy. The Argentan-Falaise Gap was the gap
between the Canadian and American forces in France in August 1944.
292 'Kleve,' 'Emmerich': towns close to one another in West Germany
292 'Groningen': Dutch city in the province of that name
293-7 A comparison of the 'music' of the returning servicemen's deeds
to great music. 'Eroicas' suggest Beethoven's Eroica symphony; this
is apt, as 'eroica' is the feminine form of the Italian word 'eroico,'
meaning 'heroic.' 'Chorals' may refer to Beethoven's Choral sym-
phony, 'Passions' perhaps to J.S. Bach's Passion of St Matthew,
and 'Pathétiques' to the Pathétique of either Beethoven or
Tchaikovsky.

Behind the Log

For four accounts of the background and genesis of the poem, see *OHLP*
133–44.
105 'Fisher': British Admiral Sir John Fisher (1841–1920)
106 'Jellico': John Rushworth, 1st Earl (1859–1935), Commander in Chief
of the British fleet in World War I
108 'Coronel': port on the Pacific Ocean, site of a naval battle in 1914 in
which the British were defeated
132–3 'Rear Admiral Sir Francis Horatio Trelawney-Camperdown': See
OHLP 136: 'The names of the ships are authentic but the personal
names are fictitious.'
201 'da da dit dit dit': dash-dash-dot-dot-dot, the number 2 in the Morse
Code
299 'I Kan ikke ...': Translated from the Norwegian, this means 'I
cannot understand a damned word. / How in hell do they think
I can / get eight knots out of my old washtub. / I haven't had a full
crew for two years. / The devil knows what I'm going / to do. You
can all go to hell.'

315–17 'A Danish Captain ...': The Danish captain helps the Norwegian with language because Danish and Norwegian are very similar. In 316–23 the words requiring translation are *'ikke'*: not; 'vaskelbalja': washtub; *'mannskap'*: crew.

385 *'Skeena'*: HMCS Skeena, destroyer

386 *'Kenogami,' 'Orillia,' 'Alberni'*: three Royal Canadian Navy ships, all corvettes

409 'Captain of the Heads': The heads are the ship's toilets.

415 'Newfie-Crowsnest screech': Screech is overproof rum. The Crowsnest was the celebrated RCN Officers' Club in St John's, Newfoundland.

424 'Diet of Worms': meeting at Worms, Germany, of the Diet, meaning representatives of the fifteenth- and sixteenth-century German Empire. The most famous in 1521 heard Martin Luther end his defence of his position with the words 'Here I stand. I cannot do otherwise. God help me. Amen.'

462 'Asdic': device giving the range and bearing of a metallic object under water

487 'Helmholtz': Hermann von Helmholtz (1821–94), German scientist noted for his theory about the conservation of energy and for his work on nerve cells

487 'Doppler': Christian Doppler, nineteenth-century Czech scientist, who discovered the Doppler Principle that motion changes the refrangibility of light

488 'Rayleigh': John William, Lord Rayleigh, nineteenth-century English physicist

489 'Langevin': Paul Langevin (1872–1946), French mathematician who developed the Langevin theory of paramagnetism

489 'Fresnel': Augustin Jean Fresnel (1788–1827), French physicist and pioneer in optical theory

490 'Pindarics': odes in the style of Pindar (522–442 B.C.), Greek lyric poet

490 'Laplace': Pierre Simon, Marquis de Laplace (1749–1829), great French mathematician and astronomer

492 'Robert Boyle': the Honourable Robert Boyle (1627–91), Irish physicist, and a founder of modern chemistry

512 *'cordon sanitaire'*: French for 'sanitary cordon.' Russia's tsarist government collapsed in 1917 and the Bolsheviks took over. After World War II the Allies hoped the small nation states of Eastern

Europe would provide a 'cordon sanitaire' against the spread of Communism in Europe.

581 'green four-o': starboard forty degrees

582 'The ping-g-g with its death's head identity': echo from the asdic, which gives the range and bearing of a metallic object underwater – such as a submarine

587 'E.R.A.': engine room artificer

603 'Krupp's': German steel manufacturers

694 'Tirpitz': Alfred von Tirpitz (1849–1930), German admiral who began the construction of submarines in World War I

718 'bruinine': an invented word meaning 'bruinlike' or 'bearlike.' 'Bruin' was the name given the bear in the medieval English beast-fable, Reynard the Fox.

723 'herrenvolk': master race

811 'patterns': patterns of depth charges dropped by the escorting ships

816 'O.D.': ordinary seaman

816 'middle watch': midnight to four A.M.

879 'Aeneas': hero of Virgil's epic, The Aeneid, who fought against the Greeks in the Trojan war

903 'the Peggy': seaman on lookout duty, often called upon to do odd jobs in a watch

1119 Alamein': The 23–4 October 1942 Battle of Alamein in North Africa saw the British 8th Army penetrating the German commander Rommel's positions, and on 3 November the Germans started to retreat westward.

1119 'Normandy': The landings for the D-Day invasion of France were in Normandy.

Summit Meetings

7 'Caesar aut nihil': (L.) 'Caesar or nothing.' This was a motto used by Cesare Borgia (1475–1507), a Spanish noble who became Pope Alexander VI.

22 'summum': (L.) 'chief' or 'supreme'

Newfoundland Calling

20 'Matthew': name of the small ship in which John Cabot sailed in 1497 from Bristol to Canada's east coast. He landed on 24 June, but it is not established if he made his first landfall in Labrador, Newfoundland, or on Cape Breton Island.

28 'Avalonian': of the Avalon Peninsula, Newfoundland
56 'Sir Humphrey Gilbert': English seaman (1539–83) who took possession of Newfoundland for Queen Elizabeth I in 1583
56 'Captain George': Captain George Vancouver (1758–98), British navigator who explored the northwest coast of North America in 1791–2

Newfoundland Seamen
5 'Grenfell': Sir Wilfred Grenfell (1865–1940), English medical missionary who served in Labrador and Newfoundland for forty years
5 'Bartlett': Robert Abram Bartlett (1875–1965), arctic explorer, native of Newfoundland
23–4 'A rescue squad ... healing hands': Sir Frederick Banting (1891–1941), co-discoverer of insulin, and a good friend of Pratt, died in Newfoundland when the plane on which he was travelling to Britain crashed near Gander.

The Last Watch
7 'codein dots': Codein is a drug that contracts the pupils of the eyes.

Myth and Fact
26 'Cyclopean': Cyclops was a legendary giant with only one eye, in the centre of his forehead.

The Deed
For Pratt's comments on this poem, see *OHLP* 145.

Magic in Everything
For Pratt's comments on this poem, see *OHLP* 49.

Towards the Last Spike
For Pratt's accounts of the poem's genesis and intention, see *OHLP* 145–53.
40 'Thomas': See John 20:25ff.
75 'fell of Grampian rams': hide of rams in the Grampians, Scottish mountains
82 'Bannockburn': In the battle of Bannockburn, Scotland, on 24 June 1314, the Scots under Robert Bruce defeated the English forces of Edward II.

83 'Culloden': On 16 April 1746, England's Duke of Cumberland defeated the Scots under Prince Charles Edward Stuart at Culloden, Scotland.

83 'the warnings of Lochiel': See Thomas Campbell's 'Lochiel's Warning.' The hero of the poem is Donald Cameron, 'the gentle Lochiel,' who, against his better judgment, supported Prince Charles Edward Stuart at Culloden.

88 'Scots wha hae': See the 1793 poem 'Scots, Wha Hae' by Robert Burns. 'Wallace' is Sir William Wallace, c1272–1305, Scottish warrior in wars against the English.

89 'Angus': Richard B. Angus (1836–1922), banker and financier. A former general manager of the Bank of Montreal, he helped to form the Canadian Pacific Railroad syndicate in 1880 and remained a director until his death.

90 'Fleming': Sir Sandford Fleming (1827–1915), appointed chief engineer to the CPR in 1871

91 'Hector': Sir James Hector (1834–1907), geologist, discoverer, in 1857, of the Kicking Horse Pass

91 'Dawson': Simon James Dawson (1820–1902), road builder, commissioned in 1868 to build a corduroy road between Lake of the Woods and the Red River, which became known as the Dawson Route

92 '"Cromarty" Ross': James Ross (1843–1913), engineer born in Cromarty, Scotland. In 1883 he took charge of the construction of the CPR west of Winnipeg.

92 'Beatty': Henry Beatty (1834–1914), a Scot who in 1882 resigned as manager of the Northwest Transportation Company to take charge of a Great Lakes steamship line being organized by the CPR.

93 'Bruce': James Bruce, 8th Earl of Elgin (1811–63), Governor-General of Canada from 1847 to 1854

93 'Allan': Sir Hugh Allan (1810–82), financier who with the backing of American financiers founded the Canadian Pacific Railway Company in 1871, of which he was president from 1872 to 1873, when the Pacific Scandal broke in the House of Commons

93 'Galt': Sir Alexander Tilloch Galt (1817–93), first minister of finance in the new Dominion, a man with strong interests in the Grand Trunk Railroad

93 'Douglas': Sir James Douglas (1803–77), the 'Father of British Columbia,' first governor of the province from 1858 to 1863

94 'Stephen': Sir George Stephen (1829–1921), president of the CPR
1881–8. A Montreal businessman, president of the Bank of Montreal,
he, along with Richard Angus and Donald Alexander Smith,
formed the syndicate that organized the CPR in 1880.

94 'Smith': Sir Donald Alexander Smith, Lord Strathcona (1820–1914),
commissioner of the Hudson's Bay Company 1870–4. As indepen-
dent MP for Selkirk, 1871–88, he voted against Macdonald in the
debate over the Pacific Scandal. As a member of the syndicate he
gave crucial support to the CPR in 1880 and drove the last spike in
1885.

100 'Sir John A.': Sir John A. Macdonald (1815–91), first Prime Minister
of Canada

112 bull's beef': bully beef, which is canned beef

131 'Tupper': Sir Charles Tupper (1821–1915), premier of Nova Scotia
1864–67, a Father of Confederation, MP 1867–84. As Minister of
Railways and Canals, 1879–84, he introduced the bill that gave the
CPR its charter in 1881.

131 'Cartier': Sir George Etienne Cartier (1814–73), Joint Premier of
United Canada 1857–62 and Father of Confederation, one of
Macdonald's chief supporters in building the CPR

151–4 'Hudson ... McClintock of *The Search*': a roll-call of Arctic
explorers, which includes Henry Hudson (?–1611), John Davis
(c1550–1605), William Baffin (c1584–1622), Sir Martin Frobisher
(c1535–94), Sir John Franklin (1786–1847), Sir James Clark Ross
(1800–62), Sir William Edward Parry (1790–1855), Sir Henry Kellett
(1806–75), Robert John Le Mesurier McLure (1807–73), and Sir
Frederick McClintock (1819–1907)

159 'Dead March': from Handel's sacred oratorio *Saul*, c1739. See 2
Samuel 1:17ff.

171 'Capella': one of the brightest three stars in the northern hemisphere

172 'Cassiopeia': a constellation

174 'Aries,' 'Cygnus': constellations

183 'Selkirk': Lord Selkirk's Red River Colony, known also as the Selkirk
Settlement, was settled by Scottish immigrants in 1812.

198 'the massacre at Seven Oaks': near Winnipeg, 19 June 1816, in
which the Métis killed Robert Semple, the governor of the Red River
Colony, and twenty of his men

199 'Pemmican War': the conflict between the Northwest Company and
the Red River settlers. Pemmican was dried meat, together with

melted fat and dried fruits, pounded into a paste and made into cakes. It was originally a native Indian food.

228 'Cazadero,' 'Mendecino' (usual spelling 'Mendocino'): California towns

230 'Santa Rosa,' 'Santa Monica': California towns

234 ' "Rio de nuestra senora de buena guia"': Spanish for 'river of our lady of safe conduct'

239 'San Diego': short for San Diego de Alcala, a Spanish saint after whom San Diego, CA is named.

257 'Disraeli': Sir John A. Macdonald resembled Benjamin Disraeli, Earl of Beaconsfield (1804–81), prime minister of England in 1868 and 1874–80

Notes following 264 'Moberly': Walter Moberly (1832–1915), engineer, who in 1853 sought a route through BC for a transcontinental railway and in 1865 discovered Eagle Pass. In 1870 he took charge of mountain surveys for the CPR. 'Huntington': Lucius Huntington, Liberal MP

264 'Blake': Edward Blake (1833–1912) was premier of Ontario 1871–2. He became federal Liberal party leader in 1880, being succeeded by Laurier in 1887.

303 'Knights of Malta': Originally known as Knights Hospitallers, they were organized in the 11th century to aid Christian pilgrims in Palestine.

330 'damning correspondence': the correspondence between Sir Hugh Allan of Montreal and George W. McMullen of Chicago. McMullen and his Chicago group wanted a large part of the CPR to be in the U.S. and controlled by Northern Pacific. Sir Hugh wanted to run the line and profit from it.

331 'That Montreal-Chicago understanding': In 1871 Sir Hugh Allan signed an agreement with the Chicago group that the line would run from below Sault Ste Marie, Ontario, through the U.S. and thence up to Winnipeg.

After 351 'Mackenzie': Alexander Mackenzie (1822–92), Liberal prime minister, 1873–8

368 'loaves and fishes': See Luke 9:16ff.

370 'Where are the multitudes ...': See Luke 9:12ff.

419 'Emerson': in southern Manitoba, just above the U.S. border

444 'the Pass had its ambiguous meaning': double pun on the pass through Rockies and the 'pass' of legislation through the House

483 'coureur-de-bois': literally, 'wood runner,' an unlicensed fur trader and explorer during the French regime in Canada

487 'the title of their wings': In 1865 Walter Moberly saw eagles flying through a pass in the Gold Range of the Rockies, so named it Eagle Pass.

497 'Onderdonk': Andrew Onderdonk (1848–1905), engineer and contractor, who received from the Canadian government in 1879 the contract to build the railway through the Thompson and Fraser canyons. His headquarters for the project was in Yale, BC.

543 'Chatham': William Pitt, first Earl of Chatham (1708–78)

544 'Burke': Edmund Burke (1729–97), leader of the Whig party in England in the eighteenth century, an opponent of William Pitt and his Tory government's policy on the American colonies

552 'from sea to sea': See Zachariah 9:10.

560 'tessellated': arranged in a mosaic or chequered pattern

576 'Fundy Tide': the Bay of Fundy, an Atlantic inlet between New Brunswick and Maine on the west and Nova Scotia on the east. In its upper reaches the tides rise as much as 70 feet from low water to high.

After 580 'Pope': John Henry Pope, Macdonald's minister of agriculture

After 580 'McIntyre': Duncan McIntyre, Montreal financier and builder of the Canadian Central Railway

588–90 'when a king … His Royal Charter': charter granted to the Hudson's Bay Company on 2 May 1670. The 'king' was Charles II.

632 'Paracelsus': alternate name for Phillipus von Hohenheim (1493–1541), Swiss physician and alchemist

636 'rat-skins': muskrat pelts

647 'Tadoussac': in Quebec, near the St Lawrence

647 'Anticosti': Quebec island in the Gulf of St Lawrence

662 'Kitson': Norman Wolfred Kitson (1814–88), a fur-trader who developed the line of Red River steamers in the 1860s and later became an associate of James Hill in railway building

663 'Jim Hill': James Jerome Hill (1838–1916), railway builder

672 'Kennedy': Sir John Kennedy (1838–1921), chief engineer of the Great Western railway system, president of the U.S. Great Northern railway 1893–1907, member of the board of the CPR 1880–3.

673 'Duncan McIntyre': a native of Scotland who came to Canada in 1849. A financier and railway builder, owner of the Canada

Central line, he was one of the signatories to the preliminary agreement of 14 September 1880, for construction of the CPR.

After 683 'William Cornelius Van Horne': Van Horne (1843–1915) was appointed general manager of the CPR in 1882, was vice-president in 1884, president 1888–99, and chairman 1890–1910.

691 'Crinoids': Crinoid means 'lily-shaped' and is a term applied to fossilized sea-urchins.

691 'Perry': Albert Perry, a mountaineer who assisted Walter Moberly and was credited by him with discovering in 1866 the pass later explored by and named after Major Rogers

732 'Zuyder Zee' (usual spelling 'Zuider Zee'): Dutch for 'Southern Sea,' a former shallow inlet of the North Sea now divided by a dam

733 'Oak Lake': Manitoba town west of Brandon

773 'Rogers': Major A.B., explorer of Rogers Pass in 1881

826 'Shaughnessy': Thomas George, first Baron Shaughnessy (1853–1923), president of the CPR, 1899–1918). Having joined the company as a purchasing agent in 1882, he was credited with maintaining the flow of supplies during the construction period.

839 'fish-plates': A fish-plate is a steel plate joining two railway rails. It is secured to the sides of each rail to connect them end to end.

989 'molochs': Australian thorn-lizards

989–90 'Stay on the shore … climb the rigging': See the last four lines of the ballad 'The Wreck of the "Julie Plante",' by W.H. Drummond.

1052 'stegosaurs': huge dinosaurs

1070 'Douglases': Douglas firs

After 1102 'Skuzzy': steamboat named after a stream draining into the Fraser which served on the Fraser between Lytton and Boston Bar

1215 'diabase': dark igneous rock

1268 'bladder-wort': type of water plant with small bags, filled with air, on its roots and stems

1290 'The lady's face was flushed': Contemporary political cartoons identified the province of British Columbia as a reluctant lady and Sir John A. Macdonald as her eager suitor.

1329 'brachiapods' (usual spelling 'brachiopods)': (L.), 'arm-footed,' two-shelled water creatures are so-called because each has two spirally coiled arms around its mouth

1334 'trilobite': fossilized crustacean

1352 'mesozoic': of the geological era belonging to the age of reptiles

1404 'Riel': Louis Riel (1844–85), Métis leader of the Red River Resistance in 1870 and of the Riel Rebellion in 1885. Riel was hanged in 1885.

1409 'Scott': Irish immigrant shot by Riel's men when he attacked some of them and threatened to kill Riel

1411 'that young, tall, bilingual advocate': Sir Wilfrid Laurier, later Prime Minister of Canada

After 1483 'Revelstoke ... Baring': Lord Revelstoke, British peer, after whom Revelstoke, BC was named to honour him for his banking house, Baring's, help in financing the CPR

1485 'Athanasian': of Athanasius (c296–373), who championed the authorized Christian faith against all other interpretations, thus earning the proverb 'Athanasius contra mundum' ('Athanasius against the world')

1490 'shad-flies': flies, especially mayflies, that appear when the fish, shad, common on the Atlantic coast, are running

1507 'sparables': small, headless, wedge-shaped iron nails used in the soles and heels of boots and shoes

1593 'Flodden': In the battle of Flodden in Northumberland, 9 September 1513, English soldiers defeated James IV of Scotland's forces.

1604 'Egan': John M. Egan, General Superintendent of the CPR's western division in 1885

1615 'Cambie': Henry I. Cambie, a government engineer engaged in building the CPR

1605 'Marcus Smith': (1815–1905), engineer-in-chief of the CPR during the absence of Sandford Fleming, 1876–8

1605 'Harris of Boston': George R. Harris, a director of the CPR

1608 'Dug McKenzie': Dugald McKenzie, locomotive engineer

1608 'John H. McTavish': land commissioner, among those present at the ceremony on 26 September 1885

Appendix A: Miscellaneous Poems

E.J. Pratt published, during his lifetime, a number of occasional poems, in such sources as *World Friends* and *The Missionary Monthly*, which he clearly did not intend as part of his serious corpus. Still others, which existed in manuscript (and which Pratt never intended to publish), were published posthumously by the *Tamarack Review* in 1966. These, which we have been reluctant to include in the text of his definitive work, are offered here in the interest of a complete text.

That Night There Came to Bethlehem

That night there came to Bethlehem
Three wise men from afar,
And found the manger where He lay
Under the Eastern Star.
No flickering lamp or candle played
Its light upon the bed;
A far more lovely radiance cast
Its glory on his head.

Though sheep and cattle were inside,
Those three wise men knelt down
In adoration to a king
Who wore no earthly crown;
And out of their heart's store they gave
A love a thousand-fold
More rich than what they offered there
In incense or in gold.

10

World Friends, December 1930

January the First

My deep resolve, this New Year's Day,
As written on a page of life,
Will be with honest heart to pray
The world be cleansed of hate and strife.

Nor shall my resolution end
In empty phrases as the air –
The stranger shall become my friend,
Not less in deed than in my prayer.

There shall be neither east nor west,
Nor mountain range, nor ocean tide,   10
Where there is hunger in the breast
For that which my hands may provide.

To human need I pledge my part
This New Year's Day in loyal pact –
Lord, may the motive of my heart
Find no betrayal in the act.   *World Friends*, January 1932

Thanksgiving

Father of life that cometh from the sun
    And from the rain,
Giver of every perfect gift enwrought
    With loss and gain,
Lord of the spring-time – this we humbly ask,
Our hands be faithful to the sowing task.

Lord of the summer when with warmth and light
    The days are long,
Sustain the labourer's will, and may his faith
    Be ever strong.   10
That, with the Master's measure, shall the yield
Reward the honest tillage of the field.

Lord of the autumn, when the soul's ripe grain
  Is garnered in,
And Christ's great heart rejoices as the world
  Puts by its sin,
Into thy love shall all thy people come
With glad thanksgiving at the harvest home.

The Missionary Monthly, October 1936

Mother and Child

'We haven't a room, we haven't a bed,
The inn is full' – the keeper said.
In Bethlehem no place at all,
But a manger of straw in a cattle stall.
Not even a ray from a candle-light
To pierce the darkness of the night;
But from that manger and that stall
The world has reared a palace hall,
And from the darkness of that night
The glory of celestial light.   10
Out of the morning of that birth
The loneliest mother of the earth,
The woman of the Shadowed Face,
Of all the mothers of our race
Became the most exalted one
That human eyes have looked upon.
And the child from that lowly town
Was destined for a finer crown
Than any monarch might command
From pearls and stones of sea and land.   *World Friends*, December 1936

The Manger Under the Star

Of all the Father's children
The lowliest ever born
Was Jesus, son of Mary
On that first Christmas morn.

In a Judean stable
Far from the world's highway,
Companioned by the oxen,
And cradled in the hay!

And yet before that manger
The wisest of the earth
Came with their royal presents
To celebrate His birth;

While voices in the starlight
Rang out in glad acclaim
Hosannas in the highest
And glory to His name.

World Friends, December 1938

10

The Nativity

Around this scene our race tried to surpass
The angels in their praise, tying our tongue
To anthems, building language to amass
Our hopes and creeds: bells by the millions swung
Where statues stood and master paintings hung
And arts were found and lost in the stained glass.

With all things bright and lovely on this earth
And in the skies we made his diadem,
And then repented for the lack of worth
Within the heart-fire of each precious gem
To pay our tribute there at Bethlehem,
Hailing His coronation from His birth.

10

As Morning Star, as Sun, as King – to those
Emblems of light and honour to acclaim Him
We added the Good Shepherd to enclose
Us in His fold: still further did we name Him
By the most fragrant titles that became Him –
The Valley Lily and Judean Rose.

From crib to cross, from that three days' decrease
Of mortal breath within a mortal shrine   20
To that ascending hour of His release
We have forgotten much, but let this line
Of song – 'for He shall have dominion' – shine
On our memorial flags, O Prince of Peace!

No other name in the prophetic scroll
Carries such music to the world today.
For this, two thousand years ago, the whole
Creation groaned: for this the peoples pray.
To send this score on its triumphant way
Is still the utmost travail of his soul.
               Canadian Home Journal, December 1949

Lines on the Occasion of Her Majesty's Visit to Canada, 1959

Landfall ahead! Throughout four centuries
From deck and crow's-nest, navigators heard
That call, and sailing westward reached St John's.
So now a giant plane comes to rest on Torbay's earth
Bright with the magic omen of nature's welcome.
The fog had lifted suddenly; the clouds
Dispersed, while a shaft of sunlight turned to silver
The wings and body of the burnished sea-bird,
And Heart's Delight and Heart's Content
Were Newfoundland's once more.   10
Then through the ancient motherlands of steadfast men
The Maritimes and the princely Island
And so to Joan of Arc's sweet Canadian earth
Where old proud memories linger
And ancient faith shines forth undimmed,
Upon the St Lawrence through the locks and lakes
Each mile enshrined a human saga writ
Under a dynasty of names and deeds –
Cartier, Champlain, Brulé and Nicolet,
La Salle, La Vérendrye, Wolfe and Montcalm,   20
And names which left the loom of history

But yesterday – St Lambert's Lock which trapped
The cataracts and out-manoeuvred rapids,
The healing waters of the fraternal Seaway
Which made the inland cities ocean ports,
And brought together through Queen and President
Two nations and at their core a never fading dream
That would not die with the night.
The fervour of this international deed
Was but a symbol of the glowing family hearths   30
That greeted Queen and Prince throughout their journey.
Millions lined the streets; children would carry
In the impregnable treasure-house of their hearts and minds
The memory of a glance, a wave of the hand,
A word, a smile; singing and cheering
The grace of pity and the loveliness of flowers.
Leaving the seaways for the skies,
The Royal guests through clouds could watch
The illuminated manuscript of the prairies
Unrolling through the prelude to the foothills   40
Into the stampede's merry shivaree
And Calgary's meeting place of the clear running waters.
'Damn Braces! Bless Relaxes!' wrote William Blake
And certainly no hours in the Queen's procession
Has less protocol and pomp and so much uninhibited joy.
Much to the Queen's delight, the Prince put on
A hat which like an Arab tent enclosed
One half the dais. As he stood up to answer
A salute, the frightened horses
Threatened a premature stampede.   50
And when the song 'Home on the Range' was sung
By seventy thousand tireless throats
In stanzas endless as a sailor's song,
Its burden on the lips of those who sang
With the accents of Alberta salted with the tang of Texas
Was 'Better lo'ed ye canna' be. Will ye no come back again?'
So an unheard whisper rustled through the crowd.

From Calgary to the Foothills, and from there
The prospect of the Rockies and the Selkirks!

Range after range on to the Coastal Mountains.   60
And every mile of travel to the ranges,
Whether by train or car, had long been matched
By the feet of prospectors, pioneers
Who cut the trails through bush and forded rivers,
Turned passes into thoroughfares – Selkirk
With his small colony of Highland crofters
Made the Red River delta, with its black
Alluvial mould, the site of Winnipeg,
Then added land made fertile by the flow
Of the Assiniboine. Then Hearne, the first   70
To found the posts on the Saskatchewan,
The first to see the Great Slave Lake, the first
To trek across the Barren lands and reach
The Arctic, there to set his signature
With Davis and Baffin, Franklin, Melville and Parry.

And so it was when the Foothills had been crossed
Great things were done when men and mountains met.
At dusk the haggard hills kept their nightly vigil,
But dawn and sunlight woke their radiant grandeur.
Terror and wonder like twin signal flags   80
Flew on the peaks for men to keep their distance.
They needed miles to render up their beauty
As if the gods in high artistic moments,
Resenting the profanity of touch
Chiselled this sculpture for the eye alone.
Over the primeval way followed by David Thompson,
Indomitable, religious, just to all men,
Who mapped the lariat loop of the Columbia
And traced the Fraser to its source,
The Queen and Prince reached the sea,   90
And spanned the continent.
Fitting it is that resounding names of territories and realms
Should mark the progress of a Queen. North by east
They soared over the Coastal Range, traversed
The Yukon and the great Mackenzie River,
The Tundras to the Arctic's high auroras,
And then south-eastward to the sea again.

But it was not the spacious sense of distance,
The eagle flight of fifteen thousand feet
Above the explorers' trails   100
That made us breathless at the end.
It is not easy to define what stirs the heart
But this we know–
Whatever it is that so becomes a Queen,
Whatever it is that so becomes a Prince,
Was there at its full blossoming.
And now we offer love and cry Godspeed!
Wishing a happy journey home through untroubled skies
Nor yet is it too late to pledge their health –
The golden mintage of our common wealth.

                              CBC Information Service, August 1959

To G.B.S.

How did you learn, jester and sage,
The mood imperative of 'come'?
Irrational was it at your age
To cue your exit from the stage:
More time we wished to find our sum
Of knowledge – topsy-turvydom.
Your clothes-line humour aired our shocks
On science, social life and God,
When these were pitched upon the rocks.
O weird Hibernian paradox,   10
You smiled when cupboarding the rod –
You and your ninety years and odd.

                              Tamarack Review, Autumn 1966

The Doctor in the Boat

His talk shortened the trip across the channel.
I had the sculling oar: four others rowed.
The silent skipper cushioned in the foresheets,
His white lips like a vise, clutched at his side.

We wore forebodings like our mitts and oilskins.
A flight of waterfowl, a patch of fog,
A shape of cloud at evening, meant *Tomorrow*.
We breathed beliefs out of the air and vapour.
The doctor spent his time in shredding them.

A hundred yards ahead a bird was swimming,   10
The foulest thing in feathers – land or sea,
With sepia wings, black tips, and crest of quill.
We knew the ledge cleft where it nested, smelled
The thing before we saw it, often watched
The bird take off with slow laborious vans
Against the wind, tumbling, fumbling the air,
Until it straightened out. Now there it was,
A running blister on the water's face,
Keeping its distance, matching webs with oars,
Skiff, bird, and hospital – the same dead line.   20
An omen, sure of that. The doctor spoke
Of things like balance, purpose – balance? Yes,
We got that from a dory in a gale,
From weights and springs and piling rock in holds
Through lack of cargo. Purpose? Faith – we knew that;
Assumed it in the meshes of a net,
Or else denied it when a child was drowned.
But these were matters past the doctor's –
'Sharks too had purpose for the sea would rot
Without them.' This too strong a dose for us;   30
As well defend the devil, and this bird
Was of like brood. We knew it raised foul weather;
It would not eat clean things, lived on disease,
Decay and death. The doctor caught our thoughts
And countered them – 'And so does radium.'

The sea was blue except for streaks of red
Like gashes in an abbey afternoon,
Ripples of blood around the Mission point.
The bird still swam ahead, its purpose dark.
An automatic faith broke from our lips: 40
God moves in a mysterious way, but why

Cannot he shake this omen from our minds
Or keep that man from clutching at his side.

To D.H. Lawrence

Philosophers, what makes you so perplexed?
The record is that reason has outstripped
The midriff. Have you not misread your text?
Has the ink faded on the manuscript?

And doctors of the state who moralize
On wisdom in the higher vertebrates –
Study the jungle for an exercise
And write this older ethos on your slates.

There is a blessed mercy for the sick,
No mind engaged in vivisecting prey;   10
No needles have been found probing the quick
To linger in that luxury of delay.

Not yet evolved the ceremonial dance
When all night the raw cuts were building scars:
They say that in Malaya *kringi* ants
Shortened the route to death through jugulars.

But Mary Kept All These Things, and Pondered Them in Her Heart

Madonna! What has locked within your heart
Beyond the turn of the apostle's key,
Baffling the brushsweep, bankrupting the art
To round the *fourth* upon the symphony?
How much tomorrow was there in today?
And did your dawn herald his setting sun?

And did you know who shaped the tragic play
With the fifth act implicit in act one?

They counterpointed shadows on your face
With haloes, cherubs and angelic glory.   10
The *aves* were to find prophetic place
With the Christ-child's fulfillment of a story:
Isaiah with his blow-torch oracles,
David with lineage of loins and song,
And Jeremiah with his minute bells
Sounding a racial heritage of wrong.

'Sufficient to this day,' he might have said,
Had he but understood, could he have spoken.
The mother's cheek was pressed against his head –
Of what solicitude was this the token?   20
Not yet has the Transfiguration rhymed
The lyric manger with the epic skies,
Nor has the dusky Angelus outchimed
The murmurs of the Marian lullabies.

Sufficient! Was it not indeed enough
That his birth, life and death should be the themes
Of Israel, and not as now the stuff
Of kings – a nightmare packed in Herod's dreams?
And topping this were Caesar's bulletins
Which meant the stripes and prison to refuse: 30
The taxes cut into the household bins
And lowered the oil level in the cruse.

Did these El Greco hands tighten to clutch
Him when he stumbled? Did the heightened pace
Of pulse, the spasm of breath, call forth as much
Maternal worry as madonna grace?
Who slaked those torrid hours as they went by
Before he reached his three-years' thoroughfare,
And ended it with that Golgotha cry
Through which he passed into another's care.

Tamarack Review, Autumn 1966

The Head of the Firm

Formed out of oil and gas – his local fame,
The vulgar had it that he 'rolled in dough,'
A self-made man, such was his boast – his name
Was Puffsky, head of Fungus, Rotte and Co.

His eyes were beady and his head was swollen,
He was the law of God unto himself,
He posed alike as Croesus and as Solon,
Lord of the county town by right of pelf.

His vesper prayer was that he should increase
In wealth and power so that his name should pass   10
Around the earth – a household word for grease,
For fats and all varieties of gas.

And so one night it happened that his name
Broke through the confines of this mortal ken,
Ballooned into the stardust and became
The gossip of the gods as well as men.

Above his head, creating day from night,
The milkmaid's path shone like a drift of snow,
Millions of suns, and stars yet sending light
Had quenched their fires a thousand years ago.   20

'Who's that?' growled out the Great Bear to the Lion;
Quoth Leo, one eye cocked, 'Hanged if I know!'
But Aldebaran whispered to Orion,
'That's Puffsky, Head of Fungus, Rotte and Co.'

Tamarack Review, Autumn 1966

Appendix B: Unpublished Drama

Edited by Susan Gingell

Clay

PERSONS
Julian.
Thaddeus, a seer. ⎱ Friends of Julian.
Merrivale, a traditionalist. ⎰
Penrose. ⎱ Travellers.
Donaldson. ⎰
Voices and Echoes.

Scene: Near a village situated on the rocky shore of an island in the Atlantic.

Act I. Scene i.

Time: The fall of 1913 A.D.
Penrose and Donaldson travelling along the shore in the direction of the village.

Penrose: A lonely figure is this Julian.
He dwells somewhere along that stretch of shore,
Within a rough-shaped cabin. By himself
He lives, is not a native to these parts.
His earlier history is unknown to men
Inhabiting the coast. Some twenty years
Ago he landed here; lodged for a time

In a small village, then moved out,
Made for himself a home around those bluffs
To gain more freedom from inquiring eyes.   10

Donaldson: Has he no friends?

Penrose: But two. One – Thaddeus,
By name – as himself, who speaks
Like some great prophet of the past, whose ear,
Attuned to utterance of the winds, obeyed
Articulate voices that to common minds
Were sounds. He claims the gift of second sight,
And talks as though the future could be read
As easily as the past. He is beloved
Of Julian; comes and goes at will; for months
He may be absent, roaming, heaven knows where,   20
But ever like a tired bird he seeks
These rocks as if they were his only home.

Donaldson: But Julian? Does he not in confidence
Reveal himself? What brought him here?

Penrose: His life
Is as a folded scroll. It's said – and this
Inferred from chance remarks and acts that speak
With more insistence – that in earlier years
Sorrow had taken hold upon his heart,
Death or betrayal, ruined hopes or such,
For none has seen him laugh, or heartily   30
Enter upon those common joys that bind
Together men in groups; yet is he kind;
Men take their injured to him, for his hand
Is skilful as a surgeon's, and he knows,
They say, the secret of all herbs. He heals
Their sick, and by his silent craft he weaves
A spell upon their minds. Sometimes a lad
Is taken from the water, stiff and cold,
And drowned for aught they know. He stretches out
His body, moves his arms, and blows a stream   40

Of breath through the lad's nostrils, and the lad
Revives. They claim he calls him from the dead.
They love him with a feeling bred of awe,
For often do they see him stand at night
Upon the shore, and with no audience
But waves and rocks declaim as unto men.
Or sometimes near his hut will villagers
Pass by, and hear him holding with his friends
An eager converse.

Donaldson: Know you anything
    About the matter of their speech?

Penrose: I met   50
    This Julian once, by accident, some years
    Ago. It was while travelling down the coast,
    In search of stories of the famous wrecks
    In which these parts abound. He bade me stay
    A night before proceeding to the town
    Ten miles to the south. Of all the men
    That ever crossed my path he was the strangest.
    Guarded at all times when he thought I tried
    To stir a memory; masterful in mind
    He was, as I remember, when with speech
    Most trenchant, he descanted on those themes   60
    That ever burn within the hearts of men.
    A nature fierce and passionate; his soul
    Smoked with the hottest vapours of revolt
    Against the ground-plans of our mother-earth.
    His face was of fine cast; his stature tall;
    His eyes took on the bluer edge of flame
    Beneath grey brows; this was at times displaced
    By softer hues, for he was as a child
    In singleness of heart and guileless ways;   70
    And vulnerable to pain – another's pain.
    Strange that he looked obliquely on the world
    He lived in; everywhere that human feet
    Had trod he saw the Satyr's hoof; a core
    Malevolent inhered in life; the ape

Was grinning through men's eyes and teeth, and this
Marked all his utterance with a tragic note.

Donaldson: Has he abandoned all that men call faith
In human goals?

Penrose: Yes. It would seem that pain
Had crushed it out, nor was there, so I thought,   80
A Stoic side to which he might retreat,
As a last refuge from his ills. His head
Though bowed beneath white hair was often raised
Rebellious when I hinted at control.
Control! Restraint! That did not give but took
Away the final weapon of defiance.

Donaldson: With what new scaffolding would he then rebuild
This world, how take revenge on nature's laws,
When these are governed only by obedience?

Penrose: He may disclose that when we visit him.   90

Donaldson: What was the manner of his life when left
Alone within his house?

Penrose: He was well versed
In lore of bird and beast; a naturalist,
But with a deeper interest in the life
Of men. He studied sinews, nerves and joints,
Pored over charts of arteries and veins,
And casts of human brain and skull and heart,
His house was full of closets tenanted
By ghastly forms, some dried, some spirit-soaked–
With these his time was spent.

Donaldson: There was another   100
Of whom you spoke.

Penrose: Ah, pardon – Merrivale;
A different sort who does not understand

The moody genius of his friend, is given
To argument, is fond of statutes, saws,
Rescripts and sanctities, 'it hath been said,'
Or 'written down,' and other volubles,
Wherewith he must defend a stable world
Against this heady challenger. These three
In an odd strand of friendship mingle here
Upon occasion. I am told that now
They are here. Shall we visit them?

Donaldson: Agreed.

Act i. Scene ii.

Evening.
The shore. A storm brewing.

Julian: Swift has the darkness settled on the deep;
A moment past, and lurid streaks of day
Were casting fitful splendours on the waves.
Retiring, they have left the greying sea
Mantled in gloom. With slow and laboured hands
The crawling waters tumble round the shore,
Or swung upon the pivot of the tides
Against the frontal basement of the cliffs,
They shudder and recoil. Black fissured crags
That hugely range along the tortuous coast,   10
The eternal bulwarks of the earth's domain,
Loom silent, and with sides encased with mail
Of streaming basalt intercept the sea.
Within the narrowing gulch that sunders cliff
From cliff, the rising sea-gulls veer and scream,
And for a moment on the boulders worn
By ceaseless surge, small phantom-flitting birds
Of mottled pinions – vanguards of the storm –
Alight, and soon are gone. Now overhead
Breaks loud the thunder, and in blazing scrawl,   20
The lightning burns its signet on the clouds.
Now rain, and squally winds like birds of prey
Pounce on the feathering waves, while from the shore,

From breakers, and from lightless caverns rise
The rebel inquisitions of the night,
Strange querulous cries, half-dumb, half-understood ...
And so does man's existence find its form
Envisaged in the ocean's eyeless face
Swept by the besom of the winds. Its lines,
Its furrows, all its corrugated cares
Are mirrored in its gulfs. Dark Nature's minions   30
Break from the leash of law, and each with each
Contending, joins the universal strife;
Winds claw rebellious seas; the billows spit
Their salted rheum upon the rocks, are cuffed,
And broken in return. The Atlantic plants
Its heel of death upon the transport's hull,
Strides over the breaker's line; bludgeons the Cape,
And flung in thunder from the embattled brows
Of jag and bluff, reels with a drunkard's tread   40
Along the shore, and falls upon the beach. (Julian goes in.)

I

Voices of Wind and Wave:
  Who calls when the winds
  Sweep forth from their lair?
  What chariots are those
  That plunge through the air?

  What utterance, what mien
  Attends the wild form
  Of the rider that sits
  On the back of the storm?

  Whose feet and whose wings   50
  Contend for the prize?
  Seraphs and dragons
  Harrow the skies.

  What riot, what clamour
  Comes in from the waves?

Triton is lashing
His brook in the caves.

What medley of voices?
A strange chorus – this,   60
Anguish and rapture,
Frenzy and bliss.

Sea-nymphs are dancing
In mad festal glee,
As the winds tear down
On the face of the sea.

Loud bugles are sounding
The death of the day;
The Furies have driven
The Pities away.

Hark! through the orgy   70
Escapes a low tone;
Death draws from the heart
Of life's laughter a moan.

There – on the stones
Of a desolate shore,
A cry would out-bid
The night and its roar.

Two hands are outstretched
On the grey waters wild –
Grey waters that roll   80
By the grave of a child.

II

A man speaks: Was that a cry you say you heard?
Where? No. The winds would drown it quite.
No sound would reach the shore tonight,
Except the scream of some wild bird.

A flash you say that cut the rain
Like a red knife? It could not be;
There's nothing living in this sea.
Don't look so frightened. What – again!

The life-boat! They are hailing me.   90
They need a man for the stern oar;
The wind drives dead upon the shore;
A rudder's helpless in this sea.

A woman speaks: No. That was not a scream I heard;
One could not hear so far away.
That flash was but the breaker's spray,
That cry – the note of some wild bird.

III

Aha! the might of the winds;
They are up and awake,
On the land and the sea,   100
How they crash, how they break

On the cedar and oak,
On the pine and the elm,
On the mast and the sail,
On the boom and the helm.

They were here and are gone,
Have you hounds that may find them?
If they come when you call,
Have you cords that can bind them?

. . . . .

Be there cedars torn down   110
By the pull of the blast,
And the tempest-reared oaks
Uprooted at last?

Still shall be planted
The sapling and seed;
On the dews of the night
Shall the acorn feed.

Are there wrecks on the sea,
Is there spoil on the land,
That the lord of the storm   120
Has flung from his hand?

Yet peace shall descend
When the tempest is stilled
On the sea, and man's hands
On the land shall re-build.

. . . . .

But tell me – Can you build the heart again,
When it lies shattered by a mortal pain,
Set its wine of life a-flowing,
And the springtime breezes blowing
Through its crust?   130
Raise up the tendrils of life's young desires,
Freshen its leaves, make red its streams,
When death has crushed the trellis, when its dreams,
Its flashing ardours and exultant fires
Lie smothered in the dust?
How soothe bereaved reason
With the folded bloom of sleep,
Through winter's changeless season
And the night wind's sweep?
Call back the heart's lost passion   140
To a once triumphant throne,
That is now grey and ashen,
Untenanted, alone?
Tell how – from trampled altars
Smitten with the god's disdain,
On the dead and formless embers
Raise the sacrifice again?

IV

What is that colour on the sea,
Dotted by the white sails of ships?
It is blue, you say. We know it not, and yet   150
We know the blue of violet,
The hue of mid-day skies,
And the sapphire of young children's eyes,
But *that* we do not know – unless it be
The pallor of dead lips.

That band upon the sea?
A sash of green that in a moment's time
Becomes a girdle of wrought gold,
Held by a silver clasp of surge.

It cannot be.   160
That green is now a belt of slime,
And now – an iron-knotted scourge,
And now – the form of some anguineal fold.
That crimson core with sepia fringe,
And orange tints between,
Shows how the sun's white alchemy
Distils an aniline,
To paint a pansy on the sea.

That red is not the pansy's red,
Nor what the garden poppy shows,   170
Nor the vermilion that is spread
Upon the pastel of the rose.
But some deep smear that has its name
In the sprawled characters of the flood,
A slash of fire – a troubled flame
That takes its colour from man's blood,
Or from some wound in the sunset's side
That bled itself dry upon the tide.

V

Tarry! you flaming crests

That with spume-gathering wings,   180
Leap from the green-arched waves
In lines of python springs.

Is not your home, the sea?
Why then with clamorous greed
Do you mass upon this shore
With such insatiate speed?

There are no serpent's fangs,
As mortal as yours are,
No poison, leap and fold,
But yours are deadlier far.   190

VI

The Last Voice:
  Hush those wild strings! nor wait until tomorrow,
  The wind blows in no music from the sea,
  The bars are noises full of gusty sorrow
  That filch the waters of their harmony.

  The hours weave no web of life's young rapture,
  Caught is the spirit in a deadlier snare,
  And Time for me shall never more recapture
  Lost notes that once were resonant on the air.

  The gull shakes back the spray with shrilling laughter,
  Its grace more poignant than its gay disdain;   200
  Storm clouds are banked upon the east – and after,
  Winds barb their lyrics with unwonted pain.

  Hush then the lyre! the heart knows not its singing,
  Let the cords snap; it were better so to be,
  Than this cold lure of waters, endless, bringing
  The bye-gones of pale faces home to me.

Act I. Scene iii.

A few days later.

The house of Julian.
Enter Thaddeus.

Julian: Ah, Thaddeus, welcome! A full week has passed
  Since I expected you, and when the storm
  Broke down upon this coast I little thought
  You would be here tonight. What tidings, say?

Thaddeus: The winds have spoken ill along these shores
  Since last I left – the old and deadly feud,
  Man's hand and Nature's. Everywhere on land
  Have tempests raged. The fighting's strange at times;
  The issues so confused that one mistakes
  Alignments in the quarrels. Thunders speak   10
  Of clashes in the clouded zones of heaven;
  Lightnings are hurtled on the hills, and oaks
  Reared at the alternate knees of sun and storm,
  And brought to fullest stature have been snapped,
  As though some hand grown jealous of their strength
  Had struck them with design. Floods scoured the plains,
  And with fast-swelling rivers caught alike
  The roots of plants and trees, bearing them down
  In drift and eddy to the futile sea.
  And on the labour of man's hands was sent   20
  The hail. It threshed the summer's ripening grain
  Upon the eve of autumn's garnering.
  The worm was busy in the leaf, and frost
  Caught unawares the greenness of the herb.
  The labourer brought his horses to the stalls
  At fall of night and weary went to sleep,
  Dreaming of harvests at the morn, and woke
  To find his dreams elusive as the clouds
  That rolled their mocking shadows on the wheat
  The day before. Upon the land was lost   30
  The harvests of the fields; upon the sea,
  A vaster ruin, for the littoral
  Was strewn with broken masts and plated shards
  Of hull and funnel.

Julian: Life?

Thaddeus: The loss was great
  Beyond the count. Transport and battleship,
  Light sloop and open boat all yielded up
  Their freight of life. The weaker ships were caught
  Close to their ports and paid the penalty
  Of weakness, while the iron-framed that staked
  Their bulwarks up against the mightier winds,   40
  Lost on their daring; – so for great and small,
  A common ending.

Julian: No one yet has learned
  To trick the mastery of her clenched hand,
  By force or by evasion, whether spars
  Or heads of humans.

Thaddeus: There's no bias shown,
  No mercy but an even-graded scale
  Whereby the distribution goes to all
  Alike – unless it be for those white forms,
  The spotless models of her workmanship,
  The native sea-gulls artless as the foam   50
  On which they ride.

Julian: But other things of shape
  Less cunning, structures of the brain of men,
  Are with their authors hideous to her eye,
  Vain pictures of the things they seem, but meant
  For frolic and derision.

Thaddeus: Losses grow
  Each hour the toll comes in. The seamen ask
  Among themselves – 'Was ever such a storm?'
  Then shake their heads. Lighthouses, docks and quays
  Were washed away, and nothing left but piles
  And pitiable clumps of ruined masonry.   60
  The finest monuments of the builder's craft
  Fell far below their calculated might.

Julian: Thus ever has it been. The raft, the skiff,
  Pinnace and coracle knew no worse fate
  When men a thousand years ago tried out
  Their perilous chances on the ocean lanes.

Thaddeus: The oar, the sail, the paddle and the screw
  Are patterns of a moving tragedy
  That men misread. They think by laboured art
  They have snared the magic of the wind's uprising,   70
  And its down-sitting. Shall it blow today,
  Tomorrow and the next? They answer 'Yes,'
  Pointing to zones and pressures, isobars,
  Circles and lines they smugly pencil out
  Upon a map a hand-breadth square. 'Here are,'
  They say,'the treasuries of the snow, and here,
  The chambers of the hail and rain, and lo!
  The East will soon be garmented with clouds,
  And a thick darkness. Then shall be driven out
  The thunders from their lair, and lightnings loosed   80
  Shall travel in these paths. The line is stretched
  Upon the flood and all the measures laid.
  Listeth the wind to blow? Nay, it is set
  By a determinate birth, passes and dies;
  So whence it comes and whither goes are known
  By place and time appointed.' While they speak,
  The winds commence to blow, and answering, say –
  'Come, we will make you one with the driven foam,
  And throw you on the breakers and the reefs,
  With our wet fingers will we comb your hair,   90
  And paint you with the blood of sea-weed, glaze
  Your brows upon the beach until they glow
  With the inveterate pallor of the coral.
  When found you out the swiftness of our feet,
  Or took the measure of our spread of wing?
  When snatched you from our hands the keys of death?
  Lo – here the gates are open, pass you through.

Julian: Aye, every step upon the grade seems vain,
  And every boast a signal of distress.

The halliard, and the rocket, roar of gun,   100
The code's weird speech that would out-wit the air
Are helpless blazons when the tempest stops
The ear and seals the sight. For now tonight,
Upon the waves, Death flags the running storm
With signs of more imperious beckoning,
Than those which from the wireless deck flash out
Their dots and dashes of a giant loss.

Thaddeus: At every gust a heart breaks.

Julian: Yes, that is
The final victim of all shock. Thaddeus! –
A gambler's been at work upon this job,   110
Or else a journeyman that did not learn
His trade too well, and left somewhere a flaw,
Spoiling a nobler plan. Look you at this,
(*Showing him the model of a heart*)
This crimson floodgate of our human life,
Where beat all mortal currents – strife and fear,
Despair and anguish, guile and false pursuits,
The sport of flotsam and of eddying ends.
Within these sluices run the world's lost tides,
Its passions smothered under stress of years
Forgotten. Shadows leap upon the floods –   120
Cain's ruthless hand still clenched in bloody thrust
Against a brother; Saul's dark javelin poised
In silhouette against a curtain fold;
The furtive bend of Borgia over a vial;
Attila's sword and heel of Tamerlaine –
All governed by this little vagus here.
Dark hidden pourings! In these cloistered depths,
What strange essay of life – the noon-tide flush
Bears the high pulse of challenge, that out-go
Of hope and purpose infinite, life's crests,   130
Its far horizons and resplendent goals.
This nerve gets weak, the tides fall to the ebb,
And the dim prescience of untrod tomorrows
Steals in upon our dreams. But wait – a drug

Is brought, a poison with your leave, and look!
What chances toss again within the veins,
An empire or a scaffold, throne or cell;
Pleasure, a foundling on the steps of pain,
Life at close grips with death; the backward sway
Of hope within a treacherous grasp; a slip,   140
An errant step that turning from the road
A hair-breadth, unretrieved, moves into night,
And vacancy, wherein no moon nor stars
Cast any light. Is it not so, my friend?
This shapely auricle, you see, is deaf
To all the tragic meanings of its beats.
What wayward laws! Whose codes? Whose fond caprice?
Where triumphs, gains, fulfilments follow sharp
Upon the heels of loss, and these again
Pursued by strivings unachieved. What race,   150
What conflict, this, wherein the one who wins
Must watch the many fall, the weary fail,
Where love must freely take, for what it gives,
Its fair requital in the loved one lost.
Who bargained for these ends, staged life's regrets,
Its issues in the gambler's leaded throw?

Act i. Scene iv.

Penrose, Donaldson and Merrivale in Julian's house.

Julian: You cleared the channel in the nick of time,
My friends. I know that piece of water; twice
I crossed it in a stouter skiff than yours,
And found that, though the wind was moderate,
The tide-rips swung the tiller side to side,
Lurching the steersman up against the gunwales.

Penrose: The glass was dropping heavily when we left,
But yet we took our chances as the wind,
Though east, and rising fast, was in our favour.

Donaldson: By the time we were half-way across, the sea   10

Was breaking high over the stern. We ran
Nigh water-logged into a neighbouring cove
Where, in a fisherman's home we stayed, storm-bound
Till yesterday.

Penrose: We go to Copper Cliff –
Donaldson has interests there – thence to Gull River,
And finally to Whale Harbour where we spend
The winter. But remembering my last trip
To this place six or seven years ago,
The shelter of this roof, I turned aside
To see you once again, and brought my friend.   20

Julian: You are welcome to what modest cheer this house
Affords.

Penrose: Your kindness leaves us in your debt.

(A little later)

Donaldson: How the sea must scourge this shore in heavy wind!
Your house withstood the storm.

Julian: That dusky crag
Lay right athwart its path and happily
Shattered its force.

Donaldson: Upon our way we saw
Many a house in ruin.

Julian: Ruin! No.
That is a word that seaman never use
For such a loss. It is too light a thing
To count when they are dragging for their dead.   30

Donaldson: Does such destruction always mark the wake
Of storms?

Julian: I have not known it otherwise.

Donaldson: I talked with old sailors as we came
    Along the shore. They spoke in simple words
    About the winds and fog and heavy seas,
    Much as they did about the calm and sunshine.
    There must be compensations in their life
    To take it so.

Julian: The words belie their feelings.
    They know one language – that of resignation.
    It is the common tongue the world, in part,   40
    Has learned. It's mastered here.

Donaldson: It is a phase
    Of struggle merely – still to be out-run;
    It's nature's way, were it so known, to match
    Each harm with good.

Julian: The key to that fine mood
    Of hers, if ever in man's grasp, is lost;
    For such a temper rarely finds its lines
    Engraved on nature's strategy. She strikes
    Beneath masked skies, and takes a fouler hold,
    When man is on his knees – a suppliant.

Penrose: I spoke to one who years ago had lost   50
    His craft in mid-Atlantic. It was manned
    By his four sons and others next of kin.
    He spoke as if his life was somehow reared
    Above the incident of pain. He lived
    Within a house so near the shore the spray
    Could swish the window-panes, and yet his eye,
    It seemed, saw not the sea, nor was his ear
    Touched by the louder winds.

Julian: I have known such eyes
    That do not see, such ears that do not hear.

Penrose: It is a discipline that men have learned –   60
    To brace the soul against life's heavier blows.

Julian: And this contentment you would make the balm
　To human ill, to live, yet to forget
　Life's sorrows as in isolation?

Penrose:　　　　　　　　　Yes.

Julian: It is a lesson that before it's learned,
　A man must first unman himself to read.
　Teach him to think without his brain, to walk
　Without his legs, to lift lead-weighted hours
　With shoulders paralysed. It is an art
　Whose subtlety is such as human wit
　May not unravel – how so to pronounce　　　　　　　　70
　Commands, 'Do this, be that,' that the achievement
　Shall follow on the vocals. Life moves not
　Upon such strange and jointless steppings. See
　That cabin yonder by that wind-torn shore.
　Till yesterday, a lamp was placed upon the sill;
　Each regular night it cast its beams to sea.
　It was a beacon to a skiff that ran
　Its daily hazards in the fog and storm.
　Last night it was not lit. Say to the heart　　　　　　80
　Of her whose care it was to tend the flame –
　'You must now journey forth alone; gird up
　Your strength; your loss is but an accident
　That touches not the vitals of your being;
　The soul may now in fortitude declare
　Aloofness to the earth; its dignity
　Is brought to stature here.' Is not the voice
　That prattles off such nursery rhymes as these
　Reduced to impotence by those stern tones,
　With which the sea makes answer to the shore?　　　　90
　The lamp is out. The heart that lighted it
　Died with the smoulder of the wick.

Merrivale:　　　　　　　　How now?
　You do not reckon well your words, nor know
　Within whose hands are light and darkness held,
　At whose command the storm leaps, by whose breath

Silence and peace, when the loud tumult ends,
Are ushered on the deep. A Monarch's voice
Speaks, and the challenged sea obeys His will.

Julian: The North wind calls the waters and they rise;
   The East wind thunders and the deeps are stirred;   100
   They know no other voice – no mastery
   Save that of wind, and man's uplifted hands,
   Clutching in frenzy at the spray, sink down
   As helpless as his cries, and there is found
   No eye to pity and no will to save.

Merrivale: Is not this treason's speech?

Julian: There is no power
   Above the winds, or else those pale drawn faces
   Would not be tossed in eddies on the waves.

Merrivale: It is not given us to understand
   Those devious paths that mark His sovereignty.   110
   His ways are dark, yet are His counsels good.

Julian: What Shepherd, this, that so attends his flocks,
   As leads them out into the wilderness,
   Up bramble-steeps and cliffs and pathless moors,
   Where they are caught within the storms white drifts,
   Or scattered by the wolves? What Father, this,
   Who cares so little for his children's fate,
   That though he holds the sea within his hands,
   He pours its floods upon their heads, lets loose
   His lightnings, blasts and stalking pestilences,   120
   Although, it's said, that by his name's great power,
   They could be held, mute, harmless, near his throne,
   Chained to its pillars? Why his children's cry
   Less urgent than the thunder's reckless laugh,
   Or the unheeding foam upon the reef?
   Who calls him Father; hears his Shepherd's voice;
   Knows him as Friend, Physician, Master, King?
   The subject's head falls crushed within the wheels

Of some immaculate law. The sower swings
A tiring arm on arid soil bestrewn
With thorns and stones. A sufferer calls in pain, 130
In the lone watches of his couch, and hears
No answer save the leaden brush of wings
Against the window-pane. The son's last right
To heirship, to inheritance of love
Is spurned upon the doorstep of his home,
His kinship cancelled, and his brother's ties
Dissolved in mutual blood. Named you him Father?
God? No. Rather a Potter with some clay.

Act II. Scene i.

Two years later.
In a small harbour town.

An old man speaks: Great lads those! Every one reliant, firm,
Steady of step – muscle and bone storm-hinged,
Yet supple as the fine battalion's lines
In which he swings. Straight-eyed with face clean-bronzed
In the clear sparkle of the morning's light.
How well the khaki takes the October sun,
Fits the square shoulders, matches cheek and hand.
That lad there, see! third line, first on the left –
Mine! youngest one of four, turned twenty-one,
Blue eyes, and hair light-brown. Two months ago, 10
He left the ship, and with two other brothers–
The second and the oldest, both big lads –
He joined the colours. Soon, at dawn, they say,
Tomorrow, they are off. God wish them well.

Fragments from a Field

1

Action – tomorrow! So the make-believe
Is ended. Well! This mock manoeuvring
Grows flat month in and out, this bodiless thrust

At sand-bags, punch and parry, battledore,
Sniping at dummies; capturing, paper-planned,
Your country's trenches. Rain, parades and mud,   20
Your daily menu. Front lines then tomorrow.
Game, are you for the show?

                           No – Yes. What's that
You said? I didn't hear. Why, yes, I'm game.
Say, did you post that letter, yesterday,
I gave you? Thanks. I wanted to make sure.

2

A dud! God! what a narrow shave. 'Twas big
Enough to clean the dug-out up, and make
A crater where a regiment could hide
At a sharp pinch. They're counter-strafing now.
Wonder how long it will last. Must be barrage.   30

3

Here – two of them. Locked close together. Ha!
Black Watch and Brandenburger. Heavens! The Scot
Knew well his bayonet's trick – Clear cut, right through;
Must have been struck himself, same time, to fall
Like that. Yes – shrapnel through the neck and shoulder,
A vicious cut. Pull back his arm and head.
You would not think they had the strength or life
To come to grips like that, after being hit.
A husky chap the Scot. The stretcher – Lift!

4

Here, on the double. Cut that out. That shell   40
Is half a mile off. What's in this pit?
A clear half-dozen – tangled up in skeins;
The first one dead, and this, ... and so, the sixth,
That's all. Make for that clump of wire.

                                        This rain
  Beats like a flood.

                          The smoke's too thick to see.
  The slime's a mile deep.

                              Here, over here,
  Three – four, alive; let's get this fellow out,
  He's got it worst.

Another – looks like dead.

  Eh? Take no chances that way. Get him out.
  They are all alike, except for size. This grime   50
  Has plastered them, you'd never know by face,
  Which one was which.

                          This fellow's come to life –
  He says his leg is broken.
                                    Easy there.

  5

(At the base)

  Gangrene! Why, how is this?

                                Must have remained
  Some time on field – Three days he must have been.
  Expected something big, but hardly thought
  The show would last so long.

                              The padres said
  They couldn't account for all. The fire was hell.

  The bases are all crammed to overflow,
  The stream's unending.

                    Will that fellow live?   60

The chances are against. Must amputate
At thigh. He'd stand a chance one out of ten,
But for his lungs. The lethal struck him hard.

6

(Next morning)

How is that fellow – number 6, Ward A?

Dead, sir. He died two hours ago. Fine lad,
Big-shouldered, tall. It's just the kind they kill;
A game sport, so they said – from overseas.
A sailor. I was near him when he died,
And heard him in his dreams talk broken words
About a ship his father owned, and seals,   70
And ice, and the big pay he got one spring.

Cries Afar Off

1

Now let the earth take
Into its care,
All that it travailed for,
All that it bare.

Leaves of the forest,
Yellow and red,
The drifting and scattered,
The dying and dead.

Grass of the hill-slopes,   80
Sickled and dried,
Vines that over-night
Blasted and died.

Blossoms and flowers
Nipped with the cold,

Trees that have fallen
A century old.

Moths of the candle-flame,
Gnats from the stream,
Wraiths from the moonlight,   90
Spectres of dream.

All that the earth gave,
All that it bare –
With all its wide kindred
Of water and air.

2

White lilies of death,
Fragrant and mild
Can you sweeten the breath
Of this little child?

Your petals so waxen,   100
So moist in the air,
Lie strewn in the flaxen
Folds of her hair.

Pale lilies, pale leaves!
Can you add to her grace,
To the paleness that cleaves
To her brow and her face?

. . . . .

Bring rather wild roses,
That the sunlight distils
From the wine of the morn,–   110
From the dew of the hills.

Quick! Scatter them faster –
On her brow and her hair,
Her face is too pale,
Her brow is too fair.

Only the red ones,
The richest, the best,
Bring hither – and shed
On her hands and her breast.

. . . . .

Blood of the rose,   120
Heart of the wild!
Why will you not beat
In the pulse of this child?

3

O rose of dreams
That blooms at night,
Shedding thy crimson
Shafts of light!

On whose dark web
Was this magic caught?
Out of what ray   130
Was this loveliness wrought?

Day – with its glooms
That wearily creep,
Night – with full colours,
Fragrance and sleep.

Rose! what legend is this?
Heartache and pain
Changed by a charlatan's touch
To garlands again.

Midnight and rest –   140
When must it cease,
This union of shadow
With gladness and peace?

Rose! thy petals are ash.

Remains now the thorn
With the passing of dreams,
With the coming of morn.

4

Snowfall on a battle-field
    Compassion of heaven,
    From night's crystal bars,
    Falling so gently   150
    In wreaths of white stars;

    Petals of mystery,
    Culled in far lands,
    Crosses of Calvary,
    Wrought by strange hands.

    Why do they lovingly
    Leave their fair home –
    These leaves of God's gardens,
    To stray on earth's loam?

    See how they hover   160
    Over faces so cold,
    How reverently cover
    The young and the old!

    Compassion of heaven,
    Tears from God's eyes,
    Falling so gently
    Out of the skies.

Act ii. Scene ii.

Julian, Thaddeus and Merrivale.

Thaddeus: The world has been in travail, Julian,
    Through many moons of blood. The sight that struck
    My eyes lay not within my dreams, and caused

My brain to stagger. Fields remote and near,
Hills, ridges, valleys, lowlands, marsh and plain,
Far to the horizon's utmost rim were filled
With clashing millions. All earth's tribes
Had by some common instinct gathered there,
Peopling the shadows of the awful zone –
The forest shades, the fissures of great rocks,   10
The caverns cut within the rotten mold;
Each nation's youth, its lithest, strongest, best,
Closed up the crimson rendezvous. The streams
That ran their livid washings through the clefts
Of spade or nature's highways, fouled and choked
With drifted foliage of a year grown old
Too soon, with autumn's hectic leaves and limbs,
And sheddings rare of dearer castaways.
As leaves fall, so upon the plains fell men;
Some tossed awhile within the gust of combat,   20
High on the sweltered air, returned to earth
As flesh and blood and bone unrecognized,
And indistinguishable dust. Some swayed,
Not knowing why they did, as if a breath
Of unnamed pestilence had touched their senses,
Robbed them of aim and guidance. Thus they drooped
And fell; and others could not die till hours
Wore into days and nights. Restless they moved,
And shuddered, clutched convulsively at stones
Or roots, and clenched their teeth upon their hands,   30
Stifling their moans. Young lads of growing years,
Who pain or weariness had never known,
Lay in strange sleep upon the fields, alone,
Or huddled up in ghastly heaps where death
Had flung them. Night winds gambolled with their hair,
Golden and brown and dark – they heeded not.
And far along the distant battle lines,
I saw the fierce insurgent tides, the rise,
The flow, the swift recessions of despair;
Huge gaps that rendered void the toil of years,   40
The lines re-formed and the price paid; strong men
Who lunged and parried thrusts and lunged again,

Struck and were struck, unknown to each the foes,
Save in the general quarrel and its cause.
And through the lulls of intermittent fight
Was blown death's bitterest music – the low sob
Of brothers mourning brothers dead, the curse
Of fallen men that had not seen their foes,
The unavailing moan that answers moan
At night in the far comradeship of wounds.
Then, strangest of all sights – the harvest moon   50
A moment broke through misty cloud, and shed
Upon the fields a sickly yellow light,
Disclosing pallid faces, blue strained lips,
And eyes that stared, amazed, through open lids
That had no time to shut – that looked and asked
But one eternal question. Then the moon
Grew dimmer as the mist increased, and showed
In hazy outlines hurrying forms that moved
In twos and threes, from place to place, and laid   60
Upon the stretchers, one by one, the dead,
Torn, jagged, mud-smeared and crumpled, carrying them
To rows of damp deep trenches newly-dug,
Where they were placed in groups of eight or ten,
In order, side by side, and face to face –
And the moon shone full again – the harvest-moon.

Julian: O Thaddeus! there is an iron in the will
  Of Him who shapes the times. His power is seen
Within the flash that cleaves the oak; it germs
Within the hidden matrix of the earth,
When cities rock before convulsing fires   70
Prepare their tombs; it lurks within the fang
Of shrike and puma, in the slanted stroke
Of the vulture's break upon the escarpment's flint,
In every coil and spring and furtive eye
Watching a desert pool. What jealous hands
Are these, that ever closing in their grasp
On bird and brute, must henceforth seek to hurl
Hell's jungle-statutes on the race of men.
What barren foot-prints, these, that mark the steps   80

Of human treading, endless labyrinths
Of fatuous gleams that beckon here and there,
Disclosing but too late the precipice.
And must life's journey by some mocking fate
Just end where it began, where men, their eyes
Blindfolded, every slip mistake for gain?
Sterile progression! where each life repeats
The racial circuit, and finds unrepealed
The acrid law by which its parent died.
Each loss, they say, is countered by its gain;   90
The steep ascent repays the mountaineer
In healthy pulse-beat, when the blue clear air
Wipes from his brow the sweat, and the high peaks
Summon his soul. Vain reason of the winds!
The height is but the instrument of the fall;
Each loss a gain, each gain a loss. How then?
What matters which goes first, a point of speech –
The fairer syllable of the two, or worse?
These never-breaking cycles yield no faith
To him who blindly trusts. The scarlet thread   100
Snaps nowhere in its bonds, and everywhere
Life bends beneath the sacrificial scourge.
Time was, when on the altar-stones, the priest
As Daysman for the multitude would place
The wheaten loaf or wine or the sweet milk
Drawn from the mountain-goat, an offering
For grievous sins, for wrath appeased,
Thanksgiving, or to send the sun and rain
Upon the seedling corn – and when the heart
In sterner syllables laid bare its zeal   110
Before the mount of Heaven, an angel spake:
'Lay not thine hand upon the lad. Behold!
A ram caught in the thicket by the horns.'
The voice speaks not again. The heavens close
Against the suppliant's cries. The long slow climb
Of all our vaunted progress leads to shame,
And Moloch's fires light up the spiral stairs
Which, being scaled, yet no alternative shows,
But horrid regress lurid with the flames. ...

There was a hill once climbed, on which the world   120
Had built the warrant of a grander faith,
A hope more excellent. A cross was raised,
And at its foot a river ran whose fount
Welled from the noblest veins that ever bore
Imperial tides. This was the last great stream;
The hill – the final altar of the world;
The tender hands upraised in death had made
High intercession, closing once for all
The scourge that bled the heart, scouring the soul. ...
O broken reed! O spirit! treble-crushed   130
By the barbed insult where the iron failed,
By dreams o'ershot and courage spent for nought;
Still are the stones laid and the shambles spread,
The candles lighted and the censer swung,
The inner courts are thronged with multitudes,
And crosses – Ah! In cluttered heaps they rise,
Stacked pile on pile, until they twist and sag
The rivets on the bolted doors of God;
And Calvary – is but a peak that flared
An evanescent torch whose light was quenched   140
In a red mist of sweat, and man's tired feet
When once they scale the summit must, in shame,
Re-walk the bloody gradient to the grave.

Merrivale: Wild words are these, that break like heedless foam
    At the wind's breath.

Julian: Was ever this wide world
    So plunged in unmeasured desolation?

Thaddeus: Death – Death stalked everywhere on land and sea,
    In clouds that banked the sun, in mists that hid
    The stars, or half disclosed the swollen moon.
    No cavern sunk beneath the earth but bore   150
    His foot-prints. Deep below the water's rim
    Great fish had trailed his scent. Earth's myriad forms
    Had felt the plague-spot of his rampant touch,
    From the small field-mouse caught within the fumes

Of sulphurous air that crept from knoll to knoll,
Withering the grass-blades, to the giant fighter
Of storm and wave, that, planked and sheathed with steel,
Felt the swift scorpion in her sides, then rocked,
And plunged with bellowing nostrils till she sank
In a wild litany of guns, with wind,   160
And night, and flame. But busier was his hand
With subtler workmanship. On eye and brow
And cheek were delved the traces of his passing –
Blindness that like a thunder-clap at noon
Closed on the sight, furrows that struck the veins,
Turning the red sap from its wonted course,
Sharp lines of pain and fury and quick hate
That on the instant changed to graven stone,
Callous and motionless. And deadlier still,
With flying leap he strode a continent,   170
Or the wide prairies of a sea, and snatched
The cup from the wan fingers of a life
That slaked its thirst upon the wine of hope;
So sure his hand – light as with finger-tips,
He touched the hair and wove the grey and white
Within the brown, or hard, with rough-spurred heel,
He mauled the bosom till its heavings ceased.

Merrivale: For every grave that's shut shall one be opened.
Hath God not spoken so? Does not each year
Declare his trumpet-pledges at the spring?   180

Julian: Think you so to convince the heart with words
Like these – to mesh it with a logic meet
For bloodless ends? What though the winds of May
Call to the springing rootlets, lure the bud
From the rose-stem, and chase the resinous sap
From the pine's trunk to branch and topmost twig –
Who yields to such delusion? Does the spring
Forget November's hecatombs, the last
Convulsion of the leaf, the gale-torn limbs
Of trees scarred to the death, the flowers that danced   190
Upon the fields scythed by the autumn's hands,

The writhen spectres of earth's quick decay
Flashed out upon the winds? All these as dust
Around the season's tombs – dust-heaps, no more;
As sands that eddy in the desert – these!
For these no resurrection. What amends
Does summer make for winter's numbing stroke?
It's death He gives, not slumber. His pale forms
Breathe not again, and eyelids that have closed
On the congealing air reflect no more   200
The warm glance of the sun. The swallows build
Their nests once more within the eaves; the thrush,
The red-breast and the lark cover again
Their young in bush and tree and meadow-grain –
They have not died. But weak ones that impaled
Upon the thorn screamed out their notes of pain,
Or dashed, wing-broken, by the wildering blast,
Fell when their strength had failed them on far plains,
On treeless hills, or dazed in homeward flight,
Fluttered and sank in furrows of the sea –   210
Their song has ended; *they* return no more.

Merrivale: There is inscrutable wisdom in His plans,
We may not read. Is not the spirit of living,
Its very essence, faith? Destroy that flame,
And this old earth becomes a charnel-house,
A tomb for slaggy refuse, embers spent
And cold.

Julian: Is faith an empty thing that needs
No richer food than the invisible air?
Must it not have embodiment; at least,
Some form from which the mind may take conviction?   220
Or is it such an alien to the mind,
That it must look as coldly on fruition
As does the cruder sense on disappointment?
Show me, I say! Let these high gifts of man,
The eye, the mind, the natural faculties –
Those, which we claim, are God's best workmanship –
Be exercised upon their functionings.

Whence did the Galilean win his right
To ground earth's faith upon a soldier's rood?
That he did earn it, none may offer question.   230
But whose the hand that made the strange award?
The prize was earned, and yet the proffered crown
Was but the shadow of the substance sought.
Who made him Conqueror, Prince of Peace, that he
Should rule a kingdom of death-skulls that stare
Rebuke at all his titles? Power to act,
To back the Cross with sovereign energy,
To mould a world as fits a monarch, fell
Most tragically in far arrear of claims.
There somewhere near the hill on which he died,   240
Does not his dust blend with the earth he loved,
But nobly failed to save? The charge, not his,
Must elsewhere lie. If God's, then sovereignty
Is as a sorry fable – shells of words,
Without a kernel.

Merrivale: Does the fault not rest
    At mortal doors?

Julian: Then wherefore speak of hope?
    Since, if you will or not, the thing goes out
    On two disastrous counts. What follows hard,
    You say, as consequence, has happened – graves,
    And jungle-heaps, foul pits whose stench exhausts   250
    The lavender of heaven. If the one,
    Who was the very rose-ray of all dreams
    The world's imagination fed upon,
    Yearned for through centuries before he came,
    And raised in retrospect to rank of God,
    Worshipped by many whom the world, in turn,
    Has canonized as saints and demi-gods,
    Crowned with a lustre comparable with the might
    Imputed to him – if he failed, as failed
    He has with the momentum of the years   260
    Of twenty centuries to make his name
    The lode-star of the race – pray, tell me then,

Is there another yet to come, endowed
With more resistless weapons of offence,
With panoply more cunningly devised
To stay the onslaught?

Merrivale: No, that may not be.
The mind collapses at the effort made
To frame a nobler mould.

Julian: Then ruin waits
Upon his shrine, and dogs all pilgrim steps
That, flocking thither, search for peace and rest.   270

Act ii. Scene iii.

A year later.

Thaddeus: Like some fair crocus in the swamps of spring,
I saw life push its way through mire of death,
Triumphant.

Julian: How?

Thaddeus: A ship lay motionless,
Not anchored, nor becalmed, but held in spell
Of some great shock. She listed heavily,
As though a wound had gripped her loins.
And in the rain and chill were lowered boats,
So filled, they lacked the margin of an inch
To meet the water's edge. A law well known
To men who live upon the sea, here ran   10
Its old and honoured course. The boats were few
And small, and there was left upon the deck
A sturdier throng who stretched out willing hands
To save the weak. One boat hung yet suspended,
Filled short of obvious risk, and a slim girl
Stepped out, and gave an aged woman left
Unnoticed in the crowd, her place. Her lips
Were closed, and her face pale, but yet a smile

Made soft and sweet the pallor of her cheeks.
Then out into the night the boat was rowed,   20
Steadily and silently. No clamour broke
The stillness on the deck, nor was there sound
Of voiced farewell, but here and there,
A hand was raised, and a white fluttering
Answered the distant rhythm of the oars.

Julian: Chaos indeed may well disclose a star,
    Caught unawares within the tangled drift
    Of cloud and chasing glooms. Earth's wastes are full
    Of miry swamps and quicksands. Compensates
    The flower, rare and lovely though it be,   30
    For the death-suctions of the stretching void?
    It lessens not; it only swells the sum
    Of terrors. Then the virtue lies in this –
    The rarity of the bloom, for were it much,
    Our mourning for the good would never cease.
    But if the great destroyer rake the earth,
    It were better that he gather verminous leaves,
    And chaff and sapless roots than opening buds
    With the bright light of morn upon their dew.

Donaldson: Rare? No, not rare indeed. The firmament   40
    Is studded with its stars untold, and flowers
    Thrive hardiest near huge boulders, hemming them
    With softest hues, or where damp airs invite
    Their subtler fragrance.

Thaddeus: Look upon the plains
    Again. Charred ruins not of nature's hand
    Lie deep within unfathomable slime.
    How foul the wreckage stands – a spectacle
    So ill that it might seem to bar forever
    The lily's right to grow therein again.
    And yet a few short hours before when death   50
    Was taking in his most exacting toll
    Of this, his bloodiest year, were women seen –
    Strange forms indeed, with red insignia

Stamped clear upon their brows, fulfilling well
Their pledge of office. Lovingly their hands
Cooled the hot flush of temple and of wound,
Made by the steel of surgeon and of foe.
They beat the angels, at the angels' game –
These women. God might well His embassage
Forego – His feudals of pure space – and take   60
In chartered ministry those lovelier forms,
That know the ravelled driftings of our life,
And hence God's art of salvage all the more.

Julian:
    These are fine colours woven in the grey
    And tattered fabric.

Thaddeus: Grant you not as well
    The value of the life that's lost. The lad
    That struck out in the storm without a star,
    Or faintest glimmer of a port, that took
    His orders with blanched cheeks yet with a heart
    That pumped its resolution through young limbs,   70
    Untaxed till now by paths wherein the errand
    Failed by fore-doom of the sure goal – think you,
    That with his eyes made blind before he struck
    The highway, when his senses clouded fast
    With the delusions of ungoverned winds;
    That falling here somewhere around the place
    Of starting, he should then be counted out,
    His life not worth the value of a smile,
    Much less redeemed by forfeit? Is there not,
    In the unvisioned queries of our faith,   80
    A phrase whose pregnant utterance commends
    The will, exalts the aim, wherein the power
    To do falls heavily short of its achievement;
    Whose bare pronouncement is the servant's meed,
    Albeit the drought consumed the harvest yield,
    And the far labour of the spring appeared
    But days of idle story, hours devoid
    Of mirth and promise, without song or dreams.

Julian: Of what account the sowing when the grain
  Is threshed by hail, or the young blade is nipped   90
  By the quick frosts of night? Does courage tell
  In the last sum of things when strength is gone,
  And the rent form resigns its shredded flesh
  To the planned stealth of him whose wiles outmatch
  The weaker's zest? What does the partridge gain
  With its wild flap and rush against the hound,
  When brood and mother fail despite the dare
  Of helpless wings? Is there for human kind
  A scale that weighs the profit differently,
  A higher calculus that measures loss   100
  By hidden worths and meanings to the brute
  Denied? Those bones out yonder to the earth
  Give up their lime; their rotted flesh transforms
  By subtler alchemies the laboured soil,
  Until from grass and shrub and flower the air
  Is scented with rich odours. Is the gain
  Not this, and this alone?

Thaddeus: Were this the end,
  That one might take the overplus of might,
  Transmute it into something handled, seen,
  Bow down before its image, whether stone,   110
  Iron or gold and say – 'Let this be Good,
  Or God,' call it what name you please, 'The Law,
  The Natural Statute, That by which the race
  Is ruled, by which it comes to be.' Were this
  The sum of all advantage that a slip
  On ground unequal gives the victor right
  To wear his laurel, while the soul of contest
  Is pushed aside by rude arbitrament
  Of power, or blackened so that greed alone
  Is common by acknowledgement, the Earth   120
  Might justly say to all her seedlings – 'Grow!
  Let the herbs multiply their kind; the grass
  Make yet more beautiful its green; the trees
  With unaccustomed pride spread to the winds
  The glory of their foliage; let the grape

Take from the soil its redder sap, for now
The ground is succulent with buried weeds –
Things that possessed no function when alive,
But to despoil the tiller of his bread
With stifling growths, but dead they serve the spade   130
Of nature in the turn-out of her seasons.'
Were this the sequel of man's birth, the shrub
Could boast a fairer destiny, could call
Him 'servant' without jester-play of rank.

Julian: Does not the fact overwhelm the abstract right,
    Clad as it is in robes of tragedy?
    Look well upon the plains. There sinews, bones
    Of friend and alien fast are interlocked
    In mutual conquest. There the overlord
    Of this fair earth's the grave. Lo! triumphs there   140
    The worm, and evolution reaches thus
    Its final phrasing – 'From the dust to dust.'
    The purple rots into the matted clay,
    And majesty is a weak word that, cut
    Adrift from sounding consonants and vowels,
    Is but an echo of the noise it made.
    So Death still keeps its ancient sting, the Grave
    Its victory. Man's proud investiture
    Of place and species, title, dignity
    Are mock heroics playing round his name,   150
    Whose birth is in the winds, whose death rides out
    Upon the whirlwind.

Donaldson: Do these human dreams
    Long cherished at exhausted wells, by paths
    That form and close within stark desert sands,
    On which the sun beats down his pitiless ray,
    Portray their night's dark origin when morn,
    That should bring light, strips them of beauty, shows
    How truth is but the dupe of fancy's making,
    That colour is destroyed by light of which
    It should be author? Mad the artisan,   160
    Who slays while fashioning, that turns the axe

Upon his chiselled models. Then the dream
Is less than parable; then priest and seer,
Bound to this world by ties of prayer and promise,
Have found their moorings, threads of gossamer,
That snapped as the grey light of morn revealed
The snare. It cannot be. The heart knows not
Such cordage.

Julian: If the dream be ne'er fulfilled,
But ever broken with the reassertion
Of day's compelling hours, what reasoning   170
Shall buoy the heart with tidings more assured,
That the hid future shall awake with joy,
Than those on which its hopes had split
And foundered? Ground the future in the past;
What warrant had those great historic hopes.
Failure is writ upon them, nor need be
Erased the word on those that come. Belief,
A wish, a dream – where is its leverage
To raise the dead, to make those bones knit joint
To joint and leap, to pry until the mountains   180
Remove their base, or force the heart's wide wastes,
Where hate was sown, that love shall blossom there.
What has been, will be. Time has proved it so.

Donaldson: Marks he the issue well, who sees here naught
Save huge world-fires upon whose smouldering ruins
Man's hand has lost its cunning to re-build,
Or that the piles new-reared shall fall once more
In the mad blasts that periodic run
Their cycles of decay? May not the eye
Range over those dun fields of death, and see   190
From vile putrescence, Beauty rise in light
Unquenchable? May not the scars remind
The sufferer of his healing as of wounds?

Julian: Man's life feeds like a fever on his hopes;
Eternal yearning gnaws his heart – a plague,
More than a blessing when the end he seeks

Becomes a withering drought. What plan is this,
So wise and fair, as can with beauty clothe
Those bleached frames that rattle in the air,
When the winds swoop. Enswathe it as you may,   200
That touches it.

Thaddeus: No. Lime and ash tell not
The story of all struggle. Causes lost
Awhile on earth, at stake or cross, try out
On new arenas fiercer qualities.
They are re-born upon the air; they storm
The souls of men; find homes in thunder-peals;
Are hitched to lightnings. Slain, they rise again
With such forged temper that they turn aside
The opposing edge of armouries of steel.   210
And every life that guideless though it seemed,
And blinded to the very sockets, joined
The losing issue swings again to play,
With falcon vision and its speed of wing,
A winning game.

Penrose: Reasons that manifold
Lie in the petty judgments of man's mind,
That crawl from step to step, prompting the sight,
That the touch apprehends, that hearing, taste
Admit as natural, known – these may be weighed,
And counted as a string of silver coins,   220
Figures that undisputed draw the lines
Of profit set against minuter loss.
Herein the argument – 'This is currency;
Behold the stamp, the image genuine,
Safe venture, this! The morning's sun or rain
Is in the evening's tracery of the West.
May one not read the signs? A fool may read.'

Julian: The latter is our human heritage.
Why given eyes and ears, fingers that touch
Sharp thorns and bleed may man not feel   230
His pain? It's his to avoid the edge. His tongue

Abhors the myrrh, the bitter cup. Why place
The poison to his lips? The end of fire
Is flesh consumed, is charcoal cold and dead.
Gold purified is allegory in life,
A myth for blooded things. Man's step is short,
His vision bounded, why then make him leap?

Penrose: The leap's the symbol of his daring. More!
　　There are great promptings planted, mightier
　　Than what the sense enfolds; they bid him cross 240
　　Spans unexplored, gulfs where the plumb-line hangs;
　　Try for vast title-holdings where the hands
　　Are bankrupt for the bids. Hence will the fires
　　Burn until all the dimmer eye beholds
　　As left, is what a half-filled urn contains –
　　Charred residue. So will be welcomed pain,
　　And wounds, hunger and the hot coals of thirst,
　　Outlawry, persecution, banishments,
　　Lapsed friendships, open enmities and hate –
　　All that may follow life to sepulchres. 250

Julian: This to what end? Is pain an element
　　In which he lives, or that to which perhaps
　　He would return therein to find his pleasure,
　　As some gill-breathing creature strayed to sea
　　Might with as good a reason seek the land?
　　Is beggary a choice, and nakedness,
　　And homeless sojourn?

Penrose:　　　　No – but if the goal
　　Dark, heavily clouded as it is, demands
　　Those unblazed trails, those foot-falls by the way,
　　The challenge is the warrant in itself 260
　　For the adventure. Does the heart not know
　　Such voices, whether in the blasts they come
　　Like stern reveilles at the dawn, or low
　　Like inarticulate sounds that rise at night
　　From the deep swellings of a quiet sea?

Julian: And the answer is a sea that's strewn with spars
    And riven hulls. And yet were waves and gales
    The only agents of man's ruin, then
    The chances range upon his side; the fight
    With nature grows more simple every hour   270
    Her ways are known, but when the struggle takes
    Hell's routes and ends in bloody fratricide –
    Not once, nor twice, as though an incident
    Of casual kind had touched man's history,
    But as a baffling epidemic strikes
    A thousand times his life, failing of cure;
    How strike this foul insistent integer
    Clean from his life? The taint is in the blood,
    Try surgery there! Find the right scalpel first.

Act II. Scene iv.

Julian, Penrose, Donaldson and Merrivale.

Merrivale: Only a man whose soul was sick to death
    Would so bedaub this world with drab. The face
    Would always turn to sunlight, were the eyes
    Not blind.

Penrose (to Merrivale): There is a sickness that yields not
    To acids.

Donaldson: It's a deeper malady.

Julian: My step is slow, and a thick film over-spreads
    My sight, yet does my mind bend back its gaze
    With an unwonted keenness on the past
    For nearly twice a score of lonely years.
    I travelled far through many lands and knew   10
    This earth as well as most that travel it;
    I knew its peoples, and their customs, ways
    Of living. Life was like an open road –
    A glorious highway, with by-paths that stirred

The mettle of adventure. Then the winds
Such as the desert only feels swept down;
Yet as a pool within the sands was left
A solace, a companion, one who kept
A memory green who, as he grew, became
A very fountain of live hope. Time seemed   20
To shape itself about his future; years
Were planned without misgiving. Here was one –
So ran my thought – who would in time achieve
The promises that lay within his youth,
·And these were golden. Never was a nature
More finely strung to touch or glance or word,
For like a harpsichord it registered
All moods – the flame of passion in just cause,
Anger and quick revulsion when a deed
Showed foul at core, and yet his soul could breathe   30
Such adoration for a cherished friend,
Such warmth of fealty for a cause held high,
That he could lose the temper of restraint
With lavish offering; as generous in heart,
As keen in mind. Then suddenly, well … a blank,
A veil hangs that may not be lifted here. …
I saw him dead, his face all passionless, cold.
The luminous shafts that kindled in his eyes,
Sparkless as flint in loam, his head, his brow,
The flexions of his body – graven stone.   40
So cloud and dust have since companioned me;
There's nothing left.

Donaldson: The memory of love
Remains. His was a nature that you prized,
That having loved was worth the years of living.
Is it not so?

Julian: Worth? Who may speak of worth,
When the wrought gem is cast into the sea?
Where is its value if you may not take
That self-same jewel in your hands and let
Its facets glow in sunlight?

Donaldson: Would you then
  Have been the richer had it not been yours   50
  To have and lose?

Julian: How otherwise? I am
  The poorer for the loss, have suffered more,
  And mark you – that fine quality of your code
  That makes his rarer attributes a gain
  For him, a virtue as you smoothly say,
  Was his undoing. I could tell you now,
  Were but my heart to speak, how that high pride
  Of his, that scorn of baser things that stamped
  His sterling put the anguish in his soul
  When fires played at last upon his will.   60

Donaldson: Would you have had him formed of rougher grain,
  Safer perhaps for life as living goes,
  But with wings clipped or leaden, vision dulled?

Julian: Where is the ground of preference if his life,
  Being fashioned like a sensitive plant, should die
  By some rude sting, having but known the power
  To feel the wound?

Donaldson: The coarser fibre stands
  The keenness of the cut; as well knows not
  The joy unfolded in achievement.

Julian: Ah!
  Within that word lies all the bitter root.   70
  Where has great striving ever found its goal
  Save in mischance? These more than four-score years
  Have taught their lessons. If this baffling life
  Could give the lie to age, and prove mistrust
  A whim, with youth's fair hopes well realized,
  And courage laurelled on the hard-fought field,
  A father mourning for a son laid low
  Might lift his head. But no – the tides are set.
  Out there upon the shore today they move,

With fixity of bounds as yesterday.   80
And so within the veins the lines are drawn
As hard, as fast, and hidden processes
In cell and tissue play their destined part.
This organism dies; its functions called
By divers names as goodness, duty, right –
These fail; the other lives because to it
Was added marrow. Bring then sackcloth – ash.

Act III. Scene i.

A Later Spring

A flash of indigo in the air,
A streak of orange edged with black!
A blue-bird skimmed the spruces there,
A redstart followed in his track.

The light grows in the eastern skies,
The deeper shadows are withdrawn,
From marsh and swamp the vapours rise,
In the cool cloisters of the dawn.

What loom – a-weaving on the land,
Such colour and fragrance fuses,   10
Magenta and white on moss and sand
Azaleas, arethusas?

And higher up along the steeps,
The pink of mountain-laurel;
While lower down the yellow creeps
From celandine and sorrel.

Sea-foam or snow-drift – flecked with spurt
Of flame – upon the grasses spread;
The snow is foam of mitre-wort,
The flame – the ragged robin's red.   20

. . . . .

Where sips the lily of the morning dew
When light winds waken,
And gems that the violets hold
Gently are shaken
To crystalline purple and blue;
And emerald, crimson and gold
From the heart of the rose unfold,
And burst into view:

There at the dawn's first blush
The notes of a brown thrasher fall,   30
And the importunate voice of the thrush
Blends with a tanager's call;
There under a dragon-fly's wings
A stream carols by with sweet noise,
And slowly a daffodil swings
Beneath a humming-bird's marvellous poise.

(Thaddeus, walking through a field in the direction of Julian's home.
The day is warm and sunny. A rapid stream, a short distance away,
flows through a valley whose banks slope down from small hills covered
with evergreen. Afar off, the land is high and forest-clad. At a bend of
the stream he suddenly meets Julian.)

Thaddeus: There is a quality in this air that stirs
The blood as readily as the balsam sap.
What brow, what chemistry; what hand is this
That grips the pestle? Never was the grass   40
Throughout arterial nature marble-cold,
And pale, are heard the joyous sounds of life
Revived; earth's wells are opened in the vales;
Through ice-clad mountains chiselled by the hands
Of northern blasts the gurgling waters run,
In stream and torrent, and in the mad plunge
Of cataract. Beyond the snow-capped ranges,
Lusty young rivers tear and strain at the dugs
Of the foot-hills, and parting force their pace   50
Through gorge and valley to the open sea.
Life boundless, keen, ecstatic, uncontrolled!

Vast, heaving, surging life, strung to great thews,
Rapt in wide wonderments. Hail, life of Spring!
Born of prophetic gales and plangent shocks,
That rouse the torpor of earth's granite veins,
And sluggard eyes. Glorious in resurrection!
Thou peerless colourist of nature's life!
With what unrivalled hands the lines are drawn,
The shadows set, and the rich hues enwrought   60
Upon how great a canvas! The far climb
Majestic of fresh-foliaged ash and elm
Along the mountain crags; the river banks
Where the white spray falls softly on the iris,
And violets creep along the sides; the gift
Of minted treasure on the open fields
Where bloom those golden legions of the earth –
The daffodils and lowland marigolds –
Cerulean tints that light our common paths,
That bless our road-sides, cheer our vacant wastes;   70
Bluets and hare-bells and the lilac bloom;
Orchards aflame beneath a setting sun –
And trailing slow around moss-covered rocks,
The flower of May superlatively veined.
Come! Leave your tents, O mortals, gather here
In Nature's high rotunda crystal-domed,
And offer praise!. ... O Julian, give me   ·
Your hand. We meet under new skies today.
The times are changed; the earth renews her face;
There is a fine contagion in the spring   80
For heavy hearts.

Julian: You would infect the blood
   Of an old man.

Thaddeus: Come, Julian! In this life,
   There is an unslain good that has outlived
   All floods and fires. There are undaunted spirits
   The age has not destroyed. I have seen them breathe
   Upon dry bones until they leaped with sinew;
   Even flotsam by their touch was salvable.

No life however craven at the face
But found a courage stirring at the core.
The groundwork's there to build a structure on;   90
The hand that yesterday tore like an eagle's claw
Now pours in balm today, blesses and cures.
There is a restoration in a smile
We knew not of; we had forgotten it –
But wings unseen were flying in the night.

Julian: I would there was a rock from which man's hopes
    Might never more be swept, or that his blood
    Might always bathe his heart with healthy stream.
    But those alternate currents like the seasons
    Have been our fateful legacy through all time.   100
    What power is this you speak of that the dark
    May sudden blaze with light before the morn
    Is ushered in at nature's call? Is this
    The ultimate conquest of her will that day
    Shall not know supersession by the night,
    With earth's diurnal axis over-ruled?

Thaddeus: Have you not noticed, standing in the aisles
    Of some high-vaulted temple when the massed
    And reverent throngs were hushed in expectation,
    How a great organ poured forth like a flood   110
    Its spells of music as the master's hands
    Swept the wide boards? What power over the soul
    To lift its hopes, to plant its aspirations
    In the rich soil of heaven came from the touch!
    But let untutored fingers meet the keys,
    And the rapt ear is split by discords, airs
    That bray their grovelling kinship with the clay.
    Are not the strings, the instrument, the same
    With either press? But how extremes depend
    Upon the craft of him who plays. Life's songs   120
    From baser jars and fretted failures range
    Along the gamut of their enterprise,
    In spiral movement to such high refrains
    As could, with buoyant amplitude of roll,

Lift up the souls of sinking men, and float
The world's grey cares on seas of evening calm. ...
Have you not heard God's music when His winds
Are given boundless space wherein to blow
Upon the greenness of the earth? They pass,
And from the meadows and the valley-slopes   130
The latent rhythms of the daisies blend
With the low rustle of the sedge. They pass
Again, and lo, in grander orchestra,
The pines lift up their voices on the hills. ...
The human heart is such a lute, a harp
Of many strings, an organ that may roll
To the strong pull of a mighty diapason.
Today, the keys are pressed and a sharp hiss,
As of some jealous flame leaps on the sense,
And the bewildered mind is stung by jets   140
Of unexpected pain. Tomorrow comes,
And the vexed reeds acclaim a nobler master.
Vibrating passions purged of gross appeal
Move up along the pipes, and storm the nave
And the far arches. There is not a scale
Can measure the full quality of life's deeds
When human souls, that hitherto had known
But wayward flaws and barren purposes,
Are touched to wonder by those knowing hands,
And motivated by his breathings. Acts that loom   150
High on the horizon of our mortal range,
That never pale in retrospect of time,
While others blur on faded scrolls, take on
The ripened glow and colour of their greatness
From this, the self-same source of all that holds
Its upward course in human destiny.

Julian: Dust gathers in my mouth. I cannot speak
    What I would say. Whether it is the drought
    Of age, or some strange filtrate of the past
    That sets a parched seal upon the lips,   160
    I do not know. It may be that from thistles
    I tried to gather figs, or, where I looked –

Before I plucked, I said the vines were dry.
Now I am old. I find the roadways blocked,
And memory ranging through the fungus years
Finds but the husks where it would take the fruit.
And yet, there is a knocking in this clay –
A restless flame – something that, if it could,
Would leap the grammared confines of slow speech,   170
And give the echo to your dancing words.

Act III. Scene ii.

Two days later.
(Penrose and Donaldson about to take their final departure from the coast.)

Donaldson: Well, Penrose, how the last five years have sped!
    They should be rather scaled as centuries
    In calendars of deeds and thoughts and passions;
    I did not think – that day you brought me here –
    I would have been so often to this coast,
    Lured by that lonely sage. Is this the last
    That we shall see of him?

Penrose: The last – I fear.
    We must be gone some time. Should we return,
    At length, we shall not find him here. He is old,
    Beyond the age of men. Did you not see   10
    How yesterday he scarcely spoke a word,
    When we were there? His step was weaker far,
    His face, though kindly as before, was changed,
    And when we shook his hand and said 'Farewell,'
    His speech was thick.

Donaldson: Thaddeus remains with him?

Penrose: Yes – to the end.

Donaldson: He loves him as he would
    A father.

Penrose: Thaddeus is no longer young;
   But he maintains a gracious blend of years
   And hope, of seer and child – a crutch of love
   To the old man. ... This way – our boat has come.   20

NOTES

This text of *Clay* is based on a complete typescript (referred to below as 'ts 1') in the E.J. Pratt Collection (Box 8, No. 62) at Victoria University Library. The spelling has been made consistent with that of the poems, a few obvious typographical errors have been silently corrected, and a small number of format and essential punctuation changes made. Pratt did not include act designations for each new scene, but for clarity's sake these have been added. For similar reasons, Pratt's erratic changes from Arabic to Roman numerals for scene designations have not been preserved; otherwise the text remains unaltered. There is also an incomplete typescript of *Clay* ('ts 2') in the same file, and parts of the verse drama were published as individual poems in *Newfoundland Verse* (1923).

I.i. The identification of Thaddeus as 'seer,' Merrivale as 'traditionalist,' and Penrose and Donaldson as 'travellers' were holograph additions to ts 2.

I.ii.heading. 'The Rocky shore upon an island in the Atlantic. Evening,' ts 2

I.ii.82–97. These lines were published as 'On the Shore,' *The Rebel* (1920), reprinted as 'Later,' *NV* (1923), and as 'Signals,' *VS* (1930). See Bibliography.

I.ii.148–78. These lines were published as 'The After-Calm,' *NV* (1923).

I.ii.178–9. Between these two lines, in ts 2, there was a heading: 'A woman's voice (Still later. Chanted).'

I.iii.53. In ts 1 'hideous' was inserted over crossed-out 'gargoyles.'

I.iii.114. This line was added to ts 1, written at the bottom of the page, its place being indicated by an arrow.

I.iii.121ff. Cain is the Biblical archetype of the fratricide (Genesis 4:1–17); the Israelite king Saul, jealous of the favour David (the future king) had found with Saul's people and the Lord, thrice attempted to slay his rival with a javelin (1 Samuel 18:7–16 and 19:8–10); Cesare Borgia (1476–1507), son of Pope Alexander VI, was a notorious criminal and murderer. The historically unsubstantiated tradition exists that the Borgias possessed the secret of a mysterious deadly poison, which they used to promote selfish interests and papal power; Attila the Hun (A.D. 406?–453), notorious for ravaging the Byzantine Empire, earned the epithet 'Scourge of God'; Tamerlaine (d.1405), a corruption of Timur-Leng, meaning Timur the Lame, employed terror and devastation to extend his rule to include Turkestan, Siberia, Persia, and India.

I.iii.126. The vagus nerve innervates the larynx, lungs, heart, esophagus, and most of the abdominal organs.

II.i.71–94. These lines, with the addition of an eight-line closing stanza, were published as 'A Dirge,' NV (1923).

II.i.147–66. These lines, with the addition of an extra stanza between two and three, were published as 'Snowfall on a Battlefield,' NV (1923).

II.ii.4–66, 147–77, 181–211; II.iii.1–28, 45–77, 203–79; III.i.1–134, 157–70 were, with added material to aid transition, published as 'Fragment From a Story,' NV (1923).

II.ii.113. See Genesis 22:12–14.

II.ii.117. Moloch was a Semitic deity whose worship required the sacrifice of children.

II.iii.142. Pratt is here paraphrasing a passage from 'The Burial of the Dead' in The Book of Common Prayer. See also Genesis 3:19.

II.iii.148. See 1 Corinthians 15:55.

II.iii.183. See Ecclesiastes 1:9.

II.iv.15. 'the winds': 'cloud and wind,' ts 2

III.i.1–36. These lines were published as 'Anticipations,' CF (June 1921), and then as part of 'Fragment From a Story,' NV (1923).

III.i.75. 'tents, O mortals': 'tents, mortals,' ts 2

Appendix C: Unpublished Poetry

Edited by Susan Gingell

Poems included in this section, found among Pratt's manuscript materials (housed in the Pratt Library, Victoria University), are those which are either in manuscript or holograph form or are seemingly fair copies. The numbers in square brackets refer to the Pratt Collection listing (see Bibliography) except those numbered [7.50 Un] which are from Viola Pratt's private collection.

To Pelham Edgar

Pelham, old dear, if I only knew
Some kind of a drink which in your view
Possessed the kick of a kangaroo,
A fiery draught that might outdo
The strength and taste of The Witches' Brew,
And raise the hell of a hullabaloo,
How gladly I'd pass it on to you.   [1.4.150]

A Breadliner's Prayer

Forgive O Lord if one presumes
To ask a question over-bold,
Why wool and cotton glut the looms
And yet our children die from cold?

'Give us this day our daily bread' –

There was a need for such a prayer
When thy disciples went unfed
Because of withered harvests there –

But here with world bins stacked and crammed
I cannot feed my family;   10
Forgive me Lord but I am damned
If I can keep from blasphemy.   [2.14.86]

A Strip of Sea Coast

Come life or death, come peace or war,
The moon has never failed the tide
Here where the ocean meets the shore.
On this forsaken coast
Only the ancient things abide:
The blue-green-salmon tints in the glide
And dive of the dolphin;
The silver of the gull's ride
Outmatching the sun's rays
On the foam against the black   10
Of the basalt boulders;
The down on the curlew's breast,
The vertical cut of her wings
Back to back
And tip to tip
Before resolving into rest
As the last wave curls on the beach.
These have remained,
And shall remain
While human blood boils in its pain   20
And the adagio of the dulse
Rebukes the fevers of our pulse.
Here shall the sea
Answer our tossing nights
With patience in its face,
And in the Logos of its voice,
Its co-eternal cool antistrophe.   [4.30.181]

But One Way

If you should go to meet your enemy,
Go not encumbered with your wrongs and causes,
Nor let your reinstating pardon be
Conditioned by the damnatory clauses;
Nor halt your steps upon the road, mid-way,
Hailing him from afar in battle-mood
To come and take your wrath before the day
Descend upon a longer sterner feud.
And if you go to take *his* anger, go
Unhelmeted, and the full road, prepared   10
With all the odds conceded to his blow
But fear – hands empty, heart and body bared:
Then watch the sword of the antagonist
Waver and clatter from his nerveless wrist.   [7.50.Un]

[Today and Yesterday]

Today

To the 'jet,' the riding lord of the continents,
The plane far below him which stumbles and crawls
Is an eagle left-banking over the Falls
With a brood of fifty attached to her ligaments.
To the bird those are beetles and ants that are scurrying
To their hills and holes upon the earth's floor –
Those men that are chasing the hours and worrying
About God and the devil and atoms and war.

Yesterday

With the rise of the curtain the years take flight
From the Hydro back to the candlelight.   10
The birds that make up the sky's patrols
Are thrushes and robins and orioles.
The ear-drums are safe from the static and yammer

In the throats of the radio gramophones.
Rather the ring of the blacksmith's hammer
Is heard on the axles of carioles
Twisted by jolts from the cobblestones.

At the corner store with a lull in the trade,
The son of a Family Compact dictator
Fights with a miller in a word fusilade   20
On the treatment of Gourlay of the *Spectator*.
The miller is losing, until a debater
Trained by a Methodist comes to his aid
With the Irish Chief of the Fire Brigade.
Lured by the swing of a hurricane lamp
They swarm to the tavern on Saturday nights
To evaporate Niagara damp,
And to hear the latest account of the fights –
How Foul Weather Finnegan and Pat McGuire
Bore the whole brunt of the Waterloo fire,   30
How Hector, a sabre-trenched guardsman, won a
Commission for holding the rear at Corunna.
And the air becomes thick like the speeches, while
Becky the barmaid serves Demerara
To a handsome creature called Captain O'Hara
Or 'chin-chucking Charlie,' late of the Nile.

With Sunday morning's release from work,
The country and town turn out to the Kirk,
And envy is stamped on the rustic faces
At all the imported wealth of attire –   40
At the march of the satins and silks and laces,
At every poke-bonnet as tall as a spire.
Curved like a staircase, in Empire style,
The wife of the Colonel glides up the aisle,
Attended by fighting Patrick McGuire.
The daughter comes next in a brilliant tiara,
Leading the dandy, Charlie O'Hara,
But salter by far than the waters of Marah
Is the worship divine to Captain O'Hara,
For the sermon is preached by no less a person   50

Than the Reverend Jasper Andrew MacPherson.
He takes as his text 'the sheep and the goats,'
Dividing them up with stern canonicity,
And after two hours he adds a few notes
Of his own containing a blast of publicity
On captains and drummers, and the town's use
Of taffeta, perfumes, and Sabbath abuse.
And damning them all to extreme infelicity,
He closes his sermon with thoughts on lubricity,
And the unrepentant churchful of sinners,   60
Smelling of brimstone, go home to their dinners.   [7.50.Un]

'First-Born of England'

First-born of England! Lo, out there she lies!
Storm-flung upon the Western world, apart,
Rooked in the thunder, 'neath the clouded skies,
The foster-waif of the Atlantic's heart;
Laired in the surges where the Gulf Stream joins
The torpid clasp of the great Arctic's hand.
Mothered of Britain, sprung of Nature's loins,
Isled in the Ocean's grandeur – Newfoundland.

Well had she stood the capital tests of Time,
The urge of tempest and the roll of flood,   10
Her sailor sons were nurtured in a clime
That forged the iron deep within the blood;
Stripped were her ramparts all along her shores,
Scatheless beneath the brunt of ageless shocks,
The billows ripping up the ocean floors
Were rent in smitten fragments on her rocks.

Four centuries of rich full-tided life
Had beat within her ports, had winged the seas,
Had triumphed over Nature's winds and strife,
Outsped her chariots, probed her mysteries,   20
Roamed o'er the ice floes of the frozen North,
Had pierced Gibraltar, and the Eastern world,
Had touched the Indies, and had voyaged forth
Under the banners of the South unfurled.

To struggle was the birthright of her race,
The glory of their failure and their gain,
To fight against great odds, strongly to brace
The soul's undaunted sinews under strain
Of tide and tempest; faith unquenchable
Was theirs; it drew the sunlight from the clouds,　　　　30
It spoke of dawn whenever midnight fell,
It brought forth music from the whistling shrouds.

Life had they known, its bounding pulse, its feel
Of vibrant wonder, morning and the call
Of waters springing at the vessel's keel,
The eager hoist of sail, and the proud haul
Of ensign to the mainmast top, the flap
Of canvas toying with the rising breeze,
The answering plunge of the ship's bows, the snap
Of ruddy spray slung by the chasing seas.　·　　　　40

Love had they known, for under winter skies
The hearth was warm, and tender light undying
Shone from the stainless iris of blue eyes
To the leal gaze of other eyes replying;
And they had heard the laugh of children, known
The soft press of a babe's cheek, the strong grip
Of brother's hand – life's richest gifts bestrown
Within the haven of love's comradeship.

Death had they known – those lads of Newfoundland –　　　　50
The bitter sweetness of its sacrifice,
Well had they learned in that high hour to stand
Unbleached upon the ships, and pay the price
It sought, and when the night from evening came,
And the swift darkness wrapped up Nature's form,
They sank with noble, unrecorded fame,
Clothed in the grand insignia of the storm.

·　·　·　·　·

Fell the great storm of ages! Broke amain
The thunder from the hills, and from the skies

Once more the wind and hail and once again
The lightning: and above them all the cries   60
That spring from shattered bulwarks. Far away
The flooded waters heaved, and ever higher,
Stabbing the East – its dark and trackless grey,
The signal rockets of a world on fire.

And those who life and love had known and death
Within the island compass of their home,
Now felt upon their face a ruder breath
Than ever scoured a thousand leagues of foam;
And once again the parting kiss was given,
As round the altars of their homes they met,   70
For life and love with death once more had striven,
And once again their children's eyes were wet.

They sailed again – those lads of Newfoundland –
Towards the grey East with lines of flashing red,
With thrice four thousand in their gallant band,
Over the ocean's barriers they sped,
Daring the hazards of the day and night,
The baffle of the current with the blow
Of billow falling thunderous in its might,
And the swift shaft that lurked in stealth below.   80
And never was a life-boat launched and manned
On such a night and by so brave a few,
Never a rudder steered by swarthier hand,
Never returned to port so small a crew;
Never the fog so chill, never the rain,
Never the call of love with death so rife,
Never the loss so keen, never the pain,
For love through death to seek the port of life.
· · · · ·
They sleep – those island sailors – far away,
Some close to where the blue Aegean swells,   90
And where the Mediterranean waters play
Around the reaches of the Dardanelles;
Beneath the heather and the gorse they lie,
Beneath the crumpled marl and drifted sand,

It was their fortune lonely thus to die
Far from the hills and coves of Newfoundland.

And those whose lot it was, deep-scarred to foil
War's ultimate precision and its chance,
Survived but to enrich another soil
Made precious by the flowing wounds of France;   100
And round their crosses on the flowering sod
The hare-bells and the cowslips now unfold,
And everywhere the roses grow – and God
Has added daisies with their hearts of gold.
And others are there yet who sleep apart
Beneath the North Sea's wide and roughening wave,
Within the shadow of great England's heart,
They did not seek a more triumphant grave;
For out of the winds and out of the tides they came,
Out of the waters rolling full and free,   110
Back to the tides again their life, their name,
Back to their cradle first and last – the sea.   [7.50.Un]

Moonlight

A magic lake the heavens! No rude stir
Flutters a fragile cloud that sleeps on high –
A weft of frosted rue and gossamer.
The greater stars in tints of gold,
Sprinkling the far-off spaces,
Hang pendulous like jonquils of the sky,
And silent, soon,
In slow ascent crawls the moon,
And golden, too, its face is.

Upon the sea,   10
Vast replica of the arch of night –
Silence and light.
Stilled now upon its tongue
Its ponderous rune,
Unsung

Its harp-caught melody,
Its throbbing bars
Closed. On its face
The heavens trace
The cloudlet and the moon,   20
And the bright stars.

Upon the land – one sound,
One strain of music falling
Tremulously,
The waters of a brooklet calling
To the sea.

One light,
One lamp alone.
Steadily
Its gleams are thrown   30
Clear out to sea.
Long does it burn,
Watchful and bright,
Will he return?...
Late is the night.   [7.50.Un]

The Fisher Boy

The moon has come up
Like a silver-wrought crown,
The stars have come out,
The wind has gone down;
Bestrewn is the ocean,
With diamonds afloat,
No foam and no motion,
And still is the boat.

With his day's work all over,
To the cuddy he crept,   10
Lay down 'neath its cover,
And dreamless he slept;

Close, close to his father,
His head near his breast,
So deep in his slumber,
So sweet in his rest.   [7.50.Un]

[The Toucan]

If you go to a place along the shore
Of a region known as Ecuador
And enter the fringe of the forest you can
Discover a creature called Toucan.
Of all wild birds the greatest freak
Its voice can range from chatter to roar,
No matter how long and far you seek
There's nothing can match its terrible beak.   [7.52.39]

(To Cornie)

An arc of azure dipping from the sky,
Fringed by green hills and glades and rising brake,
Changing to orange as the sunbeams die –
   It is the lake.

A curve of sapphire with a splash of green,
The form of some sleek serpent coiled in slumber,
There, through the tangled trees it may be seen –
   It is the Humber.

A quiet haunt where friends are wont to stay,
It lies upon the Humber's crested dome,
There glad ones greet you at the close of day –   10
   It is the home.   [7.52.51]

The Inexpressible

There is no earthly shrine which may enfold

A worship of this spirit flight, whose aim
Would soar above all symbols that proclaim
A love the heart itself could never hold.
For words and looks and gestures are a mould
Too frail to stand the casting of a name,
Which in the tropic centre of its flame
Would make a deed involving death seem cold.
Therefore, let not these holy vows be scarred
By flint of speech, by priests put on parade   10
Before stone altar-steps, witnessed and marred
By oath, but given under an acolade
Of night with its unuttered language starred
Against a deep Uranian facade.   [7.52.53]

The Yeas and the Nays

(The Yeas)
They dotted i's and crossed the t's,
Secured the periods and apostrophes
Within their credal paragraphs of power.
And with their affirmations of salute
They slew their souls down to the root.
Then with their hands withered by spoil
They found their hour
Of death in spate of blood and rut of soil.

(The Nays)
These are the recusants who, having learned
The negatives of speech and spurned   10
The articles of power,
Have joined the hosts
Who gave their bodies to be burned.
They took their hour
Of life in death,
Bartering the vapour of their breath
For immortality
On roads starred with direction posts –
Nach DACHAU, à ROUEN, to CALVARY.   [7.52.57]

His Last Voyage

Batten down the hatches; reef the sails,
And knot the gaskets well. I do not know
The port that lies ahead, the seas, the gales.
But still this touch of night, this glass that's low –
Those signs that never failed my senses yet –
Won't fail them now. Come bosun! Have me feel
The lead of your hand to the aftdeck, then let
The cable slip and lash me to the wheel.   [7.53.12]

The Osprey

He swept the full circumference of the lake,
With leisured flight,
Then with a light
And careless spiral swung
To the centre where he hung
One hundred feet above the water,
At perfect rest.

He dropped and dived:
And when he rose he flung
A colour riot through the air –   10
Brown of his wings, white of his breast,
Gold of the lilies, green of the pads,
And the silver flash
Of a bass
Against the backdrop of a rainbow
Woven by the sun with the threads of the splash.   [7.57.1]

St John's, Newfoundland: Steep Are Thy Cliffs

Steep are thy cliffs that stand like bolted doors,
Hinged to the iron columns of the earth,
Encircled by the sea thy tortuous shores,
Like those of that far-off isle that gave thee birth;

The north winds girt thee with their rougher mail,
The east winds drench thee with their climbing foam,
The surge of tidal wave, the thresh of hail
Have battered at the lock-gates of thy home.

But not within thy jagged thews alone,
Thy strength resistant; for these latter years –   10
When bugle notes across the sea are blown,
And the loud surge with unfamiliar tears
Is piping –have revealed how strong thou art,
How staunch the granite fibres of thy heart.   [8.62.92]

TEXTUAL NOTES

To Pelham Edgar
Occurs as a holograph on the inside back cover of a notebook
but in a more final form on a fly-leaf of *The Witches' Brew*
presented to Pelham Edgar, now in the possession of his daughter,
Jane Conway of New Westminster, British Columbia.

A Breadliner's Prayer
4 Pratt wrote and then crossed out 'sleep' before settling
on 'cold.'

A Strip of Sea Coast
11 The word 'sleek' is written in the left-hand margin beside this
line and was perhaps to have been inserted before 'basalt.'
21 'adagio' was written in over the crossed-out words 'slow rhythms.'
21–2 In the holograph these lines actually appear in parentheses
after line 25, but their present position is indicated by an arrow.
27 'The echo of its cool antistrophe' crossed out

[Today and Yesterday]
One complete and two incomplete typescripts are extant. Ts 1 (the
copy text) is a xerox of an unidentified copy; ts 2 is p. 2 of an
earlier typescript; ts 3 is identical to ts 2 but also contains a
third page. The Pratt Collection has xerox copies of ts 2 and ts 3, the
originals being in the possession of Viola Pratt.

3 'To soften the chill of Niagara damp' crossed out
23 'Methodist' written over crossed-out 'parson'

First Born of England
Taken from a typescript in the possession of Viola Pratt

Moonlight
Taken from a typescript in the possession of Viola Pratt

Fisher Boy
Taken from a typescript in the possession of Viola Pratt

The Toucan
Taken from a holograph; the poem was written to accompany Viola Pratt's collection of bird stamps. For each stamp Mrs Pratt sought a poem about the bird depicted on it, but unable to find one about the toucan she pressed her husband to write one.

(To Cornie)
Taken from a typescript (7.52.51), the poem is a companion piece to 'In a Beloved Home' published in *Newfoundland Verse* (1923). In the typescript this latter title heads the two poems or sections which bear the dedications '(To Cornie)' and '(To Hubert).' Cornie and Hubert are Cornelia and W. Hubert Greaves.

The Osprey
Taken from a framed typescript (7.57.1), the poem was written for Pratt's friends, Mr and Mrs Robert Fennell. It was also used on a card illustrated with a woodcut by Claire Pratt.

St John's, Newfoundland: Steep Are Thy Cliffs
Taken from a typescript (8.62.92), the words in the title, 'St John's, Newfoundland,' are written in.

Descriptive Bibliography

Lila Laakso

INTRODUCTION

This bibliography consists of seven sections:

A / *Books and Pamphlets* arranged in chronological order. The quasi-facsimile transcriptions are based on Fredson Bowers' *Principles of Bibliographical Description* (Princeton 1949). For each entry, the following information is provided whenever possible: quasi-facsimile transcription of title page; collation (with height measurement given first); contents supplemented by a literary contents note in quasi-facsimile transcription; typography and paper, with all paper being white wove unwatermarked unless otherwise indicated (all laid paper is machine-made); all pagination is centred at foot of page unless otherwise noted; illustrations; description of binding and dust wrappers utilizing the system outlined by G. Thomas Tanselle in 'The Bibliographical Description of Patterns' (*Studies in Bibliography*, 23 [1970], 71–102); the colour designations follow the ISCC–NBS Centroid Color Charts as outlined by Tanselle's 'A System of Color Identification for Bibliographical Descriptions' (*SB*, 20 [1967], 203-34); publication information; publishing history notes; manuscript collections (since most of Pratt's books are available in major libraries across Canada, only the locations of copies examined are indicated). Publication dates are given whenever known. When they are unknown, and often when known, other dates are also given: date printed, date delivered to publisher from printer, date review copies mailed, date copies were made available to dealers, and date when copies were made available to the public.

B / *Broadsides* chronologically arranged. Broadsides with unknown publishing dates are arranged alphabetically by title following the chronological listing.

c / *Individual Poems in Books and Periodicals* is a chronological listing of every Pratt poem with its transmission history for the authoritative period. Anthology occurrences are listed here only when a poem appears for the first time in such a work. See Section F for anthology contributions. Manuscript locations are noted.

d / *Prose Published in Books and Periodicals* is a chronological listing of all first appearances in print of Pratt's prose material. Unsigned book reviews have been attributed to Pratt by Mrs Viola Pratt.

e / *Audio and Video Recordings, Sheet Music, and Miscellaneous*. This section includes dramatizations of Pratt's works, poems set to music, pageants and hymns written by him, readings of his work (by himself), interviews with Pratt, and tributes to him.

f / *Poems in Anthologies and Textbooks* inclusive to 1967 is arranged chronologically and alphabetically within a particular year.

g / *Pratt as Editor and Consultant*. Because of space limitations books edited by Pratt are presented in a brief bibliographical listing (not in quasi-facsimile) with publishing history notes. Where Pratt's name does not appear on the title page, his involvement in the editorial work has been verified by actual notes in extant copies, by correspondence in the Macmillan Archive (OHMA) and by Mrs Pratt.

h / *Manuscript Sources* is a guide to holdings of manuscripts and correspondence; detailed finding aids exist in each of the libraries which house the manuscripts.

An Index of Titles and Names concludes the bibliography.

It is not our purpose to include secondary materials; these are available in Volume II of *The Annotated Bibliography of Canada's Major Authors*, edited by Robert Lecker and Jack David (ECW Press 1980).

ACKNOWLEDGEMENTS

From the beginning of my bibliographic work on Pratt I have had the support of the late Mrs Viola Whitney Pratt and Miss Claire Pratt. For their interest and assistance in answering innumerable questions, and for calling to my attention information which I could not have known about, I am deeply grateful.

In the preparation of this bibliography I have had the generous assistance of many librarians and institutions, and although individually unnamed, I wish to acknowledge my indebtedness to them. For help and advice provided in various ways, I wish to express gratitude to Sandra Djwa, a General Editor of *The Collected Works of E.J. Pratt*, Susan Gingell, Rachel Grover, Richard Landon, Douglas Lochhead, Desmond Neill, and

Bruce Whiteman. I wish to thank the following: for their co-operation, book-dealers Nelson Ball, William Hoffer; for their research help, Debbie Green, Janice Lavery, Don McLeod; for her typing, Gwen Peroni. To my co-workers, the staff of the E.J. Pratt Library, Victoria University, I extend my appreciation. I am grateful to Victoria University for its support of this project.

Finally I wish to offer special thanks to Robert Brandeis, Chief Librarian, Victoria University, for invaluable assistance; Gordon Moyles, a General Editor of *The Collected Works of E.J. Pratt*, for expertise and patience; Jean Wilson and Gerry Hallowell of the University of Toronto Press for professional assistance; David G. Pitt for his timely additions and advice; Raymond, my husband, for unfailing support.

Location Abbreviations

BVAU	University of British Columbia, Vancouver
BVIV	University of Victoria, Victoria
LML	Collection of Lila Laakso
MWU	University of Manitoba, Winnipeg
OHMA	Archives and Special Collections Division, McMaster University, Hamilton
OKQ	Queen's University, Kingston
OONL	National Library, Ottawa
OTMC	Massey College, Toronto
OTMCL	Metropolitan Toronto Library, Toronto
OTNY	North York Public Library, Willowdale
OTR	Ryerson Polytechnical Institute, Toronto
OTU	University of Toronto, Toronto
OTUTF	Thomas Fisher Rare Book Library, University of Toronto
OTV	Victoria University, Toronto
OTW	Wycliffe College, Toronto
VCP	Collection of Claire Pratt

A / Quasi-Facsimile Title Pages of Published Works

A1 **Studies in Pauline Eschatology** 1917

STUDIES IN / Pauline Eschatology / AND ITS BACKGROUND / By / EDWIN J. PRATT, M.A., Ph.D. / Accepted by the University of Toronto as a Thesis / for the Degree of Doctor of Philosophy / [rule 2.1 cm.] / TORONTO / WILLIAM BRIGGS / 1917

(Cut: 19 × 12.5 cm.) 1–13^8 [$1 (–1, 2)], 104 leaves, pp. [1–2] 3 [4] 5–203 [204–208].

P. 1: title page as above; p. 2: [lower left margin] 'Copyright, Canada. 1917, / by EDWIN J. PRATT.'; p. 3: contents; p. 4: blank; pp. 5–10: introduction; pp. 11–203: text; pp. 204–208: blank.

Signatures at foot of page against inner margin; running titles on verso; running chapter titles on recto.

Facing p. 11, three tipped-in folding charts entitled: 'FROM THE MIDDLE OF THE FIRST CENTURY B.C. TO THE DESTRUCTION OF JERUSALEM 70 A.D.' [25.3 × 73.5 cm.]; 'ANALYSIS OF THE CONCEPTS IN THE APOCALYPTIC PERIOD FROM THE RISE OF THE MACCABEES TO THE MIDDLE OF FIRST CENTURY B.C.' [24.1 × 73.5 cm.]; 'ANALYSIS OF JEWISH RELIGIOUS CONCEPTS FROM THE EIGHTH CENTURY B.C. TO THE BEGINNING OF THE GREEK PERIOD.' [21.6 × 73.5 cm.]

Material: diagonal fine rib (102be), dark olive green (Centroid 126); upper cover: [enclosed within a frame, 3.3 × 9 cm.] 'Studies in [underscored] PAULINE / ESCHATOLOGY; [enclosed within a frame 1.7 × 9 cm.] E.J. PRATT'; [the whole enclosed within frame, 5.5 × 9 cm.]; all in gilt; spine: [lettered horizontally in gilt] 'Studies in / Pauline / Eschatology / [rule 6 mm.] / E. J. Pratt / [at foot] BRIGGS'; lower cover: blank. Dust wrapper: not seen.

200 copies published in 1917 at $1.00.

Notes: Lorne Pierce (January 12, 1932) asked Pratt for 'written authority ... to consign your Pauline Eschatology to the Eschatological incinerator.' Pratt replied, 'You are most welcome to consign these Eschatological monstrosities to the everlasting flames where they should have gone in the first place ... This is your authorization to give them a hasty and fiery despatch' (Lorne Pierce Collection, OKQ).

In a letter to E.K. Brown (April 20, 1942) Pratt details how Pauline Eschatology was published: 'In an unguarded moment I consented with the publisher; Ryerson against the victim.' He also confides to Brown that he would like to have forgotten this work because it 'was done to a formula – and not a naked expression of the spontaneous poetic spirit.' Mrs Viola Pratt related how two hundred copies were published by Pratt on the promise that the Methodist Church would advertise and sell them for $5.00 a copy. In error, the book was advertised and sold at $1.00. Pratt was out of pocket for the publication; in 1925, tired of the whole project, he burned fifty of the books.

Copies examined: OTV (2); OTU; OTW; OONL; MWU; BVAU; VCP.

As above except for title page as follows:
STUDIES IN / PAULINE ESCHATOLOGY / AND ITS BACKGROUND / By / EDWIN J. PRATT, M.A., B.D. / A Thesis / Submitted in Conformity with the Requirements for / the Degree of Doctor of Philosophy in / the University of Toronto / February, 1917 / [rule 2.1 cm.] / TORONTO / WILLIAM BRIGGS / 1917

Copies examined: OTUTF; OTU.

A2   **Rachel: A Sea Story of Newfoundland in Verse** 1917

As there is no title page, the following description is taken from the cover: [within a single-rule frame (14 × 7.7 cm.) all enclosed within a double-rule frame (15.6 × 9.3 cm.)] 𝕽𝖆𝖈𝖍𝖊𝖑 / 𝕬 𝕾𝖊𝖆 𝕾𝖙𝖔𝖗𝖞 𝖔𝖋 𝕹𝖊𝖜𝖋𝖔𝖚𝖓𝖉𝖑𝖆𝖓𝖉 / 𝖎𝖓 𝖛𝖊𝖗𝖘𝖊 / [flower ornament] / [all in gilt]

(Cut: 18 × 12 cm.): [unsigned, 1^8], 8 leaves, pp. 1–15 [16].

P. 1: title as above at head of text; pp. 2–15: text; p. 16: blank. Material: printed wrappers (morocco 402), black (Centroid 267), stapled; upper cover: as described above in quasi-facsimile; lower cover: blank.

500 copies privately printed in New York, 1917.

Notes: an ornament (1.3 × 1.3 cm.) appears at the end of the poem, p. 15. An insert consisting of one leaf (18.5 × 11.5), double rule at top and foot of page [8.9 cm.], untitled page (35 lines of text) of biographical information on Pratt. Insert seen only in OTV copy.
    In a letter to Viola Whitney (July 5, 1917) Pratt writes: 'I have just finished typewriting "Rachel," and am now sending a copy to your dear self. I am also this morning sending one to Dr. Edgar at Camp

Kapuskasing. I am anxious to see what he has to say. Shall send you his report just when I get it' (OTV).

Pratt wrote in a letter to E.K. Brown in April 1942 that 'It was a private printing limited to 500 copies and done in New York' (OTV). In a letter to David G. Pitt, dated 18 February 1958, he stated that 'A few friends of mine got together, and unknown to me, printed privately 500 copies in New York for personal and non-commercial distribution.' Mrs Pratt claimed that only 100 copies were printed and considering the scarcity of the poem, this figure seems correct.

Manuscripts, typescript: OTV, Box 1.1, 1.2, 8.62.

Copies examined: OTV; OTUTF; OTNY; OHMA.

A3   A / **Newfoundland Verse** 1923

[Within ornamental frame 15 × 9.6 cm.] Newfoundland / Verse / *by* / E [dot] J / Pratt / DECORATIONS / BY [dot] FREDK [dot] H / VARLEY / [illustration 2.5 × 2 cm.] The [dot] Ryerson [dash] Press / Publishers [dash] Toronto

(Cut: 18.5 × 12.5 cm.) $[1]^{10}$ $2-9^{8}$ [\$1 signed, −1] 74 leaves, pp. [i–vi] [1–4] 5–6 [7–8] 9–140 [141–142].

Pp. i–iv: blank; p. v: half-title [double rule thick thin 4.6 cm.] / 'NEWFOUNDLAND / VERSE'; p. vi: blank; p. 1: dedication [begins 6.3 cm. from top of page], '*To my* [star-shaped decoration 2.2 × 3.8 cm.] / MOTHER' [underlined with ornamental rule 4.2 cm.]; p. 2: blank; p. 3: title page as above; p. 4: at lower left margin [rule 3.2 cm.] / 'COPY-RIGHT, CANADA, 1923 / BY THE RYERSON PRESS'; pp. 5–6: contents; p. 7: fly-title [double rule thick thin 4.6 cm.] / 'NEWFOUNDLAND / VERSE'; p. 8: blank; pp. 9–140: text; p. 141: 'THIS BOOK IS A PRODUCTION OF / THE RYERSON PRESS, / TORONTO, CANADA'; p. 142: blank.

Contents: 9: 'Sea Variations'; 15: 'The Toll of the Bells'; 17: 'The Ground-Swell'; 18: 'Magnolia Blossoms'; 20: 'The Ice-Floes'; 27: '?'; 28: 'The Shark'; 30: 'The Fog'; 31: 'The Big Fellow'; 33: 'The Morning Plunge'; 34: 'In Absentia'; 35: 'The Flood Tide'; 36: 'The Pine Tree'; 37: 'In Lantern Light'; 38: 'The Secret of the Sea'; 40: 'Loss of the Steamship Florizel'; 41:

'The Drowning'; 42: 'Monologues and Dialogues / I / CARLO'; 46: 'II / OVERHEARD BY A STREAM'; 47: 'III / OVERHEARD IN A COVE / (The Old Salt Talks Back)'; 63: 'IV / THE PASSING OF JERRY MOORE / (*Juniper Hall answers the critics*).'; 71: 'V. / THE HISTORY OF JOHN JONES'; 73: 'Creatures of Another Country / I / THE BIRD OF PARADISE'; 74: 'II / THE EPIGRAPHER'; 77: 'Ode to December, 1917'; 87: 'Newfoundland'; 91: 'Flashlights and Echoes / From the Years of 1914 and 1915 / I / A COAST'; 92: 'II / LATER / (*A man speaks*)'; 93: 'III / (*A woman speaks*).'; 93: 'IV / MORNING'; 94: 'V / GREAT TIDES'; 94: 'VI / THE AFTER-CALM'; 96: 'VII / SCENES FROM AFAR / (*A Battlefield*)'; 99: 'VIII / A DIRGE'; 100: 'IX / THE SEED MUST DIE'; 102: 'X / COME NOT THE SEASONS HERE'; 103: 'XI / ON THE SHORE'; 104: 'XII / BEFORE A BULLETIN BOARD / (*After Beaumont-Hamel*)'; 105: 'XIII / BEFORE AN ALTAR / (*After Gueudecourt*)'; 106: 'XIV / SNOWFALL ON A BATTLE-FIELD'; 108: 'The Great Mother'; 110: 'In Memoriam'; 112: 'The Hidden Scar'; 113: 'Evening'; 114: 'In a Beloved Home / (*To w. h. g.*)'; 115: 'The Conclusion of "Rachel" / (*A story of the sea*)/ IN MEMORY OF R. S. LE D.'; 122: 'A Fragment from a Story / I / (THADDEUS, *a traveller, speaking to Julian, / an old man*)'.

Pagination at bottom right margin of type page on recto and at bottom left margin of type page on verso; headlines on recto and verso of poem titles; signed on inner margin of type page on recto. Top edge tinted light reddish brown (Centroid 42).

Material: printed imitation black quarter binding which extends 2.8 cm. on to upper and lower covers; paper covered boards with whorl pattern (412) greyish brown (Centroid 61); upper cover: [lettered in black within a light yellowish brown (Centroid 76) scroll-designed compartment (10.5 × 9 cm.)] 'NEWFOUNDLAND / VERSE / [illustration of seagulls 4.6 × 4 cm.] / *by* E / J / Pratt'; lower cover: blank; spine: paper label (9.6 × 2.2 cm.) whorl pattern (412), greyish brown (Centroid 61) [ornamental rule (1.3 × 2 cm.) greyish yellow (Centroid 90)] 'NEW / FOUND / LAND / VERSE / [illustration of seagulls (2 × 1.5 cm.] / by / EDWIN / J / PRATT' [ornamental rule (1 × 2 cm.) greyish yellow (Centroid 90)]; at foot of spine: paper label (2 × 1.3 cm.) greyish brown (Centroid 61) with publisher's device, '*The* [illustration] / Ryerson / Press / Founded / 1829'; endpapers: [within frame (17.7 × 24 cm.) extending over two pages, (sepia) illustration of seashore and seagulls in slightly yellowish brown (Centroid 74) on whorl pattern (412) paper, greyish yellow (Centroid 90)]; signature in lower left-hand corner,

'F.H. / VARLEY / . . . . 23'. Dust wrapper: not seen. ('Paper jacket' referred to in a note in the McGraw-Hill-Ryerson archival copy.)

1,000 of contracted 2,500 printed in April 1923 at $1.50 (the number printed was given to David G. Pitt by Mrs Viola Pratt in an interview in 1969).

Notes: The contract for the publication of *Newfoundland Verse* was signed in January 1923. The royalty was set at 10% for the first 2,500 copies sold and 15% for the rest. The illustrator was named in the agreement as F.H. Varley (McGraw-Hill Ryerson Archives, Toronto).

In a letter to Lorne Pierce (January 16, 1923) Pratt noted that Varley was almost finished his designs. He had indicated to Varley that he preferred 'a design having the quality of spaciousness befitting ocean themes.' He also warned Pierce that in publicity he wished not to be identified by 'such an ugly, stiff term as "Professor" ... the term is sufficient to stultify any poetic claims which a writer may, in all modesty, put forth.' A week later Pierce replied that Varley's sketch for the end-papers and other material for *NV* were satisfactory. He continued: 'I shall do my best to secure for your book an English publisher and have their name associated with ours in the first edition. We were unsuccessful a week ago in New York.'

On March 16, Pierce wrote to Pratt that he had seen 'a sample page of your book this morning ... [Publication] is earmarked for Easter; [our] salesmen [will] dodge around the city and load up the Merchants here in plenty of time.' After publication, Pratt wrote Pierce (May 16) that before a 'second edition or a first English or American Edition, I'd like to make a few small but important corrections. "Magnolia Blossoms" must certainly be integrated. "Newfoundland" must have its last stanza spatially articulated to the body of the poem. Two or three mis-spellings and some punctuations must be corrected. Wherever the errors are due to my oversight in proof, I shall gladly put up the coin.'

A Ryerson Press production sheet for *NV* (February 29, 1924) records the binding of 512 copies at 20 cents each for Educational Department purchase. This lot was indicated to be the 'balance of [the] edition' (Lorne Pierce Collection, OKQ).

Manuscripts, typescript: OTV, Box 1.2; Lorne Pierce Collection, OKQ, Box 72.003.

Holograph draft: OTV, Box 7.52.
Typescript drafts: OTV, Box 7.54, 7.55, 8.62.
Holograph commentaries: OTV, Box 6.44, 7.60, 8.63, 9.63, 9.64, 9.86.5.

Copies examined: McGraw-Hill Ryerson Archives; OTNY; MCL.

B / Identical to A except for:
(Cut: 18.5 × 12.5 cm.) [1 $(-1_{3-4} + 1_3)^{10-1}$] 2–9^8 [$1 signed, −1] 73 leaves,
pp. [i–iv] [1–4] 5–6 [7–8] 9–140 [141–142].

Pp. i–iv: blank; p. 1: dedication [begins 13.3 cm. from top of page]; p. 2:
blank; p. 3: title page as above; p. 4: copyright as above; pp. 5–6:
contents; p. 7: half-title [double rule thick thin 4.6 cm.] / 'NEWFOUND-
LAND / VERSE'.

Copies examined: OTV (3); OTU; OONL; OKQ; VCP.

C / Identical to B except for:
(Cut: 18.5 × 12.8 cm.): [1^8] 2–9^8 [$1 signed, −1] 72 leaves, pp. [i–ii] [1–4]
5–140 [141–142].
Pp. i–ii: blank; p. 1: dedication [begins 11.8 cm. from top of page].

Copies examined: OTV (2); OTU; OTMCL; OTNY; OHMA; VCP; LML.

Notes: The states of this issue can probably be attributed to dissatisfac-
tion with the placement of the dedication and the additional half-title;
amending these necessitated the changes indicated in the collations. In
the first state, the dedication appears 6.3 cm. from the top of the page;
it was then moved to 13.3 cm. from the top, and finally to 11.8 cm. from
the top. The additional half-title was removed. The width of the page
also changed from 12.5 to 12.8 cm. The changes appear to have been
made very early in the issue as the McGraw-Hill Ryerson file copy is
the first state and is designated 'first copy' by an in-house note inserted
into the copy. In addition, very few copies of the first state appear to
have been issued.

A4   A / **The Witches' Brew** 1925

THE WITCHES' BREW / BY / E.J. PRATT / With Decorations / *BY JOHN*

AUSTEN / [engraving of a black cat 2 × 3.8 cm.] LONDON: / SELWYN &
BLOUNT, LIMITED, / 21, York Buildings, Adelphi, W.C. 2.

(Cut: 18.2 × 12 cm.): 1-2^8, 16 leaves, pp. [1–8] 9–31 [32].

P. 1: half-title, 'THE WITCHES' / BREW'; p. 2: '*By the same Author* / NEW-
FOUNDLAND VERSE / By E.J. PRATT / With Decorations / By
FREDK. H. VARLEY / *The Ryerson Press* / *Toronto.*'; p. 3: blank; p. 4:
frontispiece; p. 5: title page as above; p. 6: [at centre] '*First Printed in
1925* / [at foot of page] *Made and Printed in Great Britain by* / *John Wright &
Sons Ltd., Stone Bridge, Bristol*'; p. 7: dedication, 'TO MY WIFE'; p. 8:
blank; p. 9: engraving of underwater scene of fish, seaweed, sunken
ship (5 × 7.5 cm.), above 'THE WITCHES' BREW / E.J. PRATT' followed
by text; pp. 10–32: text.

Contents [Section Headings]: 13: 'OTHER INGREDIENTS'; 16: 'DEFENSIVE
MEASURES'; 17: 'THE SEA-CAT'; 18: 'THE FLIGHT OF THE IMMORTALS'; 19:
'INVENTORY OF HADES'; 20: 'AN HOUR LATER'; 22: 'THE MIDNIGHT REVELS AS
OBSERVED / BY THE SHADES'; 25: 'THE CHARGE OF THE SWORDFISH'; 27:
'THE SUPREME TEST'; 31: 'THE RETURN OF THE CAT'.

Signed numeral at foot of page against outer margin. Pagination
enclosed in brackets centred at foot of page.

Frontispiece only (12 × 9 cm.) facing title page (p. 4): engraving of three
witches by John Austen.

Material: light greyish brown (Centroid 60) paper covered boards;
printed pale orange yellow (Centroid 73) paper label on upper cover (6.4
× 7.9 cm.) [within a double ruled frame; outer frame very red
(Centroid 11), 2 mm. wide; inner frame thin black rule] 'THE / WITCHES'
BREW / BY E.J. PRATT' / [an engraving in a triangular shape (2.6 × 5.3
cm.) of three women with long, flowing hair]; spine: sand patterned
cloth (408), black (Centroid 267), which extends 1.8 cm. to front and
back covers; printed paper label (4 × 1 cm.) horizontal letters [1 cm.
double rule: ornamental red and thin black] / 'The / Witches' / Brew /
[5 mm. rule] / E.J. / Pratt' / [1 cm. double rule: thin black and ornamental
red]; lower cover: blank. Glassine wrapper.

1,000 copies were to be published February 1926 and sold for one half-crown (60 cents) (letter, Pratt to Pierce, Sept. 24, 1924); of these, 520 copies were sent to Macmillan of Canada.

Notes: On January 17, 1924 a letter to Ryerson Press from a representative of Frederick A. Stokes Co., New York, refused *The Witches' Brew*: 'I really do not think there would be a market for this volume, so I am returning the manuscript to you herewith.'

Writing to Lorne Pierce (Sept. 24, 1924), Pratt stated that Selwyn & Blount would 'instantly ... publish one thousand copies, cloth cover with illustrations. Professor Gordon of Oxford wrote enthusiastically about it and sent a copy of it to Squire of the Mercury. Squire may print it in parts. In any case it took well wherever it was presented, both in London, Oxford and Leeds. Selwyn & Blount were to write you to see if you would represent it over here.' (Evidently Pratt paid 50 pounds to Selwyn & Blount for publishing the poem [receipt, dated Sept. 1, 1924].)

In a letter (Dec. 16, 1924) headed 'PROFESSOR! HOW COULD YOU?', Pierce wrote that 'The general feeling is that a publishing house so closely connected with the Methodist Church could not very well act as Canadian distributor of [*The Witches' Brew*]. Personally, I should like very much to be able to do something for you with this book ... I hope that the timidity of our house is not prevalent among other publishers in town. ... There is only one change that I would make if I were you. On page two I would strike out your name and on page 9 I should do the same kind service.' Pratt replied (Dec. 18): 'Sorry the vintage proved a little too stimulating for regular consumption. I understand the situation in which you are placed, as a firm, by reason of ecclesiastical affiliations' (Lorne Pierce Collection, OKQ).

Manuscripts, holograph, drafts: OTV, Box 1.3, 1.4.
Typescripts: Lorne Pierce Collection, OKQ, Box 72.004.

Copies examined: OTV (2); OTMC; OHMA; OONL; VCP; LML .

B / **The Witches' Brew** – First Canadian Edition – 1926

THE WITCHES' BREW / BY / E.J. PRATT / With Decorations / *BY JOHN AUSTEN* / [engraving of a black cat 2 × 3.8 cm.] TORONTO / THE MACMILLAN COMPANY OF CANADA, LTD., / AT ST. MARTIN'S HOUSE. / MCMXXVI.

Identical to the London edition except for title page reset imprint at foot: 'TORONTO: / THE MACMILLAN COMPANY OF CANADA, LTD., / AT ST. MARTIN'S HOUSE. / MCMXXVI.'

520 copies published in 1926 at $1.00.

Copies examined: OTV (2); OTMCL; OTNY (2); OTUTF; OHMA; VCP; LML.

A5   A / **Titans** 1926

[The whole within thick-thin rule (13.8 × 8.3 cm.)]: TITANS / By / E.J. PRATT / [acorn ornament 7 × 5 mm.] / MACMILLAN & CO. LIMITED / ST. MARTIN'S STREET, LONDON / MCMXXVI

(Cut: 18.5 × 12.7 cm.): A-D^8 E^4 [$1 signed], 36 leaves, pp. [1–6] 7 [8] 9–67 [68-72].

P. 1: half-title, 'TITANS'; p. 2: in upper left corner, '*Author of* / "Newfoundland Verse" / "The Witches' Brew"'; p. 3: title page as above; p. 4: at centre, 'COPYRIGHT / [at foot of page] 'PRINTED IN GREAT BRITAIN'; p. 5: dedication, 'TO / THE BOYS / OF THE / STAG PARTIES'; p. 6: acknowledgement, '*The Author begs to acknowledge permission / to reprint "The Cachalot," which appeared / in "The Canadian Forum" for / November 1925*'; p. 7: contents; p. 8: blank; pp. 9–68: text; p. 69: blank; p. 70: [at centre] publisher's ornament [1.9 × 1.5 cm.] / 'The Westminster Press / 411a Harrow Road / London W.9'; pp. 71–72: blank.

Contents: 9: 'THE CACHALOT'; 27: 'THE GREAT FEUD / (*A Dream of a Pleiocene Armageddon*)'; 43: [Section Heading] 'WITH THE PASSAGE OF THE MOONS / THE MUSTER'.

Signed upper case Roman letters at foot of type page against outer margin. Laid paper, vertical chain lines 2.4 cm. apart. Watermark of a crown above '𝔄𝔟𝔟𝔢𝔶 𝔐𝔦𝔩𝔩𝔰 / 𝔊𝔯𝔢𝔢𝔫𝔣𝔦𝔢𝔩𝔡'.

Material: linen cloth (304); black (Centroid 267); printed paper label on upper cover very reddish orange (Centroid 34) (6.2 × 8.6 cm.) [within double rule (5.6 × 8 cm.)] 'TITANS: / TWO POEMS / [rule 1.7 cm.] / E.J. PRATT'; spine: printed paper label very reddish orange (Centroid 34) (3.3 × 1.3 cm.), horizontally lettered [double rule 1 cm.] 'TITANS: / TWO / POEMS / [6 mm. rule] / PRATT / [1 cm. rule] / MACMILLAN' / [double rule 1 cm.]; lower cover: blank; endpapers: wove paper yellowish white (Centroid 92). Dust wrapper: on upper cover: in black, red and green on white, a prehistoric animal surrounded by rock, crossing over crevice with a large moon in background; [overprinted at bottom right] 'TITANS / [in greyish yellow green (Centroid 122)] BY / E.J. PRATT.' [in white] / initials 'ERA' [in black]; spine: [horizontally lettered] 'T/I/T/A/N/S/ E.J. / PRATT' / [publisher's device (.9 × .9 cm.)]; lower cover: blank; inside front flap: Price $1.00; back flap: blank.

750 copies printed for Macmillan in London and sent in sheets to Macmillan, Toronto, Oct. 29, 1926. The first 450 were bound in December 1926, and 296 in March 1927. The copy in the possession of Claire Pratt is dated (in Pratt's hand), 'January 18, 1927'.

Manuscripts, holograph drafts of *The Great Feud*: OTV, Box 1.3, 1.4, 1.5.
Typescript of *The Cachalot*: OTV, Box 1.7.
Holograph notes of *The Cachalot*: OTV, Box 2.15.
Holograph commentaries on *The Great Feud*: OTV, Box 1.5, 9.63.
Typescript commentary on *The Great Feud*: OTV, Box 1.6.

Copies examined: OTV (6); OTMCL (2); OTNY (3); OTMC; OHMA (2); VCP.

B / Variant binding: bound in paper boards, not embossed, brownish orange (Centroid 54) with dark grey (Centroid 266) pattern; printed paper label on front cover yellowish white (Centroid 92) (3.2 × 5 cm.) [within rule (3.4 × 1.7 cm.) broken by a central dot, and with four corner ornaments] 'TITANS / [dot] / E.J. PRATT'; rule, ornaments and lettering in dark green (Centroid 146); fore-edge: untrimmed; spine: printed paper label (5.3 × 1.2 cm.) yellowish white (Centroid 92) [within ornamental rule (5.1 × 1 cm.) horizontally lettered] 'T/I/T/A/N/S/ E.J. / PRATT'; rule and lettering in dark green (Centroid 146); lower cover: blank. Dust wrapper as above except lower cover contains notice about other Macmillan poetry publications by A.E., James Stephens, Wilfrid Gibson, John Freeman, W.S. Gilbert and W.B. Yeats. On inside front flap: 3/6 net.

Copies examined: OTV; OTUTF; OONL.

C / Reissued in 1961 by Macmillan, London [not seen].

A presentation binding for E.J. Pratt done to Macmillan's special order in fine straight-grain morocco (404b), deep yellow green (Centroid 118); gilt ornaments on upper cover, spine and lower cover; gilt lettering on upper cover, 'TITANS'; on spine, 'TITANS / [ornament] / E.J. / PRATT'. In the collection of Claire Pratt.

A6 A / **The Iron Door (An Ode-)** 1927

THE IRON DOOR / [within ornamental brackets] *An Ode- / by E.J. Pratt /* [engraving 7.5 × 5.4 cm.] / *Toronto: The Macmillan Company of / Canada Limited, at St. Martin's House /* MCMXXVII

(Untrimmed: 19.3 × 12.9 cm.) 1-4⁴ [$1 signed, −1], 16 leaves, pp. [1–8] 9–30 [31–32].

P. 1: half-title, 'THE IRON DOOR / [within ornamental brackets] *An Ode- / by E. J. Pratt*'; p. 2: [at upper right on page] '*Mr. Pratt has also written: / Newfoundland Verse / The Witches' Brew / Titans*'; p. 3: blank; p. 4: 'One thousand copies of "The Iron Door / (An Ode)" by E.J. Pratt, with decorations by / Thoreau MacDonald, and Jacket design by E.R. / Arthur, have been printed for the Publishers by / Warwick Bros. and Rutter, Limited, Toronto. / Nine hundred copies are on Byronic White / Laid Paper made in Canada. / One hundred copies, of which ninety only are / for sale, are on English Handmade Paper, and are / numbered and signed by the author.'; p. 5: title page as above; p. 6: [at centre] 'Copyright, Canada, 1927 / By The Macmillan Company of / Canada Limited / Toronto / [at foot of page] Printed in Canada'; p. 7: dedication, '*To some very dear memories.*' [with vignette of a pine branch (3.7 × 2.4 cm.)]; p. 8: blank; pp. 9–30: text, with title at head of text and drawings on pp. 10, 15, 19, 25, 28; p. 30: semi-circular vignette (2.8 × 5.4 cm.) at end of text; pp. 31–32: blank.

Signed numerals at foot of type page against inner margin. Pagination at outer margin at foot of type page. Laid paper, vertical chain lines 2.5 cm. apart; watermark of beaver superimposed on an S, both enclosed within a circle with 'MADE IN CANADA' around bottom half of circle and 'Byronic Book' beside it; edges: top edge trimmed, fore and bottom edges untrimmed.

All drawings by Thoreau MacDonald (except dust wrapper which is by Eric R. Arthur) printed for the publisher by Warwick Bros. and Rutter, Ltd., Toronto. Size of drawings on pp. 10, 15, 19, 25 and 28: 7.6 × 7.6 cm.

Material: paper covered boards, medium greenish blue (Centroid 173);
upper cover: [centred near top] 'THE IRON DOOR / [enclosed within
ornamental brackets] *An Ode-* / *by E.J. Pratt*' / [semi-circular vignette (1.4
× 2.8 cm.)] all in gilt; spine: [vertically lettered in gilt] '*The Iron Door*
[dot] *by E.J. Pratt* [dot]; lower cover: blank; endpapers: same as text.
Dust wrapper: engraving by Eric R. Arthur in black (Centroid 267) on
medium greenish blue (Centroid 173): a stone structure with a massive
door containing a cross design with a skull above it on the door frame;
clusters of figures standing before the door; [overprinted at top] 'THE
IRON DOOR / BY / E.J. PRATT' [in strong red (Centroid 12)]; spine:
[vertically lettered in black] 'THE IRON DOOR / [ornamental dash
8 mm.] / PRATT'; lower cover: blank; inner front flap: biographical note
on Pratt; back flap: publisher's advertisement for Pratt's books.

900 copies (and an additional 100 copies numbered and signed as
described below) published Sept. 23, 1927. Price: $1.25 (limited, $2.50).

Notes: Pratt, when sending *A Vision of An Iron Door (An Ode)* to Lorne
Pierce (July 15, 1927), claimed: 'You are responsible for the 2nd and
3rd stanzas on page 4. I have never written anything which came so
naturally from my heart ... Last night a whole crew of people came up
to my house to hear it read ... and it was their common judgment that
the ode was the best thing I had done, by a long chalk ... Eayrs is going
to publish it immediately in book form and get the English Macmillan's
to publish it over there.' Pratt planned to make the ode his 'chief item'
on his forthcoming Western tour (Lorne Pierce Collection, OKQ).
   William Arthur Deacon (August 25, 1927) begged Pratt for a 'short
poem that would do in the Literary Section [of the *Globe and Mail*].' He
scolds Pratt for not letting him know of and have some lines from *The
Iron Door* that could be published in advance of the book: 'It would be
a good announcement of the book.' But the limited edition was then out
and Deacon, in a second letter (August 29), reported that he had
ordered it. He also thanked Pratt for having sent him the manuscript: 'I
like it very much' (Deacon Manuscript Colection 160, OTUTF).

Drawings recorded in *Thoreau MacDonald: A Catalogue of Design and Illus-
tration* by Margaret E. Edison (Toronto: University of Toronto Press,
1973), p. 68.

Manuscripts, holograph draft: OTV, Box 1.5.

Typescript: Lorne Pierce Collection, OKQ, Box 2.009; Deacon Manuscript Collection, 160, OTUTF.
Holograph commentary: OTV, Box 1.5.

Copies examined: OTV (2); OTUTF; OTMC; OTNY; OHMA (2); VCP.

B / **The Iron Door (An Ode-)** – Limited Edition –1927

The first limited edition of 100 copies of which 90 were for sale (at a price of $2.50) is identical with the first trade edition except for:

p. 4: edition statement followed by Copy Number and E.J. Pratt's signature.

English handmade paper: Hayle (Barchum Greene), vertical chain lines 4 cm. apart, watermarked with hand and framed head.

Material: paper covered boards, greenish grey (Centroid 155) quarter bound white linen grain cloth (304) which extends 1.3 cm. to front and back covers (titles identical to trade edition). Dust wrapper: identical except printed on greenish grey (Centroid 155) paper same as boards. Slipcase (28 × 14 × 1 cm.): case paper covered, greenish grey (Centroid 155); upper cover, spine and lower cover: blank.

Copies examined: OTV (Nos. 31 & 38); OTUTF (No. 66); OTMC (No. 92); OTMCL (No. 90); OHMA (No. 33); OONL (Nos. 93 & 94); VCP (Nos. 1 & 91).

A7   A / **The Roosevelt and the Antinoe** 1930

THE ROOSEVELT / AND THE ANTINOE / By E.J. PRATT / THE MACMILLAN COMPANY / NEW YORK MCMXXX

(Untrimmed: 22.3 × 16 cm.) [unsigned, $1–3^8$], 24 leaves, pp. [1–8] 9–44 [45–48].

P. 1: half-title, 'THE ROOSEVELT AND THE ANTINOE'; p. 2: 'BY E.J. PRATT / NEWFOUNDLAND VERSE / THE WITCHES' BREW / TITANS / THE IRON DOOR / VERSES OF THE SEA (Preparing)'; p. 3: title page as above; p. 4: 'COPYRIGHT, 1930, / BY THE MACMILLAN COMPANY / [rule 9 mm.] / ALL RIGHTS RESERVED, INCLUDING THE RIGHT OF / REPRODUCTION IN WHOLE OR IN PART IN ANY FORM. / [rule

9 mm.] / Set up and printed. / Published February, 1930.' / [at foot of page] 'PRINTED IN THE UNITED STATES OF AMERICA / BY T. MOREY & SON'; p. 5: dedication, 'TO MY BROTHERS / JIM, ART AND CAL'; p. 6: blank; p. 7: pronunciation, '"Antinoe" is pronounced here An'-ti-no, / as in popular usage'; p. 8: blank; pp. 9-44: text [with title at head of text on p. 9]; pp. 45-48: blank.

Pagination at bottom outer margin. Laid paper vertical chain lines 1.8 cm. apart; unwatermarked; edges: untrimmed.

Frontispiece: on coated paper, facing title page, entitled 'THE ROOSEVELT STANDING BY THE ANTINOE IN THE JANUARY STORM OF 1926' [9.7 × 16.7 cm.]; [above title]: 'Reproduced by permission of J.W. Dearden'; 'From the painting by Charles Dixon R.I..'

Material: calico-texture cloth (302), dark red (Centroid 16); upper cover: [within a blocked compartment (4.5 × 8.1 cm.)]: printed pale orange yellow (Centroid 73) paper label (4.2 × 8 cm.) [within a very red (Centroid 11) ornamental frame (3.5 × 7.3 cm.)] 'THE ROOSEVELT / AND THE ANTINOE / [red rule 8 mm.] / E.J. PRATT'; spine: blank; lower cover: blank. Dust wrapper: greyish yellow (Centroid 90); upper cover: 'THE ROOSEVELT / AND / THE ANTINOE / BY / E.J. PRATT' [all enclosed in an ornamental frame (10.5 × 14.9 cm.) very red (Centroid 11) on upper half of wrapper]; spine: [ornamental rule same design as the ornamental very red (Centroid 11) frame on front cover 1.5 cm.] [vertically lettered] 'THE ROOSEVELT AND THE ANTINOE / [rule 5 mm.] / PRATT / MACMILLAN' / [ornamental rule as above]; lower cover: blank; inner front flap: publisher's note about the poem; back flap: blank.

Published February 18, 1930 at $1.50 (limited, unknown). No. of copies unknown.

Notes: With The Roosevelt and the Antinoe Pratt had a new experience: publishers were interested before the poem was completed. In a letter to Pelham Edgar (August 6, 1929) he explained that Hugh Eayrs of Macmillan 'had mentioned [his] intention to Harper's and to Macmillan's of United States and they were anxious to take a look at the poem ... though it was much against my grain ... I sent [the unrevised main part] to Harper's and ... to Macmillan's ... Harper's made me an immediate offer ... Quite enthusiastic they were. Next week comes an offer from Macmillan.' Macmillan's reader, Edwin Arlington Robinson, gave 'the most whole-hearted commitment I have ever received in my life.' The Canadian publication was postponed until February because editorial work 'and other things' had not allowed Pratt to finish the poem. Pratt also reported to Edgar that the postponement would not interefere with a recital of the poem (OTV).

On October 11, 1929, Pratt sent William Deacon two complimentary tickets to his Oct. 16th recital. He also informed Deacon that the poem would be published in the United States by Macmillan in January 1930 (OTUTF/160). The Canadian launching was celebrated with a dinner hosted by Macmillan on Feb. 28, 1930.

Manuscripts, holograph drafts: OTV, Box 1.5, 2.8.
Typescript: OTV, 2.9, 2.10.
Holograph notes and commentary: OTV, Box 9.64, 9.65.
Typescript commentary: OTV, Box 2.11, 2.12.

Copies examined: OTV (3); OTUTF; OTMC (2); OTMCL (2) OTNY (6); OHMA (2); OONL; VCP; LML.

B / The Roosevelt and the Antinoe – Limited Edition –1930

The first limited edition of 100 copies is identical with the first trade edition except for:
[Unsigned, π^2 1–3^8] 26 leaves, pp. [i–iv] [1–8] 9–44 [45–48].

P. i: blank; p. ii: blank; p. iii: 'THIS EDITION OF THE ROOSEVELT AND THE ANTINOE IS LIMITED / TO ONE HUNDRED COPIES SIGNED BY THE AUTHOR / THIS IS NUMBER ____.' [number in ink and signature of E.J. Pratt]; p. iv: blank.

Material: quarter bound black calico cloth (302) which extends 1.5 cm. to upper and lower covers; cracked surface texture paper over boards, deep red (Centroid 13); upper cover: [within a blocked compartment 4.5 × 8.1 cm.] printed pale orange yellow (Centroid 73) paper label as in trade edition; lower cover: blank; top of pages gilt. Dust wrapper: as trade edition except colour is light grey (Centroid 264).

Copies examined: OTMCL (No. 56); OTUTF (No. 38); OTV (No. 85); BVIV (No. 17).

A8   **Verses of the Sea** 1930

[The whole within an ornamental frame 14.7 × 9.2 cm.]: *St. Martin's Classics* [underscored] / VERSES OF THE SEA / *By* / E.J. PRATT / *With an introduction by* / CHARLES G.D. ROBERTS / *and notes by the Author* / [publisher's device 1.9 × 1.5 cm.] / TORONTO: THE MACMILLAN COMPANY OF / CANADA LIMITED, AT ST. MARTIN'S HOUSE / 1930

(Cut: 16.7 × 11.3 cm.): [unsigned, 1-6^8 7^{10}], 58 leaves, pp. [i–iv] v–xv [xvi] [1–2] 3–97 [98–100].

P. i: half-title [series title]: '*St. Martin's Classics* / VERSES OF THE SEA'; p. ii: blank; p. iii: title page as above; p. iv: 'Copyright, Canada, 1930 / by / THE MACMILLAN COMPANY OF CANADA LIMITED / [at foot of page] PRINTED AND BOUND IN CANADA / BY THE HUNTER-ROSE CO., LIMITED'; pp. v–xiv: introduction; p. xv: contents; p. xvi: blank; p. 1: fly-title, 'VERSES OF THE SEA'; p. 2: blank; pp. 3–72: text; pp. 73–96: notes; p. 97: illustration; pp. 98–100: blank.

Contents: 3: 'THE ICE-FLOES'; 10: 'THE TOLL OF THE BELLS'; 12: 'THE GROUND SWELL'; 13: 'THE SHARK'; 15: 'THE FOG'; 16: 'IN LANTERN LIGHT'; 17: 'THE BIG FELLOW'; 19: 'THE MORNING PLUNGE'; 20: 'CARLO'; 25: 'GREAT TIDES'; 26: 'OVERHEARD BY A STREAM'; 28: 'THE HISTORY OF JOHN JONES'; 30: 'THE FLOOD-TIDE'; 31: 'NEWFOUNDLAND'; 35: 'SIGNALS'; 36: 'ON THE SHORE'; 37: 'THE GREAT MOTHER'; 39: 'IN ABSENTIA'; 40: 'THE CACHALOT'; 62: 'DAWN'; 63: 'THE RITUAL'; 65: 'THE SEA-CATHEDRAL'; 67: 'THE LEE-SHORE'; 68: 'THE BURIAL SERVICE / From *The Roosevelt and the Antinoe*'.

Pagination in headline against outer margin of type page; running-titles in roman caps: 'VERSES OF THE SEA' on recto and verso (except pp. vii–xiii; recto: 'INTRODUCTION'; pp. 75–95, recto: 'NOTES').

Diagrams on p. 97: 'GREENLAND (RIGHT) WHALE' 'SPERM WHALE (CACHALOT)'; 'Normal position of harpoon head'; 'Position after entering whale'.

Material: calico-texture cloth (302), very red (Centroid 11); upper cover: [the whole within 2 mm. thick blind stamped frame (16.8 × 10.3 cm.)] at centre: [publisher's device (3.4 × 2.7 cm.)] in gilt; spine: [ornamental rule 2 cm.] / [horizontally lettered] 'ST. MARTIN'S / CLASSICS / VERSES / OF / THE SEA / [at foot] MACMILLAN' / [ornamental rule 2 cm.] all in gilt; lower cover: blank; endpapers: white wove, unwatermarked.

Published in 1930 at 50 cents. No. of copies unknown.

Copies examined: OTV; OTUTF; OTMCL; OTNY (3); OONL; VCP; LML.

A9   **Many Moods** 1932

MANY MOODS / By / E.J. PRATT / TORONTO / THE MACMILLAN COMPANY / OF CANADA LTD. / AT ST. MARTIN'S HOUSE / 1932

(Untrimmed: 22 × 14.2 cm.) π^4 1–3^8 4^4 [$1,2 (–$4_2$)], 32 leaves, pp. [i–iv] v–vi [vii–viii] 1–53 [54–56].

P. i: half-title, 'MANY MOODS'; p. ii: 'By E.J. PRATT / *Newfoundland Verse / The Witches' Brew / Titans / The Iron Door / The Roosevelt and the Antinoe / Verses of the Sea.*'; p. iii: title page as above; p. iv: dedication, 'To / VIOLA / and / CLAIRE'; pp. v–vi: contents; p. vii: fly-title, 'MANY MOODS'; p. viii: blank; pp. 1–53: text; p. 54: 'PRINTED BY / WALTER LEWIS, M.A., AT / THE UNIVERSITY PRESS / CAMBRIDGE, ENGLAND'; pp. 55-56: blank.

Contents: 1: 'A REVERIE ON A DOG'; 9: 'SEA-GULLS'; 9: 'THE WAY OF CAPE RACE'; 10: 'EROSION'; 10: 'THE SEA-CATHEDRAL'; 11: 'A PRAIRIE SUNSET'; 12: 'THE DEPRESSION ENDS'; 19: 'OUT OF STEP / (1931 A.D.)'; 20: 'THE MAN AND THE MACHINE'; 20: 'A PUZZLE PICTURE'; 21: 'THE PARABLE OF PUFFSKY'; 23: 'FROM STONE TO STEEL'; 23: 'OLD AGE'; 24: 'BLIND'; 25: 'A LEGACY'; 25: 'THE DECISION / (To L.R., a college athlete who died May, 1923.)'; 26: 'THE LOST CAUSE'; 26: 'TO AN ENEMY'; 27: 'WHITHER?'; 27: 'THE HIGHWAY'; 28: 'PUTTING WINTER TO BED'; 33: 'CHERRIES'; 34: 'A FELINE SILHOUETTE'; 34: 'THE CHILD AND THE WREN / (To Claire)'; 35: 'FROST'; 36: 'A NOVEMBER LANDSCAPE'; 36: 'MAGIC'; 37: 'COMRADES'; 38: 'ONE HOUR OF LIFE'; 38: 'HORIZONS'; 39: 'DOORS'; 39: 'THE ARMISTICE SILENCE'; 40: 'DREAMS'; 40: 'TIME-WORN'; 41: 'TO ANGELINA, AN OLD NURSE'; 44: 'JOCK O' THE LINKS'; 45: 'TATTERHEAD'; 46: 'THE CONVICT HOLOCAUST / (Columbus, Ohio, 1930)';

47: 'THE DRAG-IRONS'; 47: 'A LEESHORE'; 48: 'THE PURSUIT'; 48: 'THE FUGI-
TIVE'; 49: 'THE 6000'; 52: 'THE RITUAL'.

Signatures at foot of page against outer margin. At left of direction line
the letters 'MMM' on first page of each signature. Laid paper, vertical
chain lines 2.5 cm. apart; watermark of a crown above '𝔸𝔟𝔟𝔢𝔶 𝔐𝔦𝔩𝔩𝔰 /
𝔊𝔯𝔢𝔢𝔫𝔣𝔦𝔢𝔩𝔡'; edges: top edge trimmed, fore-edge and bottom untrimmed.

Material: quarter bound criss-cross cloth (120), pale yellow (Centroid 89)
which extends 3.4 cm. to upper and lower covers; linen grain cloth
(304), very deep purplish red (Centroid 257); upper cover: [lettered in
gilt, within a blocked compartment (4.5 × 8.6 cm.)] 'MANY MOODS /
E.J. PRATT'; spine: [lettered vertically in gilt] 'MANY MOODS / [5 mm.
rule] PRATT / [at foot] MACMILLAN'; lower cover: blank; endpapers:
white wove unwatermarked. Glassine wrappers [not seen].

753 copies printed in England and sent in sheets to Macmillan, Toronto,
October 26, 1932. The first 250 were bound and recorded as delivered
by Nov. 21, 1932 and the balance by Feb. 3, 1933. Price: $1.50.

Notes: The search for a title elicited 'Sea Foam and Star Shine' from
Macmillan, titles which, Pratt confided to Hugh Eayrs (July 9, 1932)
delighted both him and his wife. He suggested that the book have a
'jacket without decoration but with a few comments on the earlier
poetry.' He should like, he added, to have the comments of C.P. Scott of
The Manchester Guardian, who 'wrote a gorgeous thing ... on the
Roosevelt and on Titans ... somewhere in the advertisement.' In a reply
(July 15, 1932) Eayrs requested that Pratt allow 'For Better or Worse' and
'The Decision' to be omitted because neither is 'up to your standards
[but] are trite compared with the rest ... I am holding the two poems
here ... I have decided to have the book set at the Cambridge Univer-
sity Press ... There are no printers in the world like Cambridge'
(Macmillan Archive, OHMA). ('For Better or Worse' did not appear in
Many Moods but 'The Decision' did.)
    In a letter to Pelham Edgar (August 26, 1932), Pratt stated that he had
submitted *Sea and Sky* as a title for the book, but 'it was used on
another recent volume ... Many Moods was finally decided on.'

Manuscripts, holograph drafts: OTV, Box 2.13, 2.14, 2.15, 4.30, 9.65.

Holographs of individual poems: Lorne Pierce Collection, oKQ, Box 72.004.
Macmillan Archive, oHMA, Box 128.7.
Holograph notes: oTV, Box 4.29, 7.51.
Holograph commentaries: oTV, Box 2.14, 2.15, 6.44, 7.60, 9.63, 9.65, 9.68.3.

Copies examined: oTV (3); oTUTF; oTMCL (3); oTNY (2); oHMA (2); oONL; VCP; LML.

A10   **The Titanic** 1935

THE TITANIC / By E.J. PRATT / [publisher's device 2 × 1.5 cm.] / TORONTO: THE MACMILLAN COMPANY OF / CANADA LIMITED, AT ST. MARTIN'S HOUSE / 1935

(Untrimmed: 23.5 × 15.5 cm.), [unsigned, 1–3⁸], 24 leaves, pp. [i–vi] [1–2] 3–42.

P. 1: half-title, 'THE TITANIC'; p. ii: [at centre] 'BY E.J. PRATT / NEW-FOUNDLAND VERSE / The Witches' BREW / TITANS / THE IRON DOOR / THE ROOSEVELT AND THE ANTINOE / VERSES OF THE SEA / MANY MOODS'; p. iii: title page as above; p. iv: [at centre] 'Copyright, Canada, 1935 / by / THE MACMILLAN COMPANY OF CANADA LIMITED / All rights reserved – no part of this book / may be reproduced in any form without per- / mission in writing from the publisher, except / by a reviewer who wishes to quote brief / passages in connection with a review written / for inclusion in magazine or newspaper.' / [at foot of page] 'Printed in Canada / The Armac Press Limited, Toronto'; p. v: dedication, 'TO MY FATHER'; p. vi: 'ACKNOWLEDGMENT / The author and the publisher gratefully acknowledge the / permission of the Holloway Studio, Ltd. to use the two illus- / trations in this volume.'; p. 1: fly-title, 'THE TITANIC'; p. 2: blank; pp. 3–42: text [with title at head of text on p. 3].

Laid paper, vertical chain lines 2.3 cm. apart; watermark of beaver superimposed on an S, both enclosed within a circle with 'MADE IN CANADA' around bottom half of circle and '*Byronic Book*' beside it; edges: top edge trimmed, fore and bottom edges untrimmed.

Tipped-in frontispiece on coated paper facing the title page, two oval-shaped photographs of icebergs: top photograph (6.6 × 10 cm.) '... had stratified / The berg to the consistency of flint.'; bottom photograph (6.9 × 10 cm.) '... palaeolithic outline of a face / Fronted the trans-atlantic shipping route.'

Material: diagonal fine rib (102be), dark blue (Centroid 183); upper cover: [on upper half of cover, lettered in gilt] 'THE TITANIC / E.J. PRATT'; spine: blank; lower cover: blank. Cellophane wrappers [not seen].

752 copies printed October 25, 1935 by The Armac Press, Toronto for Macmillan of Canada with 250 bound and recorded as delivered by Nov. 5, 1935 and the balance by April 3, 1936. Price: $1.50.

Notes: On April 6, 1935 Pratt read from *The Titanic* for the first time to 'the boys': 'It was a joy to read it ... and receive such overwhelming responses.' Discussing its theme, Pratt talked of being 'swept away ... as I was in the Roosevelt only to a vaster extent. It is so much more complex, involving so many more philosophic, economic and artistic issues ... [It reveals] crescendos of cries and fears approaching panic, the terrible silences and innuendos, the tensions, the inward voiceless struggles that issued in decisions, the stark outlines of the iceberg remaining immovable while the ship takes her plunge, grim, alone and triumphant ... I hope to get ... it out as a fall book.' He promises to send Deacon a typed carbon copy in advance and should be glad to 'get any advice upon the construction so I may make any necessary adjustments before it goes to proof' (Macmillan Archive, OHMA).

Manuscripts, holograph drafts: OTV, Box 3.16, 3.17.
Holograph commentaries: OTV, Box 3.16, 3.17, 6.44.
Typescript commentary: OTV, Box 3.18.

Copies examined: OTV (3); OTUTF; OTMCL; OTNY (3); OHMA (4); OONL; VCP; LML.

Variant binding: (1) deep blue (Centroid 179): OTV; (2) blackish blue (Centroid 188): OHMA; LML.

A presentation binding for E.J. Pratt done to Macmillan's special order in fine morocco (402b), dark bluish green (Centroid 165); gilt decoration on upper cover, spine and lower cover; [gilt lettering on upper cover] 'THE / TITANIC / [rule .7 cm.] / E.J.PRATT'. Inscribed: 'This, the first copy off the press of "*The Titanic*" is signed for the author by a group of his friends gathered together to tell him how much they think of him. St. Martin's House / Toronto November 15, 1935.' [In the collection of Claire Pratt]

A11 **The Fable of the Goats and Other Poems** 1937

THE FABLE OF THE GOATS / AND OTHER POEMS / By / E.J. PRATT / [publisher's device 2 × 1.5 cm.] / TORONTO: THE MACMILLAN COMPANY OF / CANADA LIMITED, AT ST. MARTIN'S HOUSE / 1937

(Untrimmed: 22.9 × 15.1 cm.) [unsigned, 1–3^8], 28 leaves, pp. [i–vi] vii [viii] 1–47 [48].

P. i: half-title, 'THE FABLE OF THE GOATS'; p. ii: 'By E.J. PRATT / *Newfoundland Verse / The Witches' Brew / Titans / The Iron Door / The Roosevelt and the Antinoe / Verses of the Sea / Many Moods / The Titanic*'; p. iii: title page as above; p. iv: [at centre] 'COPYRIGHT, CANADA, 1937 / BY / THE MACMILLAN COMPANY OF CANADA LIMITED / All rights reserved – no part of this book / may be reproduced in any form without / permission in writing from the publishers / except by a reviewer who wishes to quote / brief passages in connection with a review / written for inclusion in a magazine or / newspaper.'; p. v: dedication, '*TO MY SISTER CHARLOTTE*'; p. vi: blank; p. vii: contents; p. viii: blank; pp. 1–47: text with title at head of text; p. 48: blank.

Contents: 1: 'THE FABLE OF THE GOATS'; 16: 'THE BARITONE'; 18: 'PUCK REPORTS BACK'; 25: 'SILENCES'; 27: 'A PRAYER-MEDLEY'; 32: 'FIRE'; 33: 'SEEN ON THE ROAD'; 34: 'THE PRIZE CAT'; 35: 'UNDER THE LENS'; 37: 'THE SEER'; 38: '(TO ANY ASTRONOMER)'; 39: 'THE TEXT OF THE OATH'; 40: 'LIKE MOTHER, LIKE DAUGHTER'; 42: 'THE MIRAGE'; 43: 'THE OLD ORGANON (1225 A.D.)'; 43: 'THE NEW (1937 A.D.)'; 44: 'THE MYSTIC'; 45: 'THE DROWNING'; 46: 'THE WEATHER GLASS'; 47: 'THE EMPTY ROOM'.

Laid paper, vertical chain lines 3 cm. apart; watermark: Supertext, 'MADE IN CANADA'; edges: untrimmed.

Material: linen grain cloth (304), medium violet (Centroid 211); upper cover: [within a blocked compartment (4.5 × 7.3 cm.) lettered in gilt] 'THE FABLE / OF THE GOATS / AND OTHER POEMS / [inverted triangle 4 × 4 mm.] / E.J. PRATT'; spine: blank; lower cover: blank; endpapers: same paper as for book. Cellophane wrappers.

752 copies printed October 28, 1937; by November 1941, 480 copies had been distributed and sold at $1.50 per copy.

Notes: In a letter of May 11, 1938 Macmillan advised Pratt that they had sent four copies of *The Fable of the Goats* to the Canadian Author's Association to be considered for the Governor-General's Award (OHMA). The book won the G-G's Award for 1937.

Manuscripts, holograph drafts: 'The Fable of the Goats': OTV, Box 3.19, 3.20.
Holograph drafts: Other Poems: OTV, Box 3.16, 7.51, 7.52, 7.53, 7.56, 7.60.
Typescript of 'The Fable of the Goats': OTV, Box 3.21; Lorne Pierce Collection, OKQ, Box 6.09.
Holograph and typescript commentary on other poems: OTV, Box 7.60.

Copies examined: OTV (3); OTUTF; OTMCL; OTNY; OHMA; VCP; LML.

Variant binding: linen grain cloth (304), very purplish blue (Centroid 194); OHMA, VCP.

A12   A / **Brébeuf and His Brethren** 1940

Brébeuf and His Brethren / BY / E.J. PRATT / [publisher's device 2 × 1.5 cm.] / TORONTO: THE MACMILLAN COMPANY OF / CANADA LIMITED AT ST. MARTIN'S HOUSE / 1940

(Cut: 21. 7 × 13.9 cm.) [unsigned, 1–4⁸ 5⁴], 36 leaves, pp. [i–vi] 1–65 [66].

P. i: half-title, 'BRÉBEUF AND HIS BRETHREN'; p. ii: '*By* E.J. PRATT / NEWFOUNDLAND VERSE / THE WITCHES' BREW / TITANS / THE IRON DOOR / THE ROOSEVELT AND THE ANTINOE / VERSES OF THE SEA / MANY MOODS / THE TITANIC / THE FABLE OF THE GOATS / AND OTHER POEMS'; p. iii:

title page as above; p. iv: [at centre] 'COPYRIGHT, CANADA, 1940 / BY / THE MACMILLAN COMPANY OF CANADA LIMITED / All rights reserved – no part of this book / may be reproduced in any form without / permission in writing from the publisher, / except by a reviewer who wishes to quote / brief passages in connection with a review / written for inclusion in a magazine or / newspaper.'; p. v: dedication, 'TO / MY FATHER'; p. vi: blank; pp. 1–65: text with title at head of text; p. 66: blank.

Contents [Section Headings]: 1: 'BRÉBEUF AND HIS BRETHREN / I'; 9: 'II'; 12: 'III'; 26: 'IV'; 30: 'V / (The Founding of Fort Sainte Marie)'; 31: 'VI / (The mission to the Petuns and Neutrals)'; 36: 'VII / (The story of Jogues)'; 45: 'VIII / (Bressani)'; 47: 'IX'; 52: 'X'; 55: 'XI'; 60: 'XII'.

Material: linen grain cloth (304), very deep red (Centroid 14); upper cover: [within a blocked compartment (4.8 × 10.5 cm.) lettered in gilt] 'BRÉBEUF / AND HIS BRETHREN / E.J. PRATT'; spine: [lettered vertically, in gilt] 'BRÉBEUF AND HIS BRETHREN / [5 mm. rule] / PRATT / [at foot] MACMILLAN'; lower cover: blank; endpapers: white wove, unwatermarked; the front and back paste down and free endpapers contain a map of Huronia (20.8 × 25.3 cm.); upper right-hand corner has a small scale inset map of surrounding area (6.9 × 8.3 cm.). Dust wrapper: brilliant yellow (Centroid 83) with black lettering; upper cover: [at top] 'BRÉBEUF / AND HIS BRETHREN / By E.J. PRATT / [at foot] MACMILLAN'; spine: [lettered vertically] 'BRÉBEUF AND HIS BRETHREN / [4 mm. rule] / E.J. PRATT / [at foot] MACMILLAN'; lower cover: [enclosed within a thick-thin rule (20.2 × 12.2 cm.)] publisher's announcement for 'THE CHAMPLAIN ROAD / By / FRANKLIN DAVEY MCDOWELL' signed 'MARGARET LAWRENCE.' On inner flap: biographical note of E.J. Pratt; on back flap: critical quotes about the works of E.J. Pratt; at foot of both flaps: 'THE MACMILLANS IN CANADA / Publishers TORONTO'.

1,042 copies were printed with 500 bound and recorded as delivered by July 8, 1940 and the balance by October 18, 1940. Price: $1.25.

Notes: On June 6, 1940 Pratt sent typed information to Ellen Elliott 'which might do for the jacket'; it was 'largely from a previous blurb [with added recent news]. I don't want to "put on the dog" too much' (OHMA). In a letter to the Edgars (July 19, 1940) he announced that

Brébeuf 'has at last come out and it looks fine in format and type' and that Grant Hall, at Queen's University, will hold 'four hundred students and visitors' for a lecture on July 28. He noted that Deacon would be reviewing the poem in the August 3 *Globe and Mail* and that Morgan-Powell 'will find it space' in the Montreal *Daily Star* (OTV).

Pratt informed Elliott (Oct. 28, 1940) that Healey Willan and Campbell MacInnes were interested in transforming *Brébeuf* into a 'Canadian Passion Play or Oratorio' and that Catholics were 'keen' to have it performed 'in the open air at Midland' (Macmillan Archive, OHMA). A musical and dramatic version of *Brébeuf*, composed by Healey Willan, was first performed and broadcast on Sept. 26, 1943 at the CBC Studios, Toronto, conducted by Ettore Mazzoleni and produced by James Finlay. The first public performance, as *The Life and Death of Jean de Brébeuf*, took place on Jan. 18, 1944 at Massey Hall, Toronto; it was performed by the Mendelssohn Choir and the Toronto Symphony Orchestra conducted by Sir Ernest MacMillan. A second version of *Brébeuf* which Healey Willan revised in 1947 for choir and organ was conducted by the composer in the Timothy Eaton Memorial Church, Toronto, in 1967.

In April 1946, Edgar received this news: 'The Harvard Speech Institute made four recordings [of Pratt reading *Brébeuf*] ... and they intend putting them on the market' (OTV). *Brébeuf* was subsequently read several times on radio (Pratt to E.K. Brown, April 27, 1948: OTV), (Pratt to Earle Birney, August 10, 1949: OTUTF/49).

Brébeuf and His Brethren won the Governor-General's Award for 1940.

Manuscripts, holograph draft: OTV, Box 3.22, 4.29.
Typescript draft: OTV, Box 3.23.
Holograph notes and commentaries: OTV, Box 3.22, 3.24.
Typescript commentary: OTV, Box 3.24, 3.25.

Copies examined: OTV (3); OTUTF; OTMCL; OONL; OHMA (2); VCP; LML.

B / **Brébeuf and His Brethren** – Second revised limited edition – 1940

Brébeuf and His Brethren / BY / E.J. PRATT / [publisher's device 2 × 1.5 cm.] / TORONTO: THE MACMILLAN COMPANY OF / CANADA LIMITED, AT ST. MARTIN'S HOUSE / 1940

(Deckled: 23.4 × 15.8 cm.) [unsigned, 1-4⁸ 5⁴], 36 leaves, pp. [i–vi] 1–66.

P. i: half-title, 'BREBEUF AND HIS BRETHREN'; p. ii: '*By* E.J. PRATT / NEWFOUNDLAND VERSE / THE WITCHES' BREW / TITANS / The Iron Door / The Roosevelt and the Antinoe / Verses of the Sea / Many Moods / The Titanic / The Fable of the Goats / and Other Poems'; p. iii: title page as above; p. iv: [at centre] 'COPYRIGHT, CANADA, 1940 / BY / THE MACMILLAN COMPANY OF CANADA LIMITED / All rights reserved – no part of this book / may be reproduced in any form without / permission in writing from the publisher, / except by a reviewer who wishes to quote / brief passages in connection with a review / written for inclusion in a magazine or / newspaper. / *Second and slightly revised edition, with new epilogue, signed by the author and limited / to five hundred copies, of which this is / No ...*' [number and signature, E.J. Pratt, in ink] / [at foot of page] 'PRINTED IN CANADA / BY / THE HUNTER-ROSE CO. LIMITED'; p. vi: dedication, TO / MY FATHER'; p. vi: blank; pp. 1–66: text with title at head of text.

Contents [Section Headings]: 1: 'BREBEUF AND HIS BRETHREN / I'; 9: 'II'; 12: 'III'; 26: 'IV'; 30: 'V / (*The Founding of Fort Sainte Marie*)'; 31: 'VI / *The mission to the Petuns and Neutrals*)'; 36: 'VII / (*The story of Jogues*)'; 45: 'VIII / (*Bressani*)'; 47: 'IX'; 52: 'X'; 55: 'XI'; 60: 'XII'; 66: 'THE MARTYRS' SHRINE'.

Laid paper, vertical chain lines 3 cm. apart; watermark: *Supertext* MADE IN CANADA; edges: top, cut; fore and bottom edges, deckle.

Frontispiece and map tipped in as follows: facing title page, on coated paper, sketch by Harry D. Wallace, 'Site of Fort Ste Marie' (8.2 × 10.2 cm.); facing p. 66, on white wove paper with watermark ('*Supertext* MADE IN CANADA'): *foldout map of Huronia* (21 × 25.5 cm.); upper right hand corner has a small scale inset map of surrounding area (6.9 × 8.3 cm.).

Material: calico cloth (302), medium reddish brown (Centroid 43) with a calico cloth (302) yellow grey (Centroid 93) strip (7.9 cm. wide) glued across the top half of the upper and lower covers and spine; upper cover: [within an ornamental frame (5.9 × 9.9 cm.) centred on yellow grey calico cloth strip] 'BREBEUF / *and his Brethren* / E.J. PRATT'; all in gilt;

spine: blank; lower cover: blank; endpapers: white wove, unwater-
marked. Slipcase: [24.8 × 16.8 × 1.5 cm.] case paper covered, patterned
sand (410), dark greyish reddish brown (Centroid 47); upper cover:
paper label (6.8 × 11.4 cm.) yellowish white (Centroid 92) pasted on
upper half of case; [enclosed within single frame (5.2 × 9.8 cm.)]
'BREBEUF / AND HIS BRETHREN / By / E.J. PRATT / (LIMITED
EDITION)'; spine: blank; lower cover: blank. Publisher's records
indicate that cellophane wrappers were supplied [not seen].

503 copies printed and bound and recorded as delivered by Nov. 14,
1940. Price: $3.00.

Notes: A new epilogue, entitled 'The Martyrs' Shrine,' has been added.
The foldout map of Huronia facing p. 66 is identical with the maps
published on the endpapers of the first edition. Some copies are signed
under the limitation statement, others on the title page.

 In a May 23, 1941 letter to John Hagedorn, proprietor of the Double-
day, Doran Book Shop, Detroit, Pratt states that 'My latest volume
Brébeuf and His Brethren sold out its first edition of 1,000 in three months.
Macmillans are out of it completely and so am I ... The special limited
edition of Brebeuf is $3.00 retail. Macmillans have a few copies left but
that may be too expensive for your customer' (OTV).

Copies examined: OTV (Nos. 110, 226, 438); OTUTF (Nos. 123, 403); OTMCL
(No. 55); OHMA (unnumbered, unsigned); OHMA (No. 40); OONL (No.
62); VCP (No. 2); LML (No. 381).

c / **Brébeuf and His Brethren** – Second trade edition –1941

Brébeuf and His Brethren / BY / E.J. PRATT / [publisher's device 2 × 1.5
cm.] / TORONTO: THE MACMILLAN COMPANY OF / CANADA
LIMITED, AT ST. MARTIN'S HOUSE / 1941

[Identical to 1940 first edition, except for reset imprint date '1941' at
foot].

P. iv: as first edition, except for additional material: '*First Edition, July,
1940 / Second and slightly revised edition, with new / epilogue, signed by the*

*author and limited / to five hundred copies, November 1940 / Second edition,
reprinted in trade format, March 1941.'*; pp. 1–66: text.

Contents: same as in second revised limited edition.

Binding: as 1940 first edition, except for dust wrapper: dark yellowish
pink (Centroid 30) with very deep red (Centroid 14) lettering as in first
edition. Lower cover and inner flap as in first edition. Back flap: critical
quotes about the poem.

1,143 copies were printed with 503 bound and recorded as delivered by
March 13, 1941. On Dec. 29, 1941 the balance were bound. Price:
$1.25.
[The Canadian trade editions sold 2,040 copies between 1940 and 1945].

Copies examined: OTUTF; OTMC; OTMCL; OTNY; OHMA.

D / **Brébeuf and His Brethren** – First American edition – 1942

Identical to the second Canadian edition, reprinted in trade format
March 1941, except for:
Title page: Brébeuf and His Brethren / (The North American Martyrs) /
BY / E.J. PRATT / [at foot of page] THE BASILIAN PRESS / 21 East
Boston Blvd., Detroit, Mich. / 1942

P. iv: 'COPYRIGHT / *First U.S.A. Edition* / THE BASILIAN PRESS, Detroit,
Mich., U.S.A. / 1942'; p. 66: 'THE MARTYRS' SHRINE / [at foot of page]
PRINTED IN CANADA'

Binding same as second Canadian edition, except for: spine: [lettered
vertically in gilt] 'BREBEUF AND HIS BRETHREN / [5 mm. rule] / PRATT /
[at foot] BASILIAN'. Dust wrapper: same, except for upper cover, reset
imprint at foot, 'THE BASILIAN PRESS'; spine: reset imprint at foot,
'THE BASILIAN PRESS '; lower cover: blank; inner and back flaps: at foot,
'THE BASILIAN PRESS / *Publishers* Detroit'. A second dust wrapper (6.4
cm. wide) white with very deep red (Centroid 14) lettering: '*Winner of /
The Governor-General's Annual / Literary Award for / Poetry, 1940*';
second wrapper placed over dust wrapper around centre of volume.

The books were to be shipped from Toronto by Oct. 1, 1942; 2,993 copies were delivered (Macmillan Archive, OHMA). Price: $1.25.

Copies examined: OTV; OTMCL (2); OHMA.

E / **Brébeuf and His Brethren** – Paperback edition –1966

Brébeuf and his Brethren / by E.J. PRATT / MACMILLAN OF CANADA

(Cut: 17.9 × 10.5 cm.) perfect binding; 40 leaves, pp. [1–10] 11–80.

P. i: half-title, '*Brébeuf and his Brethren*'; p. 2: '*The Collected Poems of E.J. Pratt / (edited by Northrop Frye) contains / all of the poet's major works.*'; p. 3: title page as above; p. 4: '©THE MACMILLAN COMPANY OF CANADA, LIMITED, 1966 / *All rights reserved – no part of this book may be reproduced / in any form without permission in writing from the publisher, / except by a reviewer who wishes to quote brief passages / in connection with a review written for inclusion in a / magazine or newspaper.*'; p. 5: dedication, '*To my father*'; pp. 6–7: map of Huronia with a small scale inset map of surrounding area (5.1 × 6.3 cm.) in upper right hand corner; p. 8: blank; p. 9: fly-title, '*Brébeuf and his Brethren*'; p. 10: blank; pp. 11–80: text.

Contents [Section Headings]: 11: '*I*'; 19: '1629 / *II*'; 23: '1633 / *III*'; 38: '*IV*'; 42: '(THE FOUNDING OF FORT SAINTE MARIE) / 1639 / *V*'; 43: '(THE MISSION TO THE PETUNS AND NEUTRALS) / 1640–1641 / *VI*'; 48: '(THE STORY OF JOGUES) / *VII*'; 58: '1646 / (BRESSANI) / *VIII*'; 60: '*IX*'; 65: '*X*'; 69: 'JULY, 1648 / *XI*'; 74: '*XII*'; 80: '(THE MARTYRS' SHRINE)'.

Paper covers in very reddish orange (Centroid 34) and dark reddish orange (Centroid 38); upper cover: a painting of Brébeuf being burned at the stake; [upper right hand corner, lettered in white] $1.95 / [lower half, below sketch, lettered in black] 'BRÉBEUF AND / HIS BRETHREN / [at foot, lettered in white] E.J. PRATT'; spine: [lettered vertically, in black] 'BRÉBEUF AND HIS BRETHREN / E.J. PRATT / Macmillan'; lower cover: publisher's note about poem and statement about Sainte-Marie and its reconstruction.

Published in 1966. Number of copies unknown. Price: $0.95, although $1.95 printed on cover.

Copies examined: OTV; OTMCL; OTNY; OHMA.

Reissued in 1967 [not seen].

F / **Brébeuf and His Brethren** – Paperback reprint –1974

Paperback reprint edition, 1974, identical to first paperback edition, except for:
P. 3: title page [at foot]: *Macmillan of Canada / in co-operation with / Historical Sites Branch, / Ontario Ministry of Natural Resources.';* p. 4: as above, with additional: 'ISBN 0 7705 0259 8 / *Reprinted 1974 / Printed in Canada.'*

As above, paper covers in very reddish orange (Centroid 34) and deep reddish orange (Centroid 36) with price deleted from upper cover; lower cover [at bottom]: ISBN 0-7705-0259-8.

According to a Macmillan memo (Dec. 7, 1973) the Ontario Ministry of Natural Resources, Historical Sites Branch, bought 1,000 copies. The reprint was to be available February or March 1974 (Macmillan Archive, OHMA). Price: $1.75.

Copies examined: OTV; OTMC; OTMCL; OTNY; LML.

A13   A / **Dunkirk** 1941

DUNKIRK / E.J. PRATT / TORONTO / THE MACMILLAN COMPANY / OF CANADA LIMITED / 1941

(Cut: 21 × 13.5 cm.) [unsigned, 1^8], eight leaves, pp. [i–ii] 1–13 [14].

P. i: title page as above; p. ii: 'Copyright, Canada, 1941 / by / THE MACMILLAN COMPANY OF CANADA LIMITED / All rights reserved – no part of this book may be reproduced / in any form without permission in writing from the publisher, / except by a reviewer who wishes to quote brief passages in / connection with a review written for inclusion in a magazine / or newspaper.'; pp. 1–13: text, with title at head of text on p. 1; p. 14: 'Printed in Canada by / Gilchrist-Wright Limited / Toronto'.

Contents [Section Headings]: 2: 'Regatta and Crew'; 3: 'The Race on the Channel'; 6: 'Heard on the Colliers'; 9: 'The Multipedes on the Roads'; 10: 'In the Skies'.

Laid paper, vertical chain lines 3 cm. apart; watermark: Supertext MADE IN CANADA.

Wrappers: laid paper, light grey (Centroid 264) vertical chain lines 3 cm. apart; watermark: Supertext MADE IN CANADA; French fold cover stapled on inside section of fold to the text; size of paper cover: 22 × 14 cm.; drawing on upper half of upper cover (11 × 5 cm.): wreath, airplanes and soldiers all in dark grey (Centroid 266); overprinted [in script], 'Dunkirk' [in very deep red (Centroid 14)]; lower half of cover: [roman, in dark grey as above] 'E.J. PRATT'; at foot of cover: [roman, in dark grey as above] 'MACMILLAN'; lower cover: blank. Paper slip case: envelope (22.2 × 14.5 cm.) wove paper, light grey (Centroid 264); watermark: Supertext MADE IN CANADA; upper left hand corner: [in very deep red (Centroid 14)] 'DUNKIRK / by E.J. PRATT'.

Published Oct. 16, 1941 at 50 cents with printings as follows:
1st printing: 1,006 copies on Oct. 16, 1941 and recorded as delivered by Macmillan.
2nd printing: 1,020 copies printed on Nov. 12, 1941 of which 715 are recorded as delivered by Macmillan; 305 copies, bound in blue hard covers with grey jackets, delivered Dec. 5, 1941.
3rd printing: 1,028 copies printed and recorded as delivered by Macmillan on Dec. 4, 1941.
4th printing: 506 copies printed and recorded as delivered by Macmillan on Jan. 26, 1942.

Notes: In a letter to Pelham Edgar (August 6, 1941) Pratt claimed he had 'worked furiously at Dunkirk which is just about finished ... The Macmillan's want it as a fall book though it is too late for the fall list ... It's shaping out into four or five hundred lines ... Dillon, the editor of Poetry (Chicago) has asked me to send some stuff ... I may send him this – abridged' (OTV). Dunkirk was published in Poetry 59, October 1941.
    Writing to Ellen Elliott on Oct. 7, 1941, Pratt suggested that, since costs were mounting, a bigger edition of his poetry (i.e., Dunkirk plus other poems) would have a 'prohibitive price.' It would be better, he

suggested, to go ahead with *Dunkirk* itself in 'soft covers.' Pratt asked for film and radio rights to be exempted from the contract: 'Brockington is looking after the radio part.' Elliott replied that Macmillan was 'going ahead with the pamphlet edition of DUNKIRK and we hope to have it ready in a week's time.'

Pratt advised E.K. Brown (Nov. 4, 1941) that *Dunkirk* was 'having a bigger sale than anything yet ... a thousand copies have been sold [in less than two weeks] ... I may get a real break.' He added: 'Brockington's reading it over the national hook-up on Armistice Day. That will help' (OTV).

In a letter to Elliott (Dec. 2, 1941) Pratt passed on the criticisms he had received from readers who complained that a large number of commas were 'scarcely distinguishable from [the] full stops,' making the poem hard to read. He suggested that if further editions were to be printed this might be made known to the printers. Elliott replied (Dec. 5): 'Our third thousand has just been printed' and added that the comma problem was due to the Goudy type; 'but we will lift out the pesky Goudy commas and put in something which looks a little more definite in our next printing.' She concludes by stating that Macmillan of New York and Random House had refused to take *Dunkirk* (Macmillan Archive, OHMA).

In a January 13, 1942 reply to John Hagedorn's request for an auto-graphed copy, Pratt stated: 'I am afraid that there are no copies of the first edition of 'Dunkirk' ... I am asking Macmillans to see if they can get a copy and if they can I shall inscribe it. The poem has now entered its fourth edition (the fourth thousand) in three months and it looks as if it might go across in a big way' (OTV).

The four Toronto printings of *Dunkirk* between October 15, 1941 and January 26, 1942 amounted to 3,560 books; sales between 1941 and 1947 totalled 3,402.

Manuscripts, holograph draft: OTV, Box 4.26, 4.29.
Author's proof copy: OTV, Box 4.27.
Holograph notes: OTV, Box 4.26, 4.29.
Typescript commentary: OTV, Box 4.28.

Copies examined: OTV (3); OTUTF (3); OTMC (2); OTMCL; OTNY (2); OHMA; OONL; VCP.

B / **Dunkirk** – Limited Edition – 1941

Title as above, except:
[Unsigned, 1^{12}], 12 leaves, pp. [i–vi] 1–13 [14–18].

P. i: 'THREE HUNDRED COPIES / of this edition of "Dunkirk" have / been printed especially for Messrs. / Johnston, Everson & Charlesworth, / Christmas, 1941. / THIS COPY IS NO. ___ [number in ink]'; p. ii: blank; p. iii: [in large script] 'Greetings *The Christmas ideal of / peace on earth may still / be far away, but we are thankful that faith persists, / that the British Commonwealth of Nations is / united in a cause vital to freemen and, above all, / that the island fortress will withstand every attack.* / [red acorn ornament 3 × 5 mm.] *Because Dunkirk was a cause for thankful- / ness, because it revealed again that indomitable / courage lives in the hearts of Britons and because it / proved that, given time, we still could keep our / liberty, we have thought it appropriate at this / Christmas season to call to mind that epic of the / beaches as commemorated by a Canadian poet of / distinction, our friend Ned Pratt.* / [red acorn ornament as above] *A wartime Christmas can never be as / merry. But we are stronger now and can look / forward with confidence to realization of our hope / that we may see in the coming year the sure signs / of an honorable and enduring peace.* / [lettered in red] J.G. JOHNSTON / R.G. EVERSON / J.L. CHARLESWORTH'; p. iv: blank; p. v: title page as in trade edition; p. vi: as p. ii in trade edition, with addition '*Reprinted 1941*'; pp. 15–18: blank.

Calico-texture cloth (302), dark blue (Centroid 183), leaves stapled and first leaf pasted to boards; upper cover: [in script, gilt] 'Dunkirk'; spine: blank; lower cover: blank. Dust wrapper: same as for trade edition; front and back flaps: blank; no slip case.

Copies examined: OTUTF (No. 10, not signed); OTV (No. 51, signed); BVIV (No. 79); OONL (No. 50, signed); VCP (unnumbered).

A14   **Still Life and Other Verse** 1943

[The whole within printer's rules, thick-thin (16.4 x 10.5cm.)]: Still Life and Other / Verse / [ornament (60 x 60 mm.): open book on stand] / E.J. PRATT / TORONTO / THE MACMILLAN COMPANY / OF CANADA LIMITED / 1943

(Cut: 21.4 × 13.5 cm.): [unsigned, 1–3^8], 24 leaves, pp. [i–viii] 1–40.

P. i: half-title, 'STILL LIFE / AND OTHER VERSE'; p. ii: list of books, *By* E.J. PRATT / Newfoundland Verse / The Witches' Brew / Titans / The Iron Door / The Roosevelt and the Antinoe / Verses of the Sea / Many Moods / The Titanic / The Fable of the Goats / Brébeuf and His Brethren / Dunkirk'; p. iii: title page as above; p. iv: 'Copyright, Canada, 1943 / by / THE MACMILLAN COMPANY OF CANADA LIMITED / All rights reserved – no part of this book / may be reproduced in any form without / permission in writing from the publisher, / except by a reviewer who wishes to quote / brief passages in connection with a review / written for inclusion in a magazine or / newspaper.' / [at foot of page] 'Printed and bound in Canada, by / T.H. BEST PRINTING CO., LIMITED / TORONTO, ONT.'; p. v: 'ACKNOWLEDGEMENT / Thanks are due to *Poetry* (Chicago), / *The Queen's Quarterly*, *Saturday* / *Night*, and *The Canadian Forum* for / permission to include in this volume / verse that originally appeared in their / pages.'; p. vi: blank; p. vii: fly-title, 'STILL LIFE / AND OTHER VERSE'; p. viii: blank; pp. 1–40: text.

Contents: 1: 'still life'; 3: 'autopsy on a sadist / (after Lidice)'; 4: 'the truant'; 11: 'the stoics'; 12: 'father time'; 14: 'missing: believed dead: returned'; 15: 'the brawler in who's who'; 17: 'the radio in the ivory tower / (1937 – Sept. 1939)'; 22: 'the submarine'; 28: 'the invaded field'; 29: 'come away, death'; 31: 'the impatient earth'; 33: 'the dying eagle'; 36: 'der fuehrer's pot-pourri'; 39: 'old harry'.

Material: patterned sand grain cloth (410), medium reddish orange (Centroid 37); upper cover: [title within a compartment (4.8 × 10.1 cm.) stamped in gilt] 'STILL LIFE / AND OTHER VERSE / [ornamental rule 8 mm.] / E.J. PRATT'; spine: [lettered vertically in gilt] 'STILL LIFE AND OTHER VERSE / [dash] / PRATT / MACMILLAN'; lower cover: blank; endpapers: white wove unwatermarked. Dust wrapper: on upper cover: [in script] 'Still Life / and / Other Verse / [in roman] E.J. PRATT'. All lettering in white on slightly bluish green background (Centroid 160) which extends to spine; spine: [in vertical letters] [roman] 'STILL LIFE [script] and [roman] OTHER VERSE [4 mm. rule] [script] E.J. PRATT / [vertical rule 7 mm.] [roman] MACMILLAN' [vertical rule 7 mm.]; lower cover: contains notice about three other Macmillan poetry publications by Frederick B. Watt, Audrey Alexandra Brown and John Coulter. On inner front flap: publisher's note about the book; on back flap: a biographical note on Pratt. All lettering on back cover and flaps in medium green (Centroid 145) on white.

Published December 1943. Number of copies unknown. Number of copies sold 1943 to 1947: 778. Price: $1.50.

Notes: On August 17, 1943 Pratt wrote to Ellen Elliott of Macmillan Canada, submitting fourteen poems including 'Still Life.' 'It is two years since Dunkirk appeared,' he wrote; 'I think I ought to be before my "constituency" ... Most of them have been printed in magazines. The very latest – "Still Life" – has not appeared. It is the poem I have put most time on, and most revision, and as it sounds a key note to the general style and content, I should like to make it the title poem.' Elliott wrote back (August 18): 'We like "Still Life" as the title poem ... hoping to produce a book [to] sell for $1.25 ... we have started the ball rolling.' In spite of Pratt's assertion that 'Still Life' had not appeared in print, a variant of the first stanza had been published in *Saturday Night*, 28 October 1939.

Knopf, New York, refused *Still Life*. Pratt concluded (Nov. 11, 1943) that 'maybe Knopf's decision is the best after all ... it would be wise to concentrate on the "Collected" ... Then we would have Knopf and Macmillan (u.s.) considering the proposition with lots of time ... It is too late in 1943 to bring out an American edition. [Let's] have "Still Life" simply as a Canadian presentation' (Macmillan Archive, OHMA).

In a letter to A.J.M. Smith (Jan. 28, 1944) Pratt related that *Still Life* had divided the 'newspaper critics very sharply ... that must always be the way with anything of an experimental character ... Saturday Night and the Globe featured it. The Montreal Gazette damned it for its obscurity ... The Hamilton Spectator was greatly puzzled over The Truant. I thought it was clear enough that I was making an indictment of Power by humanity' (OTUTF/15).

Manuscripts, holograph drafts: OTV, Box 4.29, 4.30, 4.31, 4.33.
Typescript drafts: OTV, Box 4.32, 4.34.
Holograph commentaries: OTV, Box 4.30, 4.33, 4.34, 6.44.

Copies examined: OTV (3); OTUTF (2); OTMC (2); OTMCL; OTNY; OHMA (3); VCP; LML.

A15   A / **Collected Poems** – First Canadian edition – 1944

[Within a double frame; inner ornamental frame enclosed within outer line frame, 16.5 × 9.4 cm.] COLLECTED POEMS / by / E.J. PRATT / TORONTO / THE MACMILLAN COMPANY / OF CANADA LIMITED / 1944

(Cut: 21.5 × 14.2 cm.) [unsigned, 1–10^{16} 11^4], 164 leaves, pp. [i–vi] vii–ix [x–xii] 1–162 [163–164] 165–220 [221–222] 223–236 [237–238] 239–314 [315–316].

P. i: half-title, 'COLLECTED POEMS'; p. ii: 'By E.J. PRATT / NEWFOUND-LAND VERSE / THE WITCHES' BREW / TITANS / THE IRON DOOR / THE ROOSE-VELT AND THE ANTINOE / VERSES OF THE SEA / MANY MOODS / THE TITANIC / THE FABLE OF THE GOATS / BRÉBEUF AND HIS BRETHREN / DUNKIRK / STILL LIFE'; p. iii: title page as above; p. iv: 'Copyright, Canada, 1944 / by / THE MACMILLAN COMPANY OF CANADA LIMITED / All rights reserved – no part of this book / may be reproduced in any form without / permission in writing from the publisher, / except by a reviewer who wishes to quote / brief passages in connection with a review / written for inclusion in a magazine or / newspaper.' [at foot of page]: 'Printed in Canada by / The Hunter-Rose Co. Limited, Toronto'; p. v: dedication, 'To Viola my wife / and / to Claire my daughter / this book is lovingly dedicated'; p. vi: blank; pp. vii–ix: contents; p. x: blank; p. xi: fly-title, 'COLLECTED POEMS'; p. xii: blank; pp. 1–162: text; p. 163: section title, 'NEWFOUND-LAND REMINISCENCES'; p. 164: blank; pp. 165–220: text; p. 22l: section title, 'A MISCELLANY'; p. 222: blank; pp. 223–236: text; p. 237: section title, 'EXTRAVAGANZAS'; p. 238: blank; pp. 239–314: text; pp. 315–316: blank.

Contents: 1: 'DUNKIRK'; 11: 'THE RADIO / IN THE IVORY TOWER / (1937 – Sept. 1939)'; 16: 'COME AWAY, DEATH'; 17: 'SILENCES'; 19: 'THE PRIZE CAT'; 20: 'FROM TO STONE TO STEEL'; 20: 'THE INVADED FIELD'; 21: 'COME NOT THE SEASONS HERE'; 22: 'STILL LIFE'; 24: 'AUTOPSY ON A SADIST / (after Lidice); 24: 'FATHER TIME'; 25: 'SEEN ON THE ROAD'; 26: 'THE BARITONE'; 27: 'THE STOICS'; 28: 'THE MYSTIC'; 28: 'MISSING: BELIEVED DEAD: / RETURNED'; 29: 'THE IMPATIENT EARTH'; 30: 'THE OLD ORGANON (1225 A.D.)'; 31: 'THE NEW (1937 A.D.)'; 31: 'THE SUBMARINE'; 36: 'BRÉBEUF AND HIS BRETHREN'; 95: 'BEFORE AN ALTAR / (After Gueudecourt)'; 95: 'TO AN ENEMY'; 96: 'THE EMPTY ROOM'; 96: 'FIRE'; 97: 'THE TITANIC'; 128: 'THE 6000'; 131: 'THE BRAWLER IN WHO'S WHO'; 132: 'THE DYING EAGLE'; 135: 'THE ROOSEVELT AND THE ANTINOE'; 165: 'NEWFOUNDLAND'; 167: 'THE CACHALOT'; 181: 'OLD HARRY'; 182: 'THE DRAG-IRONS'; 183: 'IN LANTERN LIGHT'; 183: 'GREAT TIDES'; 183: 'ON THE SHORE'; 184: 'IN ABSENTIA'; 185: 'THE SHARK'; 186:

'THE FOG'; 186: 'THE BIG FELLOW'; 187: 'SEA-GULLS'; 188: 'THE WAY OF CAPE RACE'; 188: 'THE FLOOD-TIDE'; 189: 'THE DROWNING'; 190: 'OVERHEARD BY A STREAM'; 191: 'THE HISTORY OF JOHN JONES'; 192: 'TO ANGELINA, AN OLD NURSE'; 195: 'THE ICE-FLOES'; 199: 'TOLL OF THE BELLS'; 200: 'THE GROUND SWELL'; 200: 'TIME-WORN'; 201: 'THE WEATHER GLASS'; 201: 'THE LEE-SHORE'; 202: 'THE RITUAL'; 203: 'ONE HOUR OF LIFE'; 203: 'EROSION'; 204: 'A REVERIE ON A DOG'; 211: 'THE SEA-CATHEDRAL'; 212: 'THE IRON DOOR / (An Ode)'; 223: 'A PRAIRIE SUNSET'; 224: 'OUT OF STEP / (1931 A.D.)'; 224: 'THE MAN AND THE MACHINE'; 225: 'THE PARABLE OF PUFFSKY'; 226: 'OLD AGE'; 227: 'BLIND'; 227: 'A LEGACY'; 228: 'THE DECISION / (To L.R., a college athlete who died May, 1923.)'; 228: 'THE HIGHWAY'; 229: 'CHERRIES'; 229: 'A FELINE SILHOUETTE'; 230: 'THE CHILD AND THE WREN / (To Claire)'; 231: 'FROST'; 231: 'COMRADES'; 232: 'JOCK O' THE LINKS'; 233: 'THE CONVICT HOLOCAUST / Columbus, Ohio, 1930)'; 234: ' THE EPIGRAPHER'; 235: 'LIKE MOTHER, LIKE DAUGHTER'; 239: 'THE WITCHES' BREW / (In celebration of a fifth wedding anniversary)'; 256: 'THE GREAT FEUD / (A Dream of a Pleiocene Armageddon)'; 289: 'THE FABLE OF THE GOATS'; 303: 'THE DEPRESSION ENDS'; 309: 'THE TRUANT'.

Frontispiece tipped in, facing title page, coated paper, 'E.J. Pratt' from the 'Portrait by Kenneth Forbes' (13.5 × 10 cm.).

Material: calico cloth (302), brilliant greenish blue (Centroid 168); upper cover [lettered in gilt within a blocked compartment (6.5 × 9.5 cm.)] 'COLLECTED / POEMS / [ornament 2 × 11 mm.] / E.J. PRATT'; spine [rule 2.7 cm.] [lettered horizontally in gilt] 'COLLECTED / POEMS / PRATT / [at foot] MACMILLAN' [rule 2.7 cm.]; lower cover: blank; endpapers: white wove unwatermarked; dust wrapper: upper cover: on light orange yellow (Centroid 70), a very purplish blue (Centroid 194) panel (13 cm. wide) extends over entire upper cover; [at top] 'COLLECTED / POEMS [at centre: drawing of three seagulls in flight (5 × 4.5 cm.)] / E.J. PRATT' [at bottom]; all lettering and drawing in light orange yellow (Centroid 70); spine: [horizontally lettered] 'COLLECTED / POEMS / [triangle 2 mm.] / E.J. PRATT / [drawing of three seagulls (1.9 × 1.7 cm.)] / [at foot] MACMILLAN'. All in very purplish blue (Centroid 194); lower cover: publisher's advertisement for 'The Letters of / ALEXANDER WOOLCOTT'. On inner flap: publisher's notice about the book; on back flap: biographical note. All lettering on lower cover and flaps in very purplish blue (Centroid 194) and very red (Centroid 11).

Published Oct. 13, 1944. Number of copies sold 1944–47: 3,434. Price: $3.00.

Notes: In a letter (Nov. 1, 1943) Pratt admitted to Ellen Elliott that he was 'most concerned about ... the "Collected" next summer or fall. That is the most important thing for me.' He believed it would sell 'in a substantial way' because so many of his books were out of print. 'I have had scores of letters asking me where the 'Titanic' might be procured' (Macmillan Archive, OHMA).

In a letter to Earle Birney (August 8, 1944) Pratt confided: 'Macmillans are bringing out my "Collected Poems" next month. They have gone to town upon the construction of it despite paper shortages, etc. The whole 12 books are to be in one volume of 350 pages.' He then corrects himself: 'I said the 12 books. I meant the best selection – many earlier verses I don't like now are excluded.' Although he felt a 'bit excited,' he tempered it with the caution that bringing out a collected edition 'is a gamble in this country' (OTUTF/49).

Manuscripts, author's proof copy: OTV, Box 4.35.

Copies examined: OTV (4); OTUTF; OTMC (2); OTMCL; OTNY (3); OHMA; BVAU; VCP; LML.

A presentation copy, binding for E.J. Pratt done to Macmillan's special order in morocco (402) and deep red (Centroid 13), upper cover and spine lettered in gilt (same pattern as in cloth binding), presented to 'Ned and Vi Pratt, Xmas 1944', is in the collection of Claire Pratt.

B / **Collected Poems** – First American edition – 1945

COLLECTED POEMS / By E.J. PRATT / [publisher's device 1.2 × 2.1 cm.] / ALFRED · A · KNOPF · NEW YORK / 1945

(Cut: 21.2 × 14 cm.) [unsigned, 1–9^{16}], 144 leaves, pp. [i–vi] vii–ix [x] xi–xv [xvi–xviii] 1–163 [164–166] 167–221 [222–224] 225–238 [239–240] 241–269 [270].

P. i: half-title, 'Collected Poems'; p. ii: 'DISTINGUISHED POETRY / [ornamental rule 9.7 cm.] / WILLIAM ROSE BENÉT / Day of Deliverance / WILLIAM ROSE BENÉT / The Dust Which is God / WALTER BENTON /

This Is My Beloved / JEREMY INGALLS / *Tahl* / DAVID MORTON / *Poems, 1920–1945* / ROBERT NATHAN / *The Darkening Meadows* / JOHN CROWE RANSOM / *Selected Poems* / JON BECK SHANK / *Poems* / [ornamental rule 9.7 cm.] / *THESE ARE BORZOI BOOKS PUBLISHED BY ALFRED A. KNOPF'*; p. iii: title page as above; p. iv: 'THIS BOOK HAS BEEN PRO-DUCED IN FULL COMPLIANCE WITH ALL / GOVERNMENT REGU-LATIONS FOR THE CONSERVATION OF PAPER, / METAL, AND OTHER ESSENTIAL MATERIALS' / [at foot of page]: '*Copyright, 1945 by Edward J. Pratt / All rights reserved. No part of this book may be reproduced in any / form without permission in writing from the publisher, except by / a reviewer who may quote brief passages in a review to be printed / in a magazine or newspaper.* / MANUFACTURED IN THE UNITED STATES OF AMERICA'; p. v: dedication, '*TO VIOLA MY WIFE. AND / TO CLAIRE MY DAUGHTER / THIS BOOK / IS LOVINGLY DEDICATED'*; p. vi: blank; pp. vii–ix: con-tents; p. x: blank; pp. xi–xv: introduction signed 'WILLIAM ROSE BENÉT / New York City / October 1944'; p. xvi: blank; p. xvii: fly-title, '*Collected Poems'*; p. xviii: blank; pp. 1–163: text; p. 164: blank; p. 165: section title, '*Newfoundland Reminiscences'*; p. 166: blank; pp. 167–221: text; p. 222: blank; p. 223: section title, '*A Miscellany'*; p. 224: blank; pp. 225-238: text; p. 239: section title, '*Extravaganzas'*; p. 240: blank; pp. 241–269: text; p. 270: 'A NOTE ON THE TYPE IN WHICH THIS BOOK IS SET / *The text of this book is set in Caledonia, a Linotype face de-* / signed by W.A. Dwiggins. *Caledonia belongs to the family / of printing types called "modern face" by printers – a term / used to mark the change in style of type-letters that occurred / about 1800. Caledonia borders on the general design of Scotch / Modern, but is more freely drawn than that letter. / The book was composed, printed, and bound by Kingsport / Press, Inc., Kingsport, Tennessee.'*

Contents: 1: '*Dunkirk'*; 11: '*The Radio in the Ivory Tower* / (1937-Sept. 1939)'; 16: '*Come Away, Death'*; 17: '*Silences'*; 19: '*The Prize Cat'*; 20: '*From Stone to Steel'*; 20: '*The Invaded Field'*; 21: '*Come Not the Seasons Here'*; 22: '*Still Life'*; 23: '*Autopsy on a Sadist* / (after Lidice)'; 24: '*Father Time'*; 25: '*Seen on the Road'*; 26: '*The Baritone'*; 27: '*The Stoics'*; 28: '*The Mystic'*; 28: '*Missing: Believed Dead: / Returned'*; 29: '*The Impatient Earth'*; 30: '*The Old Organon* (1225 A.D.)'; 31: '*The New* (1937 A.D.)'; 31: '*The Submarine'*; 36: '*Brébeuf and His Brethren'*; 95: '*Before an Altar* / (after Gueudecourt)'; 96: '*To an Enemy'*; 96: '*The Empty Room'*; 97: '*Fire'*; 98: '*The Titanic'*; 129: '*The 6000'*; 132: '*The Brawler in "Who's Who"'*; 133: '*The Dying Eagle'*; 136: '*The "Roosevelt" and the "Antinoe"'*; 167: '*Newfoundland'*; 169: '*The

Cachalot'; 183: *'Old Harry'*; 184: *'The Drag-Irons'*; 184: *'In Lantern Light'*; 185: *'Great Tides'*; 185: *'On the Shore'*; 186: *'In Absentia'*; 187: *'The Shark'*; 188: *'The Fog'*; 188: *'The Big Fellow'*; 189: *'Sea-Gulls'*; 189: *'The Way of Cape Race'*; 190: *'The Flood-Tide'*; 191: *'The Drowning'*; 191: *'Overheard by a Stream'*; 192: *'The History of John Jones'*; 193: *'To Angelina, An Old Nurse'*; 196: *'The Ice-Floes'*; 200: *'Toll of the Bells'*; 201: *'The Ground Swell'*; 202: *'Time-Worn'*; 202: *'The Weather Glass'*; 203: *'The Lee-Shore'*; 203: *'The Ritual'*; 204: *'One Hour of Life'*; 205: *'Erosion'*; 205: *'A Reverie on a Dog'*; 213: *'The Sea-Cathedral'*; 213: *'The Iron Door / (An Ode)'*; 225: *'A Prairie Sunset'*; 226: *'Out of Step / (1931 a.d.)'*; 226: *'The Man and the Machine'*; 227: *'The Parable of Puffsky'*; 228: *'Old Age'*; 229: *'Blind'*; 229: *'A Legacy'*; 230: *'The Decision / (To L.R., a college athlete who died May, 1923)'*; 230: *'The Highway'*; 231: *'Cherries'*; 232: *'A Feline Silhouette'*; 232: *'The Child and the Wren / (To Claire)'*; 233: *'Frost'*; 234: *'Comrades'*; 234: *'Jock o' the Links'*; 235: *'The Convict Holocaust / (Columbus, Ohio, 1930)'*; 236: *'The Epigrapher'*; 237: *'Like Mother, Like Daughter'*; 241: *'The Witches' Brew / (In celebration of a fifth wedding anniversary)'*; 258: *'The Depression Ends'*; 264: *'The Truant'*.

Material: calico cloth (302), black (Centroid 267); upper cover: [blind stamped design at centre (6.3 × 6.3 cm.)]; spine: [ornamental rule 2.7 cm.; lettered horizontally] 'Collected / Poems by / E.J. Pratt / [ornamental rule 2.7 cm.] [geometric pattern extending downwards 7.5 cm.] *Knopf* / [all lettering and ornament stamped in gilt]; lower cover: blank [at bottom right, blind stamp (1.3 × 1.9 cm.) of publisher's device and letters 'BORZOI / BOOKS']; endpapers: white wove unwatermarked; dust wrapper: upper cover: very pale blue (Centroid 184) with lettering and ornament in dark blue (Centroid 183); [at top] 'E.J. PRATT / [at centre, enclosed within decorative frame (8.5 × 13.1 cm.)] Collected / POEMS / [at bottom] "The most distinguished of all / contemporary Canadian poets." / -POETRY'; spine: [vertically lettered from bottom upwards] *'Alfred A. Knopf* / [publisher's device (.8 × 1.8 cm.)] / *Collected Poems* / [ornament (.6 × 2.2 cm.)] / E.J. PRATT'; lower cover: publisher's advertisement for 'This Is My Beloved / Poems by WALTER BENTON'; on inner flap: publisher's notice about the book; on back flap: portrait of Pratt from Kenneth Forbes' painting and a biographical note. All lettering and reproduction on lower cover and flaps in dark blue (Centroid 183).

3,300 copies published April 16, 1945. Price: $3.00.

Notes: In a very flattering letter ('My attention has been called to the excellence of your poetry'), Milton Rugoff of Alfred A. Knopf wrote to Pratt, offering to publish his work: 'a new volume of your verse or a selection from the verse already published' (Oct. 25, 1943). Rugoff explained: 'We are the publishers ... of many excellent American and British poets and have been hoping for some time to add a Canadian writer to that list. I therefore look forward eagerly to seeing your work.'

Pratt immediately sent off the Knopf letter to Ellen Elliott (Oct. 27, 1943) and stated that Knopf's interest had been aroused by the *Saturday Review of Literature* 'with Benet's influence.' 'This is a good chance to make a contact,' he continued, and wondered if Macmillan had any contact with Knopf so that they might encourage them to take the *Collected Poems*. Elliott came up with a scheme which she felt was 'slightly unethical' of sending Knopf a set of proofs [of *Still Life*], and 'if that doesn't come through, I can then offer it to New York (Macmillan)'. She suggested that this might prevent Knopf from insisting on a volume of selections because 'it might spoil our own market for the Collected volume ... and on that Collected we might be able to make a deal with him for sheets' (Oct. 30, 1943).

Knopf refused *Still Life*; Elliott then offered them the collected poems (Dec. 8, 1943), saying that she understood that paper rationing might make publishing from scratch 'out of the question'; she could therefore offer 'some relief by supplying you with sheets of our edition.' Alfred Knopf wrote (May 17, 1944) saying that his company had decided to publish the *Collected Poems*. Knopf would manufacture its own book following Macmillan's copy 'but omitting from the last section ... "The Fable of the Goats" and "The Great Feud",' decisions which Benét supported (Macmillan Archive, OHMA). On June 16,1944, Pratt was able to write to E.K. Brown: 'I just signed the Knopf contract today ... The contract is very favourable and the outlook is promising. The copyright, too, is in my own name.' By February 21, 1945, Pratt reported to Pelham Edgar that the judges, 'Tinker of Yale, Bush and Spencer of Harvard and Mark van Doren of Columbia sent in enthusiastic statements to Knopf'; but always on his guard against disappointment, he added: 'what will be the popular demand, who knows' (OTV).

On June 21, 1945 Ellen Elliott, after a visit to New York, reported that 'while their [Knopf's] sales of the Collected Poems hadn't been staggering in the U.S., yet the book had started off, not with a bang, but with a steady stream of orders.'

Pratt wrote Elliott on Feb. 19, 1947: 'Knopf sold over one thousand of the 'Collected' but as he expected to get rid of his 3,000 (which was the first edition) he is disappointed. Follett told me that they intended keeping it on their shelves indefinitely as they believed in it and there was a library sale which was fairly steady if it was slow. I am afraid that we can't compete with *Forever Amber* and such sellers ... I have been looking over the reviews of the Collected Poems from the American press and apart from two the reception has been all that I could desire. Yet the sales are thin. We always live in the future.'

Writing to J.M. Gray of Macmillan on July 9, 1958, Alfred Knopf refuses Pratt's second *Collected Poems* because 'we did so badly thirteen years ago ... At that time we printed some thirty-three hundred copies and had to remainder most of them' (Macmillan Archive, OHMA).

Copies examined: OTV (3); OTUTF; OTMCL; VCP.

c / **Collected Poems** – Reissue – 1946

Identical to first Canadian edition except title page imprint: '1946'.

Pp. [i–xiv] 1–162 [163–164] 165–220 [221–222] 223–236 [237–238] 239–314.

P. iv: as above, with additional 'Reprinted 1946' centred on page; pp. v–vii: contents; p. viii: blank; pp. ix–xiii: introduction, signed on p. xiii by William Rose Benét, dated New York City, October 1944; p. xiv: blank.

Illustration as above, but with dedication on recto of plate: '*To Viola my wife / and / to Claire my daughter / this book is lovingly dedicated*'.

Dust wrapper, upper cover: as above but with letters, border, and spine in light yellow (Centroid 86).

Notes: contents pages reset for 1946 reprint and introduction added.

Copies examined: OTV; OTMC; OHMA; OONL.

A16 **They Are Returning** 1945

THEY ARE / RETURNING / E.J. PRATT / TORONTO /
THE MACMILLAN COMPANY / OF CANADA LIMITED / 1945

(Cut: 22 × 14.7 cm.) [unsigned, 1^8], 8 leaves, pp. [1–4] 5–15 [16].

P. 1: half-title, 'THEY ARE RETURNING'; p. 2: blank; p. 3: title page as
above; p. 4: 'Copyright, Canada, 1945 / by / THE MACMILLAN COM-
PANY OF CANADA LIMITED / All rights reserved – no part of this
book may be reproduced / in any form without permission in writing
from the publisher, / except by a reviewer who wishes to quote brief
passages in / connection with a review written for inclusion in a maga-
zine / or newspaper.' / [at foot of page] 'PRINTED IN CANADA /
GILCHRIST-WRIGHT LIMITED / TORONTO'; pp. 5–15: text with title
at head of text; p. 16: blank.

Laid paper, vertical chain lines 2.7 cm. apart; watermark: HOWARD
SMITH / MADE IN CANADA / Byronic Text

Printed wrappers: heavy quality paper (whorl pattern 412) medium
orange yellow (Centroid 71); French fold cover stapled on the outside
section of fold to the text; upper cover: size of once folded sheet (22.7
× 15.2 cm.); [within a compartment (8.7 × 14.5 cm.) medium bluish
green (Centroid 164) stencilled in script] 'They Are Returning ...'; [at
foot of cover, within a compartment (2 × 14.5 cm.) medium bluish green
(Centroid 164), stencilled in roman] 'MACMILLAN'; [at centre, in
medium bluish green (Centroid 164)] 'E.J. PRATT'; fore-edge uncut;
lower cover: blank; top, fore and bottom edges cut.

Published in Toronto, August 10, 1945. Price: 50 cents. In a letter (June
24, 1945) Macmillan proposed to do an edition of 2,500 (see 'Notes').
Number of copies sold 1945–47: 897.

Notes: In a letter to Viola Pratt (July 27, 1944) Pratt writes: 'I am working
hard on "They Are Returning"' and by August 7 is able to report to
Pelham Edgar that he had 'almost finished – about 200 lines ...
[*Maclean's* has commissioned the poem] to celebrate the coming back of
the boys [and has contracted] to pay me $200.00 for it – the biggest

sum by far I have ever received for a single poem. They gave me $50.00 as a retainer' (OTV).

After its publication in *Maclean's* and an airing on the CBC, Pratt sent a complete copy to Ellen Elliott (June 15, 1945) to be considered for publication as a 'little chapbook or booklet.' It had received much 'favourable reaction ... I may not have another book for two or three years ... the period of the return of the men will be mainly in the next six months, and the poem will have a special application for that period.' Elliott telegraphed Pratt in Ottawa on June 21: 'Will Publish New Poem Brochure Form This Season' and followed up with a letter to Halifax with more detail: 'Luckily the paper for a little book like this doesn't present any problem, so we are going ahead with a nicely done brochure ... and I think it will look rather better than Dunkirk ... [We] will do an edition of at least 2,500 to start with, and hope to put a list price of .50 on it. Is that O.K. with you?' Pratt replied (June 24, 1945): 'While the book will not be hard cover, I think it should be more durable than Dunkirk which frayed easily, even if the price had to be 60 cents or so. You will understand this part of it better than I and I'll trust your judgement.' Pratt reveals that he is allowing Simpsons to use a small section of the poem for a July 1 advertisement for no charge since 'the whole business is a patriotic gesture' (Macmillan Archive, OHMA).

In a letter to Pelham Edgar (June 29, 1945) Pratt reported that *They Are Returning* was to receive a repeat airing by the CBC on July 1 'as a special feature ... It evidently is taking hold.' He also informed Edgar that in Nova Scotia the CBC would be airing the poem on July 26, being read by Ted Roberts (OTV).

The poem was offered to Knopf who refused (July 17, 1945) because they could 'think of nothing that [they] could do with it at the moment' (Macmillan Archive, OHMA).

Manuscripts, holograph drafts: OTV, Box 5.36.

Copies examined: OTV (3); OTUTF; OTMC; OTMCL; OTNY; OHMA (2); VCP; LML.

A17 A / **Ten Selected Poems** 1947

[Within ornamental frame 14 × 9 cm.] TEN / SELECTED POEMS / WITH NOTES / BY / E.J. PRATT / DEPARTMENT OF ENGLISH, VICTORIA

COLLEGE, / UNIVERSITY OF TORONTO / [publisher's device 2 × 1.5 cm.] / TORONTO: THE MACMILLAN COMPANY OF / CANADA LIMITED, AT ST. MARTIN' HOUSE / 1947

(Cut: 19.2 × 11.8 cm.) [unsigned, 1–3⁸, 4⁹, 5–6⁸, 7⁹, 8–10⁸], 82 leaves, pp. [i–iv] v–ix [x–xii] 1–149 [150–152].

P. i: half-title, 'TEN SELECTED POEMS'; p. ii: blank; p. iii: title page as above; p. iv: 'COPYRIGHT, CANADA, 1947 / BY / THE MACMILLAN COMPANY OF CANADA LIMITED / All rights reserved – no part of this book / may be reproduced in any way without / permission in writing from the publishers. / Mimeographing or reproducing mechani- / cally in any other way passages from this / book without the written permission of / the publisher is an infringement of the / copyright law.' / [at foot of page] 'PRINTED AND BOUND IN CANADA / T.H. Best Printing Co., Limited, Toronto'; pp. v–viii: preface; p. ix: contents; p. x: blank; p. xi: fly-title, 'TEN SELECTED POEMS'; p. xii: blank; pp. 1–132: text; pp. 133–149: notes; pp. 150–152: blank.

Contents: 1: 'THE TITANIC'; 36: 'DUNKIRK'; 47: 'THE CACHALOT'; 59: 'NO. 6000'; 62: 'THE SUBMARINE'; 68: 'THE ICE-FLOES'; 72: 'THE OLD EAGLE'; 75: 'PUTTING WINTER TO BED'; 80: 'TO ANGELINA, AN OLD NURSE'; 83: 'BRÉBEUF AND HIS BRETHREN'.

Pagination in hdl. against outer margin of type-page; running titles in roman caps: 'TEN SELECTED POEMS' on verso; individual poem titles on recto; poem lines numbered against outer margin on recto, against inner margin on verso.

Material: calico grain (302), very purplish blue (Centroid 194); upper cover: blank; spine: [vertically lettered in dark yellow (Centroid 88)] 'TEN SELECTED POEMS / [4 mm. rule] / PRATT / [at foot] MACMILLAN'; lower cover: blank; dust wrapper: upper cover: 'Ten /Selected / Poems [in script] / E.J. Pratt' [in roman]; all lettering in white on plain dark bluish green background (Centroid 165) which extends to spine; spine: [lettered vertically] 'Ten Selected Poems [in script] [two dots] PRATT [two dots] MACMILLAN'; lower cover: contains advertisement for *The Collected Poems* with quotes from two reviews; lettering in dark bluish green (Centroid 165) on white background; inner front flap:

publisher's note about the book; back flap: biographical note on Pratt; lettering on flaps in dark bluish green (Centroid 165) on white.

Published June 20, 1947. Price: $1.25. Number of copies unknown.

Notes: On July 11, 1946 John Gray informed Pratt that Mr. Knights of Macmillan's Educational Department would work with Pratt on the St. Martin's edition of selected poems. Pratt, replying on July 13, is delighted to 'co-operate with Mr. Knights as soon as I get back to Toronto.' He requests that Knights 'look through Brébeuf and advise ... what selections he thinks appropriate. The poem is on the list suggested by the Committee. I thought I would take the highlights of the poem and link them together by prose narrative to make a continuous story.' Pratt believes that the manuscript should be ready by Autumn and for sale by the Fall of 1947. He concludes: 'I am also assuming that I am doing the work on the usual 10% royalty basis and that the book would be approximately 65 cents which would govern to some extent the size of the volume. How is the paper situation shaping up? Any better?' (Macmillan Archive, OHMA).

Copies examined: OTV (3); OTMC; OTMCL (2); OTNY (3); OHMA; VCP.

B / **Ten Selected Poems** – reissue – 1947

Identical to A except for:
Title page: [the whole within ornamental frame 14 × 9 cm.] *St. Martin's Classics* [underscored] / TEN / SELECTED POEMS / WITH NOTES / BY / E.J. PRATT / DEPARTMENT OF ENGLISH, VICTORIA COLLEGE, / UNIVERSITY OF TORONTO / [publisher's device 2 × 1.5 cm.] / TORONTO: THE MACMILLAN COMPANY OF / CANADA LIMITED, AT ST. MARTIN'S HOUSE

(Cut: 16.8 × 11 cm.)

P, i: half-title, 'TEN SELECTED POEMS' [upper left-hand corner] '*St. Martin's Classics*'; p. iv: copyright statement identical except at foot of page, 'PRINTED IN CANADA'; pp. 150–152: list of other volumes in series of St. Martin's Classics.

Medium blue (Centroid 182); upper cover: at centre, publisher's device

(3.4 × 2.6 cm.) in black; spine: lettering in black; lower cover: blank. Dust wrapper not seen.

Published in 1947 at 65 cents. Number of copies unknown.

Copies examined: OTNY; LML.

c / **Ten Selected Poems** – another issue – 1947

Identical to B except for:
Title page: [the whole within ornamental frame 14 × 9 cm.] *St. Martin's Classics* [underscored] / TEN / SELECTED POEMS / WITH NOTES / BY / E.J. PRATT / [publisher's device 2.1 × 1.6 cm.] / TORONTO: THE MACMILLAN COMPANY OF / CANADA LIMITED, AT ST. MARTIN'S HOUSE.

Pp. 150–152: blank.

Copies examined: OTMC; OHMA.

D / **Ten Selected Poems** – another issue – 1947

Identical to B except for:
Title page: includes '1947' at end of imprint.

... [150–154].

Pp. 150: blank; pp. 151–153: list of other volumes in series of St. Martin's Classics; p. 154: blank.

As B above except in deep red (Centroid 13).

Copies examined: OTMC; OHMA (2).

A18 **Behind the Log** 1947

BEHIND THE LOG / *by* / E.J. PRATT / [drawing 7.2 × 6.8 cm.: sailor pulling on a rope slung over his shoulder] / DRAWINGS BY / GRANT MACDONALD / TORONTO / THE MACMILLAN COMPANY OF CANADA LIMITED / 1947

(Cut: 23 × 15 cm.) [1–4⁸], 32 leaves, pp. [i–x] xi--xiv [xv–xvi] 1–47 [48] (with illustrations on the following unnumbered pages: [xvi] [5] [9] [13] [17] [23] [29] [35] [41] [45]).

P. i: half-title, 'BEHIND THE LOG'; p. ii: blank; p. iii: 'BY E.J. PRATT / *Newfoundland Verse / The Witches' Brew / Titans / The Iron Door / The "Roosevelt" and The "Antinoe" / Verses of the Sea / Many Moods / The Titanic / The Fable of the Goats / Brébeuf and His Brethren / Dunkirk / Still Life / Collected Poems / Ten Selected Poems*'; p. iv: blank; p. v: title page as above; p. vi: COPYRIGHT, CANADA, 1947 / BY / THE MACMILLAN COMPANY OF CANADA LIMITED / All rights reserved – no part of this book / may be reproduced in any form without / permission in writing from the publisher, / except by a reviewer who wishes to quote / brief passages in connection with a review / written for inclusion in a magazine or / newspaper.' / [at foot of page] 'PRINTED IN CANADA'; p. vii: dedication, 'To / *Lorne Richardson*'; p. viii: blank; p. ix: list of illustrations; p. x: blank; p. xi-xiv: 'FOREWORD' signed by E.J. Pratt; p. xv: fly-title, BEHIND THE LOG'; p. xvi: illustration; pp. 1–47: text with title at head of text; p. 48: blank.

Ten drawings as follows: p. xvi: 'H.M.C.S. *Skeena*'; p. 5: '… they pierce horizons for the surface hulls …' signed [top right] 'Grant Macdonald / '47'; p. 9: 'The Naval Control Service Officer addresses the Masters' signed [right, two-thirds down] 'GM'; p. 13: 'Destroyer… corvettes … cargo carriers … tankers … / refrigeration ships … hybrid types' signed [right, at foot] 'GM'; p. 17: '… the asdic operator in his hut' signed [centre, at foot] 'GM'; p. 23: '… and a moon … picked out the seventy ships …' signed [left, at foot] 'GM'; p. 29: '… they ate and worked and slept' signed [right, at foot] 'Grant Macdonald / '47'; p. 35: '… hundreds of sailors un-lifejacketed clawed at the jetsam / in the oil and water' signed [right, at foot] 'Grant Macdonald '47'; p. 41: ' … wrote their own obituaries in flame' signed [right, at foot] 'GM'; p. 45: 'Spinney … does a Blue Danube on the deck …' signed [right, at foot] 'Grant Macdonald / '47'.

Material: calico-texture cloth, not embossed (302), very red (Centroid 11); upper cover: blank; spine: [vertically lettered in gilt] 'BEHIND THE LOG / [dot] / *E.J. Pratt* / MACMILLAN'; lower cover: blank; endpapers: wove unwatermarked, pale yellow (Centroid 89). Dust wrapper: on upper cover, drawing of three sailors with middle figure dominant;

coloured in bronze, black, grey, red on white; [over-printed with hand lettering at top] 'BEHIND THE LOG / by E.J. PRATT / [at foot] Drawings by Grant Macdonald'; wrapper initials: 'GM' [left, at foot of figure]; spine: [vertically lettered] 'BEHIND THE LOG / [dot] / E.J. Pratt / MACMILLAN'; lower cover contains a 22-line biographical note on Pratt and then, separated by three asterisks, an 8 1/2-line biographical note of Grant Macdonald; [at foot] 'THE MACMILLAN COMPANY OF CANADA LIMITED'. On inner front flap: publisher's note about the poem and Pratt's research methods; on back flap: a tribute to Pratt from the Royal Canadian Navy and a notice about his edition of *Collected Poems*.

Published December 1947. Price: $2.00. Number of copies unknown.

Notes: On Nov. 26, 1946 Pratt sent Earle Birney a draft of *Behind the Log* for possible publication in the *Canadian Poetry Magazine*. Birney's reply (Dec. 9) was enthusisatic: 'It is your best since Brébeuf. It is a magnificent piece of concentration and sustained dramatic tension ... I want to use it all ... we would be able to pay you $69.' As a minor complication, Pratt advised Birney that Macmillan would bring out the poem as a separate book in the fall (1947). The CBC asked for the poem for 'this coming New Year's Day ... abridge[d] here and alter[ed] there ... I am satisfied with the June issue of the c.p.m. ... I own the copyright till next September when Macmillan's take over ... I shall not allow the poem to be published even in extracts until after June' (Dec. 13, 1946: OTUTF/49).

On Jan. 28, 1947 Pratt sent a revised manuscript to John Gray: 'It has to be expanded somewhat yet but this ought to be enough to give Macdonald and New York and London an idea of the book ... I hope Macmillan's in N.Y. and London will share in the marketing.' On Feb. 7 Ellen Elliott sent the typescript to London for Daniel Macmillan's opinion. In the enclosed letter she explained that William Collins & Sons, Toronto had made 'flattering and generous overtures ... for an illustrated edition and limited edition [and] has forced our hand a little to do an illustrated edition. Pratt is undoubtedly Canada's major poet, and the response to [the] radio presentation of Behind the Log has been excellent. We are approaching Mr. Grant Macdonald ... to do the illustrations for us' (Macmillan Archive, OHMA).

In a letter to Birney (March 18, 1947) Pratt agreed to send a copy of the poem for inclusion in the *Canadian Poetry Magazine* within ten days.

He revealed that Macmillan was against the earlier publication in *CPM* because it would 'interfere with the book sales' but since 'I had decided on the C.P.M. before I submitted the ms. to the firm, they now agree.' Pratt estimates that it would take another three months before the Macmillan edition was ready (OTUTF/49).

In a letter to Elliott (April 3, 1947) Grant Macdonald makes several suggestions regarding the illustrations and requests a five hundred dollar fee for 'ten to twelve pictures, a jacket design, and a title page decoration.' By June 9, Macdonald had received a copy of the manuscript and was 'prepared to do all the drawings in "line." But if I might be allowed to do a few of them in "half-tone" ... [it] would greatly enhance the effect of studies of ships in action in which area of sky and sea are considerable.'

Pratt's satisfaction with Macdonald's illustrations was confirmed in a letter to John Gray (August 10, 1947): 'His drawings are splendid and just what I want. I suggested a couple of changes ... I hope the expense is not too great ... I trust the book can be manufactured at 2.00 at most ... If this book doesn't sell, I won't bring out another.'

On Dec. 2, 1947 John Gray sent Daniel Macmillan a copy of *Behind the Log*: 'I hope the book may have considerable sales potential in England ... I hope that in general you will find it attractive. We shall welcome your comments.' On the same day, Gray also sent a copy to H.S. Latham of the Macmillan Company, New York: 'in addition to the small quantity which you ordered ... I certainly hope you may do a great deal better with it than your House appears to anticipate on the basis of your initial order' (Macmillan Archive, OHMA). Knopf, New York, had refused the poem in February 1947.

Pratt informed Birney of the book's publication on Dec. 3, 1947: 'A thousand advance sales were recorded ... It is being released this week and Simpson's ... is giving me an autographing party.' Pratt again thanks Birney for his original criticism: 'I hope you will like the complete poem with its dramatic sketches most of which have been suggested by your good self' (OTUTF/49).

Manuscript, holograph drafts: OTV, Box 5.37, 5.38.
Typescript drafts: Box 5.38, 5.39, 5.40.
Birney Collection, OTUTF, Box 15.
Final typescript and proof paste-up: OTV, Box 5.41.
Holograph notes and commentaries: OTV, Box 5.37, 5.38.
Typescript commentary: OTV, Box 5.42.

Copies examined: OTV (5); OTUTF (3); OTMC; OTMCL (2); OTNY; OHMA (2); OONL; VCP; LML.

A19   **Towards the Last Spike** 1952

TOWARDS / THE LAST SPIKE / by E.J. PRATT / A VERSE-PANORAMA OF THE / STRUGGLE TO BUILD THE FIRST / CANADIAN TRANS-CONTINENTAL / FROM THE TIME OF THE PROPOSED / TERMS OF UNION WITH BRITISH / COLUMBIA (1870) TO THE HAM- / MERING OF THE LAST SPIKE IN / THE EAGLE PASS (1885). / MACMILLAN – 1952 – TORONTO

(Cut: 23 × 15.3 cm.) [unsigned, 1–4^8], 32 leaves, pp. [i–viii] 1–53 [54-56].

P. i: half-title, 'TOWARDS THE LAST SPIKE'; p. ii: '*Other Books by* E.J. PRATT / NEWFOUNDLAND VERSE / THE WITCHES' BREW / TITANS / THE IRON DOOR / THE *Roosevelt* AND THE *Antinoe* / VERSES OF THE SEA / MANY MOODS / THE TITANIC / THE FABLE OF THE GOATS / BRÉBEUF AND HIS BRETHREN / DUNKIRK / STILL LIFE / COLLECTED POEMS / TEN SELECTED POEMS / THEY ARE RETURNING / BEHIND THE LOG'; p. iii: title page as above; p. iv: [at centre top half of page] 'COPYRIGHT, CANADA, 1952 / BY / E.J. PRATT / All rights reserved – no part of this book may / be repro-duced in any form without permis- / sion in writing from the publisher, except / by a reviewer who wishes to quote brief pas- / sages in connec-tion with a review written / for inclusion in a magazine or newspaper. / [at foot of page] PRINTED IN CANADA'; p. v: dedication, '*To Victoria College / and / all its happy associations*'; p. vi: blank; p. vii: fly-title, 'TOWARDS THE LAST SPIKE'; p. viii: blank; pp. 1–53: text (with three asterisks on p. 52 between text and pagination); p. 54: 'SET IN 11/13 FAIRFIELD TYPE / PRINTED AND BOUND / BY THE HUNTER ROSE CO. LIMITED / TORONTO'; pp. 55–56: blank.

Contents [Section Headings]: 3: 'THE GATHERING'; 7: 'THE HANGOVER AT DAWN'; 8: 'THE LADY OF BRITISH COLUMBIA'; 9: 'THE LONG-DISTANCE PROPOSAL'; 10: 'THE PACIFIC SCANDAL'; 10: 'BLAKE IN MOOD'; 10: 'NOVEMBER 3, 1873'; 18: 'THE ATTACK'; 27: 'NUMBER ONE'; 29: 'NUMBER TWO'; 32: 'NUMBER THREE'; 35: 'INTERNECINE STRIFE'; 37: 'RING, RING THE BELLS'; 38: 'THE LAKE OF MONEY'; 41: 'DYNAMITE ON THE NORTH SHORE'; 43: 'THREATS OF SECESSION'; 44: 'BACK TO THE MOUNTAINS'; 45: 'HOLLOW ECHOES FROM THE TREASURY VAULT'; 49: 'SUSPENSE IN THE MONTREAL BOARD ROOM'; 51: 'THE SPIKE'.

Material: calico cloth (302); greyish yellow (Centroid 90); upper cover: upper half contains a drawing of a train engine surrounded by a dotted oval, 5.1 × 7.6 cm., all in a very dark yellowish green (Centroid 138); spine: [in vertical letters] 'E.J. PRATT / TOWARDS THE LAST SPIKE / MACMILLAN'; all in a very dark yellowish green (Centroid 138); lower cover: blank. Dust wrapper: in black and greyish yellow on slightly reddish brown (Centroid 40): [in greyish yellow (Centroid 90)] 'E.J. PRATT / [in black] Towards / the / Last Spike / [drawing of train engine surrounded by a dotted oval (7 × 11 cm.) all in greyish yellow (Centroid 90)] / [at foot in black] A VERSE-PANORAMA OF THE BUILDING / OF THE CANADIAN PACIFIC RAILWAY'; spine: [in vertical letters] 'E.J. PRATT / [drawing of a railway spike 8 × 4 mm.] / TOWARDS THE LAST SPIKE / [drawing of a railway spike 8 × 4 mm.] / MACMILLAN'; lower cover: in greyish yellow (Centroid 90) two verses from the poem, beginning with, 'On the North Shore a reptile lay asleep–', and ending with, 'Of Time.' Inner front flap: publisher's note about poem; back flap: publisher's advertisement about four other books by Pratt: *Collected Poems, Ten Selected Poems, Behind the Log, Brébeuf and His Brethren.*

Published June 27, 1952. Price: $2.00. Number of copies unknown.

Notes: In a letter (Nov. 26, 1951) John Gray is critical of two sections which 'fall below the level of the rest by a good deal [;] The Lady of British Columbia and the whole incident of Blake's omelette.' These he asks Pratt to reconsider. Pratt appears to have altered only the second passage.

In January, informing Gray of a write-up on the poem, Pratt enclosed a copy of *Victoria Reports*: 'Eleven thousand of these Reports go to alumni and ought to stimulate sales in the Spring.' Gray wrote back (Jan. 18), thanking Pratt for the Reports and informing him that 'very shortly ... we shall start type-setting' the poem (Macmillan Archive, OHMA).

Macmillan, looking for sales, wrote J.H. Campbell, Manager of Public Relations for the CPR (Feb. 29, 1952), sending him galley proofs: 'We shall await your comments with interest and should be glad to make a quotation on any quantity which you might like to purchase for C.P.R. distribution.' On June 4, 1952, F.A. Upjohn lets Mr. Campbell know that *Towards the Last Spike* had been printed and that Macmillan would be sending six copies for distribution to various CPR executives: 'We hope that this will lead to a decision to purchase the book in some quantity ...

We are publishing the book on June 27 at a retail price of $2.00.' On August 6, 1952, Gray sent Pratt a $150 cheque for 'your expenses in going to Banff ... legitimate public relations charge from our point of view.'

Daniel Macmillan of Macmillan, London, thanks Gray for the copy sent him (Sept. 1, 1952) but states that 'unfortunately we are not permitted under government regulations to import poetry, and I am afraid that we could not possibly undertake to print the book here' (Macmillan Archive, OHMA).

Towards the Last Spike won the Governor-General's Award for 1952.

Manuscripts, holograph drafts: OTV, Box 5.37, 6.43, 6.44, 6.45, 6.46.
Typescript: OTV, Box 6.47, 6.48.
Macmillan Archive, OHMA, Box 65.18.
Holograph notes: OTV, Box 6.44, 9.63.
Typescript commentary: OTV, Box 6.49.

Copies examined: OTV (2); OTUTF (2); OTMCL (2); OTNY (5); OHMA (2); VCP.

A presentation binding for E.J. Pratt done to Macmillan's special order in morocco (402), very deep red (Centroid 14); lettering and decoration in gilt, same pattern as in cloth binding. In the collection of Claire Pratt.

A20 **Magic in Everything** 1955

As there is no title page, the following description is taken from the wrapper: MAGIC / *in* / 𝕰𝖇𝖊𝖗𝖞𝖙𝖍𝖎𝖓𝖌 / [with black decorations around title] [at centre, in red and black, drawing of a bird (2 × 5 cm.)] / [rule 2.2 cm., space .1 cm., rule 2.2 cm.] / E.J. PRATT (Cut: 15.5 × 10.3 cm.) [unsigned, 1⁴], 4 leaves, pp. [1] 2–6 [7–8].

P. 1: half-title, 'MAGIC IN EVERYTHING'; pp. 2–7: text [with drawing of a Christmas stocking (1.8 × 4.3 cm.) on p. 2]; [drawing of Christmas bells (1.5 × 4.4 cm.) at end of text on p. 7, followed by:] 'WITH / CHRISTMAS AND / NEW YEAR GREETINGS / FROM / [space] / *The Macmillan Company of Canada Limited* / *Toronto* / IN ITS FIFTIETH ANNIVERSARY YEAR'; p. 8: blank.

Printed wrappers (16.5 × 10.8 cm.), heavy wove paper, grey greenish yellow (Centroid 105), stapled; upper cover: as described above; lower cover: blank; endpapers: none.

Sent as a Christmas card by the Macmillan Company of Canada, December 1955.

Notes: Claire Pratt advises that the following version (seen only in photostatic reproduction) was sent as a Christmas card by the Macmillan Company also, date unknown: Abridged version of poem, 1 leaf folded, printed on recto and verso of white card stock paper 13.8 × 17.6 cm. [folded size: 13.8 × 8.8 cm.]; front: [in script] 'Magic in Everything *by* E.J. Pratt'. Seen only at OTV.

Copies examined: OTV (3); OTUTF (2); OTMCL (2) OONL (2); BVAU; BVIV; VCP.

A21   **Collected Poems** – second edition – 1958

[Title page consists of the verso of the first leaf and the recto of the second leaf] [on verso of first leaf]: Published by the Macmillan Company of Canada Limited, Toronto [on recto of second leaf]: Edited with an introduction by Northrop Frye / [on recto of second leaf, sketch of a dinosaur 6.7 × 5.3 cm.] Second edition / [on verso of first leaf]: The Collected [on recto of second leaf]: Poems of E.J. Pratt / 1958

(Cut: 22.8 × 14 cm.) [unsigned, 1^{12}, 2–26^8], 212 leaves [+ tipped-in frontispiece], pp. [i–vii] viii–xxviii [xxix–xxx] [1] 2–23 [24–25] 26–33 [34–35] 36–67 [68–69] 70–78 [79] 80–105 [106–107] 108–118 [119] 120–136 [137] 138–181 [182–183] 184–209 [210–211] 212–242 [243] 244–298 [299] 300–309 [310–311] 312–343 [344–345] 346–391 [392] 393–395 [396].

P. i: half-title, 'The Collected Poems of E.J. Pratt second edition' / [drawing of train on trestle 6.7 × 4.8 cm.]; pp. ii–iii: title pages as above; p. iv: 'Copyright, Canada, 1958 / by THE MACMILLAN COMPANY OF CANADA LIMITED / All rights reserved – no part of this book may be re- / produced in any form without permission in writing from / the publisher, except by a reviewer who wishes to quote / brief passages in connection with a review written for / inclusion in a magazine or newspaper. / Printed and bound in Canada / by McCorquodale & Blades (Printers) Limited / Designed and illustrated / by Frank Davies, M.T.D.C. / Set in Baskerville type ten point on twelve point body / The handwriting of E.J. Pratt is reproduced / on the front and back covers of this book's case.'; p. v: blank; p. vi: frontispiece; p. vii: dedication, 'To Viola my wife / and to Claire my daughter / this book / is lovingly dedicated' / [at foot of page] 'Portrait of E.J. Pratt by Ashley & Crippen'; pp. viii-xi: contents; p. xii: 'EDITOR'S PREFACE'; pp. xiii–xxviii: 'EDITOR'S INTRODUCTION'; pp. xxix–xxx: blank; p. 1: fly-title, 'Part One / POEMS CHIEFLY LYRICAL / NEWFOUNDLAND VERSE / THE IRON DOOR / MANY MOODS / THE FABLE OF THE GOATS AND OTHER POEMS / STILL LIFE AND OTHER VERSE / LATER POEMS / [sketch of cliff 5.3 × 7.7 cm.] / NEWFOUNDLAND VERSE / (1923) / To my mother'; pp. 2–23: text; p. 24: blank; p. 25: fly-title, 'THE IRON DOOR / An Ode / (1927) / To some very dear memories' / [sketch of a cross and people kneeling 11 × 5.3 cm.]; pp. 26-33: text; p. 34: blank; p. 35: fly-title, 'MANY MOODS / (1932) / To Viola and Claire' / [abstract sketch 6 × 4 cm.]; pp. 36-67: text; p. 68: blank; p. 69: fly-title, 'THE FABLE OF THE GOATS / and other Poems / (1937) / To my sister Charlotte' / [sketch of out-stretched hands (8.7 × 5.4 cm.)]; pp. 7–78: text; p. 79: fly-title, 'STILL LIFE / and other Verse / (1943)' / [sketch of a vase and branches 9.4 × 8.4 cm.]; pp. 80-105: text; p. 106: blank; p. 107: fly-title, 'LATER POEMS' / [sketch of a hand, moon and sun 6.2 × 4.4 cm.]; pp. 108–118: text; p. 119: fly-title, 'Part Two / NARRATIVE POEMS / THE WITCHES' BREW / TITANS / THE ROOSEVELT AND THE ANTINOE / THE TITANIC / BRÉBEUF AND HIS BRETHREN / DUNKIRK / BEHIND THE LOG / TOWARDS THE LAST SPIKE' / [sketch of face, hands, sea-life 9 × 10.5 cm.] / [at foot of page] 'THE WITCHES' BREW / (1925)'; pp. 120–136: text; p. 137: fly-title, 'TITANS / The Cachalot / The Great Feud / (1926) / To the boys of the stag parties' / [sketch of skeletal remains 3.4 × 6 cm.]; pp. 138-181: text; p. 182: blank; p. 183: fly-title, 'THE ROOSEVELT / AND THE ANTINOE / (1930) / To my brothers Jim, Art and Cal' / [abstract sketch 6.6 × 8.3 cm.]; pp. 184-209: text; p. 210: blank; p. 211: fly-title, 'THE TITANIC / (1935) / To my father' / [sketch of iceberg 5.4 × 5.8 cm.]; pp. 212–242: text; p. 243: fly-title, 'BRÉBEUF AND HIS BRETHREN / (1940) / To my father' / [sketch of a cross 6.5 × 4.2 cm.]; pp. 244–298: text; p. 299: fly-title, 'DUNKIRK / (1941)' / [sketch of a battle scene 7.3 × 5.7 cm.]; pp. 300–309: text; p. 310: blank; p. 311: fly-title, 'BEHIND THE LOG / (1947)' / [sketch of ship equipment 7 × 5 cm.]; pp. 312–343: text; p. 344: blank; p. 345: fly-title, 'TOWARDS THE LAST SPIKE / (1952) / To Victoria College / and all its happy associations' / [sketch of railroad workers 7.8 × 2.8 cm.]; pp. 346–388: text; pp. 389-391: 'INDEX

OF TITLES'; p. 392: blank; pp. 393–395: 'INDEX OF FIRST LINES'; p. 396: blank.

Contents: 2: 'NEWFOUNDLAND'; 4: 'THE TOLL OF THE BELLS'; 5: 'THE GROUND SWELL'; 5: 'THE SHARK'; 6: 'THE FOG'; 6: 'THE BIG FELLOW'; 7: 'IN ABSENTIA'; 8: 'THE FLOOD-TIDE'; 8: 'IN LANTERN LIGHT'; 9: 'THE DROWNING'; 9: 'CARLO'; 12: 'OVERHEARD BY A STREAM'; 13: 'THE HISTORY OF JOHN JONES'; 14: 'THE EPIGRAPHER'; 16: 'GREAT TIDES'; 16: 'ON THE SHORE'; 17: 'COME NOT THE SEASONS HERE'; 18: 'BEFORE AN ALTAR / (After Gueudecourt)'; 18: 'A DIRGE'; 19: 'THE ICE-FLOES'; 26: 'THE IRON DOOR / (An Ode)'; 36: 'SEA-GULLS'; 36: 'THE WAY OF CAPE RACE'; 37: 'EROSION'; 37: 'THE SEA-CATHEDRAL'; 38: 'A PRAIRIE SUNSET'; 38: 'OUT OF STEP / (1931 A.D.)'; 39: 'THE MAN AND THE MACHINE'; 39: 'THE PARABLE OF PUFFSKY'; 41: 'FROM STONE TO STEEL'; 42: 'OLD AGE'; 42: 'BLIND'; 43: 'A LEGACY'; 43: 'THE DECISION / (To L.R., a college athlete who died May, 1923.)'; 43: 'TO AN ENEMY'; 44: 'THE HIGHWAY'; 45: 'PUTTING WINTER TO BED'; 49: 'CHERRIES'; 50: 'A FELINE SILHOUETTE'; 50: 'THE CHILD AND THE WREN / (To Claire)'; 51: 'FROST'; 51: 'COMRADES'; 52: 'ONE HOUR OF LIFE'; 52: 'TIME-WORN'; 53: 'TO ANGELINA, AN OLD NURSE'; 55: 'JOCK O' THE LINKS'; 56: 'THE CONVICT HOLOCAUST / (Columbus, Ohio, 1930)'; 57: 'THE DRAG-IRONS'; 57: 'THE LEE-SHORE'; 58: 'THE 6000'; 60: 'THE RITUAL'; 61: 'THE DEPRESSION ENDS'; 70: 'THE BARITONE'; 71: 'FIRE'; 72: 'SEEN ON THE ROAD'; 72: 'THE PRIZE CAT'; 73: 'LIKE MOTHER, LIKE DAUGHTER'; 74: 'THE OLD ORGANON (1225 A.D.)'; 74: 'THE NEW (1937 A.D.)'; 74: 'THE MYSTIC'; 75: 'THE WEATHER GLASS'; 75: 'THE EMPTY ROOM'; 76: 'THE MIRAGE'; 76: 'THE ILLUSION'; 77: 'SILENCES'; 80: 'STILL LIFE'; 81: 'AUTOPSY ON A SADIST / (after Lidice)'; 81: 'THE STOICS'; 82: 'FATHER TIME'; 83: 'MISSING: BELIEVED DEAD: RETURNED'; 84: 'THE BRAWLER IN WHO'S WHO'; 85: 'THE RADIO IN THE IVORY TOWER / (1937 – Sept. 1939)'; 89: 'THE SUBMARINE'; 94: 'THE INVADED FIELD'; 95: 'COME AWAY, DEATH'; 96: 'THE IMPATIENT EARTH'; 97: 'THE DYING EAGLE'; 99: 'OLD HARRY'; 100: 'THE TRUANT'; 108: 'THE UNROMANTIC MOON'; 108: 'THE GOOD EARTH'; 109: 'A CALL'; 110: 'A NOVEMBER LANDSCAPE'; 110: 'SUMMIT MEETINGS'; 111: 'CYCLES'; 112: 'MYTH AND FACT'; 114: 'THE DEED'; 115: 'NEWFOUNDLAND SEAMEN'; 115: 'MAGIC IN EVERYTHING'; 120: 'THE WITCHES' BREW'; 138: 'THE CACHALOT'; 151: 'THE GREAT FEUD / (A Dream of a Pleiocene Armageddon)'; 184: 'THE ROOSEVELT AND THE ANTINOE'; 212: 'THE TITANIC'; 244: 'BRÉBEUF AND HIS BRETHREN'; 300: 'DUNKIRK'; 312: 'BEHIND THE LOG'; 346: 'TOWARDS THE LAST SPIKE'.

Pagination at bottom left margin of type page; headlines on verso of poem titles.

Frontispiece facing dedication page: 'Portrait of E.J. Pratt by Ashley & Crippen'.

Material: calico cloth (302), dark grey (Centroid 266); upper cover: poem titles, beginning with 'The Convict Holocaust' and ending with 'Newfoundland Verse' in E.J. Pratt's handwriting in white centred on cover; [on top half, in very yellow (Centroid 82)]: 'The Collected Poems of E.J. Pratt second edition'; spine: [lettered horizontally in white] 'Collected / Poems / second / edition / [in very yellow (Centroid 82)] E.J. Pratt / [in white] edited by / Northrop / Frye / [at foot] Macmillan'; lower cover: poem titles, beginning with 'The Toll of the Bells' and ending with 'Time-Worn' as on upper cover; [on top half, close to spine, in very yellow (Centroid 82)] 'Macmillan'; endpapers: white wove, unwatermarked. Dust wrapper: upper cover: on medium grey (Centroid 265) a very yellow (Centroid 82); 3.5 cm. wide band, 6 cm. from top extends around wrapper; [in white lettering] 'Collected / Poems / [on very yellow band in medium grey (Centroid 265) lettering] E.J. Pratt / [in white on medium grey cover] Second / Edition / Revised and enlarged / to include all / the poet's major works / Edited with an introduction / by Northrop Frye'; spine: [vertically in white lettering] 'E.J. Pratt / [on very yellow band, in medium grey lettering]: A new / enlarged / second / edition / [in white] Collected Poems / [horizontally] Macmillan'; lower cover: [upper left-hand corner] sketch in white of laying railway track 9.6 x 7 cm.; [on very yellow band in medium grey lettering]: 'E.J. Pratt / [in white on medium grey cover] "one of the best / narrative poets of our time ... " / WILLIAM ROSE BENÉT' / lower left corner: sketch of dinosaur 5.5 × 6.7 cm.; inner flap: portrait of E.J. Pratt (4.2 × 5 cm.) same as frontispiece followed by publisher's notice about book; back flap: biographical statement about Northrop Frye and quotation from his introduction.

Published November 1958. Price: $5.00. Number of copies sold 1958–62: 3,334.

Notes: Early in 1958 J.M. Gray of Macmillan invited Northrop Frye to edit a revised edition of Pratt's collected poems. Accepting (Feb. 9,

1958), Frye suggested that the poems should appear in a 'chronological order, the different books properly separated in the table of contents and dated ... an introduction by me isn't necessary, but it could be damn useful to most of the people who would actually use the book.' He also felt that Macmillan should 'get a designer who will make the new Collected ... look like what it is, one of the essential books in Canadian literature and a definitive collection of Canada's biggest poet.'

On March 7, 1958, Frye sent Gray a table of contents; Pratt had 'wisely' chosen to omit 'The Fable of the Goats' and 'A Reverie on a Dog' but insisted on 'Carlo' and 'Putting Winter to Bed' being added. 'A Dirge,' 'The Mirage' and 'The Illusion' were added at Frye's suggestion. On June 25 Pratt also requested that 'Newfoundland Seamen' be added. In a Macmillan memo describing a meeting between Frye, Gray, and Upjohn (June 24, 1958) it is stated that Frye will edit and write an introduction which 'will run to 3,000 – 4,000 words ... in the form of a critical essay on the general theme of Pratt's poetry. It will attempt to establish his relation to the Canadian tradition of poetry and to other modern poets.'

A later memo (July 15) suggests that Pratt will look at the proofs but will not necessarily 'read every word.' But Frye did, of course, and was upset by several things, most by the attempt of Macmillan's layout artist to squeeze the introduction into narrow columns which even 'grinding poverty cannot excuse.' After an example, he asks: 'What *is* the point of such a broken-up setting? I'd much rather not see my introduction appear at all than have it appear in so preposterously unreadable a form' (letter to Upjohn, Sept. 15, 1958). The designer, Frank Davies, writing to Upjohn on Sept. 18, explained his dilemma: he had developed the format based on Pratt's poems before having seen the introduction. 'If [the introduction] had been available at the beginning the quotes with the introduction may have led to a different solution to the *entire* book.' He suggests, however, that the introduction should be set up in 'a long narrow form' similar to the poetry and that Frye should wait to see the page proofs before condemning the 'layout–man too roundly.' Davies suggests that Frye might be interested in the fall issue of 'Tamarack' which would carry his article 'on the design of the Pratt book as my main example to illustrate the approach of a book-designer to his problem.'

Frye eventually accepts Davies' arguments and agrees that he should not hold up production 'on an issue affecting only myself' (Sept. 25).

The text, he states, is 'admirable – it's hardly in the same world as the first edition – and that's all that matters.' Page proofs were returned on Sept. 29.

Knopf had refused to bring out the second edition in July, 1958. Sales of the *Collected Poems* between 1958 and 1969 were approximately 6,400 of which 100 were sold in the United States and 122 in Great Britain.

In 1969 Macmillan undertook a reprinting of the Collected. In a letter to Mrs. Pratt, Gray explained how precarious publishing in Canada had become and that 'unless the 15% royalty [were] lowered' he would have to 'consider not going ahead with the reprint.' A 10% contract was signed in December 1969. 2,500 copies were printed in 1970 (Macmillan Archive, OHMA).

Copies examined: OTV (2); OTUTF; OTMCL (2); OHMA; OONL; VCP; LML. Reissue, 1962: OTMCL; OHMA; 1970: OTV; OTMCL.

A presentation binding for E.J. Pratt done to Macmillan's special order in fine morocco (402b), very deep red (Centroid 14); lettering and ornaments on spine in gilt: [ornaments] / 'COLLECTED / POEMS / [ornamental rule] / E.J. PRATT / [ornaments] / [at foot] MACMILLAN'. In the collection of Claire Pratt.

A22   A / **Here the Tides Flow** 1962

HERE / THE TIDES / FLOW / E.J. PRATT / INTRODUCTION, NOTES AND QUESTIONS BY / D.G. PITT, M.A., PH.D. / DEPARTMENT OF ENGLISH / MEMORIAL UNIVERSITY OF NEWFOUNDLAND / ST. JOHN'S, NEWFOUNDLAND / TORONTO / THE MACMILLAN COMPANY OF CANADA LIMITED

(Cut: 18.4 × 12.2 cm.) [unsigned, 1–3^8, 4^6, 5–6^8], 92 leaves, pp. [i–iv] v–xi [xii] xiii–xiv 1–155 [156] 157–169 [170].

P. i: half-title, 'HERE / THE TIDES / FLOW'; p. ii: blank; p. iii: title page as above; p. iv: 'Copyright, Canada, 1962 / by / THE MACMILLAN COMPANY OF CANADA LIMITED / All rights reserved – no part of this book may be / reproduced in any form without permission in / writing from the publisher. / Mimeographing or reproducing mechanically in / any other way passages from this book without / the written permission of the publisher is an / infringement of the copyright law. / Frontispiece portrait of E.J. PRATT by Ashley / & Crippen. / PRINTED IN CANADA'; pp. v–vi: 'PREFACE' signed 'D.G.P.'; pp. vii–xi: 'INTRODUCTION' signed 'D.G.P.'; p. xii: blank; pp. xiii–xiv: contents; pp. 1–155: text; p. 156: blank; pp. 157–166: notes; pp. 167–169: 'QUESTIONS AND TOPICS FOR DISCUSSION'; p. 170: blank.

Contents: 1: 'NEWFOUNDLAND'; 3: 'THE TOLL OF THE BELLS'; 4: 'THE GROUND SWELL'; 5: 'THE SHARK'; 6: 'THE BIG FELLOW'; 7: 'THE FLOOD-TIDE'; 7: 'IN LANTERN LIGHT'; 8: 'THE SECRET OF THE SEA'; 9: 'LOSS OF THE STEAMSHIP FLORIZEL'; 9: 'THE DROWNING'; 10: 'CARLO'; 13: 'A COAST / (from "Flashlights and Echoes From the Years / of 1914 and 1915")'; 14: 'SEA-GULLS'; 15: 'THE WAY OF CAPE RACE'; 16: 'TIME-WORN'; 16: 'THE LEE-SHORE'; 17: 'THE RITUAL'; 18: 'EROSION'; 18: 'THE SEA-CATHEDRAL'; 19: 'TATTERHEAD'; 21: 'THE DRAG-IRONS'; 21: 'THE WEATHER GLASS'; 22: 'SILENCES'; 24: 'OLD HARRY'; 25: 'NEWFOUNDLAND SEAMEN'; 26: 'NEW-FOUNDLAND CALLING'; 27: 'PUTTING WINTER TO BED'; 32: 'DOORS'; 33: 'TO AN ENEMY'; 33: 'THE 6000'; 36: 'INVENTORY OF HADES / (from "The Witches' Brew")'; 37: 'MAGIC IN EVERYTHING'; 41: 'RACHEL / A Sea Story of Newfoundland / in Verse'; 58: 'THE ICE-FLOES'; 62: 'THE CACHALOT'; 73: 'THE TITANIC'; 97: 'DUNKIRK'; 104: 'TOWARDS THE LAST SPIKE'; 112: 'BRÉBEUF AND HIS BRETHREN'.

Frontispiece tipped in, facing title page, coated paper, portrait of E.J. Pratt by Ashley & Crippen (18.4 × 12.2 cm.).

Material: paper over board, very orange (Centroid 48) with overall pattern of publisher's circular monogram in white; upper cover: on white imitation label (9.8 × 5.1 cm.) within printer's rule, thick-thin: 'Here / the Tides / Flow / [rule 3.4 cm.] / [in roman] E.J. PRATT / [rule 3.4 cm.] / [in roman] MACMILLAN'; spine: on white imitation label, as above (1.2 × 9.8 cm.) [lettered vertically]: 'HERE THE TIDES FLOW / [dot] / E.J. Pratt'; lower cover: blank; endpapers: white wove unwatermarked.

Published in 1962. Price: $1.50. Approximately 15,000 copies published (letter D.G. Pitt, Nov. 13, 1984).

Copies examined: OTV (2); OTUTF; OTNY; OHMA; VCP.

B / Identical to first edition except for:

P. iii: title page: as above with additional 'EDITED WITH' following 'E.J. PRATT'; p. 169: as above with following numbers on line preceding pagination: 'T.H.B. 07 96 86 76 66'.

Binding as above but in brownish orange (Centroid 54).

Copies examined: OTV; VCP.

C / **Here the Tides Flow** – paperback edition – 1962

Identical to the first edition except for:
Perfect binding: 95 leaves, pp. [i–iv] v–xi [xii] xiii–xiv 1--155 [156] 157–169 [170–176].

P. iii: title page as above with additional 'EDITED WITH' following 'E.J. PRATT'; p. 169: as above with following numbers on line preceding pagination: '07 17 27 37 47 56 THB'; pp. 170-176: blank. Frontispiece: as above but paper not coated.

Paper covers, brownish orange (Centroid 54) with overall pattern of publisher's circular monogram in white.

Copies examined: OTMC; OTMCL; OHMA; LML.

A23 **Selected Poems of E.J. Pratt** 1968

Selected Poems of / E.J. PRATT / Edited and with an / introduction, bibliography, / and notes by / PETER BUITENHUIS / Macmillan of Canada / Toronto / 1968

(Cut: 17.8 × 10.5 cm.) perfect binding: 128 leaves, pp. [i–vi] vii–xxx [1–2] 3–43 [44–46] 47–221 [222–226].

P. i: half-title, 'Selected Poems of E.J. Pratt'; p. ii: blank; p. iii: title page as above; p. iv: 'The Macmillan Company of Canada Limited 1968 / All rights reserved – no part of this book may be reproduced / in any form without permission in writing from the pub- / lisher, except by a reviewer who wishes to quote brief pas- / sages in connection with a review written for inclusion in a / magazine or newspaper. / Library of Congress Catalog Card Number 68-13877 / Printed in Canada by Universal Printers Ltd. / for the Macmillan Company of Canada Limited, / 70 Bond Street, Toronto.'; p. v: preface; p. vi: blank; pp. vi–viii: contents; pp. ix–x: 'EDWIN JOHN PRATT – CHRONOLOGY'; pp. xi–xxx: 'INTRODUCTION' signed 'PETER BUITENHUIS'; p. 1: section title, 'Poems Chiefly Lyrical'; p. 2: blank; pp. 3–43: text; p. 44: blank; p. 45: section title, 'Narrative Poems'; p. 46: blank; pp. 47–206: text; pp. 207–210: bibliography; pp. 211–221: notes; pp. 222–226: blank.

Contents: [1]: 'Poems Chiefly Lyrical'; 3: '*Newfoundland Verse* / NEW-FOUNDLAND'; 5: 'THE SHARK'; 6: 'CARLO'; 9: 'COME NOT THE SEASONS HERE'; 11: '*The Iron Door* / (An Ode)'; 19: '*Many Moods* / 'THE WAY OF CAPE RACE'; 19: 'THE MAN AND THE MACHINE'; 20: 'FROM STONE TO STEEL'; 20: 'THE HIGHWAY'; 21: 'FROST'; 22: 'THE DRAG-IRONS'; 22: 'THE DEPRESSION ENDS'; 29: '*The Fable of the Goats and Other Poems* / THE PRIZE CAT'; 29: 'LIKE MOTHER, LIKE DAUGHTER'; 30: 'THE MIRAGE'; 31: 'SILENCES'; 33: '*Still Life and Other Verse* / THE STOICS'; 34: 'COME AWAY, DEATH'; 35: 'THE DYING EAGLE'; 37: 'THE TRUANT'; 43: 'THE DEED'; [45]: 'Narrative Poems'; 47: '*Titans* / THE CACHALOT'; 61: '*The Titanic*'; 93: '*Brébeuf and His Brethren*'; 152: '*Behind the Log*'; 185: '*Towards the Last Spike*'.

Paperback in dark reddish orange (Centroid 38); upper cover: colour reproduction of a landscape painting (10.1 × 9.5 cm.); [lower half of cover, lettered in white] '*Selected Poems of* / E.J. Pratt / [in black] Edited and with an introduction, biblio- / ography, and notes by Peter Buitenhuis'; spine: [lettered vertically in white] '*Selected Poems of* / E.J. Pratt / [in black] MACMILLAN'; lower cover: publisher's statement about the book (13 1/2 lines); biographical note on Buitenhuis (12 1/2 lines).

Published in February, 1968. Price: $1.95. Number of copies unknown.

Notes: Peter Buitenhuis, in a letter to John Gray (Feb. 18, 1965), proposes a Selected Pratt in paperback. Buitenhuis volunteers to select and edit: 'I knew Ned well in his last years and have had occasion to discuss his work quite a bit in recent years.' Gray makes no promises, but states that he will keep the offer in mind when a decision is made. Two years later, Gray informs Mrs Pratt that Buitenhuis is working on a selection of

Pratt poems to be published as a paperback for undergraduate and popular use (Macmillan Archive, OHMA).

Copies examined: OTV; OTUTF; OTMCL; OTR; OHMA; LML.
Reissued in 1969 and 1972.

B / Published Broadsides

The following is a complete list of single poems (or excerpts) published as single broadsides primarily to celebrate special occasions.

B1 **The Line of Ascent**

THE LINE OF ASCENT / [subtitle in very red (Centroid 11) in left-hand margin] / *A Tribute / to the / British / Stock* / [with printed signature] E.J. PRATT. *Canada, 1945* / [the following in very red (Centroid 11) at bottom of sheet] Written on the occasion of the visit of a delegation of the Publishers' Branch / of the Board of Trade (Toronto) to Britain, October 1945

Broadside: 36.2 × 26.4 cm., printed on one side only with deckled right hand edge and bottom edge.

Published October 1945 (?). Number of copies unknown.

Notes: The text is the 'Crew' section from *Dunkirk* (1941) and was therefore not 'written on the occasion' of the visit described.

Copies examined: OTV (2).

B2 **Newfoundland Calling**

[A facsimile of Pratt's holograph manuscript] Newfoundland Calling / [text in 54 lines with signature at lower right] E.J. Pratt / [at lower left] London 1949 / [at bottom centre: drawing of a flower].

Broadside: 57 × 23 cm., printed on one side only.

Published in 1949 by Macmillan, London, on the occasion of Newfoundland entering Confederation. Number of copies not known.

Copies examined: OTV (photostatic copy).

B3 A Club Inventory of Hades

A CLUB INVENTORY OF HADES / A member of the Arts and Letters Club, fifty years hence, pays a visit / to Hades to see his fellow-members domiciled in that region. They / come crowding up to greet him – and here they are. / [text in 32 lines; at lower right:] E.J. Pratt

Broadside: 27.7 × 21.6 cm., printed on one side only.

Privately printed for the fiftieth anniversary of the Toronto Arts and Letters Club, 1958. Number of copies unknown.

Copies examined: OTV; Toronto Arts and Letters Club.

B4 Inventory of Hades

[Two illustrations at the top of the sheet in gold and black with initials 'FN' in white at bottom centre of second illustration] / E.J. PRATT / INVENTORY OF HADES / [text in 23 lines with permission statement at bottom]

Broadside: 42.3 × 17.7 cm., printed on one side only.

Publication date unknown. Number of copies unknown. Frank Newfeld designed the broadside [post 1958] as his own Christmas card and gave Claire Pratt 100 for her personal use.

Copies examined: OTV (2); OTNY; LML.

B5 An Excerpt from The Truant

[Front: decoration in slightly yellow (Centroid 84) at left side, title at right side] by / the / Canadian / Poet / E.J. Pratt / an excerpt from / THE TRUANT / [at lower right, in slightly yellow (Centroid 84)] Reprinted from /

The Collected Poems of E.J. Pratt, / Revised 1958. / With the permission of / The Macmillan Company of Canada Limited / [text in 117 lines on verso of second leaf and recto of third leaf; colophon on verso of fourth leaf]

Broadside: folded size: 29.8 × 19.9 cm., printed on the outside of a single sheet folded twice. Designed by Oscar Ross; paper: Laurentic Japan; type: Deepdene and Albertus; printer: Spalding Printing Company Limited, Toronto.

Published for the International Competition for Book Designers – International Exhibition of Book Design, Leipzig, 1959. Number of copies: 1,000.

Copies examined: OTV; OTNY.

B6 The Deed

[Enclosed within illustration and scroll] EJP / [in script] The Deed / [thick and thin rule (13.8 cm.)] / [text in 32 lines with signature at lower right] E.J. Pratt / [thick and thin rule (16.1 cm.)]

Broadside: 30 × 20.9 cm., printed on one side only.

Publication date and number of copies unknown.

Copies examined: OTV (photostatic copy).

B7 In Memoriam

IN MEMORIAM / [two ornaments] / [the following a facsimile of Pratt's holograph manuscript] In Memoriam / [text in 28 lines, in facsimile, followed by two ornaments and signature] E.J. Pratt

Broadside: 39.3 × 28 cm., printed on one side only.

Publication date and number of copies unknown.

Copies examined: OTV (photostatic copy).

B8 **Sea-Gulls**

[Drawing of three sea-gulls in greyish blue (Centroid 186)] / SEA-GULLS / [text in 15 lines with drawing of waves below text in greyish blue (Centroid 186)] / [signature] E.J. Pratt

Broadside: 45.7 × 25.4 cm. in light greenish grey (Centroid 154), paper printed on one side only.

Publication date and number of copies unknown.

Copies examined: OTNY; LML.

B9 **Snowfall on a Battle-Field**

SNOWFALL ON A BATTLE-FIELD / [text in 20 lines with printed signature at lower right] E.J. Pratt

Broadside: 35.5 × 27 cm., printed on one side only.

Publication date and number of copies unknown.

Copies examined: OTV.

B10 **A Victory Message and Pledge of Friendship**

[Ensign of Canada centred at top of sheet / *A Victory Message and Pledge of / Friendship / from the Canadian People / to the U.S.S.R.* [text in 12 lines, in italic, with printed signature] E.J. Pratt / [followed by a message in 9 lines, with the ensign of the USSR centred at bottom of the sheet; printer's device and number 7 in bottom right hand corner]

Broadside: 28.5 × 14.7 cm., printed on one side only in medium reddish brown (Centroid 43).

Publication date and number of copies unknown.

Copies examined: OTV.

C / Individual Poems in Books and Periodicals

The following is a list of every Pratt poem with its transmission history for its authoritative period (i.e., during Pratt's lifetime). Anthology occurrences are listed only when a poem appears for the first time in such a work; see the Anthology section for complete anthology listing. For manuscripts, file numbers follow the decimal after box number.

C1 1909 **A Poem on the May Examinations**
Acta Victoriana, 32 (April 1909), 561–4.

C2 1914 **The Wind of the West**
Acta Victoriana, 39 (Oct. 1914), 14.

C3 **The Secret of the Sea**
Acta Victoriana, 39 (Dec. 1914), 126. [Title: 'The Sea']
Rebel, 2 (Dec. 1917), 88. [Title: 'The Sea']
Newfoundland Verse (Toronto: Ryerson, 1923), 38–9.
Here the Tides Flow, ed. D.G. Pitt (Toronto: Macmillan, 1962), 8.
Typescript: Pratt Collection, OTV, Box 1.2.

C4 1915 **Unseen Allies**
Acta Victoriana, 39 (March 1915), 331.

C5 **Evening**
Acta Victoriana, 40 (Oct. 1915), 14. [Title: 'By the Sea']
Newfoundland Verse, (1923), 113.
Typescript: Pratt Collection, OTV, Box 1.2; Box 8.62.

C6 **The Sacrifice of Youth**
Acta Victoriana, 40 (Dec. 1915), frontispiece.

C7 1916 **Dead on the Field of Honour**
Acta Victoriana, 40 (June 1916), 373.
Typescript: Pratt Collection, OTV, Box 7.52.

C8 1917 **The Seed Must Die**
Acta Victoriana, 41 (March 1917), 255.
Newfoundland Verse (1923), 100–2.
Typescript: Pratt Collection, OTV, Box 1.2; 8.62.

C9 **The Greater Sacrifice**
Acta Victoriana, 41 (June 1917), 320–1.

C10 **For Valour**
Acta Victoriana, 42 (Oct. 1917), 11–13.

C11 **The Great Mother**
Acta Victoriana, 42 (Dec. 1917), 135.

Newfoundland Verse (1923), 108.
Verses of the Sea (Toronto: Macmillan, 1930), 37.
Typescript: Pratt Collection, OTV, Box 1.2; 8.62.

C12 **The Sea-Shell**
The Poets of the Future: A College Anthology, ed. H.T.
Schnittkind (Boston: Stratford Co., 1917), 279–81.
Typescript: Pratt Collection, OTV, Box 7.52.

C13 ***Rachel: A Sea Story of Newfoundland in Verse***. New York:
privately printed, 1917.
Here the Tides Flow, ed. D.G. Pitt (Toronto: Macmillan, 1962), 41–58.
[See preceding section]

C14 1918 **The Largess of 1917**
Acta Victoriana, 42 (Feb. 1918), 248–9.

C15 **Dawn**
Rebel, 2 (March 1918), 230. [Title: 'The Angler']
Newfoundland Verse (1923), 27. [Title: '?']
Verses of the Sea (1930), 62.
Typescript: Pratt Collection, OTV, Box 1.2.

C16 **The Dear Illusion**
Acta Victoriana, 42 (March 1918), 312.
Rebel, 3 (March 1919), 218.
Dalhousie Review, 4 (Jan. 1925), 437.

C17 **Invocation**
University Monthly, 18, No. 6 (March 1918), 219–20.

C18 **The Wooden Cross**
Acta Victoriana, 42 (June 1918), 363–4.

C19 **October, 1918**
Acta Victoriana, 43 (Oct. 1918), 19–20.

C20 1919 **Amerongen**
Acta Victoriana, 43 (Jan. 1919), 157.

C21 **The Hidden Scar**
Acta Victoriana, 43 (June 1919), 332.
Newfoundland Verse (1923), 112.
Typescript: Pratt Collection, OTV, Box 1.2.

C22 **In Memoriam**
Acta Victoriana, War Supplement (Dec. 1919), 7.
Newfoundland Verse (1923), 110–11.
Broadside: Pratt Collection, OTV, n.p., n.d.
Holograph: Pratt Collection, OTV, Box 1.2.

Lorne Pierce Collection, okq, Box 72.003.

C23 **Overheard by a Stream**
Rebel, 4 (Dec. 1919), 131. [Title: 'A Dialogue by a Stream']
Newfoundland Verse (1923), 46.
Verses of the Sea (1930), 26–7.
Collected Poems (Toronto: Macmillan, 1944), 190.
The Collected Poems of E.J. Pratt, ed. Northrop Frye (Toronto: Macmillan, 1958), 12.
Typescript: Pratt Collection, otv, Box 1.2.

C24 1920 **Blow! Winds, and Roar!**
Acta Victoriana, 44 (Jan. 1920), 170.

C25 **Signals**
Rebel, 4 (March 1920), 232. [Title: 'On the Shore']
Newfoundland Verse (1923), 92–3. [Title: 'Later']
Verses of the Sea (1930), 35.
Typescript: Pratt Collection, otv, Box 1.2.

C26 **Carlo**
Canadian Forum, 1 (Nov. 1920), 55.
Newfoundland Verse (1923), 42.
Verses of the Sea (1930), 20–1.
Collected Poems (1958), 9.
Here the Tides Flow (1962), 10.
Typescript: Pratt Collection, otv, Box 1.2; 7.52.

C27 1921 **Anticipations**
Canadian Forum, 1 (June 1921), 271.
Newfoundland Verse (1923); in 'A Fragment from a Story' subtitled 'A Later Spring,' pp. 133–4.
Typescript: Pratt Collection, otv, Box 1.2.
Note: In *The Collected Works* this poem is included only as part of 'A Fragment from a Story.'

C28 **In Absentia**
Canadian Forum, 1 (June 1921), 271–2.
Newfoundland Verse (1923), 34.
Verses of the Sea (1930), 39.
Collected Poems (1944), 184–5.
Collected Poems (1958), 7.
Typescript: Pratt Collection, otv, Box 1.2.

C29 **The Flood-Tide**
Canadian Forum, 1 (June 1921), 272.

Newfoundland Verse (1923), 35.
Verses of the Sea (1930), 30.
Collected Poems (1944), 188–9.
Collected Poems (1958), 8.
Here the Tides Flow (1962), 7.
Typescript: Pratt Collection, OTV, Box 1.2.

C30   **The Pine Tree**
Canadian Forum, 1 (June 1921), 272.
Newfoundland Verse (1923), 36.
Typescript: Pratt Collection, OTV, Box 1.2.

C31   1922 **Sea Variations**
Canadian Bookman, 4 (Jan. 1922), 50–1.
Newfoundland Verse (1923), 9–14.
Typescript: Pratt Collection, OTV, Box 1.2; 7.54.

C32   **The Ice-Floes**
Canadian Forum, 2 (April 1922), 591–3.
Newfoundland Verse (1923), 20–6.
Verses of the Sea (1930), 3–9.
Collected Poems (1944), 195–8.
Ten Selected Poems (Toronto: Macmillan, 1947),
       68–72.
Collected Poems (1958), 19–23.
Here the Tides Flow (1962), 58–62.
Typescript: Pratt Collection, OTV, Box 1.2.

C33   1923 **The Ground Swell**
Acta Victoriana, 47 (Feb. 1923), 15.
Newfoundland Verse (1923), 17.
Verses of the Sea (1930), 12.
Collected Poems (1944), 200.
Collected Poems (1958), 5.
Here the Tides Flow (1962), 4.
Typescript: Pratt Collection, OTV, Box 1.2.

C34   **The History of John Jones**
Canadian Forum, 3 (Jan. 1923), 110.
Newfoundland Verse (1923), 71–2.
Verses of the Sea (1930), 28.
Collected Poems (1944), 191.
Collected Poems (1958), 13.
Typescript: Pratt Collection, OTV, Box 7.60.

c35   **A Student's Prayer at an Examination**
Canadian Forum, 3 (Jan. 1923), 111.

c36   **In Lantern Light**
Canadian Forum, 3 (Jan. 1923), 111.
Newfoundland Verse (1923), 37.
Verses of the Sea (1930), 16.
Collected Poems (1944), 183.
Collected Poems (1958), 8.
Here the Tides Flow (1962), 7.
Typescript: Pratt Collection, OTV, Box 1.2.

c37   **The Shark**
Canadian Forum, 3 (Jan. 1923), 111.
Newfoundland Verse (1923), 28–9.
Verses of the Sea (1930), 13–14.
Collected Poems (1944), 185–6.
Collected Poems (1958), 5.
Here the Tides Flow (1962), 5.
Typescript: Pratt Collection, OTV, Box 1.2; 7.60.

c38   **The Decision**
Acta Victoriana, 48 (Nov. 1923), 22.
Canadian Journal of Religious Thought, 1 (Jan./Feb. 1924), 83.
London Mercury, 17 (Jan. 1928), 244.
Many Moods (Toronto: Macmillan, 1932), 25.
Collected Poems (1944), 228.
Collected Poems (1958), 43.
Atlantic Advocate, 52 (May 1962), 23–4.
Holograph: Pratt Collection, OTV, Box 1.4.
Lorne Pierce Collection, OKQ, Box 72.004.
Macmillan Archive, OHMA, Box 128.7.

c39   **The Toll of the Bells**
Newfoundland Verse (1923), 15–16.
Verses of the Sea (1930), 10.
Collected Poems (1944), 199.
Collected Poems (1958), 4.
Here the Tides Flow (1962), 3.
Typescript: Pratt Collection, OTV, Box 1.2.

c40   **Magnolia Blossoms**
Newfoundland Verse (1923), 18–19.
Typescript: Pratt Collection, OTV, Box 1.2.

C41   **The Fog**
        Newfoundland Verse (1923), 30.
        Verses of the Sea (1930), 15.
        Collected Poems (1944), 186.
        Collected Poems (1958), 6.
        Typescript: Pratt Collection, OTV, Box 1.2.

C42   **The Big Fellow**
        Newfoundland Verse (1923), 31–2.
        Verses of the Sea (1930), 17.
        Collected Poems (1944), 186.
        Collected Poems (1958), 6.
        Here the Tides Flow (1962), 6.
        Typescript: Pratt Collection, OTV, Box 1.2.

C43   **The Morning Plunge**
        Newfoundland Verse (1923), 33.
        Verses of the Sea (1930), 19.
        Typescript: Pratt Collection, OTV, Box 1.2.
        Note: This poem is an altered version of lines 162–6 of *Rachel*.

C44   **Loss of the Steamship *Florizel***
        Newfoundland Verse (1923), 40.
        Here the Tides Flow (1962), 9.
        Typescript: Pratt Collection, OTV, Box 1.2.
        Note: This poem is an altered version of stanzas 3 & 4 of
        'Invocation.'

C45   **The Drowning**
        Newfoundland Verse (1923), 41.
        Collected Poems (1944), 189.
        Collected Poems (1958), 9.
        Here the Tides Flow (1962), 9.
        Typescript: Pratt Collection, OTV, Box 1.2.

C46   **Overheard in a Cove**
        Newfoundland Verse (1923), 47–63.
        Typescript: Pratt Collection, OTV, Box 1.2.

C47   **The Passing of Jerry Moore**
        Newfoundland Verse (1923), 63–70.
        Typescript: Pratt Collection, OTV, Box 1.2.

C48   **The Bird of Paradise**
        Newfoundland Verse (1923), 73–4.
        Typescript: Pratt Collection, OTV, Box 1.2.

C49 **The Epigrapher**
Newfoundland Verse (1923), 74–6.
Collected Poems (1944), 234–5.
Collected Poems (1958), 14–16.
Typescript: Pratt Collection, OTV, Box 1.2.

C50 **Ode to December, 1917**
Newfoundland Verse (1923), 77–86.
Typescript: Pratt Collection, OTV, Box 1.2; 7.55.

C51 **Newfoundland**
Newfoundland Verse (1923), 87–90.
Verses of the Sea (1930), 31–4.
Collected Poems (1944), 165–7.
Collected Poems (1958), 2–4.
Here the Tides Flow (1962), 1–3.
Typescript: Pratt Collection, OTV, Box 1.2.

C52 **A Coast**
Newfoundland Verse (1923), 91–2.
Here the Tides Flow (1962), 13.
Typescript: Pratt Collection, OTV, Box 1.2.

C53 **Morning**
Newfoundland Verse (1923), 93–4.
Typescript: Pratt Collection, OTV, Box 1.2.

C54 **Great Tides**
Newfoundland Verse (1923), 94.
Verses of the Sea (1930), 25.
Collected Poems (1944), 183.
Collected Poems (1958), 16.
Typescript: Pratt Collection, OTV, Box 1.2.

C55 **The After-Calm**
Newfoundland Verse (1923), 94–6.
Typescript: Pratt Collection, OTV, Box 1.2.

C56 **Scenes from Afar**
Newfoundland Verse (1923), 96–8.
Typescript: Pratt Collection, OTV, Box 1.2.

C57 **A Dirge**
Newfoundland Verse (1923), 99–100.
Collected Poems (1958), 18.
Typescript: Pratt Collection, OTV, Box 1.2.

C58 **Come Not the Seasons Here**

Newfoundland Verse (1923), 102–3.
Collected Poems (1944), 21–2.
Collected Poems (1958), 17.
Atlantic Advocate, 52 (May 1962), 23–4.
Typescript: Pratt Collection, OTV, Box 1.2.
Holograph: Pratt Collection, OTV, Box 2.14.

C59 **On the Shore**
Newfoundland Verse (1923), 103–4.
Verses of the Sea (1930), 36.
Collected Poems (1944), 183.
Collected Poems (1958), 16.
Typescript: Pratt Collection, OTV, Box 1.2; 7.60.

C60 **Before a Bulletin Board**
Newfoundland Verse (1923), 104–5.
Typescript: Pratt Collection, OTV, Box 1.2.

C61 **Before an Altar**
Newfoundland Verse (1923), 105–6.
Collected Poems (1944), 95.
Collected Poems (1958), 18.
Typescript: Pratt Collection, OTV, Box 1.2.

C62 **Snowfall on a Battlefield**
Newfoundland Verse (1923), 106–7.
Broadside: n.p., n.d., Pratt Collection.
Typescript: Pratt Collection, OTV, Box 1.2.

C63 **In a Beloved Home**
Newfoundland Verse (1923), 114.
Typescript: Pratt Collection, OTV, Box 1.2.

C64 **The Conclusion of *Rachel***
Newfoundland Verse (1923), 115–21.
Typescript: Pratt Collection, OTV, Box 1.2.
Note: this poem is included in the *Complete Poems* with *Rachel*.

C65 **A Fragment from a Story**
Newfoundland Verse (1923), 122–40.
Typescript: Pratt Collection, OTV, Box 1.2.

C66 1924 **Comrades**
Canadian Magazine, 62 (April 1924), 381.
Many Moods (1932), 37.
Collected Poems (1944), 231.
Collected Poems (1958), 51.

Atlantic Advocate, 52 (May 1962), 24.

c67 **The Frost Over-Night**
Canadian Bookman, 6 (April 1924), 87.

c68 **The Lie**
Canadian Bookman, 6 (April 1924), 88.
Holograph: Pratt Collection, oTV, Box 1.4.

c69 **One Hour of Life**
Canadian Bookman, 6 (June 1924), 135. [Title: 'The Alternative']
Many Moods (1932), 38.
Collected Poems (1944), 202.
Collected Poems (1958), 52.
Holograph: Pratt Collection, oTV, Box 1.4.

c70 **The Last Survivor**
Canadian Forum, 4 (June 1924), 274.

c71 **The Drag-Irons**
Canadian Forum, 4 (July 1924), 301.
Many Moods (1932), 47.
New Provinces: Poems of Several Authors, [ed. F.R. Scott] (Toronto: Macmillan, 1936), 47.
Collected Poems (1944), 182.
Collected Poems (1958), 57.
Here the Tides Flow (1962), 21.
Holograph: Pratt Collection, oTV, Box 1.4.

c72 **Tokens**
Canadian Forum, 4 (Sept. 1924), 365.

c73 **The Ritual**
Canadian Magazine, 63 (Oct. 1924), 347.
Acta Victoriana, 50 (Dec. 1925), 52.
Verses of the Sea (1930), 63.
Many Moods (1932), 52.
Collected Poems (1944), 202.
Collected Poems (1958), 60.
Here the Tides Flow (1962), 17.

c74 1925 **To an Enemy**
Canadian Journal of Religious Thought, 2 (Jan. 1925), 78.
Many Moods (1932), 26.
Collected Poems (1944), 95.
Collected Poems (1958), 43.
Here the Tides Flow (1962), p. 33.

Holograph: Pratt Collection, OTV, Box 1.4.
Macmillan Archive, OHMA, Box 128.7.

C75   **The Witches' Brew**
London: Selwyn & Blount, 1925.
Toronto: Macmillan, 1926.
Collected Poems (1944), 239–56.
Collected Poems (1958), 120–36.
'Inventory of Hades,' *Here the Tides Flow* (1962), 36.
Typescript: Lorne Pierce Collection, OKQ, Box 72.004.
Holograph: Pratt Collection, OTV, Box 1.3; 1.4.
Broadside: 'A Club Inventory of Hades,' Toronto Arts and Letters
    Club, 1958. Pratt Collection.
Broadside: 'Inventory of Hades,' n.p., n.d., Pratt Collection.
[See preceding section]

C76   **The Cachalot**
Canadian Forum, 6 (Nov. 1925), 47–51.
The Titans (Toronto: Macmillan, 1926), 9–26.
Verses of the Sea (1930), 40–61.
Collected Poems (1944), 167–81.
Ten Selected Poems (1947), 47–59.
Collected Poems (1958), 138–50.
Here the Tides Flow (1962), 62–72.
Typescript: Pratt Collection, OTV, Box 1.7.

C77 1926 **Tatterhead**
Acta Victoriana, 50 (Jan. 1926), 13–14.
Queen's Quarterly, 34 (April 1927), 442.
Acadie, 1 (April 1930), 13.
Many Moods (1932), 45.
Here the Tides Flow (1962), 19.

C78   **The Sea-Cathedral**
Acta Victoriana, 51 (Dec. 1926), 17.
Canadian Forum, 7 (May 1927), 237.
Verses of the Sea (1930), 65.
Acadie, 1 (May 1930), 2.
Many Moods (1932), 10.
Collected Poems (1944), 211.
Collected Poems (1958), 37.
Here the Tides Flow (1962), 18.
Holograph: Pratt Collection, OTV, Box 1.5.

c79　　　***The Great Feud***
　　　　　The Titans (1926), 27–68.
　　　　　Collected Poems (1944), 256–89.
　　　　　Northern Review, 5 (Feb./March & April/May 1952), 3–35.
　　　　　Collected Poems (1958), 151–81.
　　　　　Draft: Pratt Collection, OTV, Box 1.3; 1.4; 1.5.
c80　1927 **Cherries**
　　　　　Saturday Night (Oct. 1, 1927), 1.
　　　　　Many Moods (1932), 33.
　　　　　Collected Poems (1944), 229.
　　　　　Collected Poems (1958), 49.
　　　　　Holograph: Pratt Collection, OTV, Box 1.5.
c81　　　**The Lee-Shore**
　　　　　Canadian Forum, 8 (Oct. 1927), 406. [Title: 'A Lee Shore']
　　　　　Verses of the Sea (1930), 67.
　　　　　Onward, 42 (May 1932), 170. [Title: 'A Lee Shore']
　　　　　Many Moods (1932), 47. [Title: 'A Lee-Shore']
　　　　　Collected Poems (1944), 201.
　　　　　Collected Poems (1958), 57.
　　　　　Here the Tides Flow (1962), 16.
　　　　　Holograph: Pratt Collection, OTV, Box 1.3; 1.5.
c82　　　***The Iron Door***. Toronto: Macmillan, 1927.
　　　　　Collected Poems (1944), 212–20.
　　　　　Collected Poems (1958), 26–33.
　　　　　Holograph draft: Pratt Collection, OTV, Box 1.5.
　　　　　Typescript: Lorne Pierce Collection, OKQ, Box 2.009.
　　　　　　W.A. Deacon Ms. Collection, OTUTF, 160.
　　　　　[See preceding section]
c83　1928 **An Awakening**
　　　　　New Outlook, 4 (April 4, 1928), 12.
c84　　　**Old Age**
　　　　　Canadian Journal of Religious Thought, 5 (Nov./Dec. 1928), 463.
　　　　　Canadian Magazine, 75 (March 1931), 16.
　　　　　Many Moods (1932), 23–4.
　　　　　Collected Poems (1944), 226.
　　　　　Collected Poems (1958), 42.
c85　1929 **A Prairie Sunset**
　　　　　The Canadian Nation, 2 (May/June 1929), 19.
　　　　　Dalhousie Review, 11 (July 1931), 217.

Literary Digest, 110 (Sept. 1931), 24.
CNR Magazine (Sept. 1931), 24.
Many Moods (1932), 11.
Collected Poems (1944), 223.
Collected Poems (1958), 38.
Holograph: Pratt Collection, OTV, Box 1.5.

c86   1930 **The Convict Holocaust**

Canadian Forum, 10 (June 1930), 314. [Title: 'The Fair-Grounds Columbus, Ohio']
Many Moods (1932), 46. [Title: 'The Convict Holocaust (Columbus, Ohio, 1930)']
New Provinces (1936), 43.
Collected Poems (1944), 233.
Collected Poems (1958), 56.

c87   **Whither?**

Canadian Journal of Religious Thought, 7 (Sept./Oct. 1930), 338.
Onward, 42 (Feb. 13, 1932), 56.
Many Moods (1932), p. 27.
Holograph: Pratt Collection, OTV, Box 2.14.

c88   **The Lost Cause**

Canadian Journal of Religious Thought, 7 (Sept./Oct. 1930), 338.
Queen's Quarterly, 39 (May 1932), 209.
Many Moods (1932), 26.
Holograph: Pratt Collection, OTV, Box 2.14.

c89   **Blind**

Acta Victoriana, 55 (Dec. 1930), 23.
Canadian Forum, 11 (May 1931), 301.
Many Moods (1932), 24.
Collected Poems (1944), 227.
Collected Poems (1958), 42.
Holograph: Lorne Pierce Collection, OKQ, Box 72.004.

c90   **Sea-Gulls**

Acta Victoriana, 55 (Dec. 1930), 23.
Many Moods (1932), 9.
London Mercury, 27 (Dec. 1932), 109.
Review of Reviews, 83 (Feb. 1933), 53.
New Provinces (1936), 48.
Collected Poems (1944), 187–8.
Collected Poems (1958), 36.

Here the Tides Flow (1962), 14.
Broadside: n.p., n.d., Pratt Collection.
Holograph: Pratt Collection, OTV, Box 2.14.
Typescript: Pratt Collection, OTV, Box 7.60.

C91 **That Night There Came to Bethlehem**
World Friends, NS2 (Dec. 1930), back cover.
Note: This poem is included in the 'Miscellaneous Poems' section
of the *Complete Poems*.

C92 **The Child and the Wren**
Canadian Verse for Boys and Girls, ed. J.W. Garvin
(Toronto: Nelson, 1930), 163–4.
Onward, 42 (May 14, 1932), 158.
Many Moods (1932), 34–5.
Collected Poems (1944), 230–1.
Collected Poems (1958), 50–1.
Holograph: Pratt Collection, OTV, Box 2.14.
Typescript: Pratt Collection, OTV, Box 7.60.

C93 ***The Roosevelt and the Antinoe.*** New York: Macmillan, 1930.
Excerpt in *Verses of the Sea* (1930), 68–72.
Collected Poems (1944), 135–62.
Collected Poems (1958), 184–209.
Holograph drafts: Pratt Collection, OTV, Box 1.5; 2.8.
Typescript: Pratt Collection, OTV, Box 2.9; 2.10.
[See preceding section.]

C94 1931 **To Angelina, an Old Nurse**
Canadian Forum, 11 (Jan. 1931), 141–2.
Many Moods (1932), 41–3.
Collected Poems (1944), 192–4.
Ten Selected Poems (1947), 80–3.
Collected Poems (1958), 53–5.
Holograph: Pratt Collection, OTV, Box 9.65.

C95 **The Fugitive**
Canadian Magazine, 75 (Feb. 1931), 8.
Many Moods (1932), 48.
Holograph: Pratt Collection, OTV, Box 2.14.

C96 **Doors**
Canadian Forum, 11 (May 1931), 301.
Many Moods (1932), 39.
Here the Tides Flow (1962), 32.

C97 **For Better or Worse**
Canadian Forum, 11 (May 1931), 301.
Holograph: Pratt Collection, OTV, Box 2.14.
Macmillan Archive, OHMA, Box 128.7.

C98 **Time-Worn**
Canadian Forum, 11 (June 1931), 326.
Many Moods (1932), 40.
Collected Poems (1944), 200.
Collected Poems (1958), 52.
Here the Tides Flow (1962), 16.
Holograph: Pratt Collection, OTV, Box 2.15.

C99 **Erosion**
Canadian Forum, 11 (June 1931), 326.
Many Moods (1932), 10.
Collected Poems (1944), 203.
Collected Poems (1958), 37.
Atlantic Advocate, 52 (May 1962), 23–4.
Here the Tides Flow (1962), 18.
Holograph: Pratt Collection, OTV, Box 2.14.
Typescript: Pratt Collection, OTV, Box 7.60.

C100 **At a Sanitarium**
Canadian Forum, 11 (June 1931), 326.

C101 **Water**
Canadian Forum, 11 (July 1931), 380.
Holograph: Pratt Collection, OTV, Box 2.14.

C102 **Dreams**
New Outlook, NS7 (Nov. 25, 1931), 1117.
Many Moods (1932), 40.
Holograph: Pratt Collection, OTV, Box 2.14.

C103 **The Highway**
Acta Victoriana, 56 (Oct./Nov. 1931), 15.
Dalhousie Review, 11 (Jan. 1932), 472.
Many Moods (1932), 27.
Collected Poems (1944), 228.
Collected Poems (1958), 44.
Atlantic Advocate, 52 (May 1962), 23.
Holograph: Pratt Collection, OTV, Box 2.14.

C104 **The Armistice Silence**
Canadian Home Journal (Nov. 1931), 17.

Many Moods (1932), 39.

C105 **The 6000**
CNR Magazine (Dec. 1931), 9. [Title: 'No. 6000']
Many Moods (1932), 49.
Collected Poems (1944), 128–30.
Ten Selected Poems (1947), 59–62.
Collected Poems (1958), 58.
Holograph: Pratt Collection, OTV, Box 2.8; 2.14.

C106 1932 **January the First**
World Friends NS3 (Jan. 1932), back cover.
Note: This poem is included in the 'Miscellaneous Poems' section of the Complete Poems.

C107 **From Stone to Steel**
Canadian Journal of Religious Thought, 9 (Sept./Oct. 1932), 224. [Title: 'From Java to Geneva']
Many Moods (1932), 23.
New Provinces (1936), 44. [Title: 'From Java to Geneva']
Collected Poems (1944), 20.
Collected Poems (1958), 41.
Holograph: Pratt Collection, OTV, Box 2.13.

C108 **The Depression Ends**
Canadian Forum, 13 (Oct. 1932), 10–11.
Many Moods (1932), 12–18.
Collected Poems (1944), 303–8.
Collected Poems (1958), 61–7.
Holograph: Pratt Collection, OTV, Box 2.13; 9.65.

C109 **Putting Winter To Bed**
Dalhousie Review, 12 (Oct. 1932), 340–4.
Many Moods (1932), 28–32.
Ten Selected Poems (1947), 75–9.
Collected Poems (1958), 45–9.
Here the Tides Flow (1962), 27–32.
Holograph: Pratt Collection, OTV, Box 2.15.

C110 **A Reverie on a Dog**
University of Toronto Quarterly, 2 (Oct. 1932), 40–8.
Many Moods (1932), 1–8.
Collected Poems (1944), 204–11.
Holograph: Pratt Collection, OTV, Box 2.8; 2.13.

C111 **Bereft**
Twentieth Century, 1 (Nov. 1932), 21.
Canadian Magazine, 79 (Feb. 1933), 22.
Dalhousie Review, 14 (April 1934), 64.
Tamarack Review, 41 (Autumn 1966), 78.
Holograph: Pratt Collection, OTV, Box 7.51.

C112 **The Man and the Machine**
New Outlook, NS8, (Nov. 30, 1932), 1111.
Many Moods (1932), 20.
New Provinces (1936), 45.
Collected Poems (1958), 39.

C113 **The Mirage**
Twentieth Century, 1 (Nov. 1932), 21.
The Fable of the Goats and Other Poems (Toronto: Macmillan, 1937), 42.
Collected Poems (1958), 76.
Holograph: Pratt Collection, OTV, Box 7.51.

C114 **The Way of Cape Race**
London Mercury, 27 (Dec. 1932), 109.
Many Moods (1932), 9.
Collected Poems (1944), 188.
Collected Poems (1958), 36.
Here the Tides Flow (1962), 15.
Holograph: Pratt Collection, OTV, Box 2.14.

C115 **Out of Step**
Many Moods (1932), 19.
Collected Poems (1944), 224.
Collected Poems (1958), 38.

C116 **A Puzzle Picture**
Many Moods (1932), 20.

C117 **The Parable of Puffsky**
Many Moods (1932), 21–2.
Collected Poems (1944), 225–6.
Collected Poems (1958), 39–41.
Holograph: Pratt Collection, OTV, Box 2.13.

C118 **A Legacy**
Many Moods (1932), 25.
Collected Poems (1944), 227.
Collected Poems (1958), 43.
Holograph: Pratt Collection, OTV, Box 2.15; 9.65.
Macmillan Archive, OHMA, Box 128.7.

C119   **A Feline Silhouette**
Many Moods (1932), 34.
Collected Poems (1944), 229.
Collected Poems (1958), 50.
Holograph: Pratt Collection, OTV, Box 2.14.
Typescript: Pratt Collection, OTV, Box 7.60.

C120   **Frost**
Many Moods (1932), 35.
Collected Poems (1944), 231.
Collected Poems (1958), 51.
Holograph: Pratt Collection, OTV, Box 2.14.

C121   **A November Landscape**
Many Moods (1932), 36.
Missionary Monthly, 24 (Nov. 1949), front cover.
Collected Poems (1958), 110.
Holograph: Pratt Collection, OTV, Box 2.14.

C122   **Magic**
Many Moods (1932), 36.
Holograph: Pratt Collection, OTV, Box 2.14.

C123   **Horizons**
Many Moods (1932), 38.

C124   **Jock o' the Links**
Many Moods (1932), 44.
Collected Poems (1944), 232–3.
Collected Poems (1958), 55–6.
Holograph: Pratt Collection, OTV, Box 2.8; 2.14.

C125   **The Pursuit**
Many Moods (1932), 48.

C126   1933 **The Empty Room**
Canadian Magazine, 79 (June 1933), 8.
Fable of the Goats (1937), 47.
Collected Poems (1944), 96.
Collected Poems (1958), 75.
Holograph: Pratt Collection, OTV, Box 7.51.

C127   **Like Mother, Like Daughter**
Saturday Night, 49 (Dec. 2, 1933), Christmas Supp., p. 8.
Fable of the Goats (1937), 40–1.
Collected Poems (1944), 235.
Collected Poems (1958), 73.

C128   **A Prayer-Medley**
Canadian Forum, 14 (Dec. 1933), 92–3.
Fable of the Goats (1937), 27.
Holograph: Pratt Collection, OTV, Box 3.20.

C129   **Text of the Oath**
Acta Victoriana, 58 (Christmas 1933), 13.
New Provinces (1936), 42.
New Frontier, 1 (May 1936), 15.
Fable of the Goats (1937), 39.
Holograph: Pratt Collection, OTV, Box 7.53.

C130   1934   **To Any Astronomer**
Saturday Night, 49 (March 24, 1934), 2.
Fable of the Goats (1937), 38. [Title: '(To Any Astronomer)']
Holograph: Pratt Collection, OTV, Box 7.56.
[Title: 'A Timeless Moment']

C131   **The Mystic**
Queen's Quarterly, 41 (May 1934), 255.
[Title: 'Credo Quia Non Intellego']
Fable of the Goats (1937), 44.
Collected Poems (1944), 28.
Collected Poems (1958), 74.

C132   **The Seer**
Vox, 8 (Dec. 1934), 32.
Canadian Forum, 16 (Nov. 1936), 24.
[Title: 'The Twentieth Century Prophet']
Fable of the Goats (1937), 37.
Holograph: Pratt Collection, OTV, Box 7.52.

C133   **Fire**
Vox, 8 (Dec. 1934), 33.
Fable of the Goats (1937), 32.
Collected Poems (1944), 96–7.
Collected Poems (1958), 71.

C134   1935   **The Prize Cat**
Queen's Quarterly, 42 (Feb. 1935), 109. [Title: 'The Prize Winner']
New Provinces (1936), 41. [Title: 'The Prize Winner']
Canadian Poetry Magazine, 1 (April 1936), 23.
Fable of the Goats (1937), 34.
Collected Poems (1944), 19.
Collected Poems (1958), 72.

Holograph: Pratt Collection, OTV, Box 2.15.
Typescript: Pratt Collection, OTV, Box 7.52; 7.60.

C135 **The Weather Glass**
Canadian Forum, 14 (Nov. 1935), 362.
Fable of the Goats (1937), 46.
Collected Poems (1944), 201.
Collected Poems (1958), 75.
Here the Tides Flow (1962), 21.

C136 ***The Titanic.*** Toronto: Macmillan, 1935.
Collected Poems (1944), 97–128.
Ten Selected Poems (1947), 1–35.
Poems for Senior Students (1950), 37–77.
Poems for Upper School (1953), 27–67.
Poems for Upper School 1956–57 (1956), 15–43.
Collected Poems (1958), 212–42.
Poems for Upper School 1958–59 (1958), 26–66.
Abridgement in: *Here the Tides Flow* (1962), 73–96.
Poems for Upper School (1963), 1–41.
Holograph drafts: Pratt Collection, OTV, Box 3.16; 3.17.
[See preceding section]

C137 1936 **Silences**
Canadian Forum, 15 (March 1936), 9.
Fable of the Goats (1937), 25–6.
Collected Poems (1944), 17–18.
Collected Poems (1958), 77–8.
Here the Tides Flow (1962), 22.
Holograph: Pratt Collection, OTV, Box 7.52.

C138 **Seen on the Road**
New Frontier, 1 (May 1936), 15.
New Provinces (1936), 46.
Fable of the Goats (1937), 33.
Collected Poems (1944), 25.
Collected Poems (1958), 72.

C139 **Thanksgiving**
Missionary Monthly (Oct. 1936), front cover.
Presbyterian Message, 62 (Oct. 1952), front cover.
Note: this poem is included in the 'Miscellaneous Poems' section
of *Complete Poems*.

C140 **The Baritone**

Canadian Forum, 16 (Dec.1936),7.[Title: 'Dictator (Baritone)']
Fable of the Goats (1937), 16–17.
Collected Poems (1944), 26–7.
Collected Poems (1958), 70–1.
Holograph: Pratt Collection, OTV, Box 7.52.

C141 **Mother and Child**
World Friends, NS8 (Dec. 1936), back cover.
Greeting card illustrated by Claire Pratt, 1961.
Note: This poem is included in the 'Miscellaneous Poems' section
of *Complete Poems*.

C142 1937 **Puck Reports Back**
Canadian Poetry Magazine, 2 (Oct. 1937), 43–9.
Fable of the Goats (1937), 18–24.

C143 ***The Fable of the Goats*** in *The Fable of the Goats and Other Poems*.
Toronto: Macmillan, 1937.
Collected Poems (1944), 289–302.
Holograph drafts: Pratt Collection,OTV,Box 3.19; 3.20.
Typescripts: Pratt Collection, OTV, Box 3.21.
   Lorne Pierce Collection, OKQ, Box 6.09.
[See preceding section.]

C144 **Under the Lens**
Fable of the Goats (1937), 35–6.
Holograph: Pratt Collection, OTV, Box 7.60.

C145 **The Old Organon (1225 A.D.)**
Fable of the Goats (1937), 43.
Collected Poems (1944), 30.
Collected Poems (1958), 74.
Holograph: Pratt Collection, OTV, Box 7.52–53.

C146 **The New [Organon] (1937 A.D.)**
Fable of the Goats (1937), 43.
Collected Poems (1944), 31.
Collected Poems (1958), 74.
Holograph: Pratt Collection, OTV, Box 7.53.

C147 **The Illusion**
Fable of the Goats (1937), 45. [Title: 'The Drowning']
Collected Poems (1958), 76.

C148 1938 **The Impatient Earth**
Queen's Quarterly, 45 (Nov. 1938), 542.
Still Life and Other Verse (Toronto: Macmillan, 1943), 31–2.
Collected Poems (1944), 29.

Collected Poems (1958), 96–7.
Typescript: Pratt Collection, OTV, Box 4.32.

C149   **The Manger Under the Star**
World Friends, NS10 (Dec. 1938), front cover.
World Friends, NS26 (Dec. 1954), front cover.
Note: this poem is included in the 'Miscellaneous Poems' section
of *Complete Poems*.

C150   **The Submarine**
Canadian Forum, 18 (Dec. 1938), 274–5.
Still Life (1943), 22.
Collected Poems (1944), 31–6.
Ten Selected Poems (1947), 62.
Collected Poems (1958), 89–94.
Holograph: Pratt Collection, OTV, Box 4.30.

C151   **The Anomaly**
A New Canadian Anthology, eds. Alan Creighton & Hilda Ridley
(Toronto: Crucible Press, 1938), 158.

C152   **The Stag**
A New Canadian Anthology (1938), 159.

C153   1939   **Old Harry**
Queen's Quarterly, 46 (Feb. 1939), 66.
Still Life (1943), 39.
Collected Poems (1944), 181–2.
Here the Tides Flow (1962), 24.
Holograph: Pratt Collection, OTV, Box 4.30.
Typescript: Pratt Collection, OTV, Box 4.32; 7.60.

C154   **Still Life**
Saturday Night (Oct. 28, 1939), 3. [Variant of the first stanza of
a longer version by the same title.]

C155   **The Dying Eagle**
Queen's Quarterly, 46 (Winter 1939), 428–30.
[Title: 'The Old Eagle']
Still Life (1943), 33–5.
Collected Poems (1944), 132–4.
Ten Selected Poems (1947), 72–4. [Title: 'The Old Eagle']
Collected Poems (1958), 97–9.
Holograph: Pratt Collection, OTV, Box 4.30.

C156   **The Radio in the Ivory Tower**
Canadian Forum, 19 (Dec. 1939), 276–7.
Still Life (1943), 17–21.

Collected Poems (1944), 11–15.
Collected Poems (1958), 85–9.
Holograph: Pratt Collection, OTV, Box 4.30.

C157   1940 **Fire-Worship**
Saturday Night, 55 (Feb. 3, 1940), 1.

C158   **Dunkirk**
Maclean's, 53 (July 15, 1940), 20.
Canadian Poetry Magazine, 5 (Sept. 1940), 26.
New World Illustrated (Dec. 10, 1941), 7.

C159   ***Brébeuf and His Brethren***. Toronto: Macmillan, 1940.
Toronto: Macmillan, 1940. 2nd rev. limited edition.
Toronto: Macmillan, 1941. Detroit: Basilian, 1942.
Collected Poems (1944), 36–94.
Collected Poems (1958), 244–98.
Abridgement in: *Here the Tides Flow* (1962), 112–55.
Holograph draft: Pratt Collection, OTV, Box 3.22; 4.29.
Typescript draft: Pratt Collection, OTV, Box 3.23.
[See preceding section]

C160   1941 **The Invaded Field**
Poetry, 58 (April 1941), 1–2.
Still Life (1943), 28.
Collected Poems (1944), 20.
Collected Poems (1958), 94.
Holograph: Pratt Collection, OTV, Box 4.29.

C161   **Come Away Death**
Poetry, 58 (April 1941), 2–4.
Still Life (1943), 30–1.
Collected Poems (1944), 16–17.
Collected Poems (1958), 95–6.
Typescript: Pratt Collection, OTV, Box 4.32.

C162   ***Dunkirk***. Toronto: Macmillan, 1941.
Collected Poems (1944), 1–11.
Ten Selected Poems (1947), 36–47.
Collected Poems (1958), 300–9.
Excerpts in: *Poetry*, 59 (Oct. 1941), 10–15.
New World Illustrated (Dec. 10, 1941), 7.
Here the Tides Flow (1962), 97–103.
Broadside: *The Line of Ascent*. Toronto, 1945. Pratt Collection
[The 'Crew' section of *Dunkirk*]

Holograph: Pratt Collection, oTV, Box 4.26;4.29.
Author's proof copy: Pratt Collection, oTV, Box 4.27.
[See preceding section.]

c163   1942 **Heydrich**
Saturday Night, 57 (June 20, 1942), 14.
Holograph: Pratt Collection, oTV, Box 4.30.
Typescript: Pratt Collection, oTV, Box 7.52.

c164   **The Truant**
Canadian Forum, 22 (Dec. 1942), 264–5.
Voices, 113 (Spring 1943), 10–15.
Still Life (1943), 4–10.
Collected Poems (1944), 309–14.
Collected Poems (1958), 100–5.
Broadside: n.p., 1959. Pratt Collection.
Holograph: Pratt Collection, oTV, Box 4.33.
Typescript: Pratt Collection, oTV, Box 4.34.

c165   **The Stoics**
Queen's Quarterly, 49 (Winter 1942), 344.
Still Life (1943), 11.
Collected Poems (1944), 27–8.
Collected Poems (1958), 81–2.
Typescript: Pratt Collection, oTV, Box 4.32.

c166   1943 **Father Time**
Saturday Night, 58 (March 13, 1943), 12.
Still Life (1943), 12–13.
Collected Poems (1944), 24–5.
Collected Poems (1958), 82–3.

c167   **Autopsy on a Sadist (After Lidice)**
Voices, 113 (Spring 1943), 15.
Still Life (1943), 3.
Collected Poems (1944), 24.
Collected Poems (1958), 81.

c168   **Niemoeller**
Queen's Quarterly, 50 (August 1943), 268.
Holograph: Pratt Collection, oTV, Box 4.30.

c169   **Der Fuehrer's Pot-Pourri**
Saturday Night, 59 (Oct. 16, 1943), 40.
Still Life (1943), 36–8.
Holograph: Pratt Collection, oTV, Box 4.30.

Typescript: Pratt Collection, OTV, Box 4.32.

C170 **Still Life**
Still Life (1943), 1–2.
Collected Poems (1944), 22–3.
Collected Poems (1958), 80–1.
Holograph: Pratt Collection, OTV, Box 4.30; 4.31.
Typescript: Pratt Collection, OTV, Box 4.32.

C171 **Missing: Believed Dead: Returned**
Still Life (1943), 14.
Collected Poems (1944), 28.
Collected Poems (1958), 83–4.
Holograph: Pratt Collection, OTV, Box 4.30.

C172 **The Brawler in *Who's Who***
Still Life (1943), 15–16.
Collected Poems (1944), 131–2.
Collected Poems (1958), 84–5.
Holograph: Pratt Collection, OTV, Box 4.30.

C173 1945 *They Are Returning*
Maclean's, 58 (June 15, 1945), 5–6.
Separate edition. Toronto: Macmillan, 1945.
Holograph drafts: Pratt Collection, OTV, Box 5.36.
[See preceding section]

C174 1947 *Behind the Log*
Canadian Poetry Magazine, 10 (June 1947), 21–37.
Separate edition. Toronto: Macmillan, 1947.
Collected Poems (1958), 312–43.
Holograph drafts: Pratt Collection, OTV, Box 5.37–38.
Typescript drafts: Pratt Collection, OTV, Box 5.38–40.
Final Typescript: Pratt Collection, OTV, Box 5.41.
[See preceding section]

C175 1948 **Summit Meetings**
Outposts, 10 (Summer 1948), 6–7. [Title: 'Lake Success']
Collected Poems (1958), 110–11.
Holograph: Pratt Collection, OTV, Box 7.50.

C176 1949 **Newfoundland Calling**
The Star Weekly (March 26, 1949), 1.
Toronto Daily Star (March 31, 1949), 3.
Here the Tides Flow (1962), 26–7.

Broadside: London: Macmillan, 1949. Pratt Collection.
Holograph, Typescript: Pratt Collection, OTV, Box 7.58.

C177 **Newfoundland Seamen**
Winnipeg Free Press (March 31, 1949), 21.
Collected Poems (1958), 115.
Here the Tides Flow (1962), 25.
Holograph: Lorne Pierce Collection, OKQ, Box 72.004 [Title: 'Newfoundland Sailors'].

C178 **The Last Watch**
Canadian Poetry Magazine, 12 (Summer 1949), 5.

C179 **Displaced**
Here and Now, 2 (June 1949), 77.
Tamarack Review, No. 41 (Autumn 1966), 81.

C180 **The Nativity**
Canadian Home Journal (Dec. 1949), 9.
Note: This poem is included in the 'Miscellaneous Poems' section of the *Complete Poems*.

C181 **Blind from Singapore**
Northern Review, 3 (Dec./Jan. 1949/50), 5.
Holograph, Typescript: Pratt Collection, OTV, Box 7.52.

C182 **A Call**
Northern Review, 3 (Dec./Jan. 1949/50), 6.
Collected Poems (1958), 109–10.
Holograph, Typescript: Pratt Collection, OTV, Box 7.52.

C183 1950 **The Good Earth**
Canadian Poetry Magazine, 13 (Summer 1950), 4–5.
Collected Poems (1958), 108–9.
Atlantic Advocate, 52 (May 1962), 23–4.
Holograph: Pratt Collection, OTV, Box 7.52.

C184 1951 **Myth and Fact**
Poetry Commonwealth, 8 (Spring 1951), 2.
Collected Poems (1958), 112.
Typescript: Pratt Collection, OTV, Box 7.52.

C185 **Cycles**
Contemporary Verse, No. 36 (Fall 1951), 8–9.
Collected Poems (1958), 111–12.
Holograph: Pratt Collection, OTV, Box 7.50.

C186 1952 **The Deed**

Canadian Poetry Magazine, 15 (Summer 1952), 7.
Collected Poems (1958), 114.
Broadside, n.p., n.d. Pratt Collection.

c187 **Magic in Everything**
Mayfair (Dec. 1952), 48–9.
Collected Poems (1958), 115–19.
Issued with Christmas and New Year's Greetings from the
Macmillan Company of Canada 1955. 7 pp.
Here the Tides Flow (1962), 37–40.

c188 ***Towards the Last Spike.*** Toronto: Macmillan, 1952.
Collected Poems (1958), 346–88.
Abridgement in: *Here the Tides Flow* (1962), 104–12.
Holograph drafts: Pratt Collection, oтv, Box 5.37; 6.43–6.
Typescripts: Pratt Collection, oтv, Box 6.47–8.
Macmillan Archive, oнма, Box 65.18.
[See preceding section.]

c189 1953 **The Unromantic Moon**
Poetry, 82 (June 1953), 143.
Canadian Author and Bookman, 34 (Spring 1958), 17.
Collected Poems (1958), 108.

c190 1959 **Lines on the Occasion of Her Majesty's Visit to Canada, 1959**
[Poem commissioned by the c.b.c. and broadcast on August 1,
1959; read by John Drainie]. Issued by cbc Information Services,
August 1959.
Holograph: Pratt Collection, oтv, Box 7.59; 9.64.
Lorne Pierce Collection, okq, Box 72.004.
[This poem is included in the 'Miscellaneous Poems' section of
the *Complete Poems*.]

c191 1966 **To G.B.S.**
Tamarack Review, No. 41 (Autumn 1966), 74.

c192 **The Doctor in the Boat**
Tamarack Review, No. 41 (Autumn 1966), 76–7.

c193 **To D.H. Lawrence**
Tamarack Review, No. 41 (Autumn 1966), 77.

c194 **But Mary Kept All These Things, and Pondered Them in Her
Heart**
Tamarack Review, No. 41 (Autumn 1966), 78–9.

c195 **The Head of the Firm**
Tamarack Review, No. 41 (Autumn 1966), 80.

D / Prose Published in Books and Periodicals

D1 1910 'A Western Experience,' *Acta Victoriana*, 34 (Oct. 1910), 3–8.

D2 1913 'The Scientific Character of Psychology,' *Acta Victoriana*, 37 (March 1913), 300–4.

D3 1914 '"Hooked": A Rocky Mountain Experience,' *Acta Victoriana*, 38 (March 1914), 286–91.

D4 1918 'Introduction.' 'The Last Home Letter of Hedley Goodyear,' *Acta Victoriana*, 43 (Oct. 1918), 60.

D5 1919 'Combatting Feeblemindedness; Psychiatry in the Public Schools,' *Social Welfare*, 1 (Jan. 1, 1919), 91.

D6 1921 'Mental Measurements as Applied to a Toronto School,' *Public Health Journal*, No. 12 (1921), 148–55.

D7 'The Application of the Binet-Simon Tests (Stanford Revision) to a Toronto Public School,' *Canadian Journal of Mental Hygiene*, 3 (April 1921), 95–116.

D8 Rev. of *Memories in Melody* by A.C. Nash, *Canadian Forum*, 1 (June 1921), 280.

D9 Rev. of *Poems* by A.L. Phelps, *Canadian Forum*, 1 (June 1921), 280.

D10 1923 Rev. of *Robert Norwood* by A.D. Watson, *The Christian Guardian*, 94 (July 4, 1923), 21.

D11 1924 Rev. of *The Periodical Essayists of the Eighteenth Century* by George S. Marr, *Canadian Journal of Religious Thought*, 1 (March/April 1924), 173–4.

D12 'Thomas Hardy,' *Canadian Journal of Religious Thought*, 1 (May/June 1924), 239–47.

D13 'Golfomania,' *Acta Victoriana*, 49 (Nov. 1924), 9–13.

D14 1925 'The Loves of an Empress.' Rev. of *The Courtships of Catherine the Great* by Philip W. Sargeant, *Saturday Night*, 41 (Nov. 28, 1925), Lit. Sect. 4.

D15 1926 'An Alberta Novel.' Rev. of *New Furrows* by Flora Jewell Williams, *Saturday Night*, 42 (Dec. 4, 1926), Lit. Sect. 8.

D16 1927 'A Florentine Celebrity.' Rev. of *Life of Benvenuto Cellini* by Himself, *Saturday Night*, 42 (March 12, 1927), Lit. Sect. 3.

D17 Rev. of *Rambles in High Savoy* by F.M. Gos, trans. by Frank Kemp, *Saturday Night*, 43 (Nov. 26, 1927), Lit. Sect. 2.

D18 1928 'The Immortality of Literature.' Rev. of *Much Loved Books* by James O'Donnell Bennett, *Saturday Night*, 43 (March 17, 1928), Lit. Sect. 2.

D19   'Inside the Skin.' Rev. of *Portraits of the New Century* by E.T. Raymond, *Saturday Night*, 43 (May 19, 1928), 9.

D20   'A Poor Case for Modernity.' Rev. of *Contemporaries and Snobs* by Laura Riding, *Saturday Night*, 43 (May 26, 1928), 9, 12.

D21   'A Great Teacher.' Rev. of *Dr Arnold of Rugby* by Arnold Whitridge, *Saturday Night*, 43 (July 14, 1928), 8–9.

D22   'The Oracle of Concord.' Rev. of *Ralph Waldo Emerson* by R.M. Gay, *Saturday Night*, 43 (July 14, 1928), 10–11.

D23   'The Greatest of the Germans.' Rev. of *Goethe* by Emil Ludwig, *Saturday Night*, 43 (Oct. 13, 1928), 8.

D24   'An Intimate Autobiography.' Rev. of *The Letters of Katherine Mansfield*, ed. J. Middleton Murry, *Saturday Night*, 44 (Dec. 1, 1928), 22.

D25   1929   'Introduction' to *As You Like It* by William Shakespeare. R.S. Knox, J.M. Lothian, J.F. MacDonald, and E.J. Pratt, eds. (Toronto: Macmillan, 1929), xxxix–xlviii.

D26   'Introduction' to *Julius Caesar* by William Shakespeare. R.S. Knox, J.M. Lothian, J.F. MacDonald, and E.J. Pratt, eds. (Toronto: Macmillan, 1929), xxxlx–lv.

D27   'Introduction' to *In Caribou Land* by P. Florence Miller (Toronto: Ryerson, 1929), 5.

D28   'Introduction' to *Macbeth* by William Shakespeare. R.S. Knox, J.M. Lothian, and E.J. Pratt, eds. (Toronto: Macmillan, 1929), xxxix–lix.

D29   'Introduction' to *The Merchant of Venice* by William Shakespeare. R.S. Knox, J.M. Lothian, and E.J. Pratt, eds. (Toronto: Macmillan, 1929), xxxix–l.

D30   'Introduction' to *Moby Dick* by Herman Melville (Toronto: Macmillan, 1929), v–xvii.

D31   'The Golden Fleece.' Rev. of *The New Argonautica* by W.B. Drayton Henderson, *Saturday Night*, 44 (Jan. 26, 1929), 9.

D32   'Perilous Horizons.' Rev. of *The Persians Are Coming* by Bruno Frank, *Saturday Night*, 44 (March 16, 1929), Lit. Sect. 2.

D33   'Contemporary Verse.' Revs. of *Sonnets* by Edwin Arlington Robinson, *Angels and Earthly Creatures* by Elinor Wylie, *Wild Garden* by Bliss Carman, *The Hermit Thrush* by Kathleen Millay, and *The Devil is a Woman* by Alice Mary Kimball, *Saturday Night*, 44 (May 25, 1929), 9–10.

D34   'Whom the Gods Love.' Rev. of *A Short History of the Brontes* by K.A.R. Sugden, *Saturday Night*, 44 (Oct. 12, 1929), Lit. Sect. 19.

D35   'Philosophy and Life.' Rev. of *The Meaning of Culture* by John
       Cowper Powys, *Saturday Night*, 44 (Nov. 30, 1929), Lit. Sect. 8.
D36   Rev. of *Whiteoaks of Jalna* by Mazo de la Roche, *Acta Victoriana*, 54
       (Nov. 1929), 21.
D37 1930 'The Brownings Again.' Rev. of *Elizabeth Barrett Browning* by
       Leonard Huxley, *Saturday Night*, 45 (Jan. 4, 1930), 8.
D38   Rev. of *Youth and Other Poems* by John Linnell, *Canadian Journal of
       Religious Thought*, 7 (Jan.–Feb. 1930), 67.
D39   'Poet and Cynic.' Rev. of *Byron* by Andre Maurois, *Saturday Night*,
       45 (April 5, 1930), Lit. Sect. 3.
D40   'The Toll of the Sea.' Rev. of *Famous Shipwrecks* by Captain Frank
       H. Shaw, *Saturday Night*, 45 (July 5, 1930), 3.
D41   'An Early Imagist.' Rev. of *The Collected Poems of Stephen Crane*, ed.
       Wilson Follett, *Saturday Night*, 45 (Oct. 11, 1930), Lit. Sect. 13.
D42   'The Brownings and the Brontes.' Revs. of *Andromeda in Wimpole
       Street* by Dormer Creston, and *Three Virgins of Haworth* by
       Emilie and Georges Ramieu, *Saturday Night*, 45 (Nov. 8, 1930),
       8–9.
D43   'Queen of the Sea.' Rev. of *The Wanderer of Liverpool* by John
       Masefield, *Saturday Night*, 46 (Dec. 6, 1930), 5.
D44 1931 'The Fly-Wheel Lost,' *Open House*, eds. William Arthur Deacon and
       Wilfred Reeves (Ottawa: Graphic Pub., 1931), 246–55.
D45   'Foreword' to *The Limits of Social Legislation* by J.W. Macmillan
       (Toronto, 1931), ix–xi.
D46   'An Actor Family.' Rev. of *Broome Stages* by Clemence Dane,
       Saturday Night, 46 (Oct. 10, 1931), 4, 15.
D47   'Early Nineteenth Century.' Rev. of *Maria Edgeworth: Chosen
       Letters*, ed. F.V. Barry, *Saturday Night*, 47 (Nov. 28, 1931), 8.
D48   'The First Modern Man.' Rev. of *The Sonnets of Petrarch*, trans.
       Joseph Auslander, *Saturday Night*, 47 (Dec. 12, 1931), Lit.
       Supp. 8.
D49 1932 'Foreword' to *Our Great Ones: Twelve Caricatures Cut in Linoleum*
       by Jack McLaren (Toronto: Ryerson, 1932), n.p.
D50   Rev. of *The Montreal Poetry Year Book for 1932–33*, *The Crucible*, 1
       (Autumn 1932), 13.
D51 1933 'Canadian Writers of the Past: Marjorie Pickthall,' *Canadian Forum*,
       13 (June 1933), 334–5.
D52   'Literature: the Decay of Romance,' *Canadian Comment*,
       2 (July 1933), 24–5.

D53   'Literature: Changing Standpoints,' *Canadian Comment*, 2 (August 1933), 25.

D54   'Literature: Lord Macaulay,' *Canadian Comment*, 2 (Sept. 1933), 29.

D55   'Literature: The Nature of Poetry,' *Canadian Comment*, 2 (Oct. 1933), 26.

D56   'Literature: Francis Bacon,' *Canadian Comment*, 2 (Nov. 1933), 30.

D57   'Literature: English Meat and Irish Gravy,' *Canadian Comment*, 2 (Dec. 1933), 8.

D58   1934   Rev. of *Literature: Twenty Years A-Growing* by Maurice O'Sullivan, *Canadian Comment*, 3 (Jan. 1934), 31.

D59   'Literature: New Notes in Canadian Poetry,' *Canadian Comment*, 3 (Feb. 1934), 26-7.

D60   'Literature: The Great Diary,' *Canadian Comment*, 3 (March 1934), 26-7.

D61   'Literature: With Hook and Worm,' *Canadian Comment*, 3 (April 1934), 13.

D62   'Literature: The Dickens Vogue,' *Canadian Comment*, 3 (May 1934), 23.

D63   'Literature: Simplicity in Poetry,' *Canadian Comment*, 3 (June 1934), 22-3.

D64   'Literature: Charles Lamb,' *Canadian Comment*, 3 (July 1934), 28-9.

D65   'Literature: A Study in Poetic Development. I. The Earlier Yeats,' *Canadian Comment*, 3 (August 1934), 20.

D66   'Literature: a Study in Poetic Development. II. The Later Yeats,' *Canadian Comment*, 3 (Sept. 1934), 21.

D67   'Literature: The Drama of Ideas,' *Canadian Comment*, 3 (Oct. 1934), 17.

D68   'Literature: The Comic Spirit,' *Canadian Comment*, 3 (Nov. 1934), 17.

D69   'Literature: The Fourth Column,' *Canadian Comment*, 3 (Dec. 1934), 21-2.

D70   1935   Rev. of *Halt and Parley* by G.H. Clarke, *Canadian Comment*, 4 (March 1935), 27.

D71   'A New Book by G.H.C.' Rev. of *Halt and Parley, and Other Poems* by George Herbert Clarke, *Queen's Quarterly*, 42 (Spring 1935), 159-60.

D72   'The Titanic: The Convergence of the Twain,' *Canadian Comment*, 4 (Oct. 1935), 9-10.

D73   1936   'Foreword' (editorial), *Canadian Poetry Magazine*, 1 (Jan. 1936), 5-7.

D74   'Slang: Why and Why Not,' *Canadian Comment*, 5 (March 1936), 28–9.

D75   'Some Tendencies in Modern Poetry,' *Literary Bulletin*, 1 (Spring 1936), 8–9.

D76   'Comment' (editorial), *Canadian Poetry Magazine*, 1 (April 1936), 5–6.

D77   'Comment' (editorial), *Canadian Poetry Magazine*, 1 (July 1936), 5–6.

D78   'On Modern Tendencies,' *The Canadian Author*, 14 (Sept. 1936), 10.

D79   'Where I Stand on Spain,' *New Frontier*, 1 (Dec. 1936), 15.

D80   1937 'Life of Thomas Hardy' in *Under the Greenwood Tree* by Thomas Hardy (Toronto: Macmillan, 1937), ix–xxiii.

D81   'Brighter Days Ahead' (editorial), *Canadian Poetry Magazine*, 1 (March 1937), 5–6. Rpt. in *Canadian Author and Bookman*, 14 (April 1937), 10.

D82   'Entering the Second Year' (editorial), *Canadian Poetry Magazine*, 2 (June 1937), 5–6.

D83   'Canadian Poetry Night' (editorial), *Canadian Poetry Magazine*, 2 (Dec. 1937), 5.

D84   'Memories of Newfoundland,' *Book of Newfoundland*, ed. J.R. Smallwood (St. John's: Newfoundland Book Publishers, 1937), II, 56–7; rpt. in *A Book of Canada*, ed. William Toye (London: Collins, 1962), 206–7.

D85   1938 'Foreword' to *Down the Years* by Samuel Morgan-Powell (Toronto: Macmillan, 1938), v–viii.

D86   'Bookman Profiles: Annie Charlotte Dalton,' *Canadian Bookman*, 20 (April–May 1938), 11.

D87   Unsigned revs. of *River Without End* by Leo Cox, *Songs* by Helena Coleman, and *Stars Before The Wind* by Charles Frederick Boyle, *Canadian Poetry Magazine*, 3 (June 1938), 55.

D88   'The Third Year' (editorial), *Canadian Poetry Magazine*, 3 (June 1938), 7–8.

D89   'Canadian Poetry – Past and Present,' *University of Toronto Quarterly*, 8 (Oct. 1938), 1–10.

D90   Unsigned rev. of *Frozen Fire* by Floris Clark McLaren, *Canadian Poetry Magazine*, 3 (Oct. 1938), 54.

D91   Unsigned revs. of *The Gold of Dawn* by Dorothy Sproule, and *Legendary Lyrics* by George Kingston, *Canadian Poetry Magazine*, 3 (Oct. 1938), 54–5.

D92   1939 'In Memoriam – Albert H. Robson, 1882–1939,' *Canadian Poetry Magazine*, 3 (April 1939), 12–13.

D93   Rev. of *By Stubborn Stars and Other Poems* by Kenneth Leslie, *Canadian Poetry Magazine*, 3 (April 1939), 44–5.

D94   Unsigned revs. of *Though Quick Souls Bleed* by Gordon Le Claire, *The Wind Our Enemy* by Anne Marriott, and *Victoria Poetry Chapbook 1939–40* in *Canadian Poetry Magazine*, 4 (July 1939), 43–5.

D95   Rev. of *Cross Country* by Alan Creighton, and *Lyrics and Sonnets*, by Lilian Leveridge, *Canadian Poetry Magazine*, 4 (Oct. 1939), 45–7.

D96   1940 Rev. of *Fancy Free* by Carol Coates, *Canadian Poetry Magazine*, 4 (May 1940), 47.

D97   Rev. of *Postlude to an Era* by Verna Loveday Harden, *Canadian Poetry Magazine*, 5 (Sept. 1940), 45–6.

D98   1941 'Introduction' to *Heroic Tales in Verse*, ed. E.J. Pratt (Toronto: Macmillan, 1941), v–x.

D99   'Canadian Poetry Night' (editorial), *Canadian Poetry Magazine*, 5 (April 1941), 5–6.

D100   Revs. of *The Flying Bull and Other Tales* by Watson Kirkconnell, and *Poems* by Carol Cassidy, *Canadian Poetry Magazine*, 5 (April 1941), 53–5.

D101   Revs. of *Lords of the Air* by A.M. Stephen; *Victoria Poetry Chapbook, 1941–42* in *Canadian Poetry Magazine*, 5 (August 1941), 44–5.

D102   Rev. of *Contemporary Verse A Canadian Quarterly* in *Canadian Poetry Magazine*, 6 (Dec. 1941), 46.

D103   'Special Editorial Notice,' *Canadian Poetry Magazine*, 6 (Dec. 1941), 11.

D104   1942 Excerpt from a letter by Pratt, *Night is Ended, Thoughts in Lyric* by Joseph S. Wallace (Winnipeg: Contemporary Pub., 1942), 7.

D105   1943 'Foreword' to *Photography, a Craft and Creed* by Sir Ellsworth Flavelle (Toronto: Ryerson, 1943), [2 pp.]

D106   Rev. of *David and Other Poems* by Earle Birney, *Canadian Poetry Magazine*, 6 (March 1943), 34–5.

D107   'Saint-Denys-Garneau's World of Spiritual Communion' (editorial), *Canadian Poetry Magazine*, 6 (March 1943), 5–6.

D108   Rev. of *Tasting the Earth* by Mona Gould, *Canadian Poetry Magazine*, 7 (August 1943), 35–6.

D109   1944 'Canadian Poets in the U.S.A. – A.J.M. Smith,' *Canadian Review of Music and Other Arts*, 3 (April–May 1944), 35.

D110   Rev. of *The Hitleriad* by A.M. Klein, *Canadian Forum*, 24 (Oct. 1944), 164.

D111   'Canadian Poetry,' *Canadian Review of Music and Other Arts*, 3 (Oct.–Nov. 1944), 5.

D112   1945 'Source Material and Poetry,' *The Canadian Author & Bookman*, 21
(March 1945), 15.
D113   'The Writer and His Audience,' *The Canadian Author & Bookman*, 11
(Dec. 1945), 26.
D114   1946 'Dorothy Livesay,' *Gants du Ciel*, No. 11 (Printemps 1946), 61–5.
D115   'The Function of Criticism,' *The Canadian Author and Bookman*, 23
(Sept. 1946: Supp.).
D116   1947 'A Greeting,' *Here and Now*, 1 (Dec. 1947), 7.
D117   1949 'Foreword' to *Saint Ignace, Canadian Altar of Martyrdom*, by William
Sherwood Fox (Toronto: McClelland & Stewart, 1949), vii–viii.
D118   1950 'Foreword' to *Hidden Springs: A Narrative Poem of Old Upper Canada,
and Other Poems*, by Jenny O'Hara Pincock (Waterloo, Ont.:
n.p., 1950) vii–viii.
D119   1952 'Address Delivered at a Special Convocation of Memorial
University of Newfoundland,' *The Proceedings on the Occasion of the
Installation of the Right Honourable Viscount Rothermere of Hemsted as
First Chancellor and Raymond Gushue as Second President*, St. John's,
Memorial University, 1952, pp. 19–22. Also published in the St.
John's *Daily News*, Oct. 9, 1952, p. 5.
D120   'My First Book,' *Canadian Author & Bookman*, 28 (Winter 1952–53),
4–7.
D121   'The Poet and the University: A Symposium,' *Bulletin of the
Humanities Association of Canada*, 20 (Jan. 1957), 4–5.

E / Audio and Video Recordings, Sheet Music, and Miscellaneous

E1   1927 *United to Serve*. A pictorial presentation written for the United
Church of Canada by Denzil G. Ridout. New hymns and poetical
selections by Pratt. Music arranged by Ernest Macmillan.
[Toronto. United Church Publishing House, The Ryerson Press]
1927.
Contains by Pratt:
A / Hymns: 'Give us the zeal that never falters' [three four-line
stanzas] (p. 7); 'Father, whose strong eternal light' [three four-
line stanzas] (p. 10); 'Thou God of all the peoples' [three eight-line
stanzas] (p. 23); 'Give us the starry faith serene' [four six-line
stanzas] (pp. 24–5); 'Father whose mighty heart would hold' [four

three-line stanzas] (p. 27); 'We praise Thee that Thy spacious hand' [three four-line stanzas] (p. 28).

B / Poetical Selections: 'Come with us as we take a sacred journey' [8 lines, spoken by Prophet] (p. 3); 'It is the story of a marvellous growth' [54 lines, spoken by Christianity] (pp. 3–4); 'When once the national genius laid firm hold' [16 lines, spoken by Presbyterianism] (p. 5); 'Lo, here is one who will relate to you' [3 lines, spoken by Christianity] (p. 7); 'In the early seventeenth century was I born' [17 lines, spoken by Congregationalism] (pp. 7–8); 'Back to the life within the British Isles' [9 lines, spoken by Christianity] (p. 11); 'I would make known to you the great revival' [12 lines, spoken by Methodism] (p. 11); 'Another chapter which concerns our day' [9 lines, spoken by Christianity] (pp. 14–15); 'It is the triumph of a vital cause' [7 lines, spoken by Christianity] (p. 21); 'I saw good will and knowledge growing' [four six-line stanzas, spoken by an Ambassador] (p. 26); 'This line which marks a pilgrimage now ended' [8 lines, spoken by Prophet] (p. 27).

E2 1937 'God of All Children of the Earth.' Toronto: Woman's Missionary Society (United Church of Canada), 1937. [Part of a closing 'Ritual' on inside back cover. Written especially for *One Family* by Viola Whitney Pratt.]

E3 1942 'Keep Us Free.' Oscar Morawetz, composer. Toronto: Gordon V. Thompson, 1942. 14 pp. Sheet music. [An anthem for mixed voices with piano or orchestral accompaniment; words by E.J. Pratt.]

E4 1943 *Brébeuf.* First version, Chorus Part, engraved by John Cozens, c. 1943. 32 pp. Sheet music. Words by E.J. Pratt. Music by Healey Willan. First performed Sept. 26, 1943, CBC Studios, Toronto; produced by James Finlay; conducted by Ettore Mazzoleni. First public performance as *The Life and Death of Jean de Brébeuf*, 18 Jan. 1944, Massey Hall, by the Mendelssohn Choir and Toronto Symphony Orchestra, conducted by Sir Ernest MacMillan.

E5 *The Arts Grow Up* (Five-minute contribution by Pratt). Radio dramatization and discussion of the history of Canada's poets, painters, and composers and the present state of the arts in Canada. Broadcast by CBC, Jan. 3, 1943. CBC Toronto Ref. 430103-1D.

E6 *Brébeuf and His Brethren* (Play). Radio adaptation of Pratt's poem, with music by Healey Willan. Broadcast by CBC, Sept. 26, 1943. Total program: 60 mins. CBC Toronto Ref. 430926-1D.

E7   1947 *Brébeuf*. Second version, Chorus Part, engraved by John Cozens, revised edition 1947, 40 pp. Sheet music. Words by Pratt; music by Healey Willan. [The second version, revised in 1947 for choir and organ, was conducted by Healey Willan in the Timothy Eaton Memorial Church in Toronto in 1967]

E8   1948 *The Life and Death of Jean de Brébeuf* (Play). Recording of poem *Brébeuf and His Brethren*. Broadcast by CBC March 17, 1948. Total program: 60 mins. CBC Toronto Ref. 480317-3D.

E9   1949 *Reminiscences of Newfoundland by Professor E.J. Pratt, C.M.G.* Phonodisc. Recorded at CBC. T-9915 TO T-9924. Delivered at St. John's, Nfld., Jan. 27, 1949.

E10   *Welcome to Newfoundland*. A special radio program of welcome to Newfoundland as the newest province of Canada. Program includes commentary by Pratt and by Prime Minister St Laurent quoting from the works of Pratt. Broadcast by CBC April 1, 1949. CBC Toronto Ref. 490401-3.

E11   *E.J. Pratt Reading His Own Poems*. Harvard Vocarium Records P–1124–27. As originally recorded for the poetry room, Harvard College Library. 1949. (Record P888). Two sound discs: 78 rpm. Contents: v. 1: 'The Shark'; 'Sea-Gulls'; 'The History of John Jones'; Selections from *The Cachalot*. v. 2: Selections from *Brébeuf*.

E12   1951 'Keep Us Free.' An anthem for mixed voices. Music by Oscar Morawetz; words by Pratt. Broadcast by CBC Oct. 10, 1951. CBC Toronto Ref. S.C. 3686.

E13   1952 *Triumphs of the Faith: A Pictorial Presentation*, produced by Denzil G. Ridout. New Hymns by Pratt. [Toronto]: The United Church of Canada, n.d. Contains by Pratt:
a / Hymns (all taken from the pageant *United to Serve*, 1927): 'Give us the zeal that never falters' (p. 9); 'Father, whose strong eternal light' (p. 12); 'Lord in our worship as we sing' [three stanzas, rearranged, from the hymn beginning 'Give us the starry faith serene'] (p. 18); 'We praise Thee that Thy spacious hand' (p. 24); 'Father whose mighty heart would hold' (p. 28); 'Thou God of all the peoples' (p. 39).
b / Poetical Selections [taken from *United to Serve*, sometimes with deletions and other changes, usually minor]: 'Mine is the story of a marvellous growth' (p. 6); 'When once the national genius laid firm hold' (p. 6); 'I am Congregationalism' (p. 10); 'Back to the life within the British Isles' (p. 13); 'I would make known to

you the great revival' (p. 13); 'Another chapter which concerns our day', (p. 17).

c / Verse new to *Triumphs of the Faith*: 'The time of pioneering is not yet over' [18 lines, spoken by United Church] (pp. 20–1); 'Africa is one vast panorama of unrest' [11 lines, spoken by United Church] (p. 25); 'In Japan a restless urge' [11 lines, spoken by United Church] (p. 29); 'One of this day's most distressing needs' [10 lines, spoken by United Church] (p. 33); 'Thus in times of testing ever' [22 lines, spoken by Christianity] (p. 37).

E14   1954 *CBC Wednesday Night*. A radio program of new poems selected from material submitted by thirty poets across Canada; includes Pratt's 'The Deed.' Broadcast by CBC Oct. 13, 1954. CBC Toronto Ref. 541013-2.

E15   *Pratt Reading His Own Poems*. Recording of Pratt reading the following poems: 'Newfoundland,' 'The Way of Cape Race,' 'On the Shore,' 'The Shark,' 'The Dying Eagle' and 'To An Enemy.' Recorded by CBC in 1954. CBC Toronto Ref. 540000-2.

E16   1955 *Sept for Seven*. An entertainment for voice and musical ensemble by Alexander Brott; directed by Alexander Brott, narrated by Donald E. McGill. Words by various authors; includes Pratt's 'Erosion.' Radio-Canada Transcription (SB-1448), ca. 1955. Sound disc.

E17   1956 *E.J. Pratt Reading from His Collected Poems*. Audio tape reel-to-reel. Taped March 1956. Side 1: 'The Truant,' selections from *Brébeuf*, 'The Prize Cat,' 'The Highway,' 'The Empty Room,' 'Seen on the Road' and 'Sea-Gulls'; Side 2: 'The 6000,' conclusion of *The Titanic*, 'Erosion,' 'Old Harry,' 'The Shark,' 'The Drag-Irons,' 'From Stone to Steel,' and 'Cherries.'

E18   1958 *CBC Wednesday Night*. Radio program honouring Pratt's 75th birthday, edited and narrated by Lister Sinclair. Included in the program are Sidney Smith, Earle Birney, Cal Pratt, David Pitt, Claude Bissell, Daphne House, Arthur Phelps, Charles Comfort, Healey Willan, Northrop Frye, Morley Callaghan and others. Included are poems read by Pratt and an interview with him. Broadcast by CBC April 1, 1958.

E19   *Assignment*. E.J. Pratt with Jed Adams. A sound biography for the radio program *Assignment* produced by H.J. Boyle. Dated by CBC May 1, 1958.

E20   'Sea-Gulls.' New York: M. Witmark, 1958. 8 pp. Sheet music. Words by Pratt; music by Joseph Roff.

E21   1960 *Tribute to Arthur Meighen.* Radio obituary; includes contribution by
           Pratt. Broadcast by CBC August 11, 1960. Total program: 30 mins.
           CBC Toronto Ref. 600811-1D.

E22   *E.J. Pratt Delivering Lecture on 'King Lear.'* Audio tape reel-to-reel.
           Dated Dec. 15, 1960.

E23   1961 *Close-Up* A television interview with Pratt by Frank Willis. Dated
           by CBC Feb. 7, 1961. CBC Toronto Ref. 610207-1D.

E24   1962 *Pratt Reading His Own Poems.* 'Sea-Gulls,' 'A Feline Silhouette,' 'No.
           6000,' 'A Prairie Sunset,' 'Erosion,' selection from *The Roosevelt
           and the Antinoe.* Recorded by CBC March 7, 1962. CBC Toronto Ref.
           620307-2D.

E25   1963 *CBC Wednesday Night.* A radio program honouring Pratt's 80th birth-
           day. Poems read include: 'Erosion,' 'The Depression Ends,' 'The
           Truant,' 'Silences.' Narrator: Ronald Hambleton. Dated by CBC
           February 6, 1963.

E26   1964 *The Cachalot* (Play). Radio adaptation of Pratt's poem. Dated by CBC,
           March 29, 1964 in 'CBC Stage' Series. CBC Toronto Ref. 640320-2.

E27   1967 *National School Broadcasts Series* Includes recital of 'The Shark.'
           Dated by CBC, March 3, 1967. CBC Toronto Ref. 670303-3.

E28   'Sea-Gulls.' London, Ontario: Jaymar Music, 1967. 6 pp. Sheet
           Music. Words by Pratt; music by Jean Coulthard.

E29   *Brébeuf and His Brethren.* Musical dramatic pageant by Healey Willan;
           text by Pratt. Conducted by the composer, with David Ouchter-
           lony at the organ. Performed at the Timothy Eaton Memorial
           Church in Toronto. Music '67 Series. Dated by CBC Sept. 26, 1967.
           CBC Toronto Ref. 670926-7.

E30   TBC Recording Limited. Produced by the Department of Tourism
           and Information of the Province of Ontario. n.d. (Record 112868).
           Two sound discs: 33⅓ rpm.

E31   1968 *Landscape with Figures.* Readings from the works of Canadian
           writers, selected and commented on by Andrew Allan. Project '68
           series. Dated by CBC January 14, 1968. CBC Toronto Ref. 680114-4.

E32   *National School Broadcasts Series.* Recitals of selected Canadian poetry.
           Includes Pratt's 'Silences.' Dated by CBC, Jan. 19, 1968. CBC
           Toronto Ref. 680119-6.

E33   1970 'The Lost Cause.' In *Three Songs of Contemplation.* Scarborough
           Berandol Music, 1970. 5 pp. Sheet music. Words by Pratt; music
           by Patricia Blomfield Holt.

E34   1973 'Erosion.' In *Image Out of Season.* Words by various authors; music by Charles Wilson. Written for 4-part mixed chorus, brass quintet, 1973. Unpublished ms., Canadian Music Centre, Toronto.

E35 1974 *Rendezvous With Destiny.* Special CBC radio tribute to Newfoundland's 25th anniversary in Confederation. Program includes 'Newfoundland'. CBC Tuesday Night Series. Dated by CBC April 1, 1974. CBC Toronto Ref. 740401-9.

E36 1975 *Images of Canada.* Includes recital of *Brébeuf.* Dated by CBC June 17, 1975. CBC Toronto Ref. 750617-2(1), 750617-2(2).

F / Poems in Anthologies and Textbooks

F1 1917 *The Poets of the Future: A College Anthology for 1916–17.* Henry T. Schnittkind, ed. Boston, Mass.: Stratford Co., 1917. Contains: 'The Sea-Shell,' pp. 279–81.

F2 1922 A / *Our Canadian Literature: Representative Prose and Verse.* Albert Durant Watson and Lorne Pierce, eds. Toronto: Ryerson, 1922. Contains: 'In Memoriam,' pp. 69–70.

F3 B / 2nd edition. *Our Canadian Literature: Representative Prose and Verse.* A.D. Watson and L. Pierce, eds. Toronto: Ryerson, 1923. Contains: 'In Memoriam,' excerpt ('Morning') from 'Sea Variations,' 'Newfoundland', pp. 173–7.

F4 C / Revised edition. *Our Canadian Literature.* Bliss Carman and Lorne Pierce, eds. Toronto: Ryerson, 1935. Contains: 'The Ground Swell,' 'The Ice-Floes,' 'The Sea-Cathedral,' excerpt 'Burial at Sea' from *The Roosevelt and the Antinoe,* pp. 227–34.

F5 D / Further revised edition. *Canadian Poetry in English.* Bliss Carman, Lorne Pierce and V.B. Rhodenizer, eds. Toronto: Ryerson, 1954. Contains: in addition to the above, 'Erosion,' excerpt 'Invisible Trumpets Blowing' from *Brébeuf,* excerpt from *The Cachalot,* pp. 218–28.

F6 1924 *Shorter Poems.* W.J. Alexander, ed. [Toronto]: T. Eaton Co., Ltd., 1924. Contains: 'The Ice-Floes,' pp. 114–19.

F7 1925 *Canadian Singers and Their Songs.* Edward S. Caswell, ed. Toronto: McClelland & Stewart, 1925. Contains: 'The Ground Swell,' p. 165.

F8 1926 *Canadian Poets.* John W. Garvin, ed. Toronto: McClelland & Stewart, 1926. Contains: 'The Ground Swell,' 'Sea Variations,' pp. 470–4.

F9 1928 *Newfoundland Literature Course,* Book 2. London: Thomas Nelson & Sons, n.d. [c1928]. Contains: 'Snowfall on a Battlefield,' p. 147.

F10   1930 *Canadian Verse for Boys and Girls*. John W. Garvin, ed. Toronto: Nelson, 1930. Contains: 'The Shark,' 'The Child and the Wren,' pp. 162–4.

F11   1932 *A Pedlar's Pack*. Adrian Macdonald, ed. Toronto: Macmillan, 1932. Contains: excerpt from *The Cachalot*, 'The Ice-Floes,' pp. 181–96.

F12   1934 *A Book of Canadian Prose and Verse*. Edmund Kemper and Eleanor Hammond Broadus, eds. Revised edition. Toronto: Macmillan, 1934. Contains: *The Cachalot*, pp. 65–79.

F13   *The Canada Book of Prose and Verse*, Bk IV. C.L. Bennet and Lorne Pierce, eds. Toronto: Ryerson Press and Macmillan, 1934. Contains: 'No 6000' (prefaced by a holograph account by Pratt of the poem's origin), pp. 544–6.

F14   *The Modern Muse*. New York: Oxford University Press, 1934. Contains: 'A Prairie Sunset,' pp. 187–8.

F15   1935 *A Treasury of Prose and Verse*, Bk. I. Lorne Pierce and Dora Whitefield, eds. Toronto: Macmillan and Ryerson, 1935. Contains: 'Erosion,' p. 365.

F16   1936 *Canadian Stories in Verse and Prose*. William K. Kendrick, ed. Toronto: Clarke, Irwin, 1936. Contains: 'The Decision,' 'Erosion,' pp. 33–4.

F17   *Cap and Bells: An Anthology of Light Verse by Canadian Poets*. John W. Garvin, ed. Toronto: Ryerson, 1936. Contains: 'Jock o'the Links,' p. 8.

F18   *New Provinces: Poems of Several Authors*. [F.R. Scott, ed.] Toronto: Macmillan, 1936. Contains: 'The Prize Winner, 'Text of the Oath,' 'The Convict Holocaust,' 'From Java to Geneva,' 'The Man and the Machine,' 'Seen on the Road,' 'The Drag-Irons,' 'Sea-Gulls,' pp. 41–8.

F19   1937 *A Book of Fireside Poems*. William Ray Bowlin, comp. Chicago: Albert Whitman, 1937, Rpt. 1972. Contains: 'The Weather Glass,' p. 118.

F20   *The Book of Newfoundland*. 2 vols. J.R. Smallwood, ed. St. John's: The Newfoundland Book Publishers, 1937. Vol. 2 contains: 'Sea-Gulls,' p. 262; 'The Sea-Cathedral,' 'Erosion,' p. 265.

F21   1938 *A New Canadian Anthology*. Alan Creighton and Hilda M. Ridley, eds. Toronto: Crucible Press, 1938. Contains: 'The Anomaly,' 'At a Sanitarium,' 'The Stag,' pp. 158–9.

F22   *New Harvesting: Contemporary Canadian Poetry, 1918–1938*. Ethel Hume Bennett, ed. Toronto: Macmillan, 1938. Contains: 'The Prize

Cat,' 'Erosion,' 'Sea-Gulls,' excerpts ('The Storm' and 'Burial at Sea') from *The Roosevelt and the Antinoe*, pp. 110–28.

F23 1941 *The Best Poems of 1940*. Thomas Moult, comp. New York: Harcourt Brace and Co., 1941. Contains: 'The Old Eagle,' pp. 76–8.

F24 *Heroic Tales in Verse*. E.J. Pratt, ed. Toronto: Macmillan, 1941. Contains: *The Roosevelt and the Antinoe*, pp. 135–63.

F25 *Voices of Victory: Representative Poetry of Canada in War-Time*. Toronto: Macmillan, 1941. Contains: 'Dunkirk,' p. 81.

F26 1942 *Anthology of Canadian Poetry (English)*. Ralph Gustafson, comp. Harmondsworth, England: Penguin, 1942. Contains: excerpt from *The Cachalot*, excerpt from *The Titanic*, 'From Stone to Steel,' 'The Prize Cat,' 'Still Life,' pp. 55–60.

F27 1943 A / *The Book of Canadian Poetry: A Critical and Historical Anthology*. A.J.M. Smith, ed. Chicago: University of Chicago Press, 1943. Contains: *The Cachalot*, 'Silences,' 'The Old Eagle,' 'Come Away, Death,' excerpt from *Dunkirk*, pp. 279–91.

F28 B / Revised 2nd edition, 1948. Contains: *The Cachalot*, 'Come Away, Death,' excerpt from *Dunkirk, The Witches' Brew*, pp. 257–81.

F29 *A Little Anthology of Canadian Poets*. Ralph Gustafson, ed. Norfolk, Conn.: New Directions, 1943. Contains: 'The Prize Cat,' 'Come Away, Death,' unpaged.

F30 *Poems Worth Knowing*. Claude E. Lewis, ed. Toronto: Copp, Clark, 1941. Rpt. 1943. Contains: 'In Absentia,' 'To Angelina, An Old Nurse,' pp. 140–4.

F31 1944 *Canadian Accent*. Ralph Gustafson, ed. Harmondsworth, England: Penguin Books, 1944. Contains: 'Come Away, Death,' pp. 30–1.

F32 1945 *Spirit of Canadian Democracy: A Collection of Canadian Writings From the Beginnings to the Present Day*. Margaret Fairley, comp. Toronto: Progress Books, 1945. Contains: *They Are Returning*, pp. 200–2.

F33 *Twentieth Century Verse*. Ira Dilworth, ed. Toronto: Clarke, Irwin & Co. Ltd., 1945. Contains: 'The Prize Cat,' 'The Decision,' 'Silences,' pp. 345–52.

F34 1946 *A Pocketful of Canada*. John D. Robins, ed. Toronto: Collins, 1946. Contains: 'The 6000,' pp. 5–7; 'Sea-Gulls,' p. 28; 'Silences,' pp. 225–7; 'Erosion,' p. 227.

F35 *The Eternal Sea: An Anthology of Sea Poetry*. W.M. Williamson, ed. New York: Coward-McCann, 1946. Contains: 'The Way of Cape Race,' p. 111; 'Sea-Gulls,' pp. 275–6.

F36 1947 *The Questing Spirit: Religion in the Literature of Our Time*.

Halford E. Luccock and Frances Brentano, eds. New York: Coward-McCann, 1947. Contains: 'To an Enemy,' p. 377.

F37   *Tribute to Mary*. Gardenville, P.Q.: Harpell's Press, 1947. Contains: 'Mother and Child,' p. 21.

F38   *World Literature*. Arthur Christy and Henry W. Wells, eds. New York: American Book, 1947. Contains: 'The Man and the Machine,' p. 988.

F39   1948 *The Golden Caravan*. C.L. Bennet, J.F. Swayze, and Lorne Pierce, eds. Toronto: Ryerson and Macmillan, 1948. Contains: 'Sea-Gulls,' p. 350; 'The Ice Floes,' p. 515; 'No 6000,' p. 531.

F40   *Masterpieces of Religious Verse*. James Dalton Morrison, ed. New York: Harper, 1948. Contains: 'To an Enemy,' No. 797.

F41   *Reading for Today*. A.M. Beattie and J.F. Swayze, eds. Toronto: Ryerson, 1948, 1957. Contains: 'Silences,' p. 83; 'The Prize Cat,' p. 166.

F42   1949 *College Book of English Literature*. James Edward Tobin, Victor M. Hamm and William H. Hines, eds. New York: American Book Co., 1949. Contains: 'The Way of Cape Race,' 'Erosion,' p. 1112.

F43   *This is Newfoundland*. Ewart Young, ed. Prologue by E.J. Pratt; historical introduction by Brian Cahill; photographs by Cyril Marshall; portraits by Karsh; biographical sketches by Joseph R. Smallwood. Toronto: Ryerson, 1949. Contains: 'Newfoundland Sailors' ['Newfoundland Seamen'], as a holograph prologue.

F44   1950 *Argosy to Adventure*. C.L. Bennet and Lorne Pierce, eds. Toronto: Ryerson and Macmillan, 1950. Contains: 'Newfoundland,' p. 41; 'Erosion,' p. 151; 'The Cachalot,' pp. 568–84.

F45   *Poems for Senior Students*. Toronto: Macmillan, 1950. Contains: *The Titanic*, pp. 37–77.

F46   1951 *Ballads and Narrative Poems*. W.F. Langford, ed. Revised Canadian edition. Toronto: Longmans, Green and Co., 1951. Contains: 'The Decision,' p. 112.

F47   *A Book of Canadian Humour*. John D. Robins and Margaret V. Ray, comps. Toronto: Ryerson, 1951. Contains: excerpt 'The Shades Analyze the Reactions of Inebriated Fish' from *The Witches' Brew*, pp. 258–63.

F48   1952 A / *Canadian Poems, 1850–1952*. Louis Dudek and Irving Layton, eds. Toronto: Contact Press, 1952. Contains: 'A Feline Silhouette,' 'Erosion,' excerpt 'Invisible Trumpets Blowing' from *Brébeuf*, 'Autopsy on a Sadist (after Lidice),' 'The Decision,' pp. 47–9.

F49   B / Rev. 2nd ed., 1953. Contains (in addition to the above): 'Old
       Harry,' 'The Dying Eagle,' 'The Parable of Puffsky,' pp. 59–66.

F50 1953 *One Thousand and One Poems of Mankind: Memorable Short Poems from
       the World's Chief Literatures*. Henry Willis Wells, ed. Atlanta:
       Tupper and Love, 1953. Contains: 'Erosion,' p. 75.

F51   *Poems for Upper School*. With Notes and Questions by E.J. Pratt.
       Toronto: Macmillan, 1953. Contains: *The Titanic*, pp. 27–67.

F52   *Twentieth Century Canadian Poetry*. Earle Birney, ed. Toronto:
       Ryerson, 1953. Contains: 'Newfoundland,' pp. 11–13; 'The Prize
       Cat,' p. 30; 'Sea-Gulls,' p. 33; excerpt from *Brébeuf*, pp. 87–8;
       excerpt from *Behind the Log*, pp. 115–17; 'Erosion,' p. 121; excerpt
       from *The Titanic*, pp. 122–4.

F53 1954 *Northern Medley: An Anthology of Canadian Verse*. W.F. Langford,
       ed. Toronto: Longmans, Green and Co., 1954. Contains: 'To An-
       gelina, an Old Nurse,' pp. 42–5.

F54 1955 *Canadian Anthology*. Carl F. Klinck and Reginald E. Watters, eds.
       Toronto: Gage, 1955. Contains: 'The Ground Swell,' 'The Shark,'
       excerpt from *The Witches' Brew*, excerpt from *The Roosevelt and the
       Antinoe*, 'Sea-Gulls,' 'From Stone to Steel,' 'Erosion,' 'The Man
       and the Machine,' 'The 6000,' excerpt from *The Titanic*, 'The Prize
       Cat,' 'Silences,' excerpt from *Brébeuf*, 'The Submarine,' 'Come
       Away, Death,' pp. 234–66.

F55   *Poems to Enjoy*. W.P. Percival and J.G.S. Brash, eds. Toronto:
       Nelson and Sons, 1955. Contains: 'Sea-Gulls,' p. 193.

F56 1956 *Poems for Upper School 1956–57*. Toronto: Macmillan, 1956. Contains:
       The Roosevelt and the Antinoe, pp. 15–43.

F57 1957 *The Blasted Pine: An Anthology of Satire, Invective and Disrespectful
       Verse, Chiefly by Canadian Writers*. F.R. Scott and A.J.M. Smith,
       eds. Toronto: Macmillan, 1957. Contains: 'The Convict Holo-
       caust,' pp. 64–5; 'Text of the Oath,' p. 108.

F58 1958 *The Penguin Book of Canadian Verse*. Ralph Gustafson, ed.
       Harmondsworth: Penguin, 1958. Contains: 'Come Away, Death,'
       excerpt from *Brébeuf*, excerpt from *The Titanic*, 'The Prize Cat,'
       'From Stone to Steel,' 'Come Not the Seasons Here,' pp. 113–19.

F59   *Poems for Upper School 1958–59*. Toronto: Macmillan, 1958. Contains:
       The Titanic, pp. 26–66.

F60   *Realms of Gold*. W.F. Langford, ed. Toronto: Longmans, Green and
       Co., 1958. Contains: 'The Decision,' p. 210.

F61 1959 *Atlantic Anthology*. William Richard Bird, ed. Toronto: McClelland

& Stewart, 1959. Contains: 'The Shark,' p. 133.

F62   *A Book of Good Poems*. Charles T. Fyfe, ed. Toronto: Copp Clark, 1959. Contains: 'Erosion,' 'In Absentia,' 'The Ice-Floes,' 'Newfoundland,' pp. 334–42.

F63   1960   *The Oxford Book of Canadian Verse in English and French*. A.J.M. Smith, ed. Toronto: O.U.P., 1960. Contains: excerpt from *The Cachalot*, excerpt 'The Martyrdom of Brébeuf and Lalemant, 16 March 1649' from *Brébeuf*, 'The Truant,' excerpts 'The Gathering' and 'The Precambrian Shield' from *Towards the Last Spike*, 'Silences,' pp. 135–9.

F64   1962   *A Book of Canada*. William Toye, ed. London: Collins, 1962. Contains: excerpt 'The Precambrian Shield' from *Towards the Last Spike*, p. 23; 'A Prairie Sunset,' pp. 293–4.

F65   *Poet's Choice*. Paul Engle and Joseph Langland, eds. New York: Dial Press, 1962. Contains: 'Silences,' pp. 5–7.

F66   1963   *An Anthology of Commonwealth Verse*. Margaret J. O'Donnell, ed. London: Blackie and Son, 1963. Contains: 'The Dying Eagle,' excerpt 'March 16, 1649' from *Brébeuf*, pp. 169–73.

F67   *Poems for Upper School*. Toronto: Macmillan, 1963. Contains: *The Titanic*, pp. 1–41.

F68   1964   *An Anthology of Verse*. Roberta A. Charlesworth and Dennis Lee, eds. Toronto: Oxford U.P., 1964. Contains: 'The Iceberg' (from *The Titanic*), p. 125; 'Erosion,' p. 127; 'The Prize Cat,' p. 231.

F69   *Poems of Spirit and Action: Voice of Poetry*. William McClurg Smyth, ed. Rev. Canadian ed. Toronto: Macmillan, 1964. Contains: excerpt 'The Precambrian Shield' from *Towards the Last Spike*, p. 52; 'Erosion,' p. 57; excerpt 'In the Skies' from *Dunkirk*, pp. 82–5.

F70   1965   *Poetry of Our Time: An Introduction to Twentieth-Century Poetry, Including Modern Canadian Poetry*. Toronto: Macmillan, 1965. Contains: 'The Child and the Wren,' 'Cherries,' 'The Dying Eagle,' pp. 199–203.

F71   1966   *Great Canadian Writing*. Claude Thomas Bissell, comp. Toronto: Canadian Centennial Pub., 1966. Contains: 'Sea-Gulls,' p. 112; excerpts from *Towards the Last Spike*, pp. 113 and 118; 'The Shark,' excerpt from *The Titanic*, excerpt from *The Roosevelt and the Antinoe*, pp. 116–18; excerpt from *Brébeuf*, p. 123.

F72   1967   *A Century of Canadian Literature; Un Siècle de Littérature Canadienne*. H. Gordon Green and Guy Sylvestre, eds. Toronto: Ryerson, 1967. Contains: 'Newfoundland,' pp. 190–2.

F73   *Modern Canadian Verse, in English and French*. A.J.M. Smith, ed. Toronto: O.U.P., 1967. Contains: excerpts from *The Cachalot, Towards the Last Spike* and *Behind the Log*, pp. 1–12.

F74   *Poets Between the Wars*. Milton Wilson, ed. Toronto: McClelland & Stewart, 1967. Contains: *The Great Feud,* 'The Highway,' 'Come Away, Death,' 'The Truant,' *Towards the Last Spike*, pp. 2–80.

F75   *To Every Thing There is a Season*. Milton Wilson, ed. Photographed and designed by Roloff Beny. Toronto: Longman, 1967. Contains: excerpts from *Towards the Last Spike* and *Brébeuf*, pp. 42 and 155.

G / Pratt as Editor and Editorial Consultant

G1   1929 Herman Melville. *Moby Dick*. With Introduction and Notes by E.J. Pratt. St Martin's Classics. Toronto: Macmillan, 1929.

G2   1932 *A Pedlar's Pack*. Adrian Macdonald and [E.J. Pratt], eds. St Martin's Classics. Toronto: Macmillan., 1932. Note: According to Viola Pratt, E.J. Pratt co-edited this collection although his name does not appear on the title-page. John Gray of Macmillan, in a June 14, 1963 letter to Pratt, in which he encloses a royalty cheque for *A Pedlar's Pack*, writes: 'Isn't it fun to see A PEDLAR'S PACK which you and Adrian Macdonald and Frank Upjohn and I planned more than thirty years ago still selling cheerfully' (Macmillan Archive, OHMA).

G3   1934 *A Book of Canadian Prose and Verse*. Edmund Kemper Broadus and Eleanor Broadus, eds. Toronto: Macmillan, 1934. Rev. ed. Note: Although E.K. Broadus and his wife are listed as the compilers of this 'new and completely revised with additional material' edition, it was in fact Pratt who undertook the revision. In a Feb. 24, 1934 reply to Macmillan's Hugh Eayrs regarding the revision of the anthology,Pratt stated: 'If you would revise it, I would undertake to get the favourite authors, works and selections from the other members of the staff. Would Broadus consent to have the revision left in Macmillan hands and still allow his name, as at present? For very obvious reasons I want my own name, that is, if I do the revision, absolutely out of the job.' Eayrs replied (Feb. 27): 'If he [Broadus] is agreeable, then we shall turn to you and ask you to do the revision for us upon an honorarium basis.' Pratt did the revision and in a letter to Eayrs (March 27) wrote: '... we want to make a definitive anthology which would throw into the shade all prospective competitors.' Although Hugh Eayrs's contribution is acknowledged in the Preface, Pratt's role as editor is unacknowledged. (Macmillan Archive, OHMA)

G4   1936 *New Provinces: Poems of Several Authors.* Toronto: Macmillan, 1936. Note: In his 'Introduction' (p. x) in the University of Toronto Reprint of *New Provinces* (1976), Michael Gnarowski writes that F.R. Scott sent letters to A.J.M. Smith and E.J. Pratt enlisting their help in 'assembling and examining material for a small anthology of representative Canadian verse.' Begun in Montreal, it 'extended beyond the Montreal nucleus, so much so that by 2 January 1934 E.J. Pratt had become an important part of the scheme and Scott was writing to ask him to invite Robert Finch into the project.'

Poems to be included by the six poets (Finch, Pratt, Scott, Smith, Leo Kennedy, A.M. Klein) were discussed, agreed upon, and changed. Scott wanted Macmillan to publish the book; Smith and Scott wanted an introduction written by Smith that would picture the group's newness, their radicalism and knock the 'Confederation poets out of the ring' (Gnarowski's introduction). Finch and Pratt disagreed, and found an ally in Hugh Eayrs who made a short introduction by Scott one of the conditions of publication by Macmillan: 'There are two points: 1. Pratt and Finch, and I, all feel the long introduction should go and a brief not too provocative one page introduction be substituted, preferably written by you. 2. The best estimate we can get to do a nice book would mean that your group would need to pay us $250., in return for which we would supply you with 250 books. On the balance of the edition we would pay you a royalty of 15% of the list price, the list price being $2.00. For models I suggest either WINGED CHILD or MOUNTAINS AND MOLEHILLS, (copies of which went to you by last night's mail), varied in colour of binding and jacket to suit your taste' (Jan. 16, 1936: Macmillan Archive, OHMA).

Scott in a letter to Eayrs (Jan. 24) quickly agreed to the Macmillan proposal: 'If Ned Pratt feels it is satisfactory also you can accept that as the basis of publication.' He pleaded for a lower price and promised a one-page preface 'shortly.' Eayrs then advised Pratt that the project would go ahead and Macmillan would list the book 'in the Spring.' (Macmillan Archive, OHMA)

G5   1937 Thomas Hardy. *Under the Greenwood Tree*. Edited with Introduction by E.J. Pratt. St Martin's Classics. Toronto: Macmillan, 1937.

G6   1941 *Heroic Tales in Verse*. Edited, with Preface and Notes by E.J. Pratt. St Martin's Classics. Toronto: Macmillan, 1941; rpt. 1943. Rpt. 1977 by Granger Books, Florida, USA. Note: The Pratt copy contains emendations by Pratt on title page: replace 'E.J. PRATT / DEPARTMENT OF ENGLISH, VICTORIA COLLEGE, / UNIVERSITY OF TORONTO' with 'the Macmillan Editors'.

G7   1950 *Poems for Senior Students*. Toronto: Macmillan, 1950. [Not explicitly attributed to Pratt, but the notes in this edition are exactly the same as those in the 1953 text.]

G8   1953 *Poems for Upper School*. With Notes and Questions by E.J. Pratt. Toronto: Macmillan, 1953. OTV copy contains changes by Pratt in his hand on the cover and the title page to replace 'Notes & Questions by E.J. Pratt' with 'Notes by the Macmillan Editors.' Thereafter the school texts prepared by Pratt have that statement.

G9   1956 *Poems for Upper School 1956–57*. With Notes and Questions by Charles W. Dunn and the Macmillan Editors. Toronto: Macmillan, 1956.

G10 1958 *Poems for Upper School 1958–59*. With Notes and Questions by Gordon H. Bailey and the Macmillan Editors. Toronto: Macmillan, 1958.

G11 1963 *Poems for Upper School*. With Notes and Questions by the Macmillan Editors and Julia Gray. Toronto: Macmillan, 1963.

H / Manuscript Sources

I / E.J. PRATT LIBRARY
VICTORIA UNIVERSITY
TORONTO, ONTARIO

A / Pratt Manuscript Collection (OTV)

The following outline of this major collection of manuscripts lists only the most important items in the boxes; the *Inventory of the E.J. Pratt Collection of Manuscripts* provides a complete listing. The items in Boxes 1–6 include notebooks, typescripts, printer's proofs.

Box 1
Rachel. A Sea Story of Newfoundland in Verse: typescripts.
Newfoundland Verse: typescript.
Titans: draft, notes, and an address.
The Witches' Brew: drafts.
The Iron Door: An Ode: draft and commentary.

Box 2
The Roosevelt and the Antinoe: partial draft, typescripts, and address.
Many Moods: draft poems.

Box 3
The Titanic: drafts, notes, and an address.
The Fable of the Goats: draft and notes.
Brébeuf and His Brethren: draft, notes, typescript.

Box 4
Dunkirk: drafts, page proofs, and introductory material.
Still Life: draft poems and typescripts.
Collected Poems: proof sheets.

Box 5
They Are Returning: draft and notes.
Behind the Log: draft, typescripts, proof sheets, and an address.

Box 6
Towards the Last Spike: drafts, notes, typescript, and an address.

Box 7
Holograph and typescript drafts of individual poems, some which had been published in earlier works, plus some written after *Collected Poems* (1958) and previously unpublished. Includes: 'Cycles,' 'Bereft,' 'The Empty Room,' 'The Deed,' 'The Human Doctor,' 'Carlo,' 'Blind From Singapore,' 'The Shell,' 'The Osprey,' 'Sea-Variations,' and 'Newfoundland Calling.'

Box 8
Photocopy of typescript of Pratt's M.A. Thesis, 'The Demonology of the New Testament [Synoptics] in its Relation to Earlier Developments, and to the Mind of Christ,' University of Toronto, 1912; typescripts of unpublished verse drama *Clay*.

Box 9
Notes and drafts for academic lectures on English literature; public lectures, formal and informal speeches, toasts and introductions.

Box 10
Notes and drafts for lectures on Shakespeare, courses on American literature, radio broadcasts, essays, and book reviews.

Box 11
Correspondence: letters to and from E.J. Pratt.

Box 12
Scrapbook on Pratt 1923–64, compiled by Mrs Viola Pratt, consisting of press cuttings and articles.
Typescripts of interviews, talks, and tributes to Pratt; programs, announcements, cards, brochures of dinners, receptions, and autographing sessions.
Typescript of *The Silent Ancestors: The Forebears of E.J. Pratt*, by Mildred Claire Pratt. Related correspondence.
Microfilm, audio recordings, tapes and cassettes.
Formal studio portraits; informal photographs and illustrations.
Woodcuts by Claire Pratt.

B / *Edgar Collection*

Correspondence: E.J. Pratt to Pelham Edgar.

II / MILLS MEMORIAL LIBRARY
    ARCHIVES AND SPECIAL COLLECTIONS DIVISION
    MCMASTER UNIVERSITY
    HAMILTON, ONTARIO

Macmillan Archive
Correspondence, including E.J. Pratt to staff at Macmillan of Canada; typescript; holographs of individual poems; production and publicity files; clippings and other miscellaneous material.

III / QUEEN'S UNIVERSITY ARCHIVES
    KINGSTON, ONTARIO

Lorne Pierce Collection
Manuscripts of individual poems, notes, other prose, typescripts; correspondence.

IV / THOMAS FISHER RARE BOOK LIBRARY
 UNIVERSITY OF TORONTO
 TORONTO, ONTARIO

W.A. Deacon Papers, Manuscript Collection 160 (OTUTF/160)
Correspondence between Deacon and Pratt.

Birney Collection, Manuscript Collection 49 (OTUTF/49)
Correspondence between Earle Birney and Pratt.

A.J.M. Smith Papers, Manuscript Collection 15 (OTUTF/15)
Correspondence: Pratt to Smith.

V / UNIVERSITY OF SASKATCHEWAN LIBRARY
 SASKATOON, SASKATCHEWAN

Gustafson Collection
Correspondence between Ralph Gustafson and Pratt.

Index of Titles and Names in the Bibliography

The name in parentheses following a title is that of the author,
editor, or corporate producer. If the title is not followed by a name,
E.J. Pratt is the author or editor.

Index of First Lines

Index of Titles in Parts 1 and 2